Mastering Endpoint Management using Microsoft Intune Suite

Learn **Everything About Intune** Suite

Saurabh Sarkar

Rahul Singh

‹packt›

Mastering Endpoint Management using Microsoft Intune Suite

Portfolio Director: Kartikey Pandey
Relationship Lead: Prachi Rana
Project Manager: Sonam Pandey
Content Engineer: Sayali Pingale
Technical Editor: Simran Ali
Copy Editor: Safis Editing
Indexer: Rekha Nair
Production Designer: Deepak Chavan
Growth Lead: Shreyans Singh

First published: November 2025

Production reference: 1241125

Published by Packt Publishing Ltd.
Grosvenor House
11 St Paul's Square
Birmingham
B3 1RB, UK.

ISBN 978-1-80602-195-6
www.packtpub.com

To my wife, Shirsha: for your unwavering support, trust, and love.

To my parents and sister. And to my niece, for keeping me young at heart.

To my amazing managers/mentors: Ian Bartlett, Shammi Dua, Nishat Desae, and Scott Breen, for always inspiring me and setting the bar so high!

Lastly, to the incredible Intune community, whose inspiration and guidance have shaped my journey and motivated me to give back.

– Saurabh Sarkar

In the age of the cloud, authoring a technical book requires perseverance, patience, dedication, and discipline. I would like to take this opportunity to thank my lovely parents, who I have been blessed with by the Divine, as without their support, I would not have been able to be a part of this amazing project.

– Rahul Singh

Foreword

Endpoint management has reached a stage where identity, compliance, privilege control, application delivery, and analytics must operate together without gaps. Most people now work remotely or move between locations throughout the day. Home, office, customer site, and public Wi-Fi—it shifts constantly. Devices rarely sit on a trusted network anymore, and the old assumption of having an on-premises PKI or local infrastructure nearby no longer matches how people work. Expectations stay the same. Everything must function instantly and securely. This is why the Intune Suite has grown so quickly. It brings the essential components together in one platform instead of relying on scattered tools and licenses.

EPM shows this growth the clearest. Local admin rights have been a major weakness for years, yet taking them away often creates more problems than leaving them in place. Users get blocked, workflows stall, and admin rights quietly return. EPM fixes that. It gives a controlled elevation model that fits how people actually work. It is preferred because it reduces risk without slowing anyone down. With the new option to run elevation under the signed-in user instead of the isolated virtual account, one of the biggest practical gaps is finally closed. Profile access, user context, and application behavior stay intact.

EPM is also the first feature in the Intune Suite that benefits directly from the move toward the new MMP-C architecture and the WinDC channel. The book covers this shift as well. The modern platform handles elevation rules through declarative device management instead of the older request-based approach. The device knows the required state and keeps it aligned without waiting for a scheduled sync. Rules arrive when they should, and they behave the same every time. This stability is a direct result of the new management model and dual enrollment.

Cloud PKI resolves another long-standing issue. Certificate-based authentication used to depend on on-premises PKI even when devices no longer lived inside corporate networks. Cloud PKI removes that dependency and makes certificate deployment straightforward, especially in remote-first environments.

The same shift appears across the other parts of the suite. Enterprise App Management cuts out the constant packaging work that slowed everything down. Advanced Analytics fills the visibility gap that made troubleshooting guesswork. Remote Help and Microsoft Tunnel handle support and access in a way that fits with how people work today. Together, they replace the scattered solutions that never kept up with devices living outside traditional networks.

This book covers these areas in a way that matches real behavior. The content goes deep into architecture, flows, design reasoning, and the steps you need to take when something does not behave the way you expect. It fills the knowledge gap that many teams encounter the moment they start deploying EPM, Cloud PKI, or Enterprise App Management. I appreciate the detail around EPM because it explains what matters on the device, not just the concept.

Saurabh and Rahul bring experience from both sides of the platform. One builds it inside Microsoft. The other implements it with customers under real constraints. That mix produces explanations that are accurate and practical.

If you want a clear view of EPM, the surrounding Intune Suite features, and what the move to declarative device management changes behind the scenes, this book provides it.

Rudy Ooms

Content Creator at Patch My PC, Microsoft MVP, Community Contributor

Reflecting on my journey as a device management professional over the last 20 years, adaptability to new tech is the only thing that matters. The landscape of modern endpoint management is transforming with greater speed, which demands not only keeping up but staying ahead. The line between device management and security is getting thinner as we move forward at a faster pace. The Microsoft Intune Suite has emerged as a catalyst for security and management.

For years, IT teams struggled with disjointed tools: one for privilege management, another for PKI, and yet another for third-party app management and patching. The Intune Suite helps organizations to streamline all these critical functions for Zero Trust architecture without sacrificing user experience.

The Intune Suite comes out as the real winner to get rid of the friction between security and productivity. On-premises PKI normally takes more than a month to set up, whereas Cloud PKI simplifies the process to a greater extent and makes it simpler to secure identity and devices. It's almost the end of the tug of war between locking down the devices and giving end users a better user experience with **Endpoint Privilege Management** (**EPM**).

The repackaging and patching of third-party vendor applications on Windows devices has been a painful process for ages. With Enterprise App Management automation, you can ensure that the business apps are always secure and up to date. These features fundamentally change the role of the Device Management or Security Admin from a firefighter to a strategic enabler.

Mastering Endpoint Management Using the Microsoft Intune Suite is here to take admins to the next level with advanced capabilities. This book dives deep into the specific, high-value components of the suite: Cloud PKI, EPM, and Enterprise App Management.

What I appreciate most about this book is that it fills a critical knowledge gap for professionals who are comfortable with core Intune features but need to master the "suite" to take their environment to the next level.

Saurabh and Rahul have over 30 years of combined experience that complements the real-world architectural and implementation experience gained from deploying these solutions in complex environments. Together, they offer a different blend of engineering depth and on-field tested strategy. I encourage you to approach this book not just as a technical manual but as a stepping stone for your own career growth.

Anoop C Nair

Senior Workplace Architect and Microsoft MVP, HTMD Community

Contributors

About the authors

Saurabh Sarkar is a content writer and product manager for Intune at Microsoft, with over 14 years of experience. He currently works with his team at Microsoft on developing, improving, and deploying Intune for large-scale customers. Previously, at Microsoft, he held various positions focusing on Intune, such as support engineer, intern technical advisor, and service engineer.

Additionally, he manages a YouTube channel and blog site (named "EverythingAboutIntune") where he provides tutorials, demos, and walk-throughs on Intune at Level 200+. He is also an active member of the HTMD user group community, which offers free online and offline sessions and community events for tech enthusiasts. Saurabh resides with his family in Noida, Uttar Pradesh.

Rahul Singh is a seasoned IT and Cybersecurity Architect with more than 18 years of industry experience. He holds numerous certifications across the Microsoft technology stack and has been an MCT since 2020. Rahul is deeply passionate about technology and excels at demystifying complex technical architectures through various pedagogies and a systems-based learning approach, making learning an enjoyable and enriching experience.

About the reviewers

Ola Ström works as a chief technical architect within the workplace area at Advania Sweden, a Nordic Microsoft partner, where he guides and advises their customers around moving to cloud-based services such as Microsoft Intune and Windows 365.

Ola has worked within the Microsoft Intune space since 2013 and has worked for both Microsoft and the customer side before moving to a Microsoft partner. Since 2022, he has been a Microsoft MVP within Windows & Devices (Windows 365 and Windows). Ola regularly shares his experiences and expertise on his blog (olastrom.com) and at community events.

I would like to thank the authors for giving me the opportunity to help out by being a technical reviewer of this book. I would also like to thank my fiancé, Emma, for putting up with me spending time reviewing this book.

Jon Jarvis is a Microsoft MVP for Security and Windows & Devices/Windows 365, and serves as a security solutions architect at Advania UK. With over a decade of experience in the Microsoft cloud ecosystem, he began by helping organizations migrate to Exchange Online and now leads secure modern workplace strategies, focusing on Microsoft Intune, Microsoft Defender for Endpoint (XDR), and Windows 365 Cloud PC deployments.

Recognized as the first Windows 365 Microsoft MVP in the UK, his dual-award status underscores his community leadership in endpoint security and device management. He regularly presents at international conferences and publishes technical articles that translate Microsoft's best-practice guidance into real-world implementations.

Joost Gelijsteen is a specialist in the modern workplace and security landscape. At Secure at Work, he guides organizations in taking clear control over a safe and forward-looking digital environment. His background spans more than 25 years of hands-on experience with large-scale workplace deployments and deep technical work in Windows management, Intune, and identity-driven security. As a Microsoft MVP, he follows new developments from close by, studies how features behave inside the platform, and turns that knowledge into practical steps that teams can apply without noise or guesswork. He also writes an in-depth technical blog at joostgelijsteen.com, where he publishes research, analysis, and practical insights for engineers.

Joost values clarity. A modern workplace should be automated, secure, productive, and pleasant to use. Achieving that balance requires technical depth combined with persistence and curiosity. He brings that mix to every project and aims to help organizations build workplaces that remain strong, simple, and ready for what comes next.

Table of Contents

Chapter 3: Streamlining Application Deployment with EAM   115

Chapter 6: Empowering Support from Anywhere with Remote Help 275

Chapter 7: Go-To Resources for Intune Mastery   341

Chapter 8: Unlock Your Exclusive Benefits   351

Other Books You May Enjoy   357

Index   361

Preface

In today's rapidly evolving digital landscape, effective endpoint management and security are more critical than ever. This book delves into the comprehensive capabilities of the Microsoft Intune Suite, offering you an in-depth guide to mastering this powerful toolset. Designed for professionals who have a basic understanding of device management, it provides a thorough understanding of backend architecture, logs, registry, and troubleshooting approaches necessary to resolve related issues.

Unlike other introductory books, this guide goes deeply into the flow, architecture, logs, and registry of each topic, reaching a highly technical level. Rich with screenshots and figures, it provides detailed block diagrams explaining the backend architecture, making it easier for you to relate. Drawing from our experience, the book includes in-depth knowledge and undocumented concepts, offering a unique perspective that sets it apart from other resources.

The book is structured to provide a logical progression from foundational concepts to advanced topics. Each chapter begins with an overview explaining the need for the feature (the *Why*), builds on the feature's capabilities, and establishes an end-to-end flow by examining logs at each step, which is essential for IT admins. Special focus is given to logs and the registry, along with troubleshooting approaches. The book also includes tips for feature rollout and a section titled *Our two cents*, offering our unfiltered take on the product, its missing capabilities (if any), and areas of improvement.

By the end of this book, you will have a comprehensive understanding of the Microsoft Intune Suite and be well prepared to implement, manage, and troubleshoot it effectively within your organization.

Who this book is for

This book is intended for IT admins, UEM admins, security admins, endpoint consultants, Entra admins, security/solution architects, and anyone involved in managing enterprise mobility. You should have a basic understanding of MDM and device management in order to efficiently grasp the concepts of Intune Suite.

What this book covers

Chapter 1, Securing Digital Identities with Cloud PKI, covers PKI fundamentals and certificate deployment, starting with traditional on-premises NDES before transitioning to Microsoft Cloud PKI. Learn about backend architecture, setup, reporting, and post-deployment configurations for Radius/NPS, along with practical insights in the *My 2 cents* section.

Chapter 2, Elevating Endpoint Privilege Management with Control and Security, explains the importance of EPM within Microsoft's Zero Trust framework, compares it with third-party tools, and teaches you how to deploy and troubleshoot EPM policies. The chapter concludes with deployment strategies and practical takeaways on real-world usability.

Chapter 3, Streamlining Application Deployment with EAM, explores EAM's use cases, deployment, and update processes for enterprise apps. Learn about background workflows, Graph API integration, and troubleshooting, alongside comparisons with tools such as PatchMyPC and a preview of newly added features, wrapped up with practical insights.

Chapter 4, AI-Driven Insights with Endpoint Analytics and Intune Advanced Analytics, covers advanced analytics, single and multi-device queries, and the Intune resource graph. Learn how to set up analytics, write KQL queries, and use Security Copilot to generate KQL from natural language, with comparisons to endpoint analytics and implementation details.

Chapter 5, Enabling Secure Connectivity with Microsoft Tunnel for MAM, explains how Microsoft Tunnel provides secure, lightweight VPN access for iOS and Android devices, supporting BYOD and modern authentication. The chapter covers the setup, configuration, and user experience for secure, flexible mobile connectivity.

Chapter 6, Empowering Support from Anywhere with Remote Help, describes the setup and cross-platform capabilities of Remote Help, its integration with Intune, and use on unmanaged devices. Learn about deployment, updates, reporting, and upcoming roadmap features for enhanced remote support.

Chapter 7, Go-To Resources for Intune Mastery, provides a curated list of all Intune resources, such as blog sites, YouTube channels, newsletters, and books, and makes sure you don't miss out on any new content. We also have a highly recommended list of resources that are a must-have for anyone working with the technology.

To get the most out of this book

You are expected to know the basics of Microsoft Intune. This would involve setting up an Intune tenant, assigning licenses to users, and enrolling Windows, Android, iOS, and macOS devices to Intune.

To reproduce the setup and concepts of the book, you are expected to have test devices such as Windows, Android, iOS, and macOS, along with an on-premises PKI setup.

Download the color images

We also provide a PDF file that has color images of the screenshots/diagrams used in this book.

You can download it here: https://packt.link/gbp/9781806021956.

> Due to page size constraints, some screenshot text may appear small or difficult to read. Please refer to the accompanying graphics bundle for high-resolution versions.

Conventions used

There are a number of text conventions used throughout this book.

CodeInText: Indicates code words in text, database table names, folder names, filenames, file extensions, pathnames, dummy URLs, user input, and X/Twitter handles. For example: "We will get the output in the .intunewin format in the mentioned folder."

A block of code is set as follows:

```
WindowsRegistry('HKEY_LOCAL_MACHINE\Software\Microsoft\Windows\
CurrentVersion\Run') | project RegistryKey, ValueName, ValueType,
ValueData
```

Bold: Indicates a new term, an important word, or words that you see on the screen. For instance, words in menus or dialog boxes appear in the text like this. For example: "We will have to navigate to **Tenant Administration -> Manage -> Roles -> All roles -> + Create**, as seen in the figure."

> Warnings or important notes appear like this.

> Tips and tricks appear like this.

Get in touch

Feedback from our readers is always welcome.

General feedback: If you have questions about any aspect of this book or have any general feedback, please email us at customercare@packt.com and mention the book's title in the subject of your message.

Errata: Although we have taken every care to ensure the accuracy of our content, mistakes do happen. If you have found a mistake in this book, we would be grateful if you reported this to us. Please visit http://www.packt.com/submit-errata, click **Submit Errata**, and fill in the form.

Piracy: If you come across any illegal copies of our works in any form on the internet, we would be grateful if you would provide us with the location address or website name. Please contact us at copyright@packt.com with a link to the material.

If you are interested in becoming an author: If there is a topic that you have expertise in and you are interested in either writing or contributing to a book, please visit http://authors.packt.com/.

Free Benefits with Your Book

This book comes with free benefits to support your learning. Activate them now for instant access (see the "*How to Unlock*" section for instructions).

Here's a quick overview of what you can instantly unlock with your purchase:

PDF and ePub Copies

Next-Gen Web-Based Reader

Free PDF and ePub versions

Next-Gen Reader

Access a DRM-free PDF copy of this book to read anywhere, on any device.

Use a DRM-free ePub version with your favorite e-reader.

Multi-device progress sync: Pick up where you left off, on any device.

Highlighting and notetaking: Capture ideas and turn reading into lasting knowledge.

Bookmarking: Save and revisit key sections whenever you need them.

Dark mode: Reduce eye strain by switching to dark or sepia themes.

How to Unlock

UNLOCK NOW

Scan the QR code (or go to packtpub.com/unlock). Search for this book by name, confirm the edition, and then follow the steps on the page.

Note: Keep your invoice handy. Purchases made directly from Packt don't require one.

Stay Sharp in Cloud and DevOps — Join 44,000+ Subscribers of CloudPro

CloudPro is a weekly newsletter for cloud professionals who want to stay current on the fast-evolving world of cloud computing, DevOps, and infrastructure engineering.

Every issue delivers focused, high-signal content on topics like:

- AWS, GCP & multi-cloud architecture
- Containers, Kubernetes & orchestration
- Infrastructure as Code (IaC) with Terraform, Pulumi, etc.
- Platform engineering & automation workflows
- Observability, performance tuning, and reliability best practices

Whether you're a cloud engineer, SRE, DevOps practitioner, or platform lead, CloudPro helps you stay on top of what matters, without the noise.

Scan the QR code to join for free and get weekly insights straight to your inbox:

https://packt.link/cloudpro

Share your thoughts

Once you've read *Mastering Endpoint Management using Microsoft Intune Suite,* we'd love to hear your thoughts! Scan the QR code below to go straight to the Amazon review page for this book and share your feedback.

https://packt.link/r/1806021951

Your review is important to us and the tech community and will help us make sure we're delivering excellent quality content.

1

Securing Digital Identities with Cloud PKI

In this chapter, we will understand the background, flow, and setup of Cloud PKI and get an overview of its practical implementation. The chapter begins by introducing the concept of digital certificates, detailing the authentication and authorization processes users undergo to access applications. The discussion then shifts to the advantages of **Certificate-Based Authentication (CBA)** over traditional username and password methods. A comparative analysis of SCEP and PKCS follows, outlining the strengths and limitations of each approach. The chapter then explores the conventional method of SCEP certificate delivery using on-premises NDES via Intune, providing a step-by-step breakdown of the process. This is contrasted with the modern Cloud PKI approach, emphasizing its benefits in terms of simplicity and manageability. Subsequently, the chapter presents a detailed walk-through of the SCEP certificate delivery flow using Cloud PKI, supported by logs and block diagrams at each stage. It also covers the setup process for Cloud PKI, including the various deployment models and available reporting options. Finally, the chapter examines the post-deployment phase of SCEP certificate issuance via Cloud PKI, explaining how the issued certificate can be utilized for CBA and outlining the associated connection flow.

By the end of this chapter, you will possess the knowledge and practical skills necessary to deploy Cloud PKI solutions, effectively troubleshoot existing implementations, and develop a comprehensive understanding of the processes involved in SCEP certificate delivery using Cloud PKI. Additionally, you will have gained insight into the configuration required to leverage client certificates for CBA.

The following main topics will be covered in this chapter:

- Background on certificates
- Understanding SCEP cert delivery using on-premises NDES
- The modern approach to SCEP cert delivery: Using Cloud PKI
- In-depth flow of SCEP certificate delivery using Cloud PKI
- Viewing the SCEP certificate at the device end
- Cloud PKI setup
- Reporting
- Bonus insight: SCEP certificate delivery via on-premises NDES and Intune
- The aftermath of certificate delivery using Cloud PKI
- Our two cents

Let's get started!

Free Benefits with Your Book

Your purchase includes a free PDF copy of this book along with other exclusive benefits. Check the *Free Benefits with Your Book* section in the Preface to unlock them instantly and maximize your learning experience.

Background on certificates

In the digital world, certificates are electronic credentials used to verify the identity of devices, users, or services. Client certificates authenticate individual users or devices, while trusted root certificates serve as the foundation of trust, validating the authenticity of all certificates issued by a trusted authority.

For any user to access any application, they must go through two phases, authentication and authorization, as explained next:

- **Authentication phase:** In this phase, the system verifies the user's identity to ensure they are who they claim to be. This process, known as authentication, typically involves credentials such as a username and password. It is commonly used when accessing applications, connecting to Wi-Fi networks, or establishing VPN sessions, serving as the first line of defense against unauthorized access.

- **Authorization phase**: In this phase, the user is subjected to some conditions and, depending on the output, the service determines whether the user should be given access or not. An example is the usage of a **Conditional Access (CA)** policy in Entra ID. Even after entering the correct credentials, the CA policy runs a check and only allows access to selected apps if the user is authorized to do so.

Using certificates for authentication instead of conventional username/passwords has the following advantages:

- Certificates facilitate seamless and automated authentication
- It removes the overhead for the user to enter the username/password manually
- It is more secure than passwords, which are prone to leakage

Relevant certificate types

Now let's review PKI hierarchy and the commonly used certificates by referencing the following diagram:

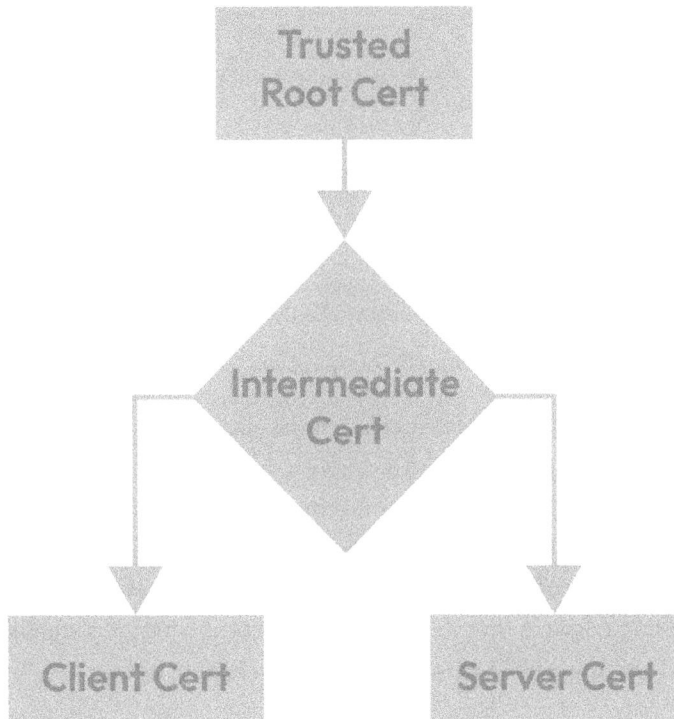

Figure 1.1: Understanding types of certificates

As illustrated in the diagram, the certificate hierarchy comprises trusted root certificates, intermediate certificates, and client/server certificates. A brief overview of each is provided next to enhance understanding of their respective roles and significance:

- **Trusted root certificates**: The root **Certificate Authority (CA)** is at the top of the certificate hierarchy. In a secure organization, there is typically a multi-tiered CA hierarchy, with the root CA kept offline to ensure its protection. A trusted root certificate is a certificate that the root CA issues to itself, meaning the issuer and the subject of the certificate are the same. The root CA and its certificates are essential components of all **Public Key Infrastructure (PKI)** setups. For example, we have trusted root certificates installed on our devices that we get from the OEM as part of a standard image. These certificates are from public PKIs such as DigiCert, Entrust, Baltimore, and GoDaddy, as seen in the following figure.

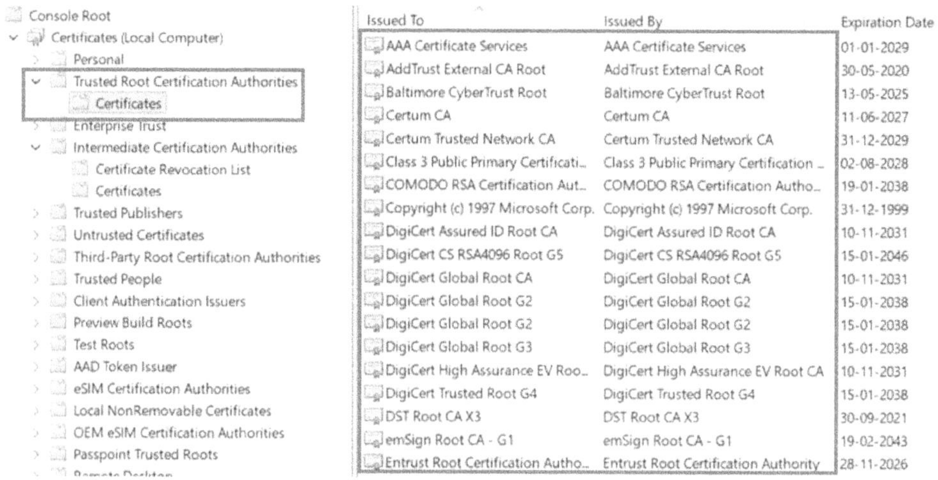

Figure 1.2: Trusted root certificates on a Windows device

- **Intermediate certificates**: Intermediate or issuing CAs are present in a two-level PKI hierarchy. They occupy the second level, with the root CA at the top. Intermediate certificates are issued by the root CA to the issuing CA, meaning the issuer of the certificate is the root CA, and the subject is the issuing CA. These intermediate certificates are crucial for building the certificate chain. For example, we also have intermediate certificates installed on our devices that we get from the OEM as a part of a standard image. These certificates are from public PKIs, as seen in the following figure:

Figure 1.3: Intermediate certificates on a Windows device

- **Client and server certificates**: Client and server certificates are at the base of the certificate chain and are issued by the intermediate or issuing CA. Client certificates are used for user authentication, while server certificates are used by servers for purposes such as SSL and website binding. For example, client certificates are usually used in organizations to automatically connect to the office network.

Now that we have understood the common types of certificates, in the next section, we will understand two key categories of client certificates that Intune can deploy, namely, PKCS and SCEP.

Client certificates: PKCS and SCEP

Via Intune, we can push two kinds of client certificates to devices, that is, PKCS and SCEP.

Both have their advantages and disadvantages but are more or less used to achieve the same use case, that is, seamless authentication.

In both cases, the end goal is delivering a certificate from an on-premises CA in the intranet to a device present anywhere in the world over the internet. The device can then leverage this certificate for any purpose. Let's understand the basics of both SCEP and PKCS:

- **SCEP:**

    - Stands for **Simple Certificate Enrollment Protocol**. It was originally developed by Cisco.

    - The protocol operates on a request-response model and uses HTTP methods such as GET and POST for communication.

    - SCEP has the private key, but the private key is not marked as exportable. This means that the private key never leaves the device, which makes SCEP more secure than PKCS.

    - An SCEP cert can be issued to a user/device or a userless device (a device without user affinity/association).

- **PKCS:**

    - Stands for **Public Key Cryptography Standard** (PKCS 12<=>PFX)
    - Initially developed by Microsoft, it is now an open standard
    - The private key is marked exportable

Understanding the similarities and differences between SCEP and PKCS is essential to identifying their appropriate use cases. The following table presents a concise comparison of the two protocols to support informed decision-making:

PKCS	SCEP (Using On-Premises NDES)
Can be deployed via Intune	Can be deployed via Intune
Used for seamless authentication to a VPN or Wi-Fi	Used for seamless authentication to a VPN or Wi-Fi
Can be issued to a user (who enrolled the device) or any device attribute	Can be issued to a user (who enrolled the device) or any device attribute
Less secure as private key is marked as exportable	More secure as private key never leaves the device
Less overhead as only the Intune connector needs to be installed	More overhead as we need a new server (NDES), IIS, app proxy, and Intune connector
Less complex to set up due to smaller footprint	More complex to set up due to larger footprint
Device talks only to the Intune service, which acts as a mediator	Device talks to NDES via an app proxy
Cannot be issued using Cloud PKI	Can be issued using Cloud PKI
Can be load-balanced, but it's not very seamless	Can be load-balanced more seamlessly

Table 1.1: Comparison between PKCS and SCEP certificate deployment via Intune

Which one to use

This is the most frequently asked question that I get as far as setting up the cert deployment via Intune is concerned. As seen in the preceding comparison, both have their advantages and disadvantages.

On one side, PKCS is easier to deploy and has fewer components involved. On the other, SCEP is more secure but has an added overhead of more components, as discussed. Both the certs can be used to achieve seamless auth to Wi-Fi and a VPN (except PKCS can't be used with userless devices).

My recommendation would be to use SCEP if you can afford the added infrastructure overhead, given that it is more secure and can be deployed to userless devices, unlike PKCS. Otherwise, PKCS would suffice in most use cases. However, it's always best to discuss this with the networking folks and the CA admin to see what kind of certificate they are looking for that the **Remote Authentication Dial-In User Service (RADIUS)** server would authenticate. We must remember that Intune is a delivery mechanism responsible for (in this case) delivering a certificate. Once the certificate has been delivered to the device, it's pretty much up to the device to present it in order to prove its authenticity.

Up to this point, we have developed a foundational understanding of digital certificates—their types, benefits, and a comparative analysis of key protocols. In the following section, we will shift focus to the SCEP certificate delivery process via Intune. We will begin by examining the traditional deployment method, which involves using on-premises NDES as the CA integration point.

Understanding SCEP cert delivery using on-premises NDES

Cloud PKI is the modern way of deploying an SCEP cert via Intune; however, before we understand it in detail and identify its advantages, it's very important to get a basic understanding of how an SCEP certificate was delivered traditionally using on-premises NDES via Intune—when there was no option of Cloud PKI.

A brief overview of on-premises NDES

On-premises NDES is a conventional way of distributing SCEP certificates to devices. The devices can reach out to the NDES server, which in turn goes to the issuing CA and grabs the certificate on the user's behalf. The NDES server is bound to the CA; hence, both need to be in the same on-premises domain. As devices reach out to the NDES server over the internet, NDES needs to be publicly available.

To achieve this, the on-premises NDES is front-ended by an app proxy, which routes the traffic from the internet to NDES.

> To understand the background flow and delivery of an SCEP certificate using on-premises NDES, refer to the *Bonus insight: SCEP certificate delivery via on-premises NDES and Intune* section later in this chapter.

In the next section of this chapter, we will understand the detailed SCEP certificate flow using Cloud PKI and understand how it makes troubleshooting easier by removing the dependency on many components.

The modern approach for SCEP cert delivery: Using Cloud PKI

Before we get started, here's some background on Cloud PKI.

Microsoft announced Cloud PKI as an upcoming offering in August 2023. In March 2024, Cloud PKI became generally available for usage, allowing us to manage the full life cycle of issued certificates for Intune-managed devices. Microsoft Cloud PKI is a fully cloud-native solution designed to streamline and automate the entire certificate life cycle for devices managed through Microsoft Intune. It delivers a dedicated PKI tailored to your organization's needs—eliminating the complexity of deploying and maintaining on-premises servers, connectors, or specialized hardware. This service seamlessly manages certificate issuance, renewal, and revocation across all platforms supported by Intune, ensuring secure and scalable identity management without the traditional overhead.

Traditionally, admins had an option of doing this via an on-premises NDES server, which was cumbersome to set up and troubleshoot.

Using Microsoft Cloud PKI, organizations can simplify their certificate management with minimal effort. The overhead of managing and maintaining an on-premises CA is removed/reduced using the SaaS-based certificate registration authority, which is hosted in Azure on behalf of the customer. As the service is hosted in Azure, it's highly available, and we don't have to worry about its load balancing.

Comparison: On-premises NDES versus Cloud PKI

Let's conduct a detailed comparison between the delivery of SCEP certificates via Cloud PKI and the traditional method of deploying SCEP certificates using on-premises NDES through Intune:

Criteria	On-Premises NDES	Microsoft Cloud PKI
Manageability (components to be managed)	Management is difficult– NDES server, issuing/root CA, app proxy, Intune connector.	Management is easy– nothing needs to be managed on-premises.
Deployment	Deployment is complex.	Deployment is straightforward.

Load balancing/redundancy	We need to spin up multiple NDES instances on-premises.	As it's SaaS on Azure, it's highly available, hence load balancing is not needed.
Supported devices and certificates	Can be used to supply certs to all kinds of devices. Also, we can issue almost all kinds of certs.	(As of the time of writing) can supply certs to Intune-managed devices only. Also, only client authentication certs can be issued. SSL certs/SMIME cannot be issued.
Control (over attributes)	More granular control/customization available.	Less granular control/selection available.
Cost	No additional licensing cost except cost of managing the NDES server and CA.	Extra licensing cost—$2/user/month.
Troubleshooting	As many components are on-premises, the customer can check and troubleshoot them at their end.	Not much troubleshooting can (or has to) be done at the customer's end due to components of SaaS.

Table 1.2: Comparison between on-premises NDES and Cloud PKI

Based on the factors outlined in the table—such as setup costs (including component requirements), the desired level of control over certificate attributes, and the available resources for implementation—we can determine whether an on-premises NDE or a Cloud PKI solution is more suitable.

So far, we have explored the foundational concepts of Cloud PKI and conducted a comparative analysis with on-premises NDES across various parameters. In the next section, we will take a detailed look at the SCEP certificate delivery workflow using Cloud PKI, correlating each step with relevant logs to provide deeper operational insight.

In-depth flow of SCEP certificate delivery with Cloud PKI and log insights (L200)

Now, let's refer to the following diagram to understand the detailed background flow during SCEP certificate delivery via Cloud PKI and correlate each step with the corresponding logs.

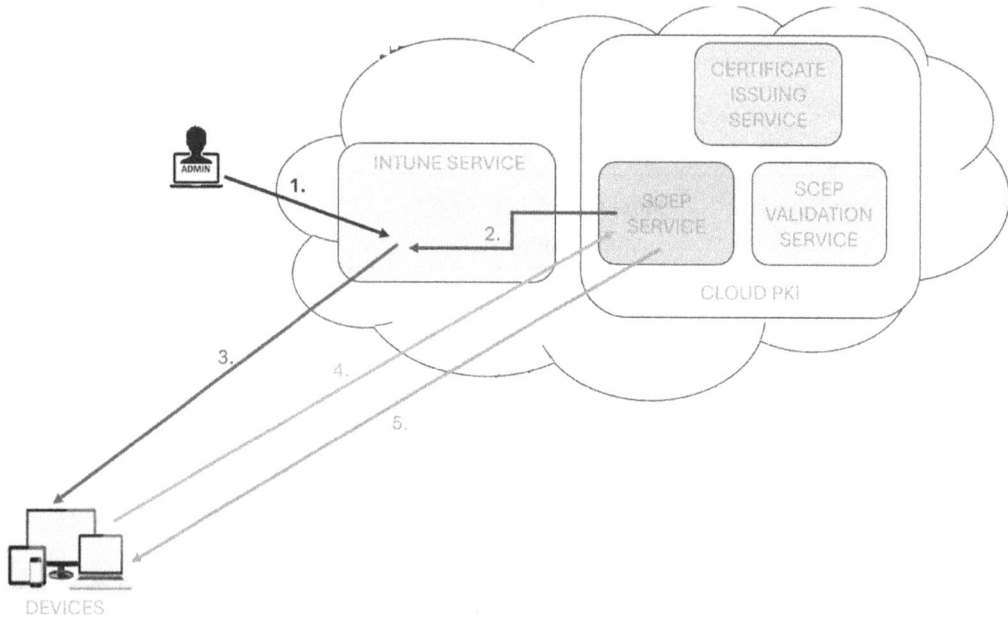

Figure 1.4: (Part 1) Flow behind SCEP cert delivery using Cloud PKI

Here are the components of the diagram:

- The **Intune admin**, who is making the SCEP profile and managing its assignment·
- The **end devices**, which are enrolled to Intune and have internet connectivity
- The **Intune service** and **Cloud PKI service**, which is SaaS on EntraID

The following sections outline the key stages involved in the SCEP certificate delivery process using Cloud PKI based on the preceding diagram.

Step 1: Admin creates and assigns the SCEP profile

In the initial step, the admin creates and assigns the SCEP profile. This is the very first step in the flow that needs to be carried out by the admin.

Once the SCEP profile has been assigned, Intune reaches out to Entra and identifies the effective applicable users. It then fetches the **Common Name** (**CN**) of the members.

It also evaluates the group association, making sure that the SCEP profile and the trusted profile are both deployed to the exact same group (and not nested groups).

Step 2: SCEP challenge generation

In the next step, the Intune service reaches out to the SCEP service (hosted in Cloud PKI), requesting a challenge password.

The challenge password is a unique challenge string (such as a **one-time password**, or **OTP**) that is generated per user per SCEP profile configured in Intune.

The challenge, the thumbprint of the issuing CA, and the timestamp are sent by the SCEP service. This is equivalent to manually generating a challenge from the NDES server by browsing to the mscep_admin URL in NDES, which is `https://<NDES FQDN>/certsrv/mscep_admin`, as shown in the following image:

Network Device Enrollment Service

Network Device Enrollment Service allows you to obtain certificates for routers or other network devices using the Simple Certificate Enrollment Protocol (SCEP).

To complete certificate enrollment for your network device you will need the following information:

The thumbprint (hash value) for the CA certificate is: **5F1501F1 C1F82B1C CD1BC807 C393E7F9** — *Thumbprint of the issuing CA*

The enrollment challenge password is: **1AB1BFF61436AD6E** — *Challenge Password*

This password can be used only once and will expire within 60 minutes.

Each enrollment requires a new challenge password. You can refresh this web page to obtain a new challenge password.

For more information see Using Network Device Enrollment Service.

Figure 1.5: Replicating SCEP challenge generation using on-premises NDES

Before we proceed, let's take a brief detour to understand how the SCEP protocol functions and what the challenge password is—explained in the following section using an analogy.

How does SCEP work? A 1,000-foot overview

The simplest way to understand how SCEP works is through the following analogy:

- Consider making a purchase on an e-commerce website using a card. We visit the website, place an order, and enter our card details for payment. Subsequently, we receive an OTP from the bank via text or call, which serves as a challenge password. This OTP is a secret provided by a trusted source.

- To complete the payment, we must enter the received OTP on the transaction page of the website. Several checks are performed to ensure the OTP is valid, including matching the OTP sent by the bank with the one we entered on the website. Additionally, the OTP has a **Time to Live (TTL)**, typically 10 minutes, meaning the transaction will still fail even if the correct OTP is entered after this period.

Applying this analogy to SCEP, the NDES server generates a challenge password and sends it to the device via the Intune service along with the SCEP payload. The device then contacts the NDES server/SCEP service and presents the same challenge. The SCEP service validates the challenge password and checks other relevant attributes. Once verified, the request is forwarded to the CA.

Step 3: Delivery of the SCEP payload to the device over the internet via Intune

Now the SCEP policy payload will be delivered to the device by Intune over the internet. This process can be monitored in real time by running a SyncML trace on the device, which will display the incoming SCEP payload, as seen in the following screenshot:

```
<Item>
<Target>
  <LocURI>./User/Vendor/MSFT/ClientCertificateInstall/SCEP/ModelName_AC_8dbf03ab-f625-4076-b74b-bbd9543986ba_LogicalName_09cdbc12_58f4_4fa4_953e_4ee10a8fc127_Hash_-1727961139/Install█████</LocURI>
</Target>
<Data>https://fwf.msuc02.manage.microsoft.com/TrafficGateway/PassThroughRoutingService/CloudPki/CloudPkiService/Scep/9dbf03ab-f625-4076-b74b-bbd9543986ba/8595667a-3c16-47b0-a369-11b570c9811█</Data>
<Item>
<Place>
```

Figure 1.6: SyncML trace from device targeted with a Cloud PKI-based SCEP profile

In the preceding figure, we can see that other attributes of the SCEP payload, such as the SAN, key usage, key size, **Extended Key Usage (EKU)**, validity, and challenge password, are also deployed to the device as a part of this MDM session using the SyncML tool.

Step 4: Device generates and sends the GetCACert and GetCACaps request

After receiving the SCEP payload in the previous step, the device is now going to make use of it. As a part of the SCEP protocol, the device now needs to do a `GetCACert` and `GetCACaps` request. This request will be sent to the NDES server via the app proxy URL, which was delivered to the device in the SCEP payload in the previous step. The following two points illustrate the processing that occurs at this stage.

- The response to `GetCACert` is the two **Registration Authority (RA)** certificates, which are binary-encoded. These are the CA certificates that will be used later by the device.

- SCEP uses the CA certificate in order to secure the message exchange for the **Certificate Signing Request (CSR)**. The response for a `GetCACaps` message is a list of CA capabilities in plain text, which is usually as follows:

Keyword	Description
`"AES"`	CA supports the AES encryption algorithm.
`"DES3"`	CA supports the triple DES encryption algorithm.
`"GetNextCACert"`	CA supports the GetNextCACert message.
`"POSTPKIOperation"`	CA supports PKIOperation messages sent via HTTP POST.
`"Renewal"`	CA supports the Renewal CA operation.
`"SHA-1"`	CA supports the SHA-1 hashing algorithm.
`"SHA-256"`	CA supports the SHA-256 hashing algorithm.
`"SHA-512"`	CA supports the SHA-512 hashing algorithm.
`"SCEPStandard"`	CA supports all mandatory-to-implement sections of the SCEP standard. This keyword implies "AES", "POSTPKIOperation", and "SHA-256".

Figure 1.7: List of possible responses to GetCACaps operations showing a CA's capabilities

We have determined that in *step 4*, the device sends `GetCACert` and `GetCACaps` requests to the NDES server to obtain the RA certificates and the CA's capabilities. This step is crucial because the device requires the NDES server's RA certificate later and needs to verify that the CA can issue the type of certificate the device ultimately needs. Therefore, this check is performed at this stage.

Step 5: Device receives the response

The device now receives the response for GetCACaps. To manually replicate this, you can navigate to the following URL in a browser, which will display the CA's capabilities, as shown next. This is how the GetCACaps response appears:

```
https://{{CloudPKIFQDN}}/TrafficGateway/PassThroughRoutingService/CloudPki/
CloudPkiService/Scep/8dbf03ab-f625-4076-b74b-bbd9543986ba/8595687a-3c16-47b0-a300-
13b570c90813?operation=GetCACAPs.
```

Here, {{CloudPKIFQDN}} is the MSU where our Cloud PKI instance is hosted. In the following example, the MSU is fef.msuc02.manage.microsoft.com.

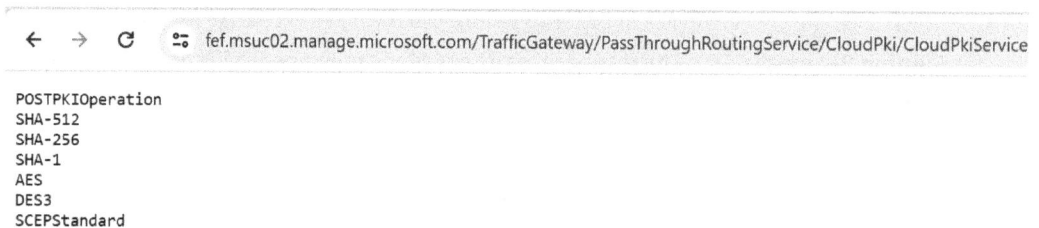

```
POSTPKIOperation
SHA-512
SHA-256
SHA-1
AES
DES3
SCEPStandard
```

Figure 1.8: Replicating the GetCACaps response in the web browser

The device also receives the response for GetCACert. To manually replicate this, you can navigate to the following URL in a browser, which will display the RA certificates that will be downloaded by the browser:

```
https://{{CloudPKIFQDN}}/TrafficGateway/PassThroughRoutingService/CloudPki/
CloudPkiService/Scep/8dbf03ab-f625-4076-b74b-bbd9543986ba/8595687a-3c16-47b0-a300-
13b570c90813?operation=GetCACert
```

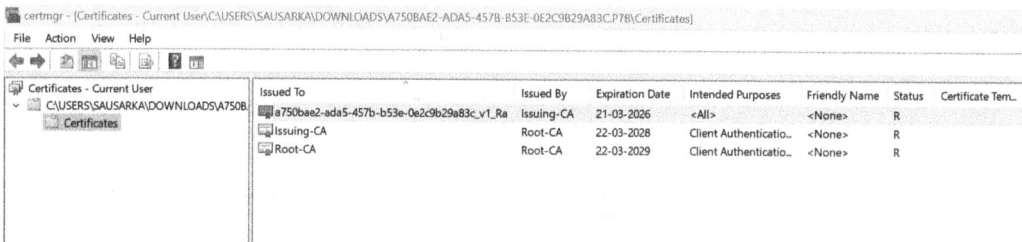

Figure 1.9: Replicating GetCACert capabilities in a browser

For Android and iOS devices, this step is also logged in the Company Portal logs, as illustrated in the following figure:

```
Extract of CP logs for Android Device.
#Needs to be checked only when the cert has been pushed by the CA
#Can be tracked in the OMADMLog_0 via the Thumbprint of the cert/policy id.

#1- <NDESUrl>https://ndes-
nuggetlabs.msapproxy.net/certsrv/mscep/mscep.dll</NDESUrl></NDESUrls><CAThumbprint>16F2644246C2434C54EC8F73FDC058601D18190A</CAThumbprint><ValidityPeriod>1</ValidityPeriod><ValidityPeriodU
nit>Years</ValidityPeriodUnit><EKUMapping><EKUMap><EKUName>Client Authentication

The request to the external url is being picked up from the SCEP profile pushed to the device.
The profile is linked with a trusted root. Over here it is refering to the thumbprint of the trusted root cert.Hence it is important to have the trusted root successfully delivered to the
device before hand.

2019-02-11T21:46:22.7020000    VERB    com.microsoft.omadm.platforms.android.cert=gr.CertificateEnrollmentManager    27185   05314   Trying to enroll pending SCEP certificates for user:1

2019-02-11T21:46:23.7100000    VERB    org.jscep.transport.UrlConnectionGetTransport   27185   05314   Sending GetCACaps(ca) to https://ndes-
nuggetlabs.msapproxy.net/certsrv/mscep/mscep.dll?operation=GetCACaps&message=ca

2019-02-11T21:46:25.5840000    VERB    org.jscep.transport.UrlConnectionGetTransport   27185   05314   Received '200 OK' when sending GetCACaps(ca) to https://ndes-
nuggetlabs.msapproxy.net/certsrv/mscep/mscep.dll?operation=GetCACaps&message=ca

2019-02-11T21:46:26.1980000    VERB    org.jscep.transport.UrlConnectionGetTransport   27185   05314   Sending GetCACert(ca) to https://ndes-
nuggetlabs.msapproxy.net/certsrv/mscep/mscep.dll?operation=GetCACert&message=ca

2019-02-11T21:46:26.3390000    VERB    org.jscep.transport.UrlConnectionGetTransport   27185   05314   Received '200 OK' when sending GetCACert(ca) to https://ndes-
nuggetlabs.msapproxy.net/certsrv/mscep/mscep.dll?operation=GetCACert&message=ca

>>Then verify the certs
Looking for wifi profiles using certificate with alias: User174DC970D4DCE6C03D8223D316F4E406AD50E126

2019-02-11T21:48:02.2410000    INFO    com.microsoft.omadm.apppolicy.appconfig.AppConfigCertStateReceiver    27185   00001   Received certificate state change for alias:
User174DC970D4DCE6C03D8223D316F4E406AD50E126; new state: CERT_ACCESS_GRANTED
```

Figure 1.10: Sample Company Portal logs from Android showing GetCACert and GetCACaps operation

We have now learned about the first five steps of the SCEP certificate delivery in detail. Now, let's reference a new diagram, as seen in the following figure, to establish the flow during the SCEP certificate delivery process:

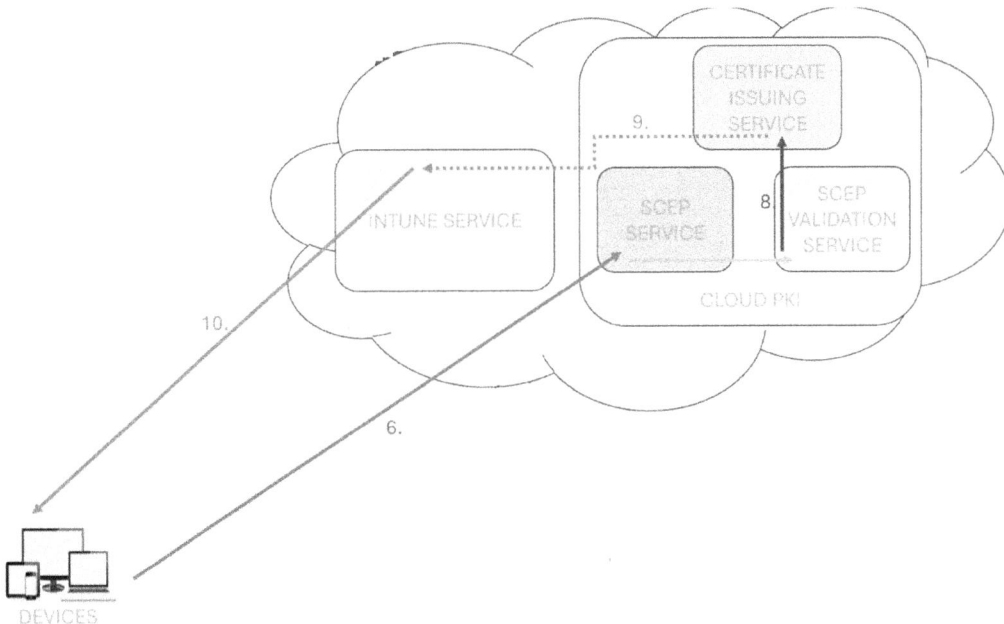

Figure 1.11: (Part 2) Flow behind SCEP cert delivery using Cloud PKI

The following steps outline the flow based on the preceding diagram.

Step 6: Device generates the CSR and sends it

The device now has all the necessary components and proceeds to generate the CSR. This CSR includes the challenge password, which the device must present to the NDES server to verify its legitimacy. Additionally, the CSR contains other essential information required by the CA for certificate issuance, such as the certificate's validity period, key usage, and other relevant attributes.

On a Windows device, this can be tracked in Event Viewer (under **Microsoft | Windows | Device Management | Enterprise Diagnostics Provider | Admin**) with event IDs 306 and 36, as seen in the following screenshot:

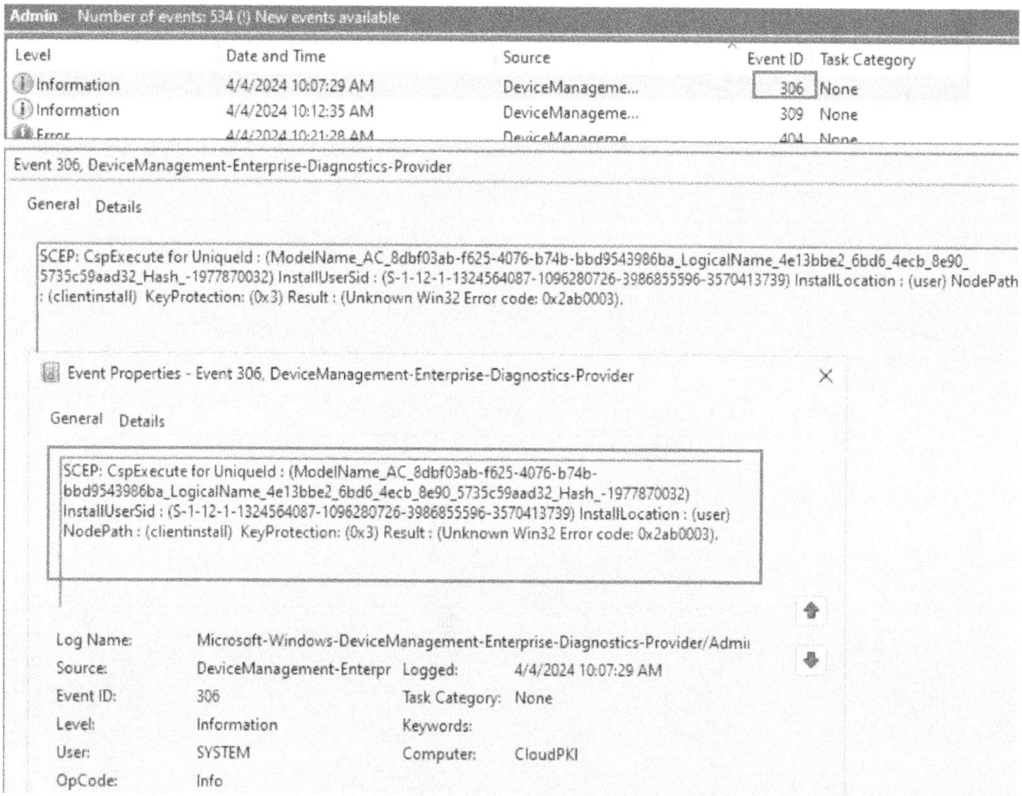

Figure 1.12: Event Viewer logs from a Windows device showing event ID 306

The following log shows the successful generation of a CSR by the device:

Admin	Number of events: 534 (!) New events available			
Level	**Date and Time**	**Source**	**Event ID**	**Task C**
ⓘ Information	4/4/2024 10:03:06 AM	DeviceManageme...	16	None
ⓘ Information	4/4/2024 10:07:33 AM	DeviceManageme...	36	None
ⓘ Information	4/4/2024 10:07:33 AM	DeviceManageme...	39	None
ⓘ Information	4/4/2024 10:07:30 AM	DeviceManageme...	43	None
ⓘ Information	4/4/2024 10:07:29 AM	DeviceManageme...	43	None

Event Properties - Event 36, DeviceManagement-Enterprise-Diagnostics-Provider ✕

General Details

SCEP: Certificate request generated successfully. Enhanced Key Usage: (1.3.6.1.5.5.7.3.2), NDES URL: (https://fef.msuc02.manage.microsoft.com/TrafficGateway/PassThroughRoutingService/CloudPki /CloudPkiService/Scep/8dbf03ab-f625-4076-b74b-bbd9543986ba/8595687a-3c16-47b0-a300-13b570c90813/pkiclient.exe), Container Name: (), KSP Setting: (0x3), Store Location: (0x1).

Log Name:	Microsoft-Windows-DeviceManagement-Enterprise-Diagnostics-Provider/Admin		
Source:	DeviceManagement-Enterpr	Logged:	4/4/2024 10:07:33 AM
Event ID:	36	Task Category:	None
Level:	Information	Keywords:	
User:	AzureAD\saurabhsarkar	Computer:	CloudPKI
OpCode:	Info		
More Information:	Event Log Online Help		

Figure 1.13: Event Viewer logs from a Windows device showing successful CSR generation

Step 7: The request is sent to the SCEP service for validation

The request for CSR validation is now sent to the SCEP service. This process is logged on the service side, where we can confirm that the CSR has been received. The SCEP service will then perform its validation, which includes the following:

- Verifying whether the timestamp of the challenge has expired or is still valid (validity is 60 minutes)
- Ensuring the challenge password is correct by matching it with the list of passwords generated by the NDES server
- Checking that the attributes for which the challenge was originally generated match those in the CSR

Unfortunately, this validation process occurs on the service side, and end customers cannot access the logs for this step, as they are stored in Microsoft's database and can only be reviewed by Microsoft's engineers using Kusto.

Step 8: Post verification, the request is sent to the issuing CA

Once verified, the request is now sent to the CA for further processing. With on-premises, we could track this step by checking the Event Viewer logs of the CA server.

Step 9: The certificate is issued as per the request

The CA now issues the certificate as per the request:

- In the request, we currently don't have the option of specifying a specific certificate template via which the cert should be issued
- CA protects the certificate package by using the device's public key (which it received in the CSR)

Step 10: The certificate is delivered to the device via the MDM channel

The certificate is now delivered to the device via Intune:

- Upon receipt, the device installs the certificate, and this action is logged across all operating systems
- This client certificate will subsequently be used by the device for authentication purposes

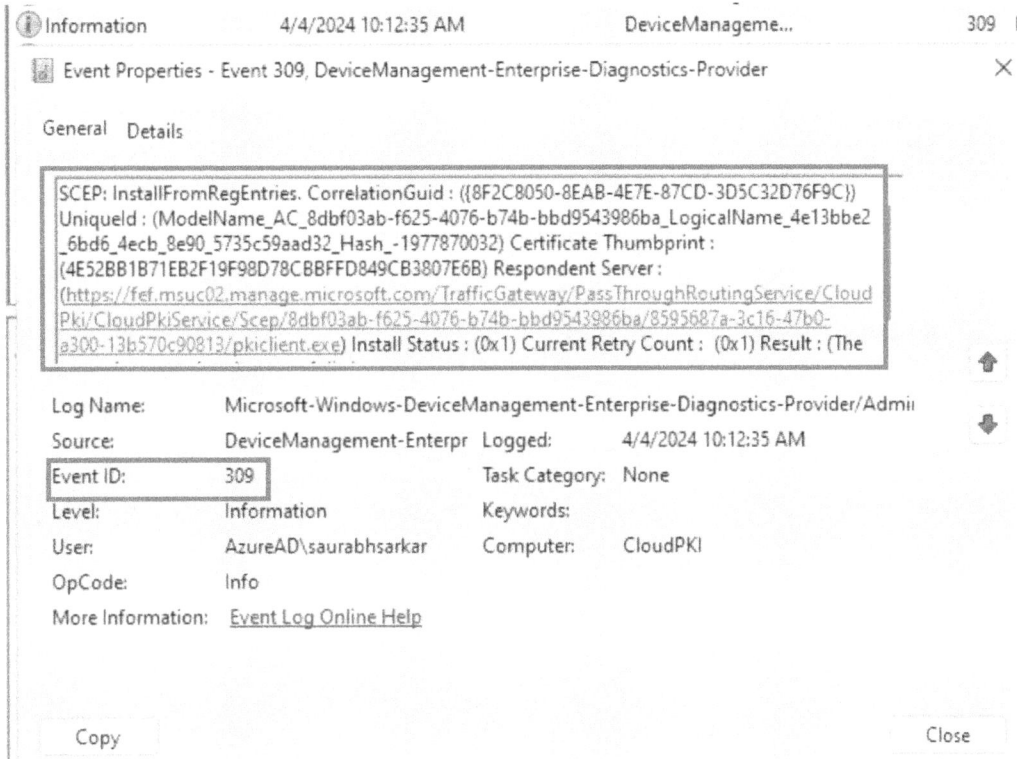

Figure 1.14: Event Viewer logs from a Windows device showing delivery of certificate

Once the certificate is installed, it can be viewed in the device's certificate store (under **Current User | Personal**), as seen in the following figure. We can see the certificate's chain as well as all of its other parameters:

Figure 1.15: Certificate store in the device showing the presence of a certificate

The successful installation of the certificate is also logged in Event Viewer with event ID 39, as seen in the following figure.

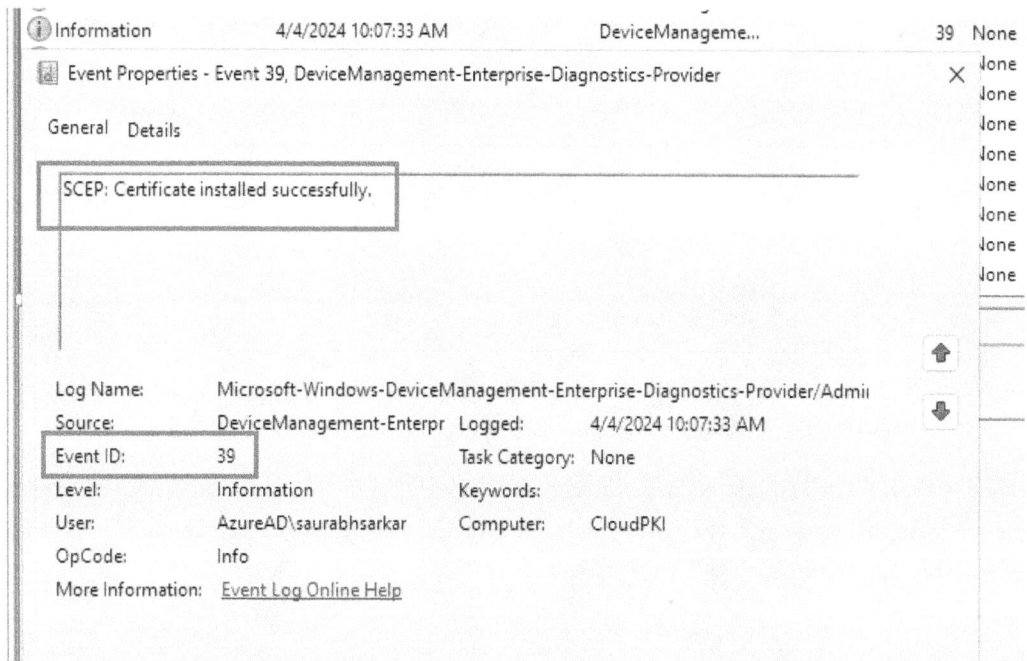

Figure 1.16: Event Viewer logs on the device showing the installation of the certificate

In this section, we explored the detailed workflow of SCEP certificate delivery using Cloud PKI. This process remains consistent across all major platforms, including Windows, Android, iOS, and macOS. There was a special focus on the certificate delivery flow in this chapter because gaining a clear understanding of this flow is essential for building a strong conceptual foundation, which in turn is critical for effective troubleshooting and issue resolution.

In the next section, we will explore the crux of SCEP certificate delivery via Cloud PKI, illustrated through a block diagram to provide visual clarity and contextual understanding.

Block diagram representation of the flow

Based on the explanation in the previous section, let's now examine a block diagram representation of the SCEP certificate flow using Cloud PKI.

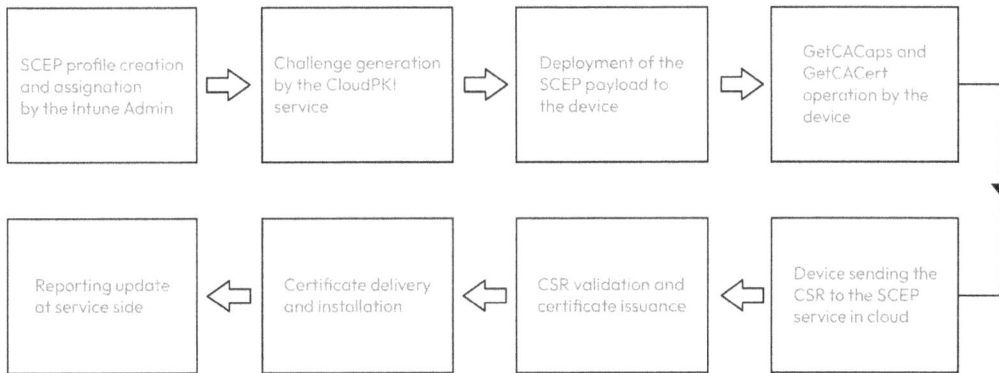

Figure 1.17: Block diagram showing an overview of the steps involved during SCEP cert delivery

At a high level, the SCEP certificate delivery process via Intune using Cloud PKI can be segmented into eight primary steps, as illustrated in the preceding block diagram. Each step is accompanied by corresponding logs, which serve as valuable tools for troubleshooting and issue resolution.

We will now explore how to locate an SCEP certificate on a device, noting that its location varies depending on the client's operating system.

Viewing the SCEP certificate at the device end

Once installed, the SCEP certificate issued by Cloud PKI is visible on the device. The location of the certificate varies depending on the operating system. The following table provides a detailed explanation:

Operating System	Location
Windows	MMC | Current User | Personal Store | Certificates
iOS	Settings | Device Management | Management Profile | More Details | Under the Certificates header, SHA-1 signifies the thumbprint
macOS	Keychains | System | My Certificates | SHA-1 signifies the thumbprint
Android	Third-party app (My Certificates application or equivalent) | User Credentials

Table 1.3: Respective locations of SCEP certificate based on operating system

When reviewing the SCEP certificate at the previously specified location, it is important to examine key attributes such as the subject name, **Subject Alternative Name** (**SAN**), validity period, key usage, and thumbprint, as these provide critical insights for validation.

In the next section, we will provide an overview of the various Cloud PKI models available to us during setup.

If the certificates are not visible on the device, it indicates a need for troubleshooting. The first step is to verify whether a certificate was actually issued for the user or device via the Intune portal, as explained in the *Reporting* section of this chapter later.

If the portal shows the certificate as issued but it still doesn't appear on the device, possible reasons could include the certificate being revoked from the portal or having expired, as illustrated in the following figure:

Home > Tenant admin | Cloud PKI > Issuing _for_BYOCA >

Issued leaf certificates   ...

() Refresh   ≡ Columns ∨

Subject name ↑	User principal name	Device name	Status	Thumbprint	Serial number	Issuance	Expiration
CN=oma, E=oma@everythingabou	oma@everythingabouti...	CLOUDPKI	Revoked	4E52BB1B71EB2F1...	00DEF76B28DFF...	4/03/2024, 23:0...	5/03/2024, 23:07:33 UTC
CN=pm, E=pm@everythingaboutin	pm@everythingaboutint...	MANIPALHOS	Expired	2A5263E7B4037E7...	65F386CE67A91...	7/09/2024, 08:3...	11/09/2024, 08:46:40 UTC

Figure 1.18: View of revoked certificates issued by Cloud PKI

If the certificate was not issued, the next step is to troubleshoot the device by revisiting the complete flow discussed in the previous section. This will help identify the exact point where the process breaks down, preventing certificate issuance.

Cloud PKI setup

Now, let's go through the steps needed for setting up Cloud PKI in the Intune portal. While doing the Cloud PKI setup, we have two options to choose from:

- **Microsoft-managed Cloud PKI root CA**: We deploy Microsoft Cloud PKI by using the root CA and issuing CAs in the cloud

- **Bring Your Own Certificate Authority (BYOCA)**: We deploy Microsoft Cloud PKI by using our own private CA

The basic difference between them is as follows:

- In the case of the Microsoft Cloud PKI root CA, there is no connection between Cloud PKI and on-premises. The root and issuing CAs are both hosted in the cloud and are managed and maintained by Microsoft.

- However, in BYOCA deployment, the issuing CA is in the cloud, and it is anchored to a root CA, which is present on-premises and maintained by us.

Here's a table outlining when to use Microsoft-managed Cloud PKI versus BYOCA to solidify your understanding:

Criteria	Microsoft-Managed Cloud PKI	BYOCA
Deployment complexity	Minimal; fully cloud-based, no on-premises infrastructure needed	Requires on-premises CA server
Maintenance overhead	Low; managed by Microsoft	Moderate; organizations are responsible for managing the on-premises CA
Use case suitability	Ideal for modern, cloud-first environments that don't want to create a CA for client cert delivery and are starting fresh	Ideal for environments with an existing on-premises CA, which can be plugged into the cloud

Table 1.4: Decision table: Microsoft Managed Cloud PKI versus BYOCA

Setting up the Microsoft-managed Cloud PKI root CA is very straightforward. However, for BYOCA, there are some additional steps. Let's take a look at both of them in the next section.

Setting up Microsoft-managed Cloud PKI

In this section, we are going to discuss how to create the root and the issuing CA in the cloud. This is a very straightforward deployment.

Creating the root CA

In order to create the root CA, we will take the following steps:

1. Go to the Intune portal, then **Tenant administration** | **Cloud PKI**, and click on **+ Create**, as shown in the following figure:

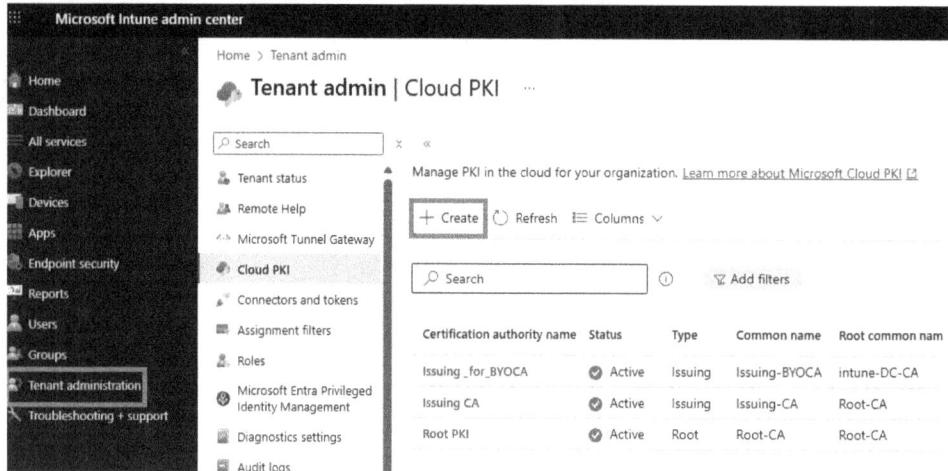

Figure 1.19: Creating a root CA in Cloud PKI

2. On the **Basics** page, provide the name of the CA.

3. On the **Configuration Settings** page, configure the CA as follows:

   - **CA type:** Select **Root CA** to create a new root CA.

   - **Validity period:** Set the validity of the root CA by choosing between 5, 10, 15, 20, and 25 years.

   - **Extended Key Usages:** We need to set the key usage types from the available options. We can also add a custom EKU by simply using the related object identifier of the EKU.

The following screenshot shows these settings in the Intune portal:

Home > Tenant admin | Cloud PKI >

Create certification authority ···

| ✓ Basics | ● Configuration settings | ○ Scope tags | ○ Review + create |

About root and issuing certificate authorities (CAs)

A root CA must be created before an issuing CA can be created. When using bring-your-own CA, a root CA is not required in Intune. Multiple issuing CAs can be contained by a root CA in Intune or bring-your-own CA. Only issuing CAs can be used to deploy leaf certificates to devices and users. Learn more about Microsoft Cloud PKI ☑

CA type *

| Root CA | ∨ |

Validity period *

| 25 years | ∨ |

Extended Key Usages *

To prevent potential security risks, each certificate authority is required to be constrained with specific purposes of use. For issuing CA, options are limited to those selected by its root CA.

| Select one | ∨ |

Type	Name	Object Identifier	
Server auth	Server auth	1.3.6.1.5.5.7.3.1	···
Client auth	Client auth	1.3.6.1.5.5.7.3.2	···
Mac address	Mac address	1.3.6.1.1.1.1.22	···
IPSEC user	IPSEC user	1.3.6.1.5.5.7.3.7	···

Figure 1.20: Configuring the properties of the root CA in the Intune portal

If you scroll further down, you'll see these options:

- **Subject attributes**: Select the CN
- **Encryption**: Select the key size algorithm by selecting between **RSA-2048 and SHA-256, RSA-3096 and SHA-384**, and **RSA-4096 and SHA-512**

Now we need to click on **Next**, as seen in the following screenshot, and then **Review + Create**.

Subject attributes

Provide details to help identify this certification authority.

Common name (CN) *

> EAI Root CA

Organization (O)

> EAI

Organizational unit (OU)

>

Country (C)

> India

State or province (ST)

> UP

Locality (L)

> Noida

Encryption

Key size and algorithm *

> RSA-4096 and SHA-512

Back   Next

Figure 1.21: Configuring the properties of the root CA in the Intune portal

Now the root CA is created, and we can view it in the Intune portal | **Tenant admin** | **Cloud PKI**, as seen in the following screenshot:

Manage PKI in the cloud for your organization. Learn more about Microsoft Cloud PKI ☑

+ Create ○ Refresh ☰ Columns ∨

🔍 Search   ⓘ   ⊽ Add filters

Certification authority name	Status	Type	Common name	Root common name	Issuance	Expiration
EAI Root CA	✓ Active	Root	EAI Root	EAI Root	10/21/2025, 04:46:39 UTC	10/21/2050, 04:46:39 UTC
Issuing _for_BYOCA	✓ Active	Issuing	Issuing-BYOCA	intune-DC-CA	3/27/2024, 12:26:34 UTC	3/27/2026, 12:36:34 UTC
Issuing CA	✓ Active	Issuing	Issuing-CA	Root-CA	3/22/2024, 04:22:56 UTC	3/22/2028, 04:22:56 UTC
Root PKI	✓ Active	Root	Root-CA	Root-CA	3/22/2024, 04:16:17 UTC	3/22/2029, 04:16:17 UTC

Newly created Root CA

Figure 1.22: Viewing the newly created root CA in the portal

If we click on the root CA, highlighted in the preceding figure, we can see all of the properties that we set during its creation, as seen in the following screenshot:

Home > Tenant admin | Cloud PKI >

EAI Root CA   ...
Root certification authority

🗑 Delete

ⓘ You can't edit the settings of a certificate authority (CA) once it's created.

Basics Edit

Name	EAI Root CA
Description	--
Status	✓ Active

Settings

CA type	Root CA
CA keys	Software
Extended Key Usages	Client auth (1.3.6.1.5.5.7.3.2) Server auth (1.3.6.1.5.5.7.3.1) IPSEC user (1.3.6.1.5.5.7.3.7) Mac address (1.3.6.1.1.1.1.22)
Validity period	25 years
Expiration	10/21/2050, 04:46:39 UTC
Common name (CN)	EAI Root
Organization (O)	EAI
Country (C)	IN
State or province (ST)	UO
Locality (L)	Noida
Key size and algorithm	RSA-4096 and SHA-512
CRL distribution point	http://primary-cdn.pki.azure.net/japaneast/crls/9e0696886262401f96353033e90cf955/0f567d24-0e1a-4e5c-a69d-c4a004869e63_v1/current.crl
Download certificate	Download

Scope tags Edit

Default

Figure 1.23: Viewing the properties of the newly created root CA in Cloud PKI

As highlighted in the preceding screenshot, once the root CA is created, we cannot edit any of its properties. Hence, it's important to make sure that we have the right settings in place during creation. We may want to include all relevant properties (e.g., EKUs) wherever possible, so we can use any of them later without needing to modify the CA, which isn't allowed.

Creating the issuing CA

Once the root CA is created, the next step is creating an issuing CA. The issuing CA is responsible for issuing certificates for Intune-managed devices. Once the issuing CA is created, it also creates the SCEP service, which we would then use in the SCEP profile in Intune, which is discussed in the following section.

We need to follow these steps in order to create the issuing CA:

1. Go to the Intune portal | **Tenant admin** | **Cloud PKI** and click on **+ Create**.
2. On the **Basics** page, provide the name of the CA.
3. On the **Configuration Settings** page, provide the CA's configuration:

   - **CA Type:** Here, select **Issuing CA**.
   - **Root CA Source:** This is going to be **Intune** as the root CA in this case is created in the Intune service.
   - **Root CA:** This would be the root CA server we created in the preceding step. Here, we are linking the issuing CA with the root.
   - **Validity Period:** We need to set the validity period of the issuing CA here.
   - **Extended Key Usage:** We need to set the purpose of the issuing CA by selecting the required key usage types. Only the EKUs selected for the root CA are available to choose from here.
   - **Subject attributes:** Specify the CN.
   - **Encryption:** This cannot be selected, and it is the same value as what we selected for the root.

The following screenshot shows these settings in the Intune portal:

Home > Tenant admin | Cloud PKI >

Create certification authority   ...

✓ Basics   ● Configuration settings   ○ Scope tags   ○ Review + create

About root and issuing certificate authorities (CAs)

A root CA must be created before an issuing CA can be created. When using bring-your-own CA, a root CA is not required in Intune. Multiple issuing CAs can be contained by a root CA in Intune or bring-your-own CA. Only issuing CAs can be used to deploy leaf certificates to devices and users. Learn more about Microsoft Cloud PKI ⧉

CA type *	
Issuing CA	⌄

Root CA source *	
Intune	⌄

Root CA *	
EAI Root CA ✕	

Common name (CN)	Status
EAI Root	active

Validity period *

10 years	⌄

Extended Key Usages *

To prevent potential security risks, each certificate authority is required to be constrained with specific purposes of use. For issuing CA, options are limited to those selected by its root CA.

Select one	⌄

Type	Name	Object Identifier	
Client auth	Client auth	1.3.6.1.5.5.7.3.2	...

Figure 1.24: Creating an issuing CA in Cloud PKI

Once these values have been set, we need to click on **Next** and **Review + create**, which would create the issuing CA for us.

Once the issuing CA is created, it will be visible under **Tenant Admin | Cloud PKI**. If we click on it, we can view all its properties by going into the **Properties** tab, shown in the following figure. This will list all the settings of the issuing CA that was created during its setup.

Home > Tenant admin | Cloud PKI >

Issuing CA ⋯
Issuing certification authority   ✕

▷ Resume   ‖ **Pause**   ⟳ Revoke   🗑 Delete

Monitor   **Properties**

ⓘ You can't edit the settings of a certificate authority (CA) once it's created.

Basics Edit

Name	Issuing CA	
Description	--	
Status	✅ Active	

Settings

CA type	Issuing CA
CA keys	Software
Root CA	Root-CA
Extended Key Usages	Client auth (1.3.6.1.5.5.7.3.2)
	Email protection (1.3.6.1.5.5.7.3.4)
Validity period	4 years
Expiration	3/22/2028, 04:22:56 UTC
Common name (CN)	Issuing-CA
Key size and algorithm	RSA-4096 and SHA-512
CRL distribution point	http://primary-cdn.pki.azure.net/japaneast/crls/9e0696886262401f96353033e90cf955/a750bae2-ada5-457b-b53e-0e2c9b29a83c_v1/current.crl
AIA | CA issuer URI	http://primary-cdn.pki.azure.net/japaneast/cacerts/9e0696886262401f96353033e90cf955/8161956f-17ae-44ca-8333-ab3ee95e9977_v1/cert.cer
SCEP URI	https://{{CloudPKIFQDN}}/TrafficGateway/PassThroughRoutingService/CloudPki/CloudPkiService/Scep/8dbf03ab-f625-4076-b74b-bbd9543986ba/a750bae2-ada5-457b-b53e-0e2c9b29a83c
Download certificate	**Download**

Properties of the Issuing CA selected during its setup

Figure 1.25: Viewing properties of an issuing CA in the Intune portal

As seen, we have the option of downloading the root certificate of the issuing CA that needs to be pushed to the device for chain building. Also, in the preceding screenshot, we can see the SCEP URI, which has been generated by the issuing CA. This is the equivalent of the NDES URL, which the end devices will reach out to, to request a client certificate. We will delve into the usage of the SCEP URI later in this chapter.

In the next section, let's briefly take a look at the configurations needed for BYOCA setup.

Setting up BYOCA

Before we set up BYOCA, let's first understand the concept. With BYOCA, we have to download a CSR from our issuing CA in the cloud, and since it is going to be anchored with the root on-premises, we need to get the CSR signed by the root (on-premises) and then upload the signed CSR back to Cloud PKI. This is done to ensure that the issuing CA in the cloud is an entity that is trusted by the on-premises root CA. Let's take a look at the following diagram, which illustrates this flow:

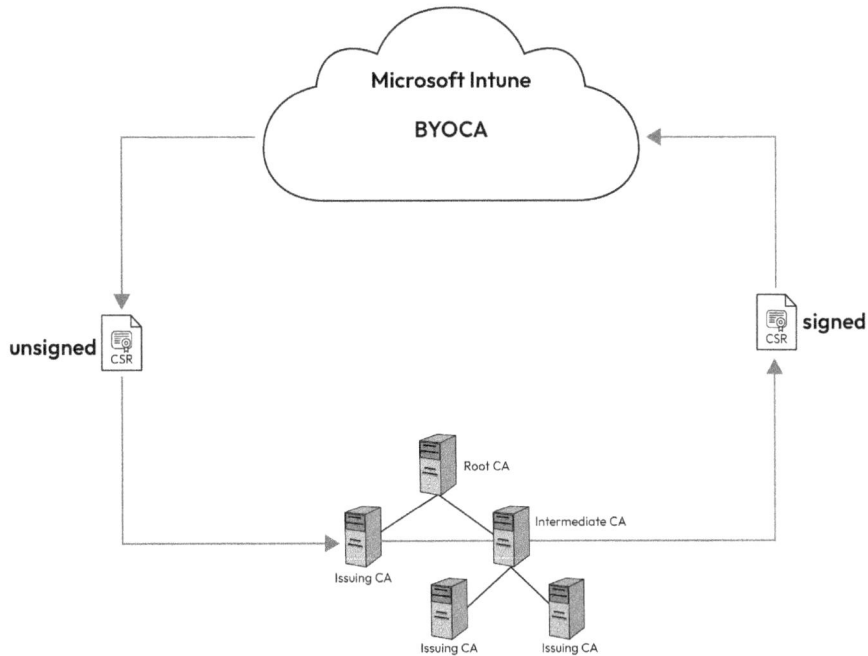

Figure 1.26: Diagram illustrating the process of signing a CSR during Cloud PKI setup

Now that we have understood the concept of the CSR signing process, let's build BYOCA in the next section.

Building BYOCA

The initial steps for building BYOCA are similar to those in the previous section:

1. Navigate to the Intune portal | **Tenant admin** | **Cloud PKI** | **+ Create**.

2. In the **Basics** tab, enter the name of the CA.

3. In the next tab, under **Configuration settings**, enter the following details:

   - **CA type**: Issuing CA

   - **Root CA source**: Bring your own root CA

   - **Validity period**: This cannot be configured, and it would be determined by the validity of the root CA on-premises

   - **Extended Key Usages**: Select from the dropdown as per your requirements

   - **Subject Attributes**: Enter the CN, country, and so on

   - **Encryption** | **Key Size**: Select from the dropdown as per your organization's requirements

The following screenshot shows these settings in the Intune portal:

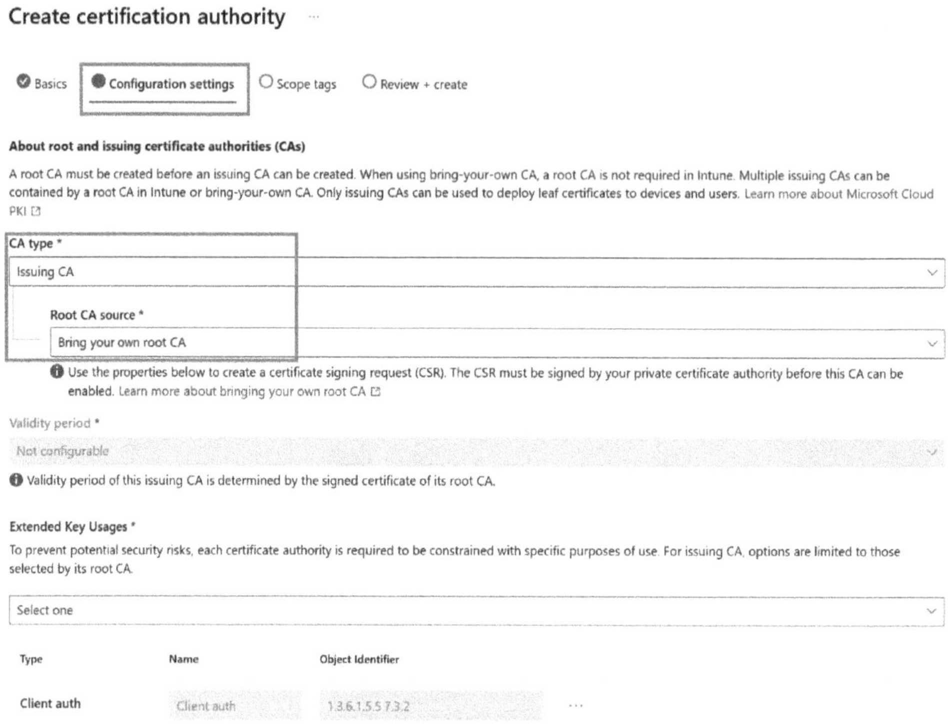

Create certification authority ...

Figure 1.27: Configuring settings for BYOCA in Cloud PKI

4. Now we just need to click on **Next** and **Create**. This will complete the initial steps of the BYOCA creation process.

However, we will notice that the CA is still not ready for issuing certificates as its CSR has not been signed by the on-premises root yet.

When we view the CA in the portal, we see **Signing required** under the **Status** column. We also have the option of downloading and uploading the CSR into the cloud CA, as seen in the following figure:

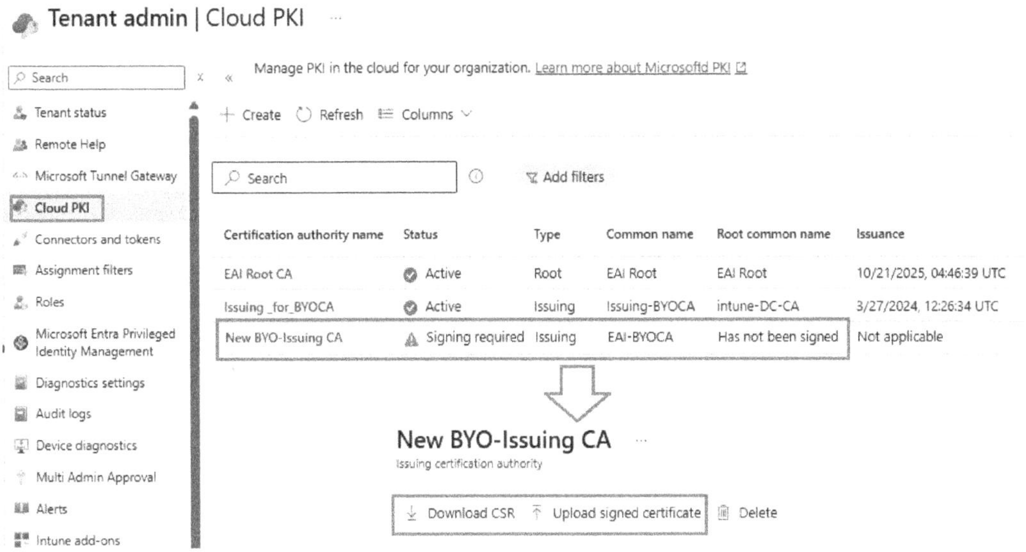

Figure 1.28: The CSR signing process during Cloud PKI setup

There are two ways of getting the CSR signed by the on-premises root CA:

- Use the CA web enrollment URL shown in the following screenshot.

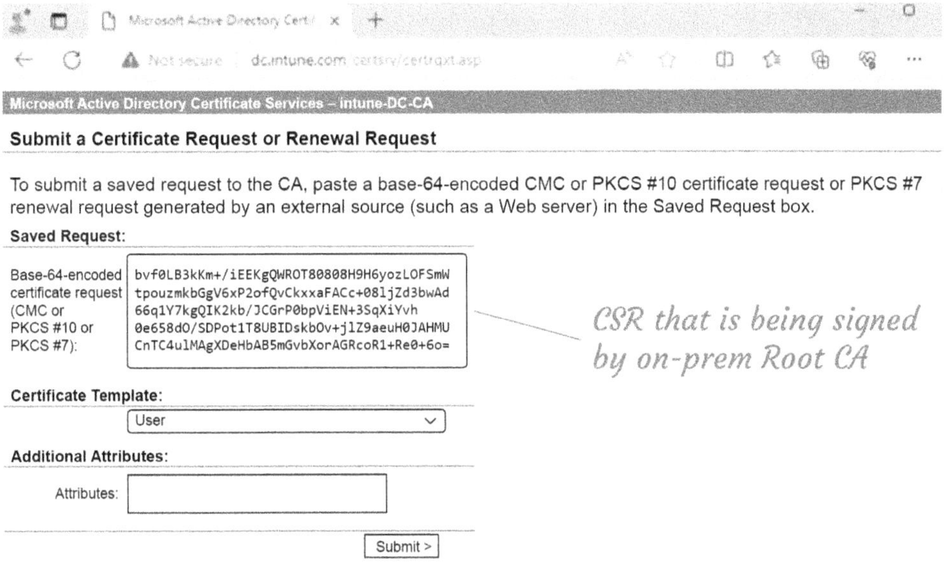

Figure 1.29: The process of signing the CSR by the on-premises CA

- We can use the `certreq.exe` command line too:

```
certreq -submit -attrib "CertificateTemplate:<template_name>"
-config "<CA_server_name>\<CA_name>" <request_file> <response_file>
```

Once the CSR is signed by the on-premises root and uploaded back to the CA in the portal, it is ready to issue certificates!

Creating an SCEP profile in the Intune portal

Now we are going to use the issuing CA in the cloud for SCEP certificate delivery to Intune-enrolled devices. This step remains the same for both BYOCA and Microsoft-managed CAs. In either case, once the issuing CA is created, we will get an SCEP URI, as seen in the following figure. The devices need to reach out to that SCEP URI in order to request a cert.

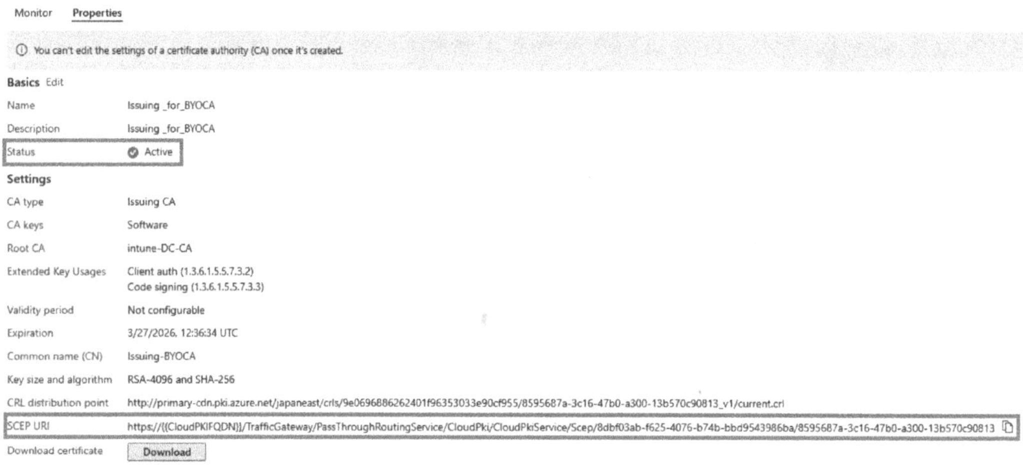

Figure 1.30: The configurations of a working Cloud PKI setup

This SCEP URI needs to be used in the SCEP profile, which we will create in the Intune portal by following these steps:

1. Go to the Intune portal | **Configuration** | **+ Create** | **SCEP certificate**, as seen in the following screenshot:

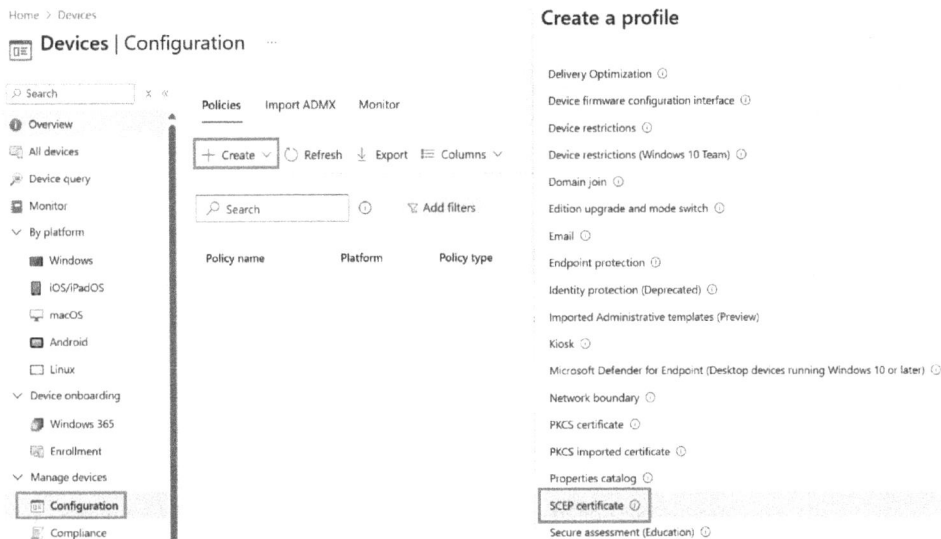

Figure 1.31: Creating an SCEP certificate profile in the Intune portal

2. Next, you'll find a screen with the following options:

   - **Certificate type**: This can be **User** or **Device**. For **User**, the subject name maps to the user's name/UPN; for **Device**, it maps to the device ID. The choice basically depends on authentication needs and RADIUS configuration.

   - **Subject name format**: CN={{UserName}},E={{EmailAddress}}.

   - **Subject alternative name**: Can be set to **User principal name (UPN)** with a dynamic value of {{UserName}}.

   - **Certificate validity period**: Can be set in days, months, or years.

   - **Key storage provider (KSP)**: Select from the dropdown as per need. We recommend setting it to **Enroll to Trusted Platform Module (TPM) KSP if present, otherwise Software KSP**.

   - **Key usage**: Select **Digital signature** and/or **Key encipherment**.

The following screenshot shows these settings in the Intune portal:

SCEP certificate   ⋯
Windows 10 and later

| ✅ Basics | ❷ Configuration settings | ③ Scope tags | ④ Assignments | ⑤ Applicability Rules | ⑥ Review + create |

| Certificate type | User | ⌄ |

| Subject name format * ⓘ | CN={{UserName}},E={{EmailAddress}} | ✓ |

Subject alternative name ⓘ

Attribute		Value	
User principal name (UPN)	⌄	{{UserName}}	✓ 🗑 •••
	⌄	Not configured	

| Certificate validity period * ⓘ | Years | ⌄ | 1 |

| Key storage provider (KSP) * ⓘ | Enroll to Trusted Platform Module (TPM) KSP if present, otherwise Software K... ⌄ |

| Key usage * ⓘ | 2 selected | ⌄ |

| Key size (bits) * ⓘ | 4096 | ⌄ |

Figure 1.32: Configuring the SCEP certificate profile in the Intune portal

The points below explain the settings that must be configured in the SCEP profile:

- **Root certificate:** We need to link the root certificate of the chain to the SCEP profile here

- **Extended key usage:** We need to add client authentication if the certificate is going to be used for Wi-Fi/VPN auth

- **Renewal threshold (%):** Leave it as the default value of **20**

- **SCEP Server URLs:** Here, we need to enter the SCEP URI that we got from the issuing CA/Cloud PKI server in the previous section

Let's take a look at these settings in the following screenshot of the Intune portal:

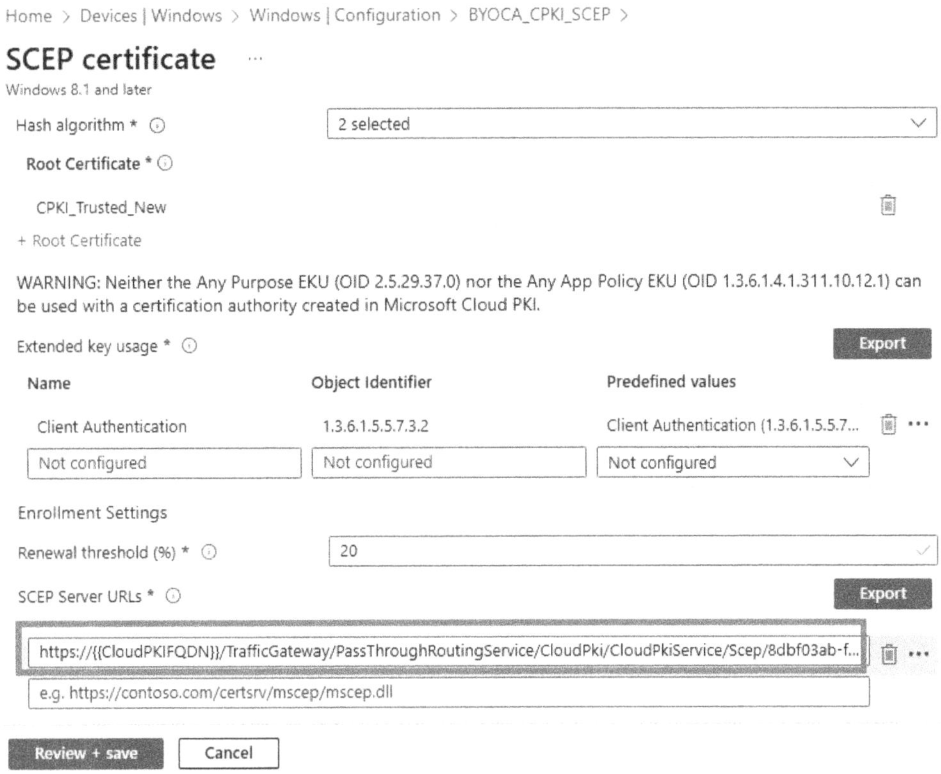

Home > Devices | Windows > Windows | Configuration > BYOCA_CPKI_SCEP >

SCEP certificate ...

Windows 8.1 and later

Hash algorithm * ⓘ	2 selected ⌄

Root Certificate * ⓘ

CPKI_Trusted_New   🗑

+ Root Certificate

WARNING: Neither the Any Purpose EKU (OID 2.5.29.37.0) nor the Any App Policy EKU (OID 1.3.6.1.4.1.311.10.12.1) can be used with a certification authority created in Microsoft Cloud PKI.

Extended key usage * ⓘ   **Export**

Name	Object Identifier	Predefined values	
Client Authentication	1.3.6.1.5.5.7.3.2	Client Authentication (1.3.6.1.5.5.7...	🗑 ···
Not configured	Not configured	Not configured ⌄	

Enrollment Settings

Renewal threshold (%) * ⓘ	20 ✓

SCEP Server URLs * ⓘ   **Export**

https://{{CloudPKIFQDN}}/TrafficGateway/PassThroughRoutingService/CloudPki/CloudPkiService/Scep/8dbf03ab-f...	🗑 ···
e.g. https://contoso.com/certsrv/mscep/mscep.dll	

Review + save   Cancel

Figure 1.33: SCEP profile in Intune using Cloud PKI URLs

The SCEP profile now just needs to be assigned to a user/device group as applicable.

> Before creating the SCEP profile, we also need to deploy the trusted root certificate profile for both the root and the issuing CA from the Intune portal. These certificates are used for chain building and establishing trust. The CSR of the root/issuing certificate needs to be uploaded to the profile.
>
> We should ensure that the same group is used for both root and SCEP certificate assignments. We should avoid using different groups, which is not recommended.

In this section, we reviewed the setup and installation of Cloud PKI, which is notably straightforward, typically taking less than 10 minutes to complete. In contrast, configuring on-premises NDES for certificate delivery is significantly more time-consuming, often requiring 2–3 hours due to the need for installing and validating multiple components individually.

In the following section, we will explore the reporting capabilities associated with certificates issued via Cloud PKI. Robust and reliable reporting is essential to validate that Cloud PKI is operating effectively and delivering the expected outcomes.

Reporting

Monitoring the certificates deployed to Intune-managed devices by the Microsoft Cloud PKI service is straightforward. Each Microsoft Cloud PKI issuing CA has a dashboard that displays the number of deployed certificates, including the following:

- Active certificates
- Expired certificates
- Revoked certificates
- Total number of issued certificates

As seen in the following screenshot, we can get details of the certificates that were issued along with their status by going to **Tenant admin | Cloud PKI | CA**. The portal itself provides the ability to revoke a certificate if needed.

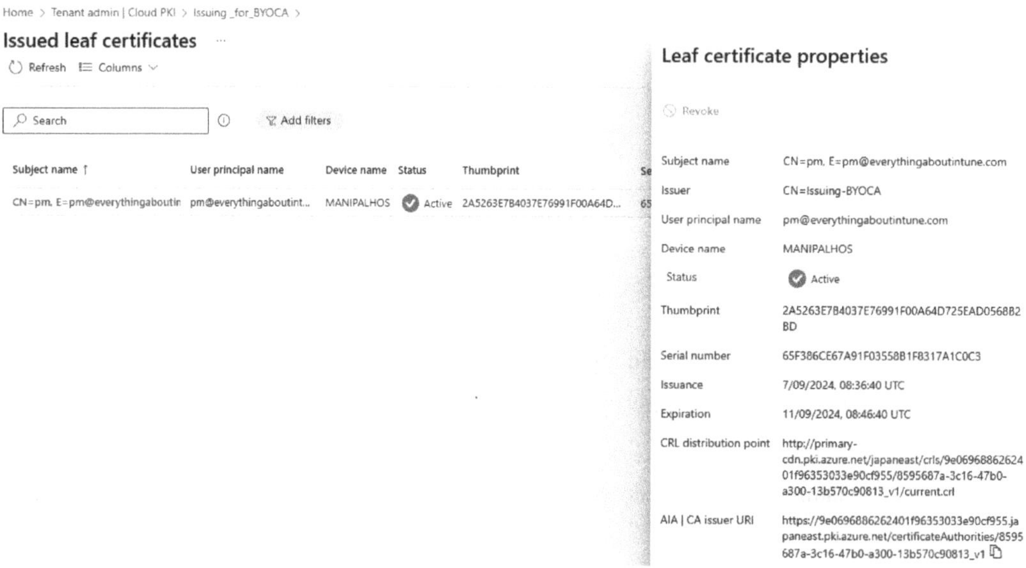

Figure 1.34: Intune portal showing Cloud PKI certificate reporting

Certificates are automatically revoked when a user or device is disabled or deleted. For devices, this also applies if they're retired or wiped. If we need to revoke a certificate manually, open the issuing CA in Intune and select **View all certificates**.

When we revoke a certificate for a user or device that still has an active SCEP profile, the next device check-in will trigger a new certificate request and issuance. To prevent this, we have to remove all SCEP policy assignments before revoking. Once revoked, the change is immediately reflected in the **Certificate Revocation List (CRL)** because the revocation triggers a CRL rebuild.

We can also go to the **Monitor** | **Certificates** section of the portal, which gives us similar reporting options to what is seen in the following figure:

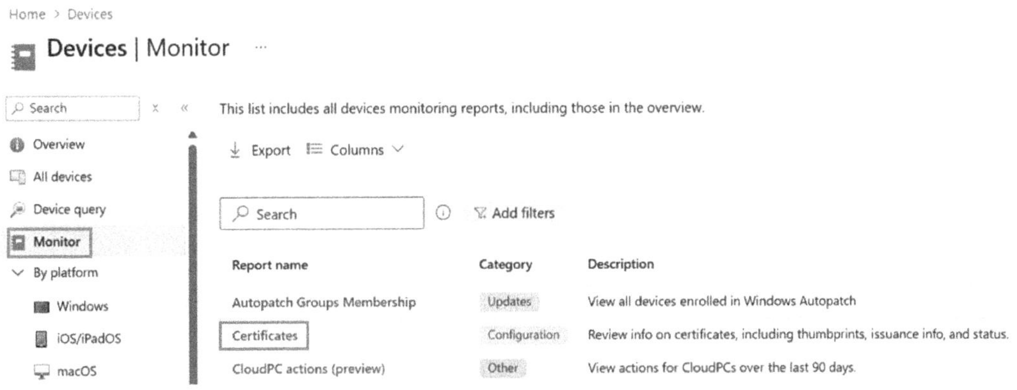

Figure 1.35: Intune portal showing Cloud PKI certificate reporting

The Intune console provides rapid and comprehensive reporting for certificates issued via Cloud PKI. These reports include key attributes such as device name/ID, username, certificate thumbprint, serial number, and SAN. Additionally, the reports can be exported for future reference and audit purposes. This is important because it enables us to keep track of all the certificates that have been issued to users/devices in our environment.

So far, we've explored the certificate delivery process using Cloud PKI in detail. To provide a more complete understanding, it's important to briefly revisit how certificate deployment was traditionally handled through on-premises NDES. A high-level overview of this legacy approach is provided in the next section.

Bonus insight: SCEP certificate delivery via on-premises NDES and Intune

Let's get a 1,000-foot overview of an SCEP certificate delivery via on-premises NDES and Intune using the following diagram. We will not be talking about the logs here as the purpose of this section is just to understand the basics.

As we'll see, the core logic behind SCEP certificate delivery remains consistent between on-premises NDES and Cloud PKI. The key distinction lies in the infrastructure: with on-premises NDES, multiple components—such as the NDES server, application proxy, and connectors—must be deployed/maintained within our on-premises environment. This added complexity increases the administrative burden during both setup and ongoing management.

The following diagram explains the steps involved in the deployment of an SCEP cert via Intune using on-premises NDES.

This section is provided for reference and aligns with the Cloud PKI flow discussed earlier in the chapter. As such, we won't delve into the detailed workings or log analysis of on-premises NDES, since that falls outside the scope of this book.

The following are the initial four steps that occur at the Intune service end and the device end to facilitate the certificate delivery.

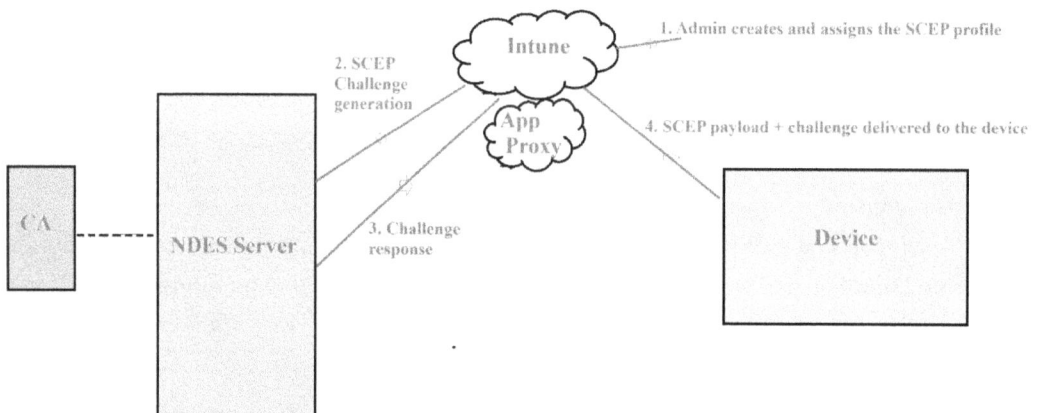

Figure 1.36: (Part 1) Flow of SCEP cert delivery using on-premises NDES and Intune

The following is an explanation of steps 1–4 in the preceding diagram:

1. Admin creates and assigns the SCEP profile.
2. SCEP challenge generation.

3. Challenge response.

4. SCEP payload + challenge delivered to the device.

Now let's refer to the following diagram to understand the next four steps:

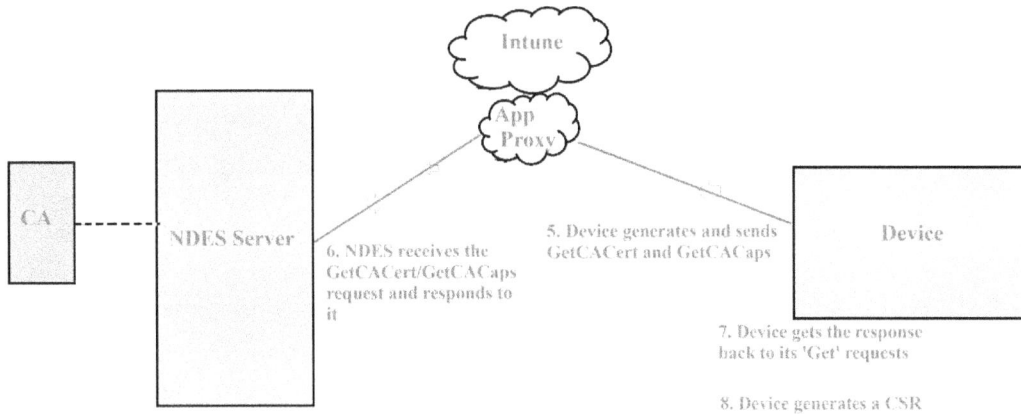

Figure 1.37: (Part 2) Flow of SCEP cert delivery using on-premises NDES

The following is an explanation of steps 5–8:

5. The device generates and sends the GetCACert and GetCACaps requests.

6. The GetCACaps and GetCACert requests are received by NDES and it responds.

7. The device receives the response to the GET request.

8. The device creates a CSR (certificate enrollment request).

Now we will refer to the following diagram to understand the next five steps:

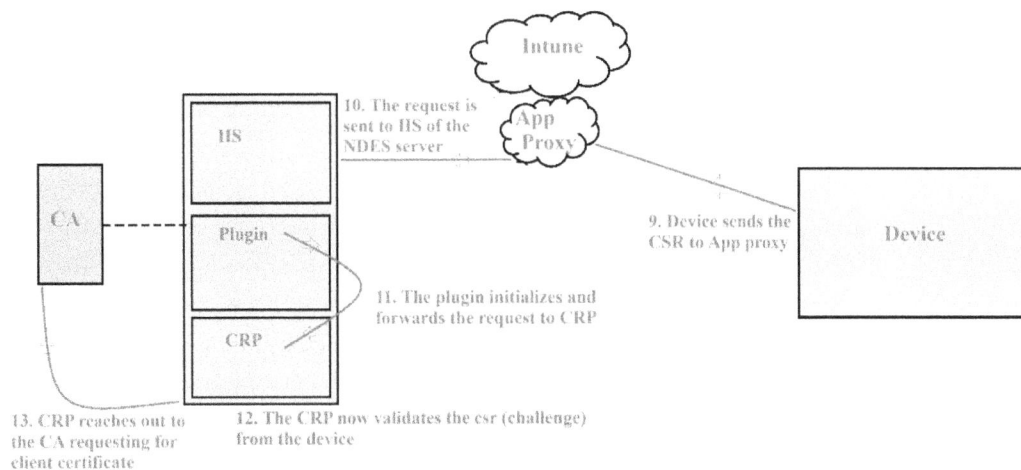

Figure 1.38: (Part 3) Flow of SCEP cert delivery using on-premises NDES and Intune

The following is an explanation of steps 9–13:

9. The device sends the CSR to the proxy.

10. The request is sent to the NDES server.

11. The plugin initializes and forwards the request to the CRP.

12. The CRP now validates the CSR from the device.

13. The CRP reaches out to the CA requesting a client certificate.

Now let's look at the following diagram, which illustrates the final four steps of the SCEP cert delivery:

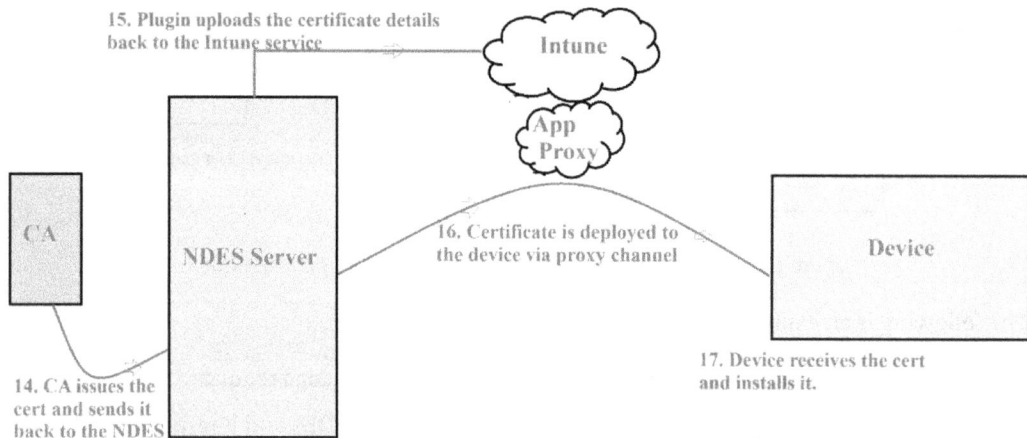

Figure 1.39: (Part 4) Flow of SCEP cert delivery using on-premises NDES

The following is an explanation of steps 14–17:

14. The CA issues the certificate and sends it back to NDES.

15. The plugin uploads the certificate details back to the Intune service.

16. The certificate is deployed to the device.

17. The device receives the certificate.

The flow of CSR validation in on-premises NDES has changed significantly with the introduction of the new unified certificate connector, which was released by Microsoft in 2022. The unified certificate connector replaced the older Intune certificate connector. The legacy connector was used to support SCEP and PKCS certificate deployment scenarios but required separate installations and configurations for different certificate types. The unified connector consolidated these capabilities into a single, streamlined solution, simplifying deployment and management.

Please refer to the following flow diagram, which provides insights into the flow with the unified certificate connector.

As we can see in step 11 of the flow, NDES is reaching out to the Intune service for CSR validation, and in step 12, the Intune service is responding to NDES with the outcome of validation (success/ failure). This change was implemented to streamline the workflow and shift part of the processing load from on-premises NDES infrastructure to the cloud, thereby enhancing efficiency.

As per the new flow with the introduction of the unified certificate connector, the SCEP challenge validation happens in the cloud, as shown:

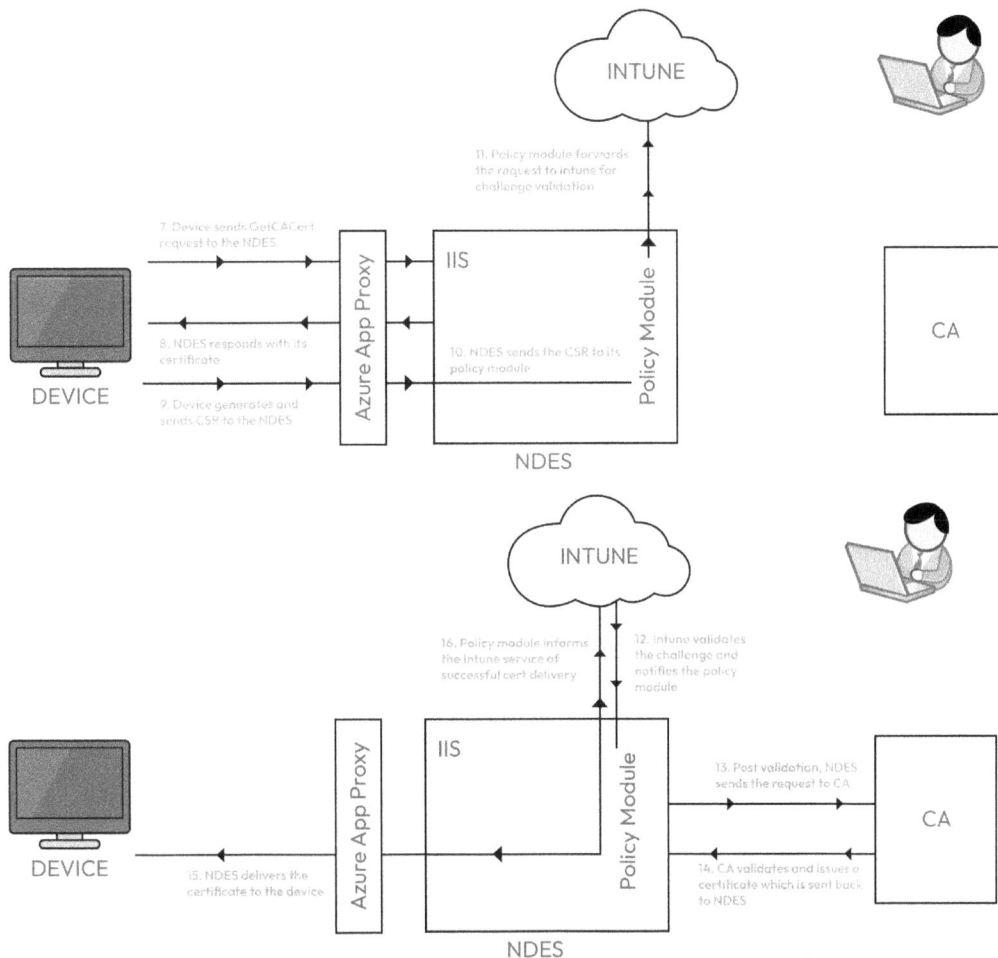

Figure 1.40: (Part 5) Flow of SCEP cert delivery using on-premises NDES and Intune

With this section, we've covered the foundational concepts of SCEP certificate delivery using an on-premises NDES setup. While the core logic and flow closely mirror what we saw with Cloud PKI earlier in this chapter, the on-premises approach involves multiple components—such as servers, connectors, and proxies—that add complexity to setup and troubleshooting. Cloud PKI simplifies this by offloading much of the infrastructure to the cloud. The purpose of this section was to provide a high-level understanding of the traditional SCEP flow, enabling a meaningful comparison with the modern Cloud PKI approach.

Once the SCEP certificate from Cloud PKI has been successfully delivered to the device, it must be utilized to establish CBA—the primary objective of the certificate issuance process. In the next section, we will explore the post-deployment phase, focusing on how the certificate is used for authentication against a RADIUS server/NPS, along with the steps involved in enabling this.

The aftermath of certificate delivery using Cloud PKI

Well, we didn't deploy the SCEP certificate using Cloud PKI to the device just because it was fun, right? The primary intention is to utilize the certificate for authentication purposes, typically for Wi-Fi authentication. Before delving into how the certificate can be used for authentication, let's understand the concept of chain building.

In the following diagram, we can see the hierarchy of a certificate. At the very bottom, we have the client certificate (SCEP certificate). The client certificate is issued to the username or device name (which is configurable) and is issued by the issuing CA/intermediate CA.

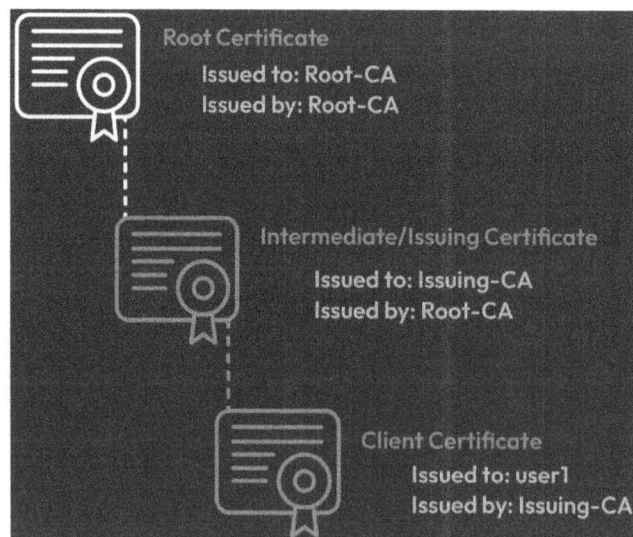

Figure 1.41: Explanation of the certificate chain

Now, let's consider a scenario where we have a RADIUS server in our environment that performs authentication before allowing devices to connect to Wi-Fi. The device will present the aforementioned SCEP certificate to the RADIUS server. However, by default, this server does not recognize or trust this certificate. The server must be configured to recognize that the client certificate presented by the device originates from a trusted source.

The server will trust the client certificate only if the chain of the user's SCEP certificate is present in the server's store. In this example, the chain of the user's SCEP certificate contains two certificates, as shown in the diagram: the root certificate (issued to and by the root) and the intermediate certificate (issued by the root and to the issuing/intermediate CA).

This means that only if these two certificates (the certificate chain) are present in the RADIUS server's certificate store will the server recognize and trust a client certificate that has originated from the same chain.

This logic applies not only to the RADIUS server but also to all types of endpoints. For example, consider our Windows devices. When navigating to an HTTPS website (i.e., one with an SSL certificate), the Windows device will only trust that certificate if its chain is already present in the device's certificate store. If the chain is not present, an error will occur, similar to what you might see when attempting to visit a website with an SSL certificate from an unknown source.

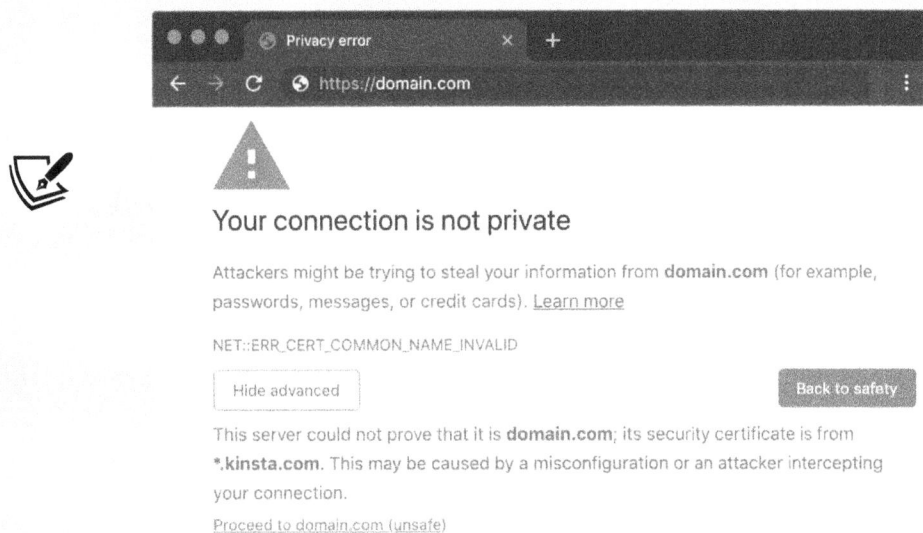

Figure 1.42: Message when accessing untrusted sites from the browser

Therefore, when we purchase a laptop, the image includes a default list of trusted root certificates from common CA vendors, such as DigiCert, Entrust, GoDaddy, Baltimore, and Microsoft. This ensures that when our device tries to access any resource with a client or SSL certificate from these providers, the device will trust them by default.

Hence, for any entity (such as a RADIUS server) to trust a certificate (SCEP certificate), it must possess the entire certificate chain (i.e., root and issuing certificates) of the certificate it needs to trust.

We will now apply this concept to two scenarios that cover how CBA occurs.

Scenario 1: CBA for a Microsoft-managed CA

We'll begin by exploring the setup of a traditional CBA in the following section. Once that's clear, we'll walk through the connection flow for a CBA.

Understanding the setup

In the following diagram, on the left-hand side, we have the device that is enrolled to Intune, and on the right-hand side, we have the Wi-Fi access point/RADIUS server.

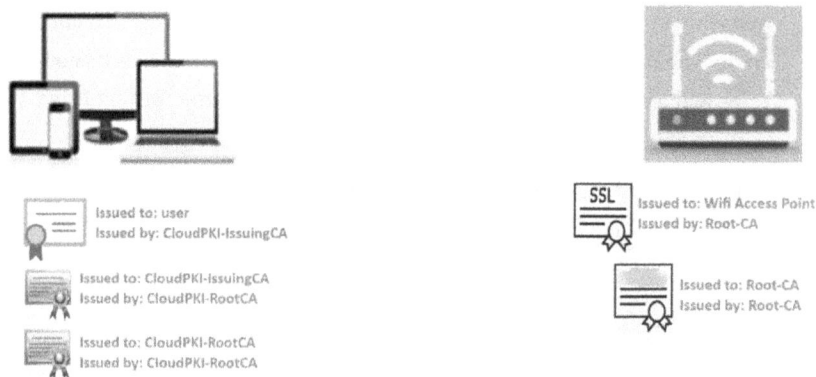

Figure 1.43: Setup for CBA for Microsoft-managed CA

The following are some key points to keep in mind from the diagram:

- The device has the SCEP cert from Cloud PKI, and this is a Microsoft-managed CA scenario (where both the root and the issuing CA are hosted on the cloud).

- The SCEP that is issued to the user and present in the device is issued by `CloudPKI-IssuingCA`.

- We also understand that for the device to trust the SCEP certificate, it must possess the entire certificate chain. This chain comprises two certificates: one issued by the root to the issuing CA, and the other a self-signed certificate issued by the root to itself.

Thus far, we have established that the device holds three certificates: one root, one intermediate, and one SCEP (user certificate).

Just as a website running HTTPS has an SSL certificate bound to it, a Wi-Fi access point/RADIUS server also has a certificate that secures the connection. Similar to a secure website, the Wi-Fi access point/RADIUS server has an SSL certificate issued by the CA and assigned to the hostname of the RADIUS server.

But who is going to issue this certificate? It is issued by our on-premises CA. The following two points outline important considerations to keep in mind in this scenario.

- Currently, Cloud PKI does not have the capability to issue certificates to non-Intune managed devices. Since a Wi-Fi endpoint cannot be enrolled in Intune, the certificate must come from our on-premises CA.

- Additionally, the Wi-Fi access point will not inherently trust this SSL certificate. Therefore, the Wi-Fi access point needs to have the certificate chain (i.e., the issuing and root certificates of the on-premises CA) that issued the SSL certificate.

Thus far, we have established that the Wi-Fi access point/RADIUS server has two certificates: the SSL certificate (issued by the on-premises CA) and the root certificate/chain for the on-premises CA. Now, let's understand how the connection happens for this scenario.

Understanding the connection flow

Let's see how the connection flow happens during a CBA by utilizing a certificate from Cloud PKI:

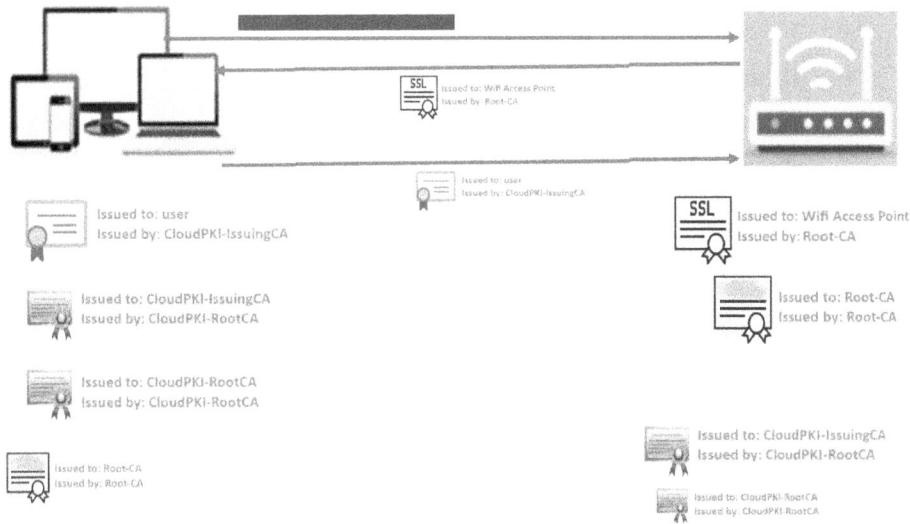

Figure 1.44: The connection for cert-based auth for Microsoft-managed CA

The following steps outline the process a device follows when attempting to connect to a Wi-Fi access point using an SCEP certificate issued via Cloud PKI:

1. When the device wants to connect to the Wi-Fi endpoint, it sends a connection request to the broadcasted Wi-Fi SSID, akin to sending a greeting message. Although a three-way handshake occurs, we will not delve into the details of it here.

2. The Wi-Fi endpoint/RADIUS responds to the device's connection request by sending the SSL certificate issued by the on-premises root CA. This certificate will be used to encrypt the communication between the Wi-Fi endpoint/RADIUS and the device moving forward.

   However, the device will not inherently trust this SSL certificate, as it was issued by an on-premises CA that the device does not recognize.

   For the communication between the device and the Wi-Fi endpoint/RADIUS to proceed, the device must trust the SSL certificate of the RADIUS server. This trust can only be established if the device already possesses the certificate chain of the Wi-Fi's SSL certificate.

   Thus, the device needs to have the root certificate of the on-premises CA (issued by the on-premises root/to the on-premises root) beforehand.

   How will the device get the root certificate of the on-premises root CA? We need to ensure it is deployed via Intune by creating a trusted root certificate profile.

   The conclusion from this step is: the device now needs to have four certificates!

   - The SCEP user cert (issued by Cloud PKI)
   - The root cert of the Cloud PKI chain
   - The intermediate cert of the Cloud PKI chain
   - The root certificate of the on-premises CA (which issued the SSL for the Wi-Fi endpoint/RADIUS)

3. In the next step of the communication, the device will present the user SCEP certificate (obtained from Cloud PKI) to the Wi-Fi access point/RADIUS server for authentication.

   However, the Wi-Fi endpoint will not inherently trust this user SCEP certificate, as it originates from the Cloud PKI CA, which the Wi-Fi endpoint is unfamiliar with.

   Therefore, for the Wi-Fi endpoint/RADIUS server to recognize and trust the user SCEP certificate generated by Cloud PKI, it must possess the certificate chain of the SCEP certificate, which is the root cert of the cloud CA (i.e., issued by the root/to the root CA) and the intermediate cert of the cloud CA (i.e., issued by the root/to the issuing CA), as shown in *Figure 1.45*.

The conclusion from this step is: the Wi-Fi endpoint/RADIUS now needs to have four certificates!

- The SSL cert (issued by the on-premises CA)
- The root cert of the on-premises CA
- The root cert of the cloud CA
- The intermediate cert of the cloud CA

Challenge: How do you get the Cloud PKI chain certs to the Wi-Fi endpoint/RADIUS server?

Well, the Wi-Fi endpoint/RADIUS is not enrolled to Intune, so we cannot leverage Intune here to deploy it. We can deploy it via a GPO, or it needs to be installed manually/sideloaded.

A RADIUS server is responsible for authenticating devices or users attempting to connect to a secure Wi-Fi network. It works alongside 802.1X and EAP protocols such as EAP-TLS, which use digital certificates instead of passwords for authentication. The RADIUS server validates the client's SCEP-issued certificate and, upon successful verification, grants access to the Wi-Fi SSID. Additionally, it enforces network policies such as VLAN assignment and access control.

To summarize, the following certificates need to be present on both parties for CBA to work in this scenario:

Device	Wi-Fi Endpoint/RADIUS
SCEP cert issued by Cloud PKI	SSL cert issued by the on-premises CA
Root cert of Cloud PKI	Root cert of the on-premises CA
Issuing cert of Cloud PKI	Root cert of Cloud PKI
Root cert of the on-premises CA	Issuing cert of Cloud PKI

Table 1.5: List of certificates needed to facilitate cert-based auth in a Microsoft-managed CA scenario

If the aforementioned certificates are deployed and installed on both parties (i.e., the end device and the Wi-Fi endpoint) in advance, we can seamlessly achieve the required CBA using the SCEP certificate originating from Cloud PKI.

Scenario 2: CBA for BYOCA

Let's keep all the concepts from the previous section in mind and examine their applicability to Cloud PKI scenarios where we have a BYOCA setup, meaning the issuing CA is in the cloud and anchored to the on-premises root CA.

Understanding the setup

In the following diagram, we have the same setup with the device on the left side and the Wi-Fi endpoint on the right. Similar to the previous scenario, the device has an SCEP certificate issued to a user by the Cloud PKI issuing CA.

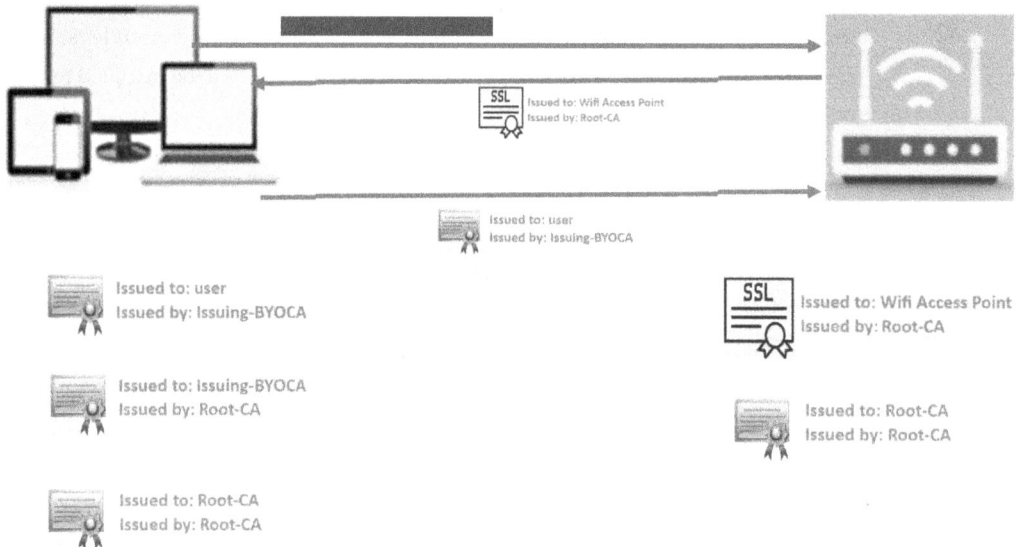

Figure 1.45: The connection for cert-based auth for BYOCA

Keep the following in mind:

- For the device to trust the SCEP certificate, it needs the certificate chain of the Cloud PKI CA. Therefore, the device must have the issuing CA certificate (issued to Cloud PKI by the on-premises root) and the self-signed root certificate of the on-premises root CA.

- On the right side, the prerequisite for the Wi-Fi endpoint/RADIUS server involves an SSL certificate issued to the Wi-Fi endpoint/RADIUS by the on-premises CA. For the Wi-Fi endpoint to trust this certificate, it must have the certificate chain of the SSL certificate, which includes the certificate issued by the root CA to itself (the same self-signed certificate that the device also needs, as mentioned previously).

The key point I want to emphasize is that the chain of the SCEP certificate obtained by the device and the chain of the SSL certificate held by the Wi-Fi endpoint/RADIUS server both originate from the same on-premises root server. This means that when the device attempts to connect to the Wi-Fi and is presented with the SSL certificate, it inherently trusts it because it already possesses the root certificate. Similarly, when the Wi-Fi endpoint/RADIUS server examines the SCEP certificate, it trusts it as well, since it also has the same root certificate.

Therefore, the conclusion is that in the case of BYOCA with Cloud PKI, there is no need to deliver or install any additional root certificates on either party for chain building, as both already have the same root certificate. In comparison, for Microsoft-managed CA scenarios, there is an overhead of manually installing an additional certificate on the Wi-Fi endpoint/RADIUS server.

Tips:

- Up to six CAs can be created within an Intune tenant.
- Intune hosts the CRL distribution point for each CA. The CRL validity period is seven days, with publishing and refresh occurring every 3.5 days. The CRL is updated with each certificate revocation.
- Intune supports RSA for signing and encryption algorithms, with key sizes of 2048, 3072, and 4096.
- Intune supports SHA-256, SHA-384, and SHA-512 for hash algorithms.
- Mixing SCEP URIs from Cloud PKI with SCEP URLs for on-premises NDES within the same SCEP profile is not supported.
- The EKU determines the intended purpose of the certificate. The EKU must be selected when creating the root CA, issuing CA, and SCEP profile. Planning ahead is essential, as the EKU list cannot be modified after CA creation in the portal.
- For security reasons, **Any Purpose EKU** is not permitted in Cloud PKI.
- The CAs created in Cloud PKI are internal to the tenant and are not public CAs.

Cloud PKI root and issuing CAs, and BYOCA issuing CAs anchored to a private CA, can exist in the same tenant because Cloud PKI can support both deployment models concurrently.

Our two cents

Cloud PKI is a valuable addition to the Intune Suite by Microsoft, offering several advantages over maintaining an on-premises NDES/PKI infrastructure. While there are minor capability gaps, many features and capabilities are currently under development and will be released soon.

We believe customers should seriously consider this solution as it represents a significant step toward becoming cloud-native and reducing the on-premises footprint. For those who wish to maintain both environments during the transition, they can utilize Cloud PKI with the BYOCA solution, where the root CA remains on-premises, and the issuing CA is hosted in the cloud. This approach allows them to benefit from the best of both worlds.

For some, the $2 pricing might seem a bit steep. However, it is important to note that this is not the final pricing, and the Microsoft Business Desk or your account team can assist in securing substantial discounts. Additionally, if you opt for the entire suite, which includes over eight product capabilities, the overall cost is significantly reduced.

Lastly, we have noticed several blogs online suggesting that Cloud PKI licensing is merely a way for Microsoft to generate additional revenue, which is perceived as unfair. However, it is important to recognize that Cloud PKI is an offering designed to make PKI management easier, faster, and more reliable, and to reduce on-premises dependency, which naturally comes with a licensing cost. Customers have the option to either adopt the cloud offering or continue using the on-premises NDES solution, which is free. Therefore, this should not be viewed as a coercive measure, but rather as a strategic direction from Microsoft toward a fully cloud-based future.

Also, having an offering from Microsoft such as Cloud Radius, in conjunction with Cloud PKI, would be highly beneficial. This would further reduce on-premises dependencies for customers, as they could use certificates issued by Cloud PKI with a cloud-based RADIUS solution, thereby eliminating the need to set up on-premises RADIUS servers for authentication. Microsoft is aware of this customer request, and based on public demand, it is hoped that a cloud version of RADIUS might be introduced in the future.

Summary

This chapter provided a comprehensive overview of client certificates, including their purpose, types, and advantages. It began by examining the traditional certificate deployment approach using on-premises NDES and contrasted it with the modern, streamlined methodology enabled by Cloud PKI. A detailed comparison between the two highlighted key differences across various operational parameters.

The chapter then delved into the end-to-end certificate delivery process, offering a step-by-step breakdown supported by illustrative diagrams and log references at each stage. It also covered the setup procedures for Cloud PKI, outlining the available deployment models and reporting capabilities.

In the latter part of the chapter, we explored how to leverage the issued SCEP certificate for CBA with a RADIUS/NPS server, detailing the connection flow and configuration steps involved. The chapter concluded with practical tips and our "two cents" to reinforce understanding and support successful implementation.

In the upcoming chapter, we'll explore how to secure Windows devices in alignment with Microsoft's Zero Trust principles by leveraging **Endpoint Privilege Management** (**EPM**).

Get This Book's PDF Version and Exclusive Extras

UNLOCK NOW

Scan the QR code (or go to `packtpub.com/unlock`). Search for this book by name, confirm the edition, and then follow the steps on the page.

Note: Keep your invoice handy. Purchases made directly from Packt don't require an invoice.

2

Elevating Endpoint Privilege Management with Control and Security

In this chapter, we will discuss the necessity of **Endpoint Privilege Management** (**EPM**) and its alignment with Microsoft's Zero Trust principle. After covering the basics, we will conduct a brief comparison of EPM with competing third-party products. Subsequently, we will provide a detailed overview of the delivery and installation process of the EPM agent on devices, including the background processing during EPM policy delivery, accompanied by logs and registry entries at each step to aid in troubleshooting EPM-related issues. Finally, we will discuss the deployment strategy to follow when rolling out this feature, concluding with our *two cents* on the practical usability of this feature.

The following main topics will be covered:

- Understanding the background and significance of EPM
- Flow during EPM agent installation and communication
- Understanding the directory, service logs, and registry
- Troubleshooting the flow
- Gathering reports and insights
- Deployment strategy
- Rolling out EPM
- When to use EPM and when not to
- Our two cents

Let's get started!

Understanding the background and significance of EPM

In the opening section of this chapter, we will explore the importance of implementing EPM and examine the potential risks and vulnerabilities that can arise in its absence within an organization.

The need for EPM

In IT administration, security professionals often advocate against granting users administrative access to their devices. This stance is rooted in the belief that admin access can expose both the devices and the enterprise to significant vulnerabilities. With admin privileges, users can inadvertently install malicious files, leading to system-level changes that compromise security.

To mitigate these risks, security administrators prefer to limit users to standard user accounts. This restriction minimizes their privileges, preventing them from installing unauthorized applications and making critical system changes.

Here are the major risks associated with granting admins privileges to users:

- Installation and execution of unauthorized processes/applications
- Installation of malware
- Disabling security and system settings
- Modification of filesystem permissions and desktop configurations

However, users often argue that the lack of admin access hampers their productivity. They seek the flexibility to install work-related applications as needed without the delays associated with administrative provisioning.

Here are the major limitations of not providing admin access to users:

- Inability to install necessary applications promptly
- Increased IT admin overhead

This situation presents a dilemma: should users be restricted to standard accounts, thereby ensuring robust security but potentially reducing productivity, or should they be granted admin access, risking non-compliance with Microsoft's Zero Trust guidelines and exposing the organization to potential attacks from malicious software?

It is not merely a binary choice, and the solution is a careful balance between maintaining security and enabling productivity by using EPM.

The goal of EPM

The goal of EPM is to strike the right balance between security and productivity while adhering to Microsoft's least privilege model (the Zero Trust model). EPM ensures that users do not have administrative access to their machines, thereby mitigating associated risks. Simultaneously, it prevents users from being restricted to standard user privileges at all times, allowing them to install or elevate applications as needed for their business requirements. This approach ensures that productivity is not compromised while maintaining a secure environment. EPM effectively finds a middle ground in this scenario.

EPM is a combination of the following two stacks:

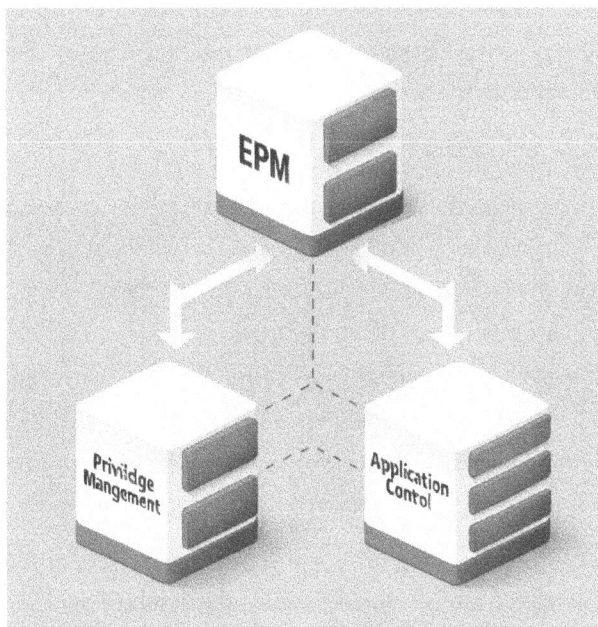

Figure 2.1: EPM stack visualization

EPM = Privilege Management + Application Control

= (managing the user's admin privileges for a specific app session)

+

(controlling which app will run on the device in admin context)

EPM plays a crucial role in mitigating attack vectors on devices. If we implement EPM for standard users, we gain several advantages:

- **Restricted installation of malicious software**: The installation of spyware, trojans, and malware is significantly limited
- **Limited system configuration changes**: End users, being standard users, are prevented from making system-wide configuration changes

These measures ensure a secure environment while maintaining the necessary balance between security and user productivity.

Key features and comparison with competitors

In this section, we will explore the key features of EPM and examine how it stands out compared to other competing products on the market.

These are the key features of using EPM:

- **Achieve least privilege in the device**: Using EPM for standard users adheres to Microsoft's standard of least privilege. Using EPM, we provide just enough access to the users for a specific application session, thereby limiting attack surfaces.
- **Seamless application control**: Using EPM, we can deliver trust-based application whitelisting with a flexible policy engine to set broad rules, choose automatic approval for advanced users – protected by full audit trails – or utilize challenge-response codes.
- **Auditing and reporting**: Using EPM, we can provide a single, unimpeachable audit trail of all user activity, speed up forensics, and simplify compliance with complete reporting for multiple stakeholders.

Here are the key advantages of using EPM over a third-party solution:

- **Integrated first-party solution with Microsoft Intune**: EPM seamlessly integrates with the Intune console, allowing administrators to manage settings without needing to switch to another console.
- **No third-party agent required**: The EPM agent, developed and owned by Microsoft, is automatically installed on devices. This eliminates any dependency on third-party agents.
- **No incompatibility issues with the OS**: The EPM agent is designed to be fully compatible with current and future OS versions, ensuring consistent performance and reliability.

EPM in the security landscape

In this section, we are going to explore how EPM fits into the security landscape and the corresponding technologies that can be used alongside it. As per our organization's requirements, we need to identify which technology to use and when. These technologies are mutually exclusive but can be used together or independently, depending on our use case:

Technology	Function	Concept
EPM	Elevates a standard user to an admin for a specific application session	• Follows Microsoft's Zero Trust model, reducing attack vectors by ensuring users are not local admins • Maintains productivity by allowing elevation to admin status for specific application sessions • Does not restrict applications from launching or running on the device • EPM essentially provides **Just-in-Time (JIT)** access to users during an application session
AppLocker and Windows Defender Application Control (WDAC)	Determines which applications can run on a device by creating rules (XMLs) to whitelist or blacklist applications	• Limits which applications can run to reduce attacks on devices • Prevents unauthorized applications from launching or running on the OS • Does not govern application installation or relate to user access levels
Local Administrator Password Solution (LAPS)	Manages and maintains the passwords of local accounts on devices	• Enforces minimum password criteria for local admin accounts, manages these passwords centrally by backing them up to Azure, and allows centralized password changes when needed • Ensures local admin account passwords are secure and centrally managed

Table 2.1: Brief of commonly used security technology in Windows landscape

Now, let's discuss the prerequisites of using EPM and the scenarios it supports.

Supported scenarios

EPM supports the following scenarios:

- **Microsoft Entra-joined or Microsoft Entra hybrid-joined devices**: Devices that are either joined to Microsoft Entra or have a hybrid configuration

- **Microsoft Intune enrollment or Microsoft Configuration Manager co-managed devices**: Devices enrolled in Microsoft Intune or co-managed with Microsoft Configuration Manager with no specific workload requirements

- **Clear line of sight on TCP port 443**: Devices must have an unobstructed connection (without SSL inspection) on TCP port 443 to the following endpoints:

  - `*.dm.microsoft.com`
  - `*.events.data.microsoft.com`

Supported versions

EPM supports the following OS versions:

- Windows 11:

  - Version 24H2
  - Version 23H2 with KB5031455
  - Version 22H2 with KB5029351
  - Version 21H2 with KB5034121

- Windows 10:

  - Version 22H2 with KB5030211
  - Version 21H2 with KB5030211

Windows 365 (Cloud PC) is supported using a supported OS version. Workplace Join devices are not supported by EPM; nor is Azure Virtual Desktop.

License and pricing

EPM requires an additional license beyond the Microsoft Intune Plan 1 license. We have two options:

- **Stand-alone license**: An add-on license of EPM is priced at $3.00/user/month.
- **Microsoft Intune Suite**: An Intune Suite license is priced at $10.00/user/month. This provides access to all the Intune Suite products.

These prices are the retail prices quoted in the official Microsoft documentation. However, they are not final. For bulk licenses, it is recommended to contact the Microsoft Business Desk/Sales team to get the best deals and applicable discounts.

Now that we have covered the background, requirements, and prerequisites, let's turn our attention to the core focus – the flow.

Flow during EPM agent installation and communication

We'll begin by examining the behind-the-scenes flow that takes place during the installation of the EPM agent on a device and its communication with the service post installation.

Agent installation flow

By default, the EPM agent is not present in the Windows OS. It is installed when the EPM elevation setting policy is deployed to the device. Let's examine the background process during the EPM agent installation using the following diagram:

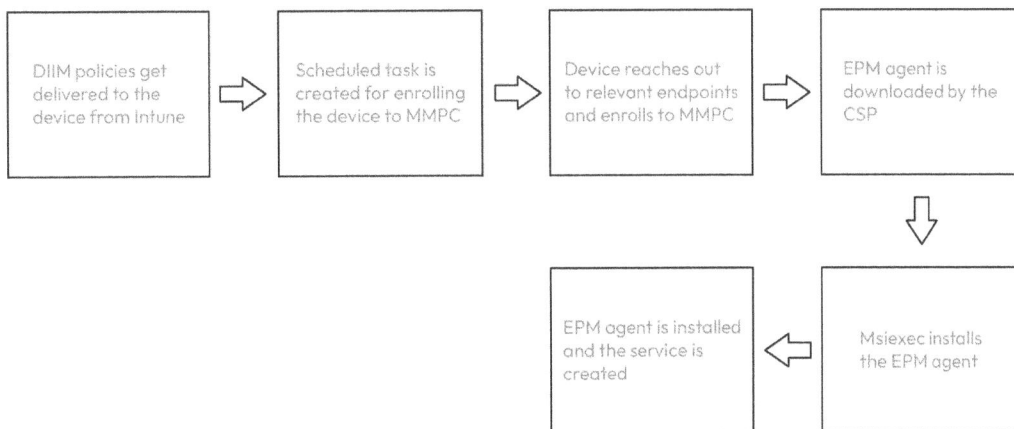

Figure 2.2: Block diagram showing the flow of EPM agent installation

With the preceding block diagram as a reference, let's walk through the background steps that lead to the installation of the EPM agent on the device:

1. When the EPM elevation setting policy is deployed to the device, it automatically sends a **Device Health Monitoring (DHM)** policy to the device from Intune. This can be tracked in real time by examining the SyncML trace on the device.

2. This policy creates a scheduled task on the device that is responsible for enrolling the device to **Microsoft Management Platform Cloud (MMP-C)** (as explained in the following section). This process is similar to how a device gets enrolled to Intune using Group Policy, where a scheduled task is created to handle the enrollment.

3. The scheduled task runs `deviceenroller.exe`, which enables the device to reach out to the MMP-C endpoints and enroll itself with the MMP-C channel.

   The following screenshot shows a successful MMP-C enrollment of a device that is logged in Event Viewer with the ID 4023:

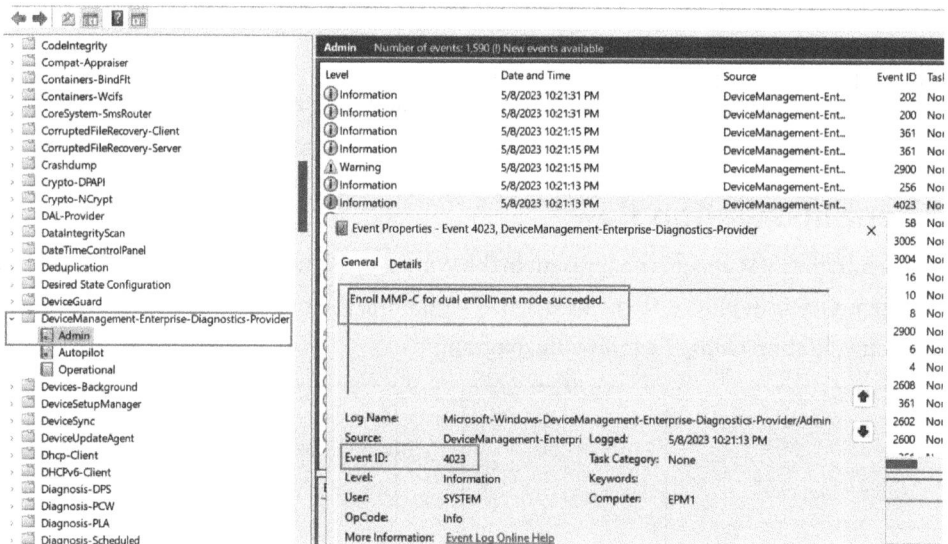

Figure 2.3: Event Viewer log from the device showing the successful enrollment to MMP-C

4. Once the device is enrolled, the EPM agent is pushed to the device. The installation process involves the device reaching out to a specific URL (`https://epmagent.manage.microsoft.com/epmagentpeeus/epmagentmsi/6.2411.82.2000/EPMAgent.msi`) to download `EPMAgent.exe`, and `msiexec` handles the installation. The EPM agent installation is executed by the same CSP that triggers the IME installation when the device is enrolled into

Intune, that is, `/Device/Vendor/MSFT/EnterpriseDesktopAppManagement/MSI.msiexec` starts installing the MSI file from the system's local `AppData` folder.

Let's take a look at the following screenshot, which displays the SyncML trace indicating this operation:

Figure 2.4: SyncML trace from the device showing the delivery of EPM agent

Once the EPM agent has been installed, we can see its version in `Computer\HKEY_LOCAL_MACHINE\SOFTWARE\Microsoft\EPMAgent`:

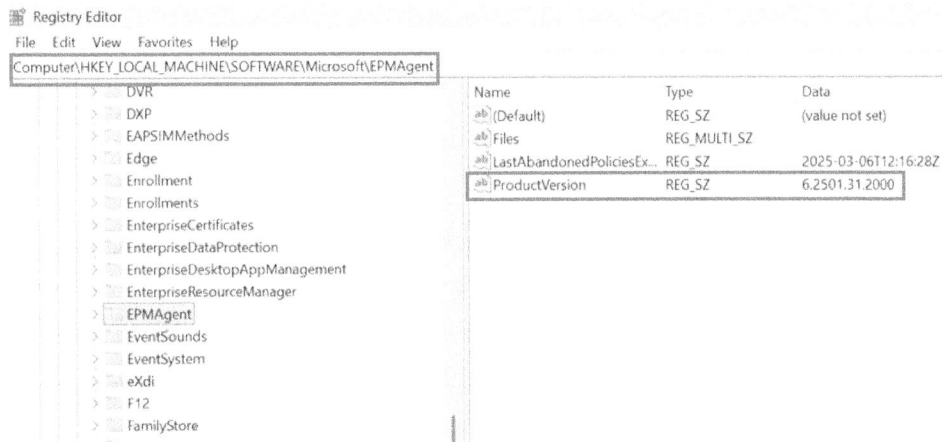

Figure 2.5: Registry location in the device showing the EPM agent version

5. After the agent has been installed, a service is created to manage the processing. The following screenshot shows the service created with the display name **Microsoft EPM Agent Service** and the location of its executable.

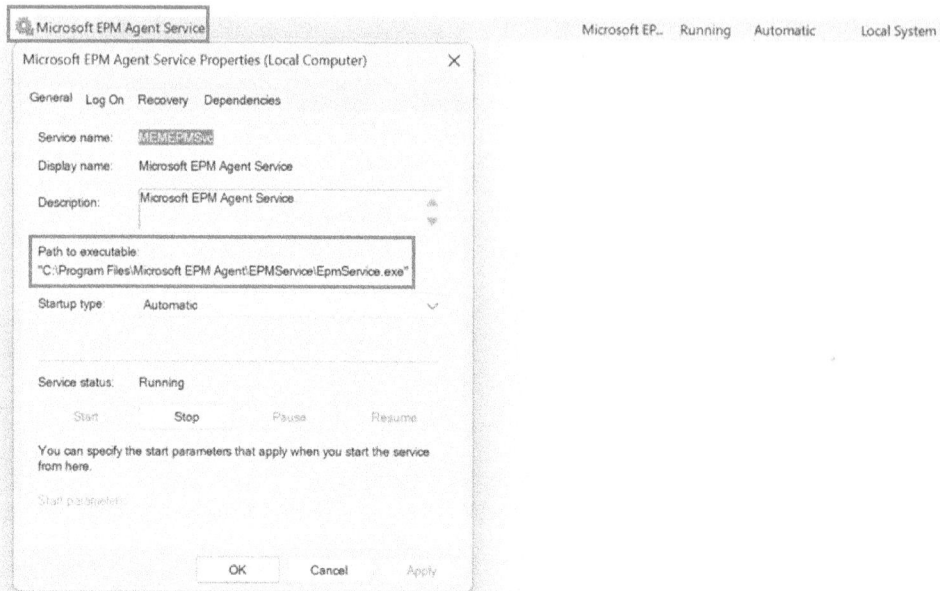

Figure 2.6: EPM service details from a device

Now that we understand the agent installation flow, in the next section, we'll take a brief look at how the EPM agent, once installed, communicates with the Intune service to retrieve policies onto the device.

Agent communication flow

Before diving into how the EPM agent functions and retrieves applicable policies, let's take a brief detour to understand the fundamentals of OMADM and MMP-C—concepts that will be valuable for grasping the EPM agent's workflow.

Microsoft Management Platform Cloud (MMP-C), also known as Windows declared configuration protocol, and **Open Mobile Alliance Device Management (OMADM)** are both frameworks used for device management, but they differ significantly in their approach and capabilities:

- **OMADM**: OMADM is an old protocol used for device management and was primarily designed for mobile devices. Key features include the following:

  - **Structured model**: OMADM follows a structured model where devices sync on a schedule, fetch policies, and apply them

  - **Policy management**: It has been the backbone of policy management in Microsoft Intune for years, providing a standardized way to manage devices

- **Mobile device focus**: OMADM was originally built for mobile phones, and while it has been adapted for broader use, it retains some limitations in flexibility and speed compared to newer methods

In short, the OMADM protocol follows the Get-Set-Get process:

- In the first Get, Intune queries the device's CSP node to check the current configuration before making changes. This is to check whether the policy has already been applied on the device and is the initial query.
- In the Set policy, Intune sends a command to update the configuration in the device (if the policy hasn't been applied as an output of the previous step). This Set query deploys the policy workload.
- In the second Get query, Intune will now check whether the policy has been successfully applied on the device in the previous step. This Get query validates whether the policy was successful.

- **MMP-C**: MMP-C is a modern cloud-based management platform designed to enhance device management and security within an organization. Key features include the following:

  - **EPM, device inventory, and MDQ**: MMP-C integrates with EPM, device inventory, and multi-device query, all utilizing the MMP-C channel for policy delivery. In the future, additional workloads may transition to MMP-C due to its numerous advantages.
  - **Declared Configuration service**: MMP-C uses the Declared Configuration service (dcsvc) for policy synchronization, which is faster, more reliable, and more secure than traditional methods.
  - **Linked enrollment**: Devices enrolled in MMP-C have a dual enrollment setup, where the primary enrollment is through Intune, and the secondary enrollment is through MMP-C.
  - **Cloud-based infrastructure**: Leveraging Microsoft's cloud infrastructure, MMP-C provides scalable and reliable management services.

The terms **Microsoft Management Platform Cloud** (**MMP-C**) and **Windows declared configuration** (**WinDC**) protocol are used interchangeably throughout this book but refer to the same thing.

We have now discussed both of the protocols and the advantages of the newer one, MMP-C. Like EPM, Microsoft might transition other policy workloads to MMP-C as well in the future.

Switching back to EPM, as illustrated in the following diagram, the device now operates with two channels: the OMADM channel and the MMP-C channel. Both channels are utilized to deliver relevant policies to the device.

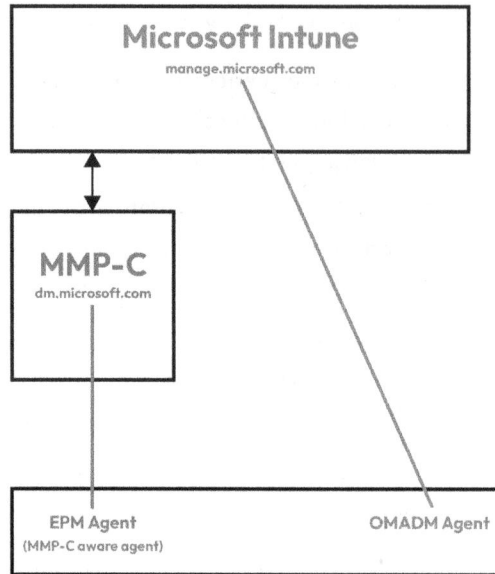

Figure 2.7: Block diagram showing the communication between the device and the Intune service

Now that we understand the basics of OMADM and MMP-C, let's do a quick comparison between them:

Features	MMP-C	OMADM
Technology and speed	Utilizes the Declared Configuration service, which is faster and more secure	Follows a scheduled sync model, which can be slower and less flexible
Enrollment	Supports dual enrollment with linked configurations, enhancing management capabilities	Traditional single enrollment focused on mobile devices
Integration	Integrates seamlessly with modern cloud services and EPM	Primarily used for mobile device management with structured policy application

Table 2.2: Comparison between OMADM and MMP-C channel

As the comparison shows, EPM uses the MMP-C channel for policy delivery, thereby enhancing security and increasing speed. In the next section, we will explore how EPM policies are deployed to the device using the MMP-C channel.

Background flow for policy delivery

Take a look at the following diagram to get an idea of the background flow involved in the delivery of an EPM elevation rule policy and the internal components at play.

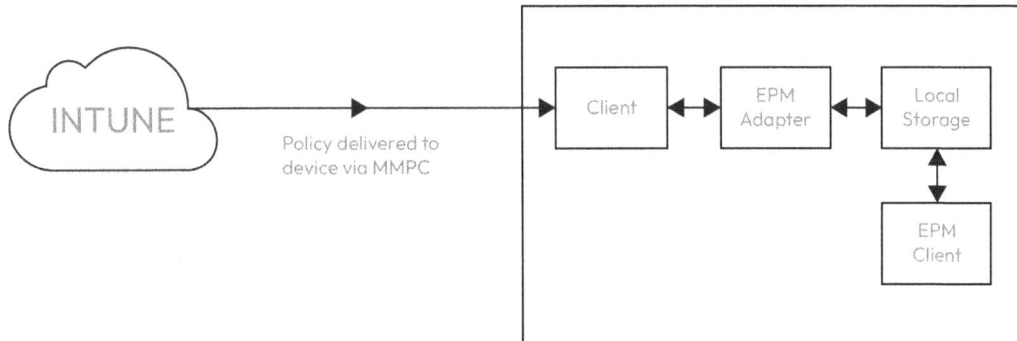

Figure 2.8: Block diagram showing the flow of EPM policy delivery

Here are the steps involved in the delivery of EPM policies to the device:

1. As established in the previous section, given that the device is MMP-C enrolled, it can now receive the EPM-related policy from Intune via the MMP-C channel, as illustrated in the preceding diagram.

2. Naturally, there must be a client on the device responsible for receiving and processing the policy. Similar to the OMADM client, which processes regular MDM policies, the WinDC client on the device is responsible for receiving the EPM-related policy via the MMP-C channel.

3. After the WinDC client receives the policy and writes it to the correct location (namespace) on the device, the EPM adapters come into play. These adapters were installed on the device when the EPM agent was installed, which occurred when the EPM setting policy targeted the device.

4. The adapter is responsible for further processing. It reads the policy values from the namespace and writes them to the local storage on the device, along with all relevant registries.

5. The EPM client then ingests this policy and enforces it whenever applicable, marking the EPM policies active. When a user attempts to elevate an application, the EPM client and the EPM service work together with the management libraries to implement the policy that was previously written to the device's local storage.

So far, we've explored how the EPM elevation rule policy is delivered to the device from the Intune service using MMP-C. In the next section, we'll delve into the processes involved in implementing the EPM rule policy on the device based on the user's actions.

Foreground flow for policy implementation

Now, let's explore the foreground flow—the steps the user takes that lead to the policy elevating a specific application—by looking at the following diagram:

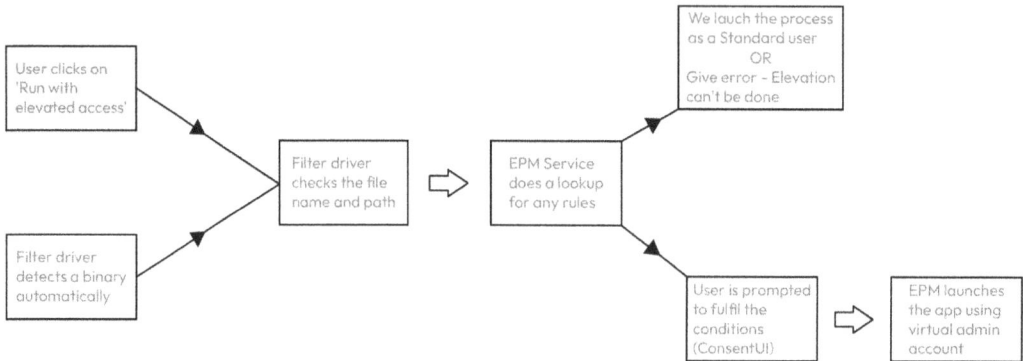

Figure 2.9: Block diagram showing the flow behind EPM initiation for an application session

The following steps align with the block diagram and illustrate the underlying process:

1. **Application detection**: This is the initial step in the foreground process. Detection can occur in the following cases:

    *   The user right-clicks on a specific application and selects **Run with elevated access**
    *   The filter driver in the OS automatically detects the application's binaries when the app is launched

    In essence, whether the user consciously tries to elevate the app by clicking **Run with elevated access** or the app is launched in an admin context by another process, the application's binaries will be detected.

2. **Confirmation of application attributes**: The filter driver verifies the application being launched, ensuring details such as the filename, location, and hash are correct. This information is double-checked and logged.

3. **Rule lookup and implementation**: Once the application has been verified, the EPM service looks up the applicable rules for that application to determine whether it should be allowed to elevate or be denied. In both cases, the action is logged in the relevant logs (explained in detail in the next section), and a consent UI appears on the screen:

- **Condition 1**: If elevation is not permitted, the user receives a prompt (generated by the consent UI) indicating that the elevation of the application is not permitted by the administrator.

- **Condition 2**: If elevation is permitted but subject to specific conditions, those conditions take effect. For example, the policy might require the user to provide a business justification or complete **multi-factor authentication** (**MFA**).

If Condition 2 is met, after fulfilling the requirements specified by the consent UI (such as MFA or justification), the EPM service launches the application session using a virtual admin account, enabling the user to enjoy admin privileges while interacting with the app during that specific session.

> An application that is elevated by the user always runs with a virtual admin account that has the admin token and the necessary privileges.

Up to this point, we've developed a comprehensive understanding of the background processes that lead to the installation of the EPM agent. We've also examined how the EPM elevation rule policy is delivered to the device and the flow involved in that process. Additionally, we have explored the foreground flow triggered when a user launches an application governed by the elevation policy.

Understanding the directory, service logs, and registry

In this section, we'll delve into the key files and .dlls involved in EPM's operation and take a closer look at the relevant logs and registry entries. This is going to be very important while troubleshooting related issues.

Working directory

The working directory for EPM is located at C:\Program Files\Microsoft EPM Agent. Within this directory, we will find many folders that are essential for the processing of EPM. These folders contain various files, including .dll, .exe, .inf, .sys, .dat, and .config files. Additionally, this directory houses the log files for EPM, which we will examine in detail in the next section.

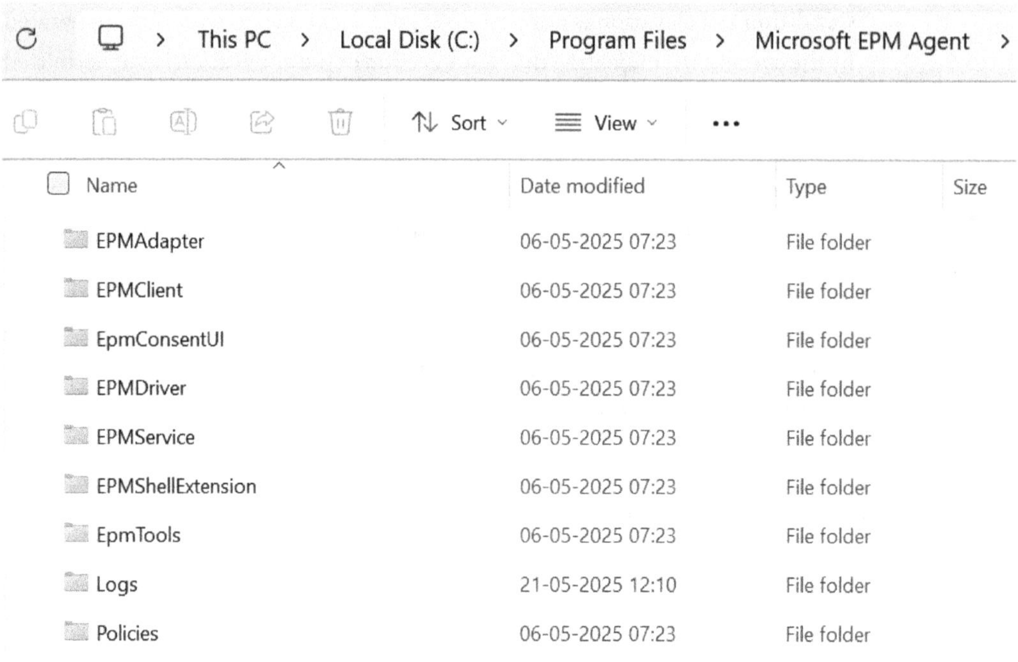
This PC > Local Disk (C:) > Program Files > Microsoft EPM Agent >
Sort
View
Name
Date modified
Type
Size
EPMAdapter 06-05-2025 07:23 File folder
EPMClient 06-05-2025 07:23 File folder
EpmConsentUI 06-05-2025 07:23 File folder
EPMDriver 06-05-2025 07:23 File folder
EPMService 06-05-2025 07:23 File folder
EPMShellExtension 06-05-2025 07:23 File folder
EpmTools 06-05-2025 07:23 File folder
Logs 21-05-2025 12:10 File folder
Policies 06-05-2025 07:23 File folder

Figure 2.10: File/folder structure for EPM

Later in this chapter, we will explore how all these files within the EPM directory structure are utilized.

EPM logs

Understanding EPM log files is crucial, as they play a key role in diagnosing issues, identifying root causes, and enabling fast resolution. When troubleshooting EPM, we need to work with the following logs, all of which are located on the device at `C:\Program Files\Microsoft EPM Agent\Logs`:

- `EPMService.log`
- `EPM.Log`
- `EPMConsentUI.log`
- `EPMServiceStub.log`
- `ElevationRules.dat`
- `MEMEPMAgent.log`

Now, let's examine all these logs in detail.

EPMService.log

This log provides detailed information on the activities of the EPM service, which handles significant tasks. It orchestrates the elevation of applications on the device according to the received policy and is responsible for telemetry. The log includes the following:

- The number of elevation rules found/targeted for the user's SSID
- The filename and the location of the application that is being attempted to be elevated
- If the EPM consent UI was launched, and if the app elevation was restricted and the user receives an error message in the consent UI, this event is also logged
- Whether the user entered justification/MFA and all token-related activities

Ultimately, it indicates whether the application session was launched in the admin context for the user. The following screenshot is from `EPMService.log` and illustrates the processing involved when the user tries to elevate any application.

```
Log Verbose: 1 : 2023-05-22 06:20:38 AM | thread[1] | Attempting to connect to EpmService...
Log Verbose: 1 : 2023-05-22 06:20:38 AM | thread[1] | Opening a handle to EpmService...
Log Information: 1 : 2023-05-22 06:20:38 AM | thread[1] | Successfully connected to EpmService.
Log Verbose: 1 : 2023-05-22 06:20:38 AM | thread[1] | Found 1 command line parameters.
Log Information: 1 : 2023-05-22 06:20:38 AM | thread[1] | Getting elevation data from EpmService.
Log Verbose: 1 : 2023-05-22 06:20:38 AM | thread[1] | Checking to ensure service is in a valid state.
Log Verbose: 1 : 2023-05-22 06:20:38 AM | thread[1] | Getting elevation data from EpmService.
Log Verbose: 1 : 2023-05-22 06:20:38 AM | thread[1] | Checking to ensure service is in a valid state.
Log Verbose: 1 : 2023-05-22 06:20:38 AM | thread[1] | Language Tag is set to en-US.
Log Verbose: 1 : 2023-05-22 06:20:38 AM | thread[1] | Attempting to convert full path of file to elevate from EpmService memory into a string.
Log Verbose: 1 : 2023-05-22 06:20:38 AM | thread[1] | Expanding environment variables.
Log Verbose: 1 : 2023-05-22 06:20:38 AM | thread[1] | Attempting to get publisher from file signature of [C:\Temp\SyncML\SyncMLViewer.exe].
Log Verbose: 1 : 2023-05-22 06:20:38 AM | thread[1] | Could not get publisher from file.
Log Verbose: 1 : 2023-05-22 06:20:38 AM | thread[1] | Attempting to get icon from file [C:\Temp\SyncML\SyncMLViewer.exe]
Log Verbose: 1 : 2023-05-22 06:20:38 AM | thread[1] | Target full path:    C:\Temp\SyncML\SyncMLViewer.exe
Log Verbose: 1 : 2023-05-22 06:20:38 AM | thread[1] | Target executable name: SyncMLViewer
Log Information: 1 : 2023-05-22 06:20:38 AM | thread[1] | Target publisher:    Unknown publisher
Log Information: 1 : 2023-05-22 06:20:38 AM | thread[1] | ConsentUI loaded successfully.
Log Information: 1 : 2023-05-22 06:20:49 AM | thread[1] | User clicked Yes to approve the elevation for [SyncMLViewer]
Log Verbose: 1 : 2023-05-22 06:20:49 AM | thread[1] | Authentication is not required for this elevation request.
Log Information: 1 : 2023-05-22 06:20:49 AM | thread[1] | Writing elevation data to EpmService.
Log Verbose: 1 : 2023-05-22 06:20:49 AM | thread[1] | Checking to ensure service is in a valid state.
Log Information: 1 : 2023-05-22 06:20:49 AM | thread[1] | Exiting application with exit code [0]
```

Figure 2.11: EPM service logs from a working device

The logs will contain numerous file hashes, which may cause some confusion. The EPM service logs the file hash of any application being elevated by the user.

Prior to this step, the EPM service launches `EpmConsentUI.exe` (located in `C:\Program Files\ Microsoft EPM Agent\EpmConsentUI`) and `EpmServiceStub.exe` (located in `C:\Program Files\ Microsoft EPM Agent\EPMService`), and their file hashes are also recorded in the log, along with any other EPM-related executables.

It is important to clarify that these hashes are not of the application being elevated by the user.

The key point is that the hash values of everything launched by EPM, whether directly (the user's application) or indirectly (EPM-related executables), are logged here.

```
CreateProcessAsUserEx: Verifying hash of file [C:\Program Files\Microsoft EPM Agent\EpmConsentUI\E
VerifyFileHash: Started.
VerifyFileHash: Getting file hash...
CCM::Utility::GetFileHash: Getting file pointer position...
CCM::Utility::GetFileHash: Current file pointer position is 0.
CCM::Utility::GetFileHash: Succeeded.
VerifyFileHash: File hash: B8FA874126CE77D5A9F72A27A41A29C32206E65C8E199C6DE44765F36F2
VerifyFileHash: Comparing file hash...
VerifyFileHash: Succeeded.
CreateProcessAsUserEx: Launch process hidden: false
CreateProcessAsUserEx: Getting SID from token...
```

Date/Time: 5/22/2023 6:18:39 AM   **Component**: EpmInterop
Thread: 5672 (0x1628)   **Source**: ElevateInterop.cpp:71

VerifyFileHash: File hash: B8FA874126CE77D5A9F72A27A41A29C32206E65C8E199C6DE44765F36F2

Figure 2.12: EPM logs showing the file hash ID of executables

In the logs, we can see a file hash ID. Upon closer inspection, we will find that the file hash ID belongs to `EPMConsentUI.exe` and not the application the user was trying to elevate:

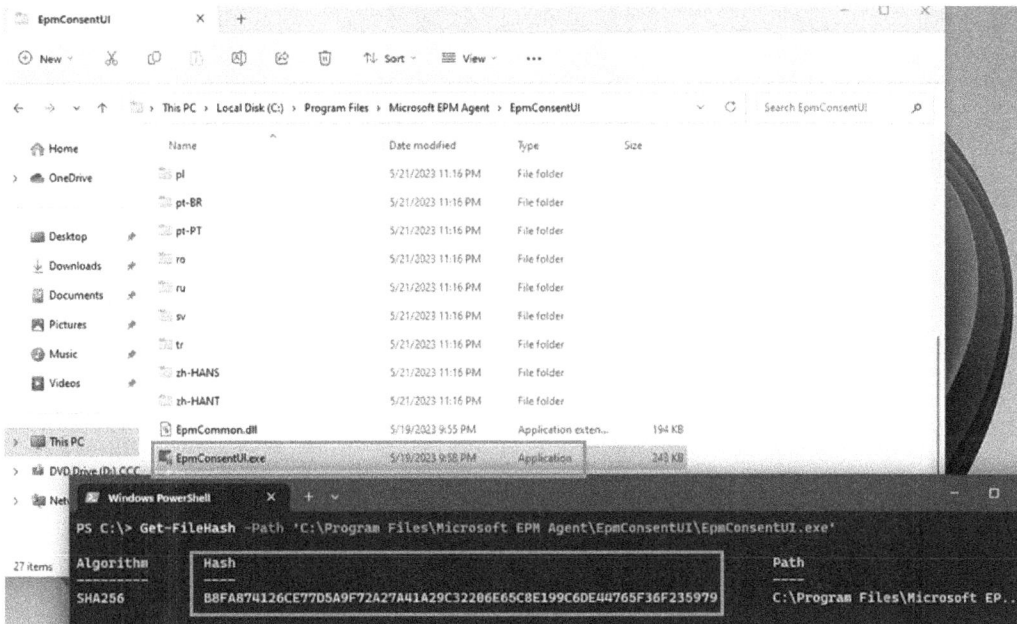

Figure 2.13: Capturing the file hash of EPMConsentUI

Similarly, we can fetch the file hash ID of `EPMClientStub.exe` using PowerShell. This file hash ID will also be shown in `EPMService.log`.

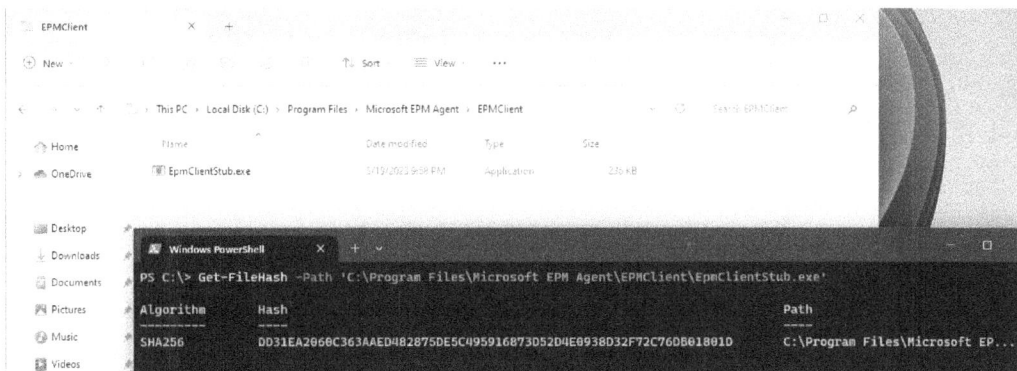

Figure 2.14: Capturing the file hash of EPMClientStub

EPM.Log

This log shows how exactly the application was detected, for example, if the user right-clicked on the app and elevated it or if it was done automatically.

EPMConsentUI.log

The system logs each instance when the EPM consent UI dialog is initiated on the device. Additionally, if a user attempts to elevate an application that is restricted by the elevation rule policy and encounters the standard error message (**Your organization doesn't allow you to run this app as an administrator**), this event is also recorded in the log.

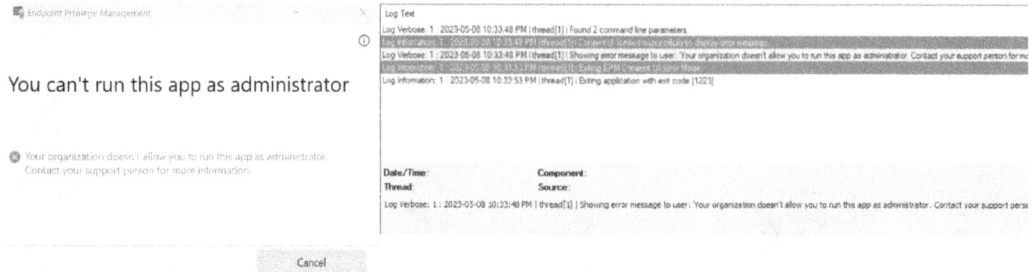

Figure 2.15: EPMConsentUI logs showing error when a restricted app is launched

ElevationRules.dat

We observe the creation of numerous .dat files in C:\Program Files\Microsoft EPM Agent\ Policies\ElevationRules. They are not exactly log files. A .dat file is a generic data file that stores information in a structured or unstructured format. However, they are important as they contain some valuable data. Let's take a look at these .dat files:

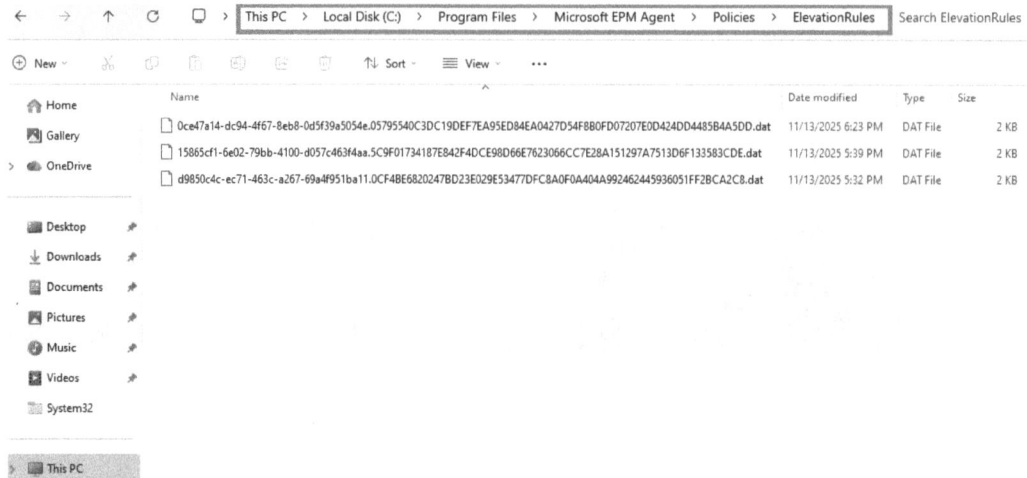

Figure 2.16: Location of .dat files for EPM

These files contain the names and information of applications targeted by the EPM policy, as well as all the settings configured within the policy. This information aligns with what was established by the administrator at the portal and what the device should have received and populated in the registry.

The content of the `.dat` file looks like the following screenshot. It contains everything configured in EPM related to the specific application. In the following example, the file is related to a rule for Notepad++.

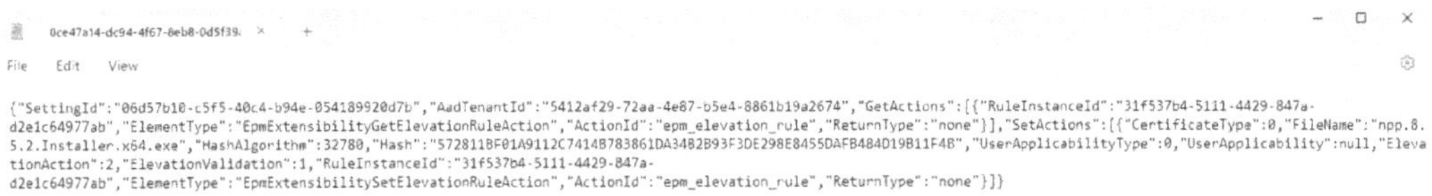
0ce47a14-dc94-4f67-8eb8-0d5f39
File
Edit
View
{"SettingId":"06d57b10-c5f5-40c4-b94e-054189920d7b","AadTenantId":"5412af29-72aa-4e87-b5e4-8861b19a2674","GetActions":[{"RuleInstanceId":"31f537b4-5111-4429-847a-
d2e1c64977ab","ElementType":"EpmExtensibilityGetElevationRuleAction","ActionId":"epm_elevation_rule","ReturnType":"none"}],"SetActions":[{"CertificateType":0,"FileName":"npp.8.
5.2.Installer.x64.exe","HashAlgorithm":32780,"Hash":"572811BF01A9112C7414B783861DA3482B93F3DE298E8455DAFB484D19B11F4B","UserApplicabilityType":0,"UserApplicability":null,"Eleva
tionAction":2,"ElevationValidation":1,"RuleInstanceId":"31f537b4-5111-4429-847a-
d2e1c64977ab","ElementType":"EpmExtensibilitySetElevationRuleAction","ActionId":"epm_elevation_rule","ReturnType":"none"}]}

Figure 2.17: Content of .dat files for EPM

MDMDiag logs

We can examine the MDMDiag logs on the device by generating a diagnostic report. In these logs, we can find the GUID for MMP-C enrollment, which should match the enrollment GUID previously identified for MMP-C. Additionally, the logs will reference the `EPMAgent.msi` that gets downloaded.

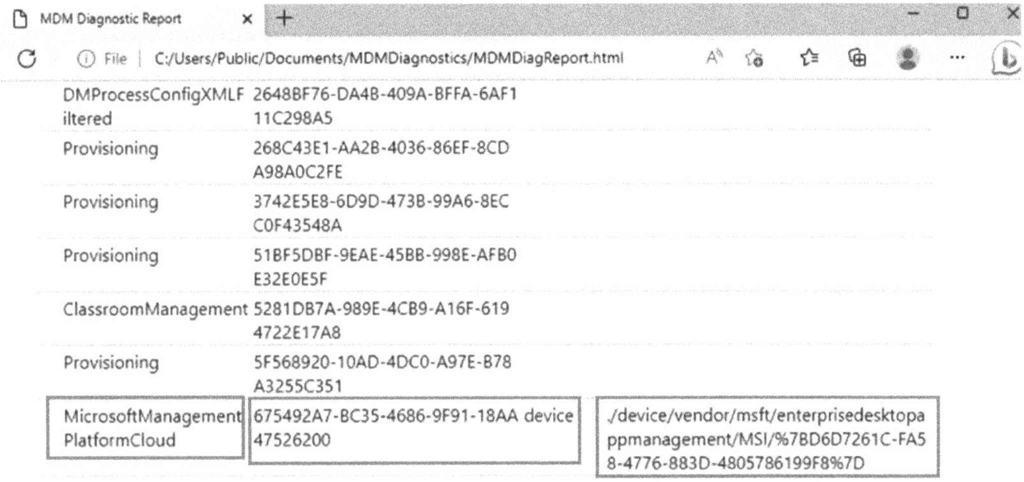
MDM Diagnostic Report
File | C:/Users/Public/Documents/MDMDiagnostics/MDMDiagReport.html
DMProcessConfigXMLFiltered
2648BF76-DA4B-409A-BFFA-6AF111C298A5
Provisioning
268C43E1-AA2B-4036-86EF-8CDA98A0C2FE
Provisioning
3742E5E8-6D9D-473B-99A6-8ECC0F43548A
Provisioning
51BF5DBF-9EAE-45BB-998E-AFB0E32E0E5F
ClassroomManagement
5281DB7A-989E-4CB9-A16F-6194722E17A8
Provisioning
5F568920-10AD-4DC0-A97E-B78A3255C351
MicrosoftManagementPlatformCloud
675492A7-BC35-4686-9F91-18AA47526200
device
./device/vendor/msft/enterprisedesktopappmanagement/MSI/%7BD6D7261C-FA58-4776-883D-4805786199F8%7D

Figure 2.18: MDMDiag logs highlight MMP-C-related information

In this section, we explored the various EPM-related log files and their significance. These logs are essential for diagnosing issues, whether related to the delivery or implementation of EPM elevation rule or setting policies, and can help pinpoint root causes and streamline troubleshooting.

Scheduled task and registry

Once a device is targeted by an EPM policy through Intune, a scheduled task is created on the device to handle its enrollment into the MMP-C channel. Let's take a closer look at this scheduled task in the following section.

Scheduled task

Let's first see a device wherein the EPM policy was not targeted. In this case, we see only one GUID entry under **EnterpriseMgmt**, which has the schedule task used for enrolling the device to Intune:

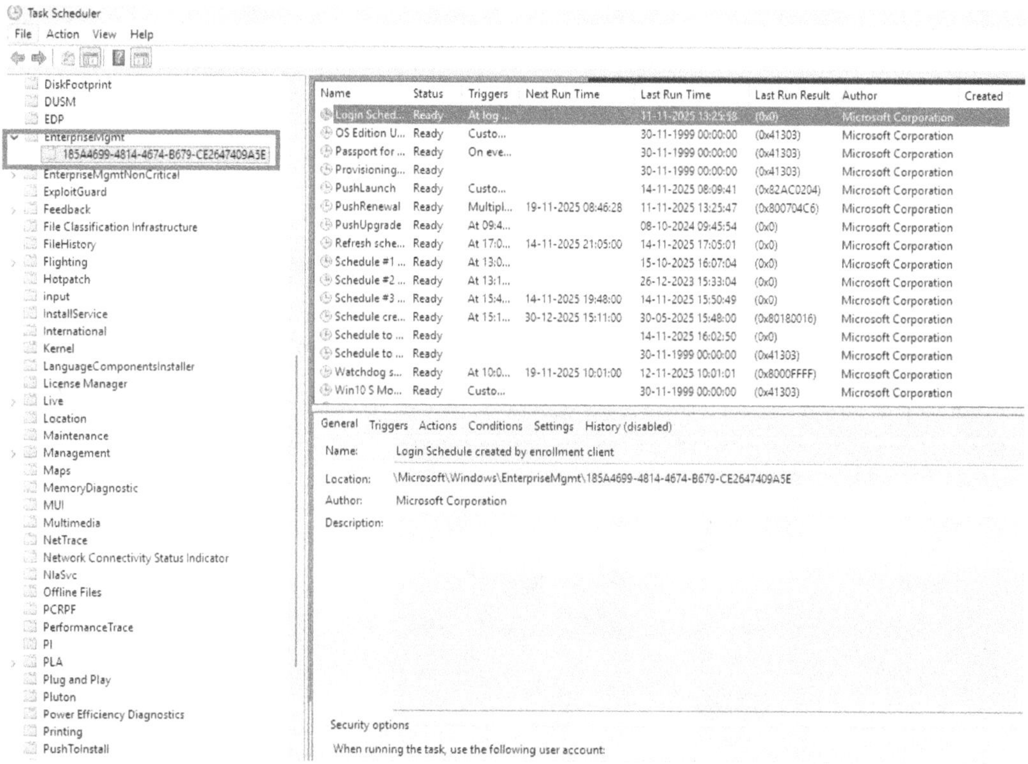

Figure 2.19: Task scheduler in a device that is not targeted via EPM policies

Now, let's see the task scheduler of a device that was targeted via an EPM policy. In this case, we see there is one more GUID under `EnterpriseMgmt`. The new GUID is for MMP-C enrollment. This GUID contains the scheduled task that is responsible for enrolling the machine with MMP-C. The device will get the EPM policy only after it has been enrolled with MMP-C. This is important.

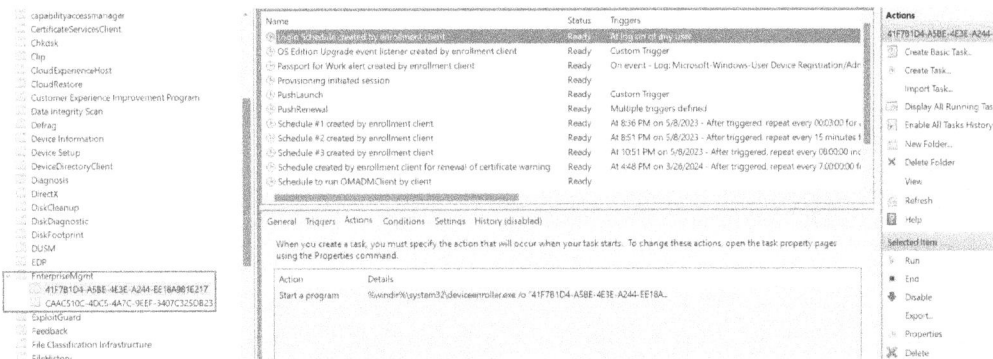

Figure 2.20: Task scheduler in a device that is targeted via EPM policies

The location of the schedule task is `Task Scheduler Library\Microsoft\Windows\EnterpriseMgmt` as seen in the preceding screenshot.

After the scheduled task runs automatically, we can verify whether the device was successfully enrolled into the MMP-C channel by checking its **Last Run Result** and the logs discussed earlier in this chapter.

In the next section, we'll delve into the key registry values that are critical in the context of EPM.

Registry

There are four critical registry entries to consider during troubleshooting EPM, as explained here:

- `Computer\HKEY_LOCAL_MACHINE\SOFTWARE\Microsoft\Enrollments\xx-yy-xx` (new enrollment GUID for MMP-C)

    After a device is enrolled in MMP-C, a new GUID (node) is created in the registry at the preceding location. Consequently, the device will have two GUIDs under the enrollment node:

    - The first GUID is the primary one, which was created when the device was initially enrolled in Intune.

    - The second GUID is created after the device is enrolled in MMP-C. The first GUID contains a reference to the second GUID.

    It is important to note that under the first GUID, there is a sub-node called **Linked Enrollment** containing a `REG_SZ` value. This value is populated with the second GUID of the MMP-C enrollment, as shown here:

> ✏️ The value xx-yy-zz is a placeholder for IDs, and its value will be different in each environment. It is used throughout this chapter for various registry locations.

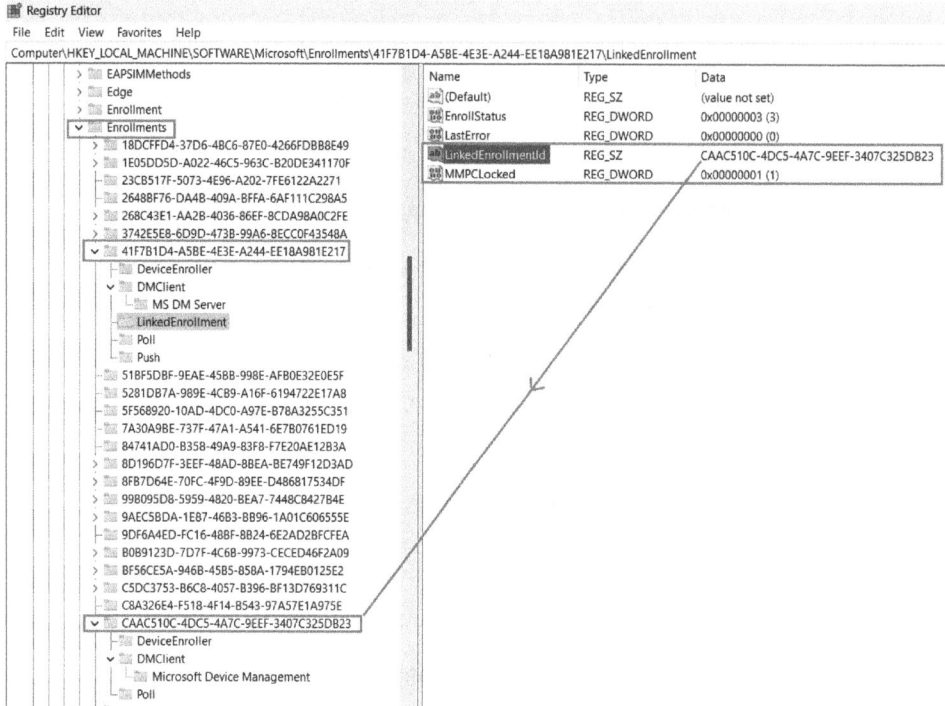

Figure 2.21: Registry in the device showing linked enrollment for MMP-C

There is also a `REG_DWORD` that gets created with the value 1 named `MMPCLocked`.

Examining the second GUID (related to MMP-C enrollment) reveals various relevant details, including the `AADResourceID`, which is the `checkin.dm.microsoft.com` endpoint, as shown here:

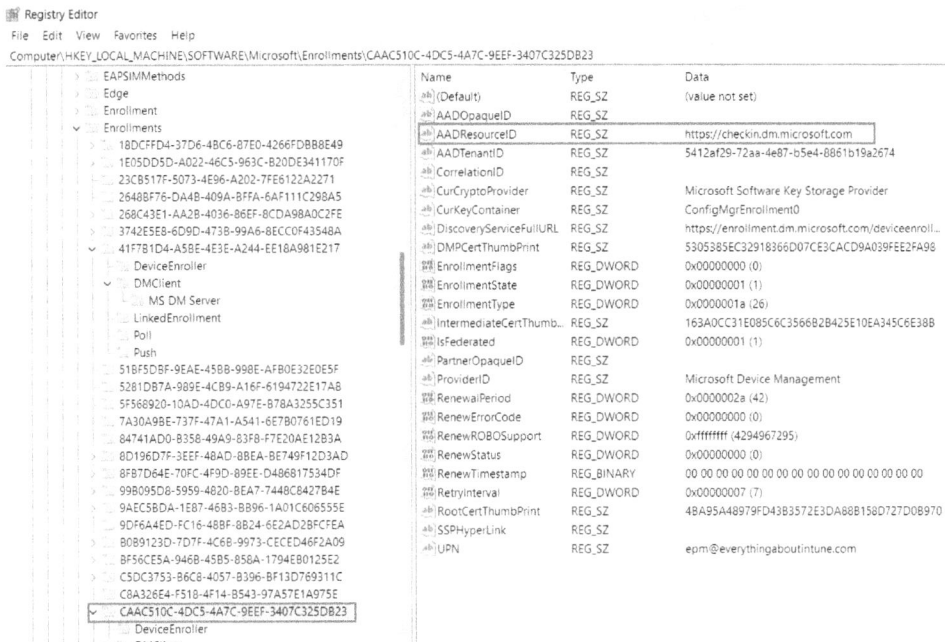

Figure 2.22: EPM-related registry in the device

This endpoint is necessary for MMP-C enrollment (and EPM) and is documented in the *Supported scenarios* section in this chapter.

> This `AADResourceID` differs from the one associated with the first GUID, which pertains to general OMADM Intune enrollment.

- `Computer\HKEY_LOCAL_MACHINE\SOFTWARE\Microsoft\EnterpriseDesktopAppManagement\S-0-000\MSI\{xx-yy-xx}`

The EPM agent will be downloaded and installed on the device. This agent is an MSI file that the device needs to download. The information about this MSI file, which is targeted via the EPM policy, is populated in the registry.

As shown in the following screenshot, a `REG_SZ` entry named `CurrentDownloadUrl` is created in the relevant registry node mentioned earlier. This URL points to the location from which `EPMAgent.msi` is downloaded by the device. This URL is probably load balanced or location specific.

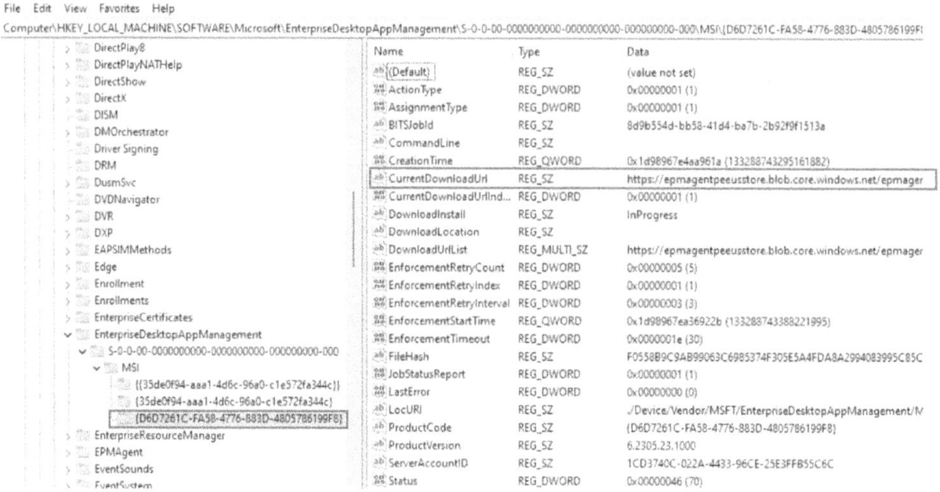

Figure 2.23: Registry in the device illustrating how the EPM agent was downloaded

If you extract this URL from the registry (e.g., `https://epmagent.manage.microsoft.com/epmagentpeeus/epmagentmsi/6.2411.82.2000/EPMAgent.msi`) and navigate to it in a browser, the browser will also download `EPMAgent.msi`, thereby validating this process.

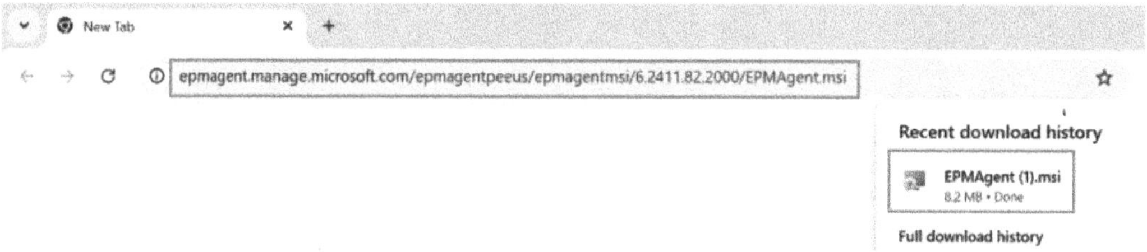

Figure 2.24: Downloading the EPM agent manually from a browser

- `Computer\HKEY_LOCAL_MACHINE\SOFTWARE\Microsoft\DeclaredConfiguration\HostOS\Config\enrollments\xx-yy-xx\SID\state\KeyValue`

In this registry hive within the user's SID, we can locate `KeyValues`. There will be a `REG_SZ` value containing the EPM policy settings that have been deployed to the device from Intune. As illustrated in the following screenshot, these settings can be opened in Notepad for verification.

For example, the device shown here has an EPM rule policy targeted at Notepad++. We can see the application filename and the detection method used, which in this case is the file hash and its value set by the admin in the portal, along with other policy settings.

Figure 2.25: Registry in the device showing the EPM policy-related settings

> If multiple applications are targeted via the EPM rule policy, their values can be checked here.

This registry entry is crucial as it ensures that the device has received the correct policy payload as configured by the admin.

- `Computer\HKEY_LOCAL_MACHINE\SOFTWARE\Microsoft\EPMAgent\RuleLookup\FileName\`

A new node called `EPMAgent` is created in the registry in this location. Within this node, there is a sub-node called `RuleLookup` that contains elevation rules for each application configured in the EPM policy in Intune. For example, I have created an EPM elevation rule policy targeting several applications, such as 7-Zip, Google Chrome, Notepad++, ProcMon, and VLC Media Player. As shown in the following screenshot, a node is created for each of these applications under the **RuleLookup** | **Filename** node.

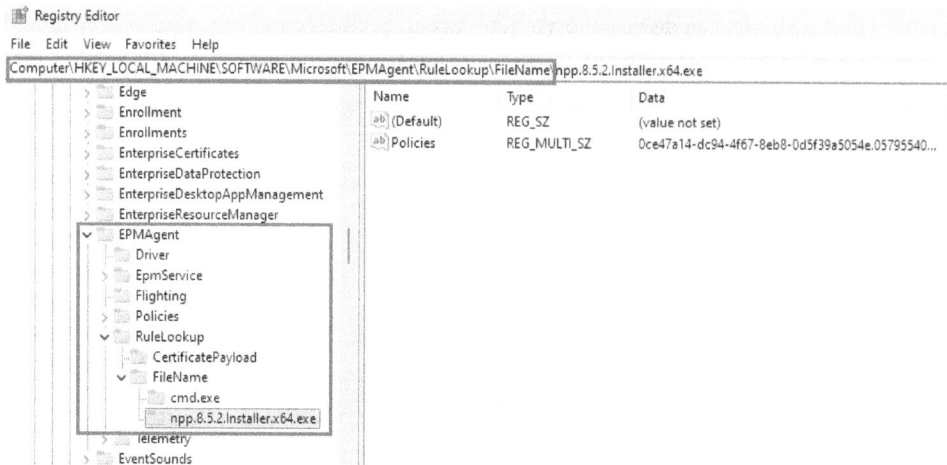

Figure 2.26: EPM-related registry in the device

This registry location is crucial as it helps us identify which applications are targeted by the EPM policy from the device's perspective, ensuring that the device adheres to the specified rules.

In this section, we covered the key registry locations relevant to EPM. Familiarity with these locations and their expected values is essential for effective troubleshooting, especially when used alongside the appropriate EPM logs.

In the next section, we will examine the EPM service, which serves as the foundation for all EPM-related operations including elevation control, policy enforcement, and reporting. These activities are comprehensively logged in the EPM logs discussed earlier in this chapter.

EPM service

As briefly discussed earlier in the chapter, after the EPM agent is installed and running on the device, a service named **Microsoft EPM Agent Service** (`MEMEPMSvc`) is created and set to automatic startup. This service runs `EpmService.exe`, located in `C:\Program Files\Microsoft EPM Agent\EPMService`, in the system context.

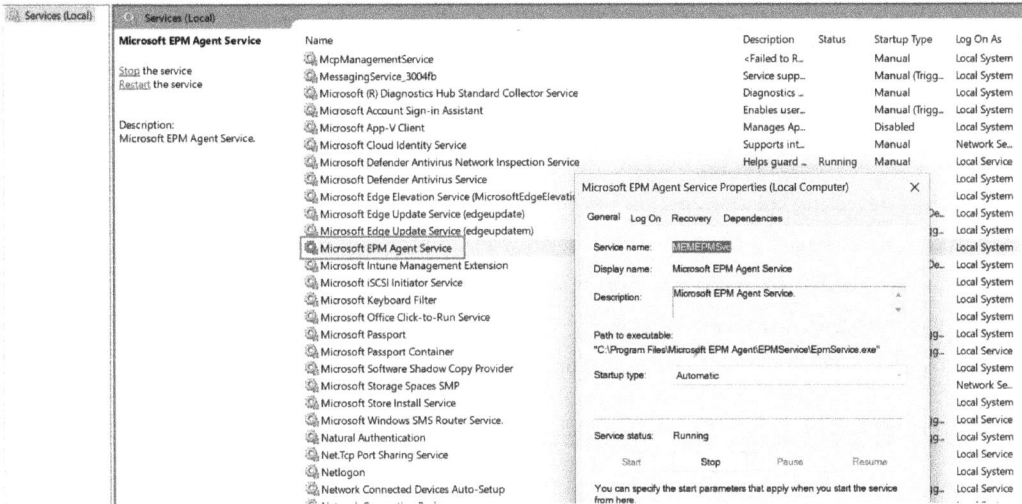

Figure 2.27: EPM service details in the device

Startup type should be set to **Automatic**, and no manual changes need to be made to its config-uration. Now that we understand the workings of EPM, in the next section, let's discuss how to troubleshoot EPM-related issues.

Troubleshooting the flow

The following diagram illustrates the troubleshooting approach we should follow when ad-dressing any EPM-related issues. It is essential to adhere to a systematic, phased approach. This troubleshooting method aligns with the flow we have established previously.

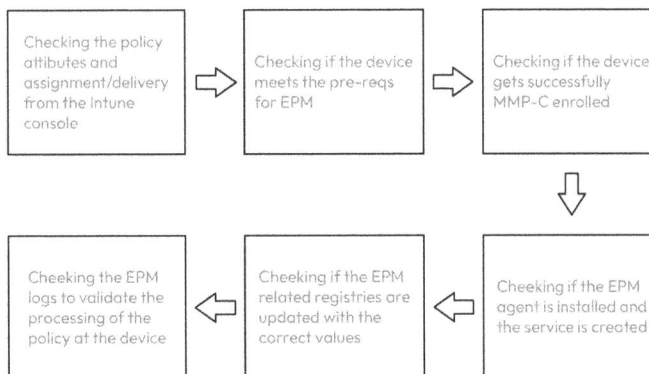

Figure 2.28: Block diagram illustrating the recommended troubleshooting approach for EPM issues

Let's now examine each component in the diagram and outline a structured approach to trou-bleshooting EPM-related issues.

Step 1: Verifying EPM policy creation

Ensure that the EPM policy has been created correctly. This involves several checks within the console. For instance, if a user is unable to elevate a specific application using EPM, begin by verifying the elevation rule policy and the elevation setting policy in the portal. Confirm that the logic for detecting the application in the EPM rule policy is accurate (e.g., validating the file hash or certificate used for the application). Additionally, check the assignment of the elevation rule and setting policy in the Intune portal, including licensing, and make sure that the device is checking in with the Intune service and that the policy deployment is successful from the Intune portal. These checks are performed at the portal level and do not depend on the user.

Step 2: Checking device-side prerequisites

If the policy is correctly created and deployed but the issue persists, focus on the specific device. Ensure that the device meets the EPM prerequisites, such as the supported OS version and required patches. Also, here we need to make sure that the device is now workplace-joined (it is either Entra ID-joined or hybrid Entra-joined and enrolled). This step involves verifying that the device complies with these requirements.

Step 3: Verifying device enrollment to MMP-C

After confirming the previous steps, check the device's enrollment to MMP-C. Verify whether the scheduled task responsible for enrolling the device to MMP-C is created. Examine the **Enterprise Diagnostic Provider** logs to determine the success of the MMP-C enrollment and ensure the relevant registry entries are populated correctly. Additionally, identify the enrollment GUID of the device in the registry.

Step 4: Confirming EPM agent download and installation

Check whether the EPM agent has been successfully downloaded and installed. Verify the presence of the EPM MSI in the registry. Confirm the creation of the EPM folder structure (`C:\Program Files\Microsoft EPM Agent`) in the filesystem and the creation of the EPM service. Successful completion of these steps ensures the correct processing and implementation of the EPM policy on the device.

Step 5: Verifying the EPM policy payload reception

Ensure that the device has received the EPM settings and rules policy payload. Check the registry to confirm that it is populated with the settings as per the policy created by the admin. Verify the creation and correct population of the relevant registry entries.

Step 6: Analyzing EPM logs for errors

If the policy is received as expected, analyze the EPM logs for any relevant errors. Review `EPM.log`, `EPMConsentUI.log`, `EPMService.log`, and `SPMServiceStub.log` located in `C:\Program Files\ Microsoft EPM Agent\Logs`. These logs will indicate any errors preventing the application from launching in the admin context.

> **Important:** Troubleshooting is about following the rule of elimination. By systematically eliminating variables through a structured approach, we can identify potential issues and resolve them effectively.

In the following section, we will explore how to access and interpret EPM-related reporting telemetry within the Intune portal, and how to derive actionable insights from this data.

Gathering reports and insights

The EPM reports are accessible from the **Reports** tab within the **Endpoint Privilege Management** node in the Microsoft Intune admin center. Navigate to **Endpoint security | Endpoint Privilege Management** and select the **Reports** tab. The report data is retained for 30 days.

We have the following categories of elevation reports:

- **Managed elevation report:** This report displays similar details to the elevation report but focuses only on elevations managed by a Windows elevation rule policy
- **Elevation report by applications:** This report provides details for all managed and unmanaged elevations, aggregated by the application that was elevated
- **Elevation report by Publisher:** This report displays details for all managed and unmanaged elevations, aggregated by the publisher of the application that was elevated
- **Elevation report by User:** This report provides details for all managed and unmanaged elevations, aggregated by the user that was elevated

The following screenshot from the Intune portal shows the EPM-related reports available and how to navigate them:

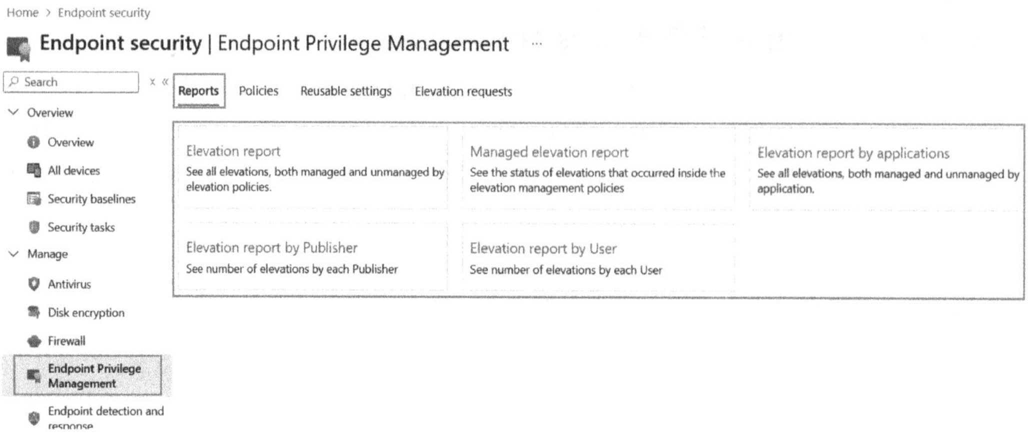

Figure 2.29: Location of EPM-related reports in the Intune portal

Now, let's take a look at an example elevation report that shows the username and the device on which the elevation happened, the application that was elevated, and the timestamp.

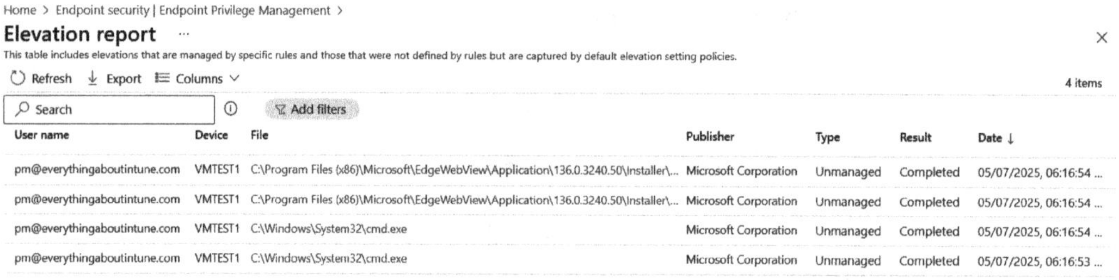

Figure 2.30: A closer look at the EPM elevation report

> Data is processed once every 24 hours, so there may be a delay before seeing data in the elevation usage reports.

Intune provides a set of tools at the device level that allow us to verify which EPM policies have been applied and to review the corresponding EPM settings. These tools are highly effective when used alongside log and registry analysis, as discussed earlier in this chapter.

In the next section, we will take a closer look at the available EPM tools and how they can support troubleshooting and validation efforts.

Using EPM tools

The EPM agent includes a PowerShell cmdlet that assists in diagnosing various issues, such as when a specific whitelisted application fails to elevate successfully. This cmdlet allows us to identify the EPM policies and settings received by the device without the need to check log files or registry locations.

The EPM tool is designed for IT administrators who are troubleshooting the device, rather than for users. IT administrators should follow the steps outlined here to utilize the EPM tools effectively:

1. **Launch PowerShell as an administrator**: The IT administrator needs to open PowerShell with administrative privileges.

2. **Import EPM agent cmdlets**: In PowerShell, navigate to `C:\Program Files\Microsoft EPM Agent\EpmTools` and import the EPM agent cmdlets by running the following command:

```
Import-Module .\EpmCmdlets.dll
```

This will import the EPM module.

```
PS C:\Program Files\Microsoft EPM Agent\EpmTools> Import-Module .\EpmCmdlets.dll
PS C:\Program Files\Microsoft EPM Agent\EpmTools> Get-Policies -PolicyType ClientSettings -Verbose
VERBOSE: Retrieving EPM Agent policies information for policy type 'ClientSettings'.
VERBOSE: Policies processed by the ClientSettings adapter, count=3

Settings              : {[EnableEpm, True]}
PolicyId              : 99c27064-47a2-4e2c-9528-99f81ea5cbe7
Version               : 6DFF82E11C9B9E644A2EDA9634EA03F47B9BBCA2A38ABF8D9BBBDCFDE21B14F0
LastWrite             : 5/9/2023 8:28:31 AM
LastVerifiedTimestamp : 5/12/2023 9:05:02 AM
UserSids              : S-1-5-18

Settings              : {[TelemetryLevel, Full]}
PolicyId              : f4617c7e-a37e-4f27-b298-13ba4f914144
Version               : 1DF3D5176FF192862AD3738E8DAD72DDACB312E48AC40FA732758988BA9BFE05
LastWrite             : 5/9/2023 8:28:31 AM
LastVerifiedTimestamp : 5/12/2023 9:05:02 AM
UserSids              : S-1-5-18

Settings              : {[DefaultBehavior, SelfElevation], [ElevationValidation, None]}
PolicyId              : 1c41d520-bfd1-431e-8d63-5568726b32d7
Version               : 78F7F1869C6C2FC34975C8C3DE925C5AB595EAAEB149B022BED0A69CE8E92FC9
LastWrite             : 5/9/2023 8:28:30 AM
LastVerifiedTimestamp : 5/12/2023 9:05:02 AM
UserSids              : S-1-5-18

PS C:\Program Files\Microsoft EPM Agent\EpmTools> Get-Policies -PolicyType ElevationRules -Verbose
VERBOSE: Retrieving EPM Agent policies information for policy type 'ElevationRules'.
VERBOSE: Policies processed by the ElevationRules adapter, count=0
PS C:\Program Files\Microsoft EPM Agent\EpmTools>
```

Figure 2.31: Using EPM tools

3. **Utilize EPM tools**: The EPM tools are now ready for use. Here are a few commands that can be executed:

   - ```
     Get-Policies -PolicyType ClientSettings -Verbose | Format-Table
     -AutoSize
     ```

   This lists all applications targeted by the EPM rule policy, along with relevant details, such as version and policy ID.

```
PS C:\Program Files\Microsoft EPM Agent\EpmTools> Get-ClientSettings

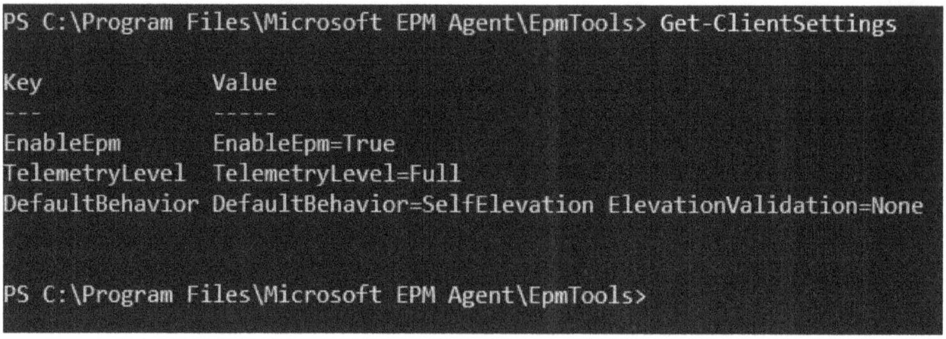

Key            Value
---            -----
EnableEpm      EnableEpm=True
TelemetryLevel TelemetryLevel=Full
DefaultBehavior DefaultBehavior=SelfElevation ElevationValidation=None


PS C:\Program Files\Microsoft EPM Agent\EpmTools>
```

Figure 2.32: Fetching the EPM settings in the device

   - ```
     Get-Policies -PolicyType ElevationRules -Verbose | Format-Table
     -AutoSize
     ```

```
PS C:\Program Files\Microsoft EPM Agent\EpmTools> Get-Policies -PolicyType ElevationRules

ExeFileNames          : Procmon64.exe,Procmon.exe,Procmon64a.exe
PolicyId              : 10995904-c7e5-4e40-b8e7-6db0aa0954e7
Version               : 9B8FBFE42E2265D4ABE9B3637133586A33FF3DB30C98E0752A7FC45AA9E1738B
LastWrite             : 5/21/2023 11:26:11 PM
LastVerifiedTimestamp : 5/21/2023 11:32:37 PM
UserSids              : S-1-12-1-3868604826-1130504159-107365766-391041882

ExeFileNames          : npp.8.5.2.Installer.x64.exe
PolicyId              : 0ce47a14-dc94-4f67-8eb8-0d5f39a5054e
Version               : B95E4436CB41EF0EB228977CE019577FB3FC9F28789DBBDF8F7B4B2DBC1C4428
LastWrite             : 5/21/2023 11:26:06 PM
LastVerifiedTimestamp : 5/21/2023 11:32:37 PM
UserSids              : S-1-12-1-3868604826-1130504159-107365766-391041882

ExeFileNames          : ChromeSetup.exe
PolicyId              : d5e10a4f-318e-44ab-9832-1d0a108c5dfb
Version               : AF285D10F3FF181272ABE17361C31A94DA1D3D9213EA185313D6ACEFDCF8879A
LastWrite             : 5/21/2023 11:26:01 PM
LastVerifiedTimestamp : 5/21/2023 11:32:37 PM
UserSids              : S-1-12-1-3868604826-1130504159-107365766-391041882

ExeFileNames          : vlc-3.0.18-win32.exe
PolicyId              : f2b310c9-bf58-497f-a8a2-95fae933d147
Version               : 555BC076C0B91921511BCB6ED25A59D45764211527C2ABA0300DBC385F7F8E12
LastWrite             : 5/21/2023 11:22:44 PM
LastVerifiedTimestamp : 5/21/2023 11:32:37 PM
UserSids              : S-1-12-1-3868604826-1130504159-107365766-391041882

ExeFileNames          : 7z2201-x64.exe
PolicyId              : f0d497f8-d467-4477-b5d8-e3001096f17b
Version               : 638CB29FF673366BDCC0E59986735F1391FEDE9DF2DF54327E20E56F8CE73A43
LastWrite             : 5/21/2023 11:21:10 PM
LastVerifiedTimestamp : 5/21/2023 11:32:36 PM
UserSids              : S-1-12-1-3868604826-1130504159-107365766-391041882
```

Figure 2.33: Getting a list of elevation rules and related applications

Now, let's take a look at the most commonly used PowerShell commands available with the EPM tools and how they are used:

Commands	Purpose
`Import-Module 'C:\Program Files\ Microsoft EPM Agent\EpmTools\ EpmCmdlets.dll'`	Loads the EPM Tools module into our PowerShell session
`Get-Policies`	Gets a list of all policies that are received by the Microsoft EPM agent
`Get-ElevationRules`	Retrieves a list of elevation rules that have been received by the EPM agent on a device
`Get-ClientSettings`	Retrieves client-specific EPM settings, such as telemetry and logging configurations

Commands	Purpose
`Get-FileAttributes`	Extracts file metadata and certificate chain information to help build accurate elevation rules
`Get-DeclaredConfiguration`	Returns the full declared configuration received from Intune, including elevation rules and client settings
`Get-DeclaredConfigurationAnalysis`	Compares the declared configuration with the current state on the device to identify mismatches or issues

Table 2.3: List of commonly used PowerShell commands related to EPM

Having now explored how to enhance EPM-related troubleshooting and log analysis using the device-side EPM tools, we will shift our focus in the next section to the recommended deployment approach for EPM. Given the complexity and multi-layered nature of EPM deployment, it is essential to follow a structured and strategic rollout plan.

Deployment strategy

Rolling out EPM to devices is not a single-step process. It is essential to conduct thorough due diligence before deploying EPM and removing admin rights from users. Here, I have outlined the steps that can serve as our deployment strategy for rolling out EPM to our production users:

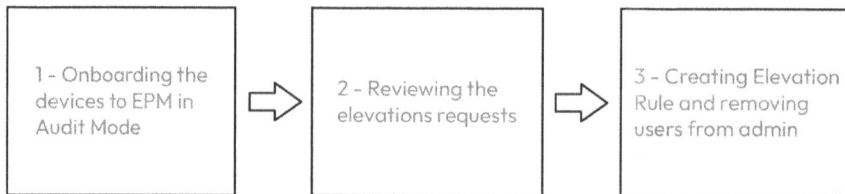

Figure 2.34: Block diagram illustrating the EPM deployment approach

Now, let's discuss each of the blocks in detail.

Step 1: Onboarding devices to EPM in audit mode

In this step, we need to create an EPM elevation setting policy in Intune and assign it to the users/devices. This will install the EPM agent on the devices, collect relevant data, and send it to Intune for the administrator to review and act. This process is hidden from the end user, who will not notice any changes.

In order to create the EPM settings policy, we must go to the Intune admin center | **Endpoint Se-curity** | **EPM** | **Policies** | **Create Policy** | **Elevation Setting Policy** and enable the following settings:

- **Endpoint Privilege Management: Enabled**
- **Default elevation response: Not configured**
- **Send elevation data for reporting: Yes**
- **Reporting scope: Diagnostic data and all endpoint elevations**

Let's take a look at these settings as configured in the EPM settings policy in the Intune portal below:

Home > Endpoint security | Endpoint Privilege Management >

Create profile ...

Elevation settings policy

✓ Basics   ② **Configuration settings**   ③ Scope tags   ④ Assignments   ⑤ Review + create

⌃ Privilege management elevation client settings

Elevation settings establish the default behaviors for the endpoint elevation client.

Endpoint Privilege Management	⬤ Enabled
Default elevation response	Not configured ⌄
Send elevation data for reporting *	Yes ⌄
Reporting scope *	Diagnostic data and all endpoint elevations ⌄

Figure 2.35: Creating an EPM settings policy from the Intune portal

Once these settings are in place, the device will be onboarded to both MMP-C and EPM. The device will then begin sending all elevation-related data to the Intune service.

Step 2: Reviewing the elevation requests

As IT admins, we can access the portal to view the reports. By navigating to **Endpoint Security** | **EPM** | **Reports**, we can see all the applications that users are elevating to the admin context within our organization.

This provides us with valuable insights into which applications generally require elevation to admin by our workforce. Based on this information, we can determine which applications need to be whitelisted via EPM.

The advantage of having devices in EPM audit mode is that it allows us to gather comprehensive insights from the end devices about the applications being elevated by users.

We can see two kinds of elevation requests in the EPM policy when we check the reports:

- **Managed elevation:** A managed elevation occurs when a file or process is elevated through an Intune EPM policy (elevation rules policy). The file matches an elevation rule defined by the admin (e.g., based on file hash, certificate, or name).
- **Unmanaged elevation:** An unmanaged elevation happens typically when a user or process elevates privileges without matching any EPM rule, such as a local administrator running an app using *Run as administrator*. This activity is logged in reports as *Unmanaged Elevation* for visibility.

Step 3: Creating an elevation rule and removing admin privileges from users

Based on the insights gathered in the previous step, we are now prepared to take action. We need to create elevation rule policies for the applications that our users require to run with admin privileges. Utilizing reusable settings can simplify the creation of these EPM rule policies.

Once these policies are established, we can proceed to remove the admin privileges from the users' machines using an Intune configuration policy.

During EPM deployment, two key configurations must be defined: the EPM settings policy and the EPM rule policy. The following table outlines the two most common values for these settings, along with their respective impacts. This comparison is intended to guide decision-making by helping determine the most appropriate configuration for various deployment scenarios.

EPM setting policy (default behavior for all apps)	EPM rule policy (behavior for whitelisted apps)	Impact
Deny All	Support Approved	This is the most restrictive combination of settings that can be chosen if the organization wants to implement strict controls. By combining these two settings, it ensures that when a user attempts to elevate to admin for whitelisted applications, they can only do so once it has been approved by the admin from the portal. This implies the highest level of control and restriction. This combination of settings ensures that IT administrators closely monitor the applications that can be elevated within the organization, and no application is elevated unless explicitly approved. If a user attempts to elevate any application that has not been whitelisted, the request is denied.
Support Approved	Automatic	This combination of settings is less restrictive. It ensures that any application deemed necessary for productivity by the admin and whitelisted will be elevated automatically when launched by the user. For any other application, when the user attempts to elevate it, the request is sent to the admin for approval. Once the request has been approved, the user can launch the application. This combination of settings is moderately restrictive. By using this approach, the admins only supervise the elevation of applications that have not been whitelisted.

Table 2.4: List of commonly used EPM settings and their impact

Now that we have reviewed the possible configuration values for EPM, the next section will focus on how to effectively roll out EPM in a production environment.

Rolling out EPM

Rolling out EPM in a production environment involves multiple steps, as illustrated in the following diagram. On the device side, it's essential to ensure that all EPM prerequisites are fulfilled and that the device is enrolled in Intune. On the administrative side, the Intune administrator must deploy EPM by configuring the appropriate policies. Finally, the rollout progress can be monitored by reviewing the logs discussed earlier in this chapter.

Figure 2.36: Block diagram illustrating the steps for EPM rollout

In this section, we are going to focus on the task at the admin end for onboarding devices to EPM.

There are two steps involved in the process.

Step 1: Creating the EPM elevation setting policy

This policy is going to enable the EPM functionality on the device. It is going to install the EPM agent and send diagnostic information from the device to the Intune service. Creating this is pretty straightforward; we just have to change a toggle to set it up. Also, in this policy, we determine the default behavior when any user tries to elevate any application (for the applications that haven't been explicitly whitelisted). The following figure shows how to navigate to the EPM policy from the Intune console:

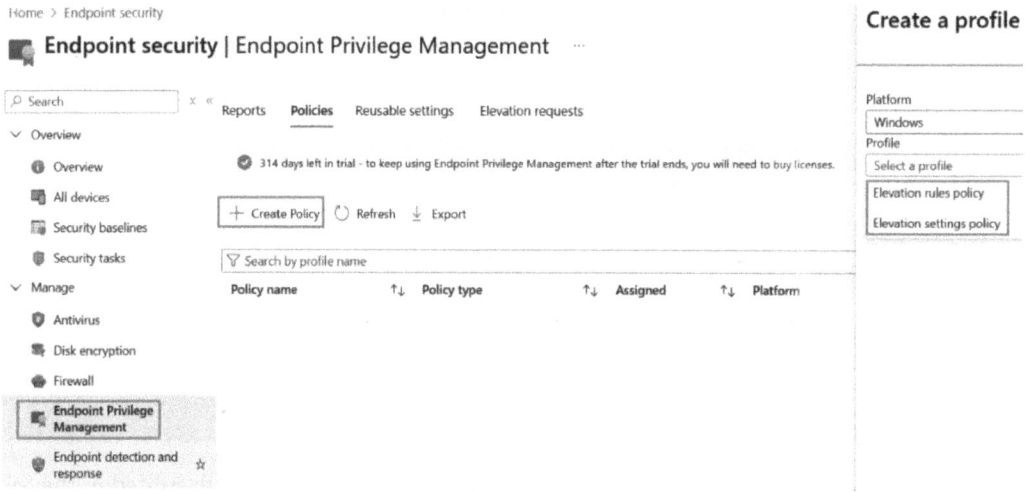

Figure 2.37: Creation of an EPM elevation rule policy in the Intune portal

We select **Elevation settings policy** on this screen and click on **Create**. This takes us to the next screen, where we define the EPM-related settings.

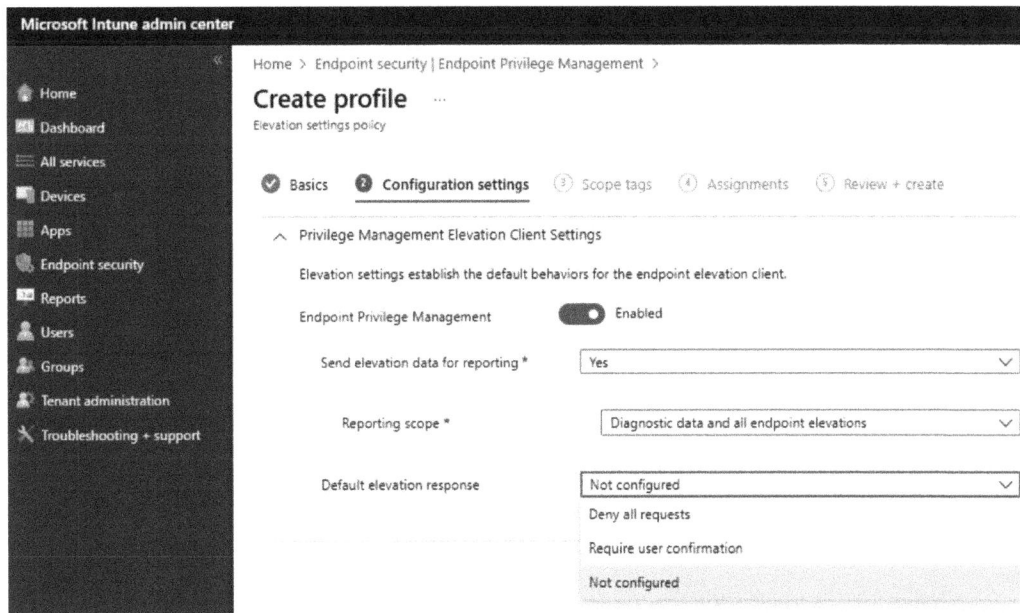

Figure 2.38: EPM settings in the Intune portal

Once the elevation settings policy is created and deployed, it will enroll the device to MMP-C and onboard to EPM by installing the EPM agent. The next step is creating an EPM elevation rule policy.

Step 2: Creating rules for whitelisting applications in EPM

There are a few decisions that we need to make when deciding on the logic for whitelisting an application in an EPM rule policy. We have to decide how we want to whitelist the applications:

- Using the filename and file hash
- Using a certificate

Both are valid options and can be used. If we want to use the filename and file hash, then we will have to get the file hash of the executable that we want to whitelist. We can get that using the Get-Filehash PowerShell command.

On the other hand, if we want to use a certificate, we can export one from the executable and upload it to the policy. To do this, we need to go to **Properties** of .exe/.msi (by right-clicking on it) and go to **Digital Signature** and then **Details**.

A new dialog box will open. Click on **View Certificate**. In the new box, click on the **Details** tab and then **Copy to File....**

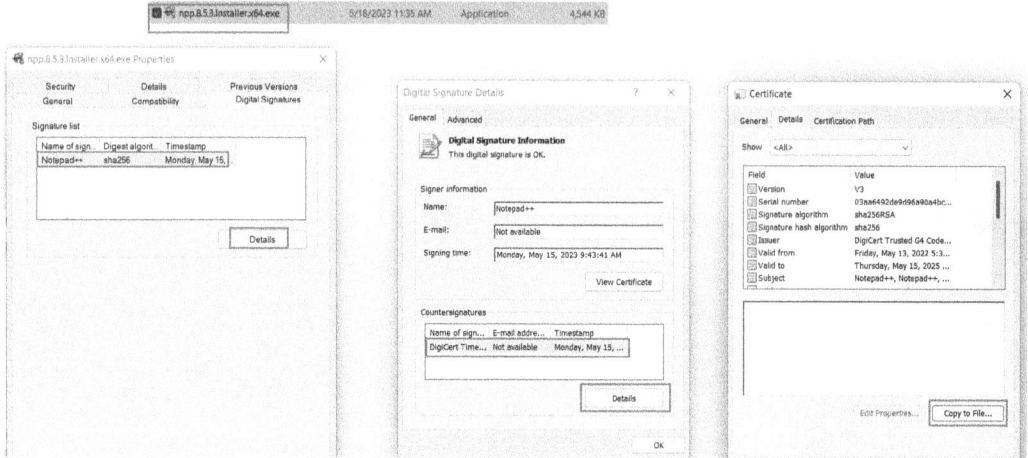

Figure 2.39: Steps for extracting the certificate of an executable for EPM rule policy creation

Now a wizard will open that will enable us to export the certificate. We need to click on **Next** and then **Select DER encoded binary X.509** and then **Browse**, and save it to the location of our choice:

Figure 2.40: Steps for extracting the certificate of an executable for EPM rule policy creation

Now the export of the file should be successful.

Figure 2.41: Successful export of the certificate

We can open the certificate and see its parameters, including the **Issued To** parameter:

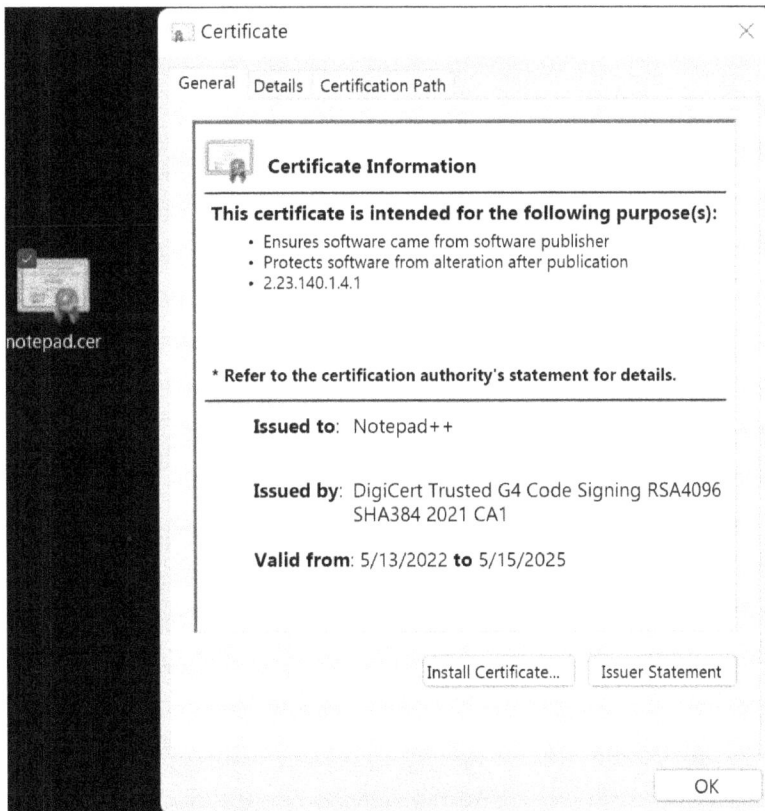

Figure 2.42: The extracted certificate to be used in EPM rule policy creation

Now, we can use the exported certificate to create an EPM rule policy. We will have to provide the elevation conditions as well as the file information, which EPM will use to detect the application when it is launched by the user.

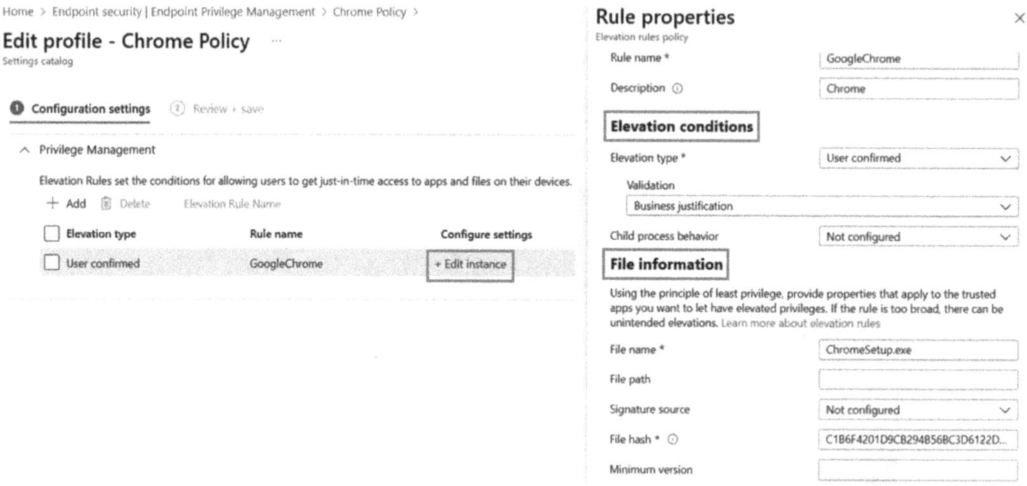

Figure 2.43: EPM elevation rule creation in the Intune portal

When to use filename/file hash and when to use certificates

We need to keep in mind that just using the filename is not sufficient because the filename can be changed by the end users. One of the caveats of using only the file hash is that it requires updates whenever the app version changes. On the other hand, new versions of the app still signed by the same certificate will still match. The best and recommended way is to use a combination of all the values whenever possible to minimize the risks.

While creating the elevation rule policy in EPM, there are some key decisions that we must make.

Other important decisions

Two additional key EPM settings—**child process behavior** and **argument list**—warrant detailed discussion for clarity. Let's examine each of them closely.

Child process behavior

Child process behavior allows us to control the context when a process elevated with EPM creates a child process. This behavior allows you to further restrict processes that would normally be automatically delegated to the context of their parent processes.

Windows automatically delegates the context of a parent to a child, so take special care to control the behavior of your allowed applications. Ensure you evaluate what is needed when you create elevation rules and implement the principle of least privilege.

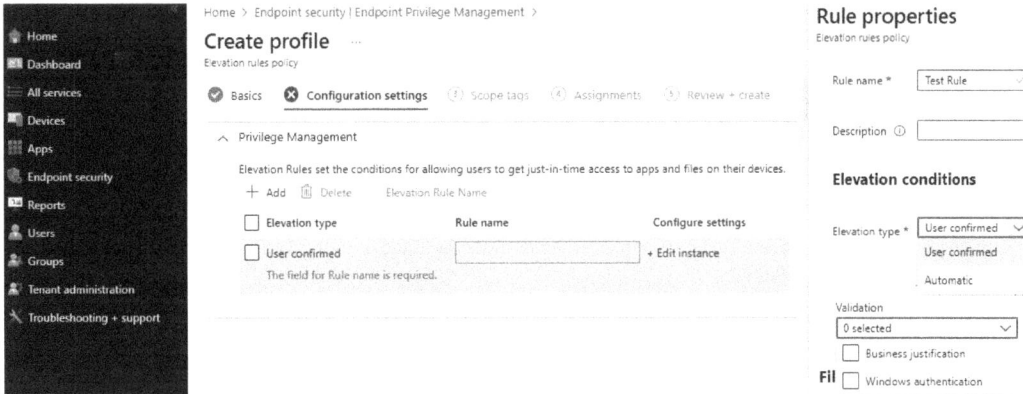

Figure 2.44: Settings while configuring your EPM rule policy in the Intune portal

In the next section, we will look at the argument list, which is another important setting while creating an EPM policy in the Intune portal.

Argument list

EPM enables the configuration of file elevation rules based on command-line arguments, offering precise control over which files can be elevated and under what conditions. Specifically, an EPM rule can be tailored to permit elevation only when a predefined argument is used. If a user attempts to elevate a file with an unapproved argument, the elevation is denied.

When a user initiates elevation, EPM evaluates the command-line argument against the rule's defined parameters. If there's a match, elevation is granted; otherwise, it is blocked.

This approach delivers the following benefits:

- Enhanced security by limiting elevation to explicitly intended use cases
- Greater administrative control through fine-tuned rule definitions
- Reduced risk of accidental or malicious elevation by enforcing argument-specific conditions

For instance, we can create an elevation rule for the dsregcmd tool, which is commonly used to assess device status in Microsoft Entra ID, by specifying approved arguments such as /status and /listaccounts. To prevent unintended actions, sensitive switches such as /leave, which unregisters a device, are excluded.

With this setup, elevation is granted only when one of the allowed arguments is used. Any attempt to run dsregcmd with an unapproved switch, such as /leave, is automatically blocked, ensuring secure and intentional use.

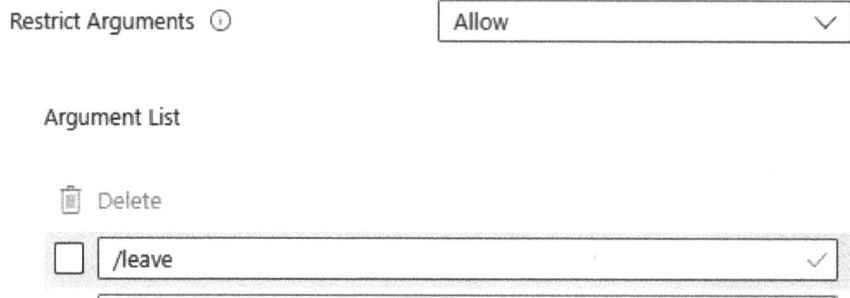

Restrict Arguments ⓘ   Allow   ∨

Argument List

🗑 Delete

☐ /leave   ✓

Figure 2.45: Option to specify an EPM argument list

EPM now supports Windows devices with ARM64 processors as well. The EPM policy supports both user and device assignments:

- **User assignment:** When the policy is assigned to a user, the EPM agent is installed, and the policy is applied after the user signs into the device.
- **Device group assignment:** When the policy is assigned to a device group, the EPM agent is installed, and the policy is applied even before the user logs in to the device.

The EPM agent is not installed as part of the Autopilot OOBE process. Consequently, the EPM policy is pushed to the device, and the agent is installed only after the device reaches the desktop screen during the Autopilot process.

There is no BYOD support for EPM. This is because the assumption is that on a BYOD device, the user would already be an admin, hence EPM is not needed in that scenario..

If we log in to a machine as an admin, then EPM is not involved.

EPM supports co-managed devices without having to move a specific workload to Intune.

Here are two good-to-have features related to EPM that might be available in the future:

- The option in EPM to create a deny rule for an application. This ensures that whenever a user attempts to elevate a specific blacklisted application to admin status, the request is denied. It is important to note that this denying feature of EPM only restricts the launch of the application in the admin context; the application can still be launched as a standard user. If the use case involves blocking the launch of the application altogether, other technologies, such as WDAC or AppLocker, should be used.

- Additionally, we have the option to determine whether the user can elevate and change system settings such as IP address, time settings, or language on the device using EPM.

In the next section, we are going to explore one of the new and powerful capabilities within the Intune portal that makes creating an EPM rule very easy for the admin.

Elevating the user's account using EPM

By default, when we use EPM and allow the end user to elevate the session for a specific application, the end user's account doesn't get elevated to an admin. There is a virtual account that is created and is used to perform actions with elevated privileges. This virtual account does not contain the identity of the logged-in standard user. This is the intended behavior for security reasons as we would want to have the elevated experience containerized and separated in a profile.

Possible issues with this approach

While in most cases the use of a virtual account with EPM elevation doesn't cause any issues and is a benefit as it creates an isolated profile for the account, there are some scenarios wherein the elevation of the application using a virtual account might cause issues. Let's look over those possible scenarios:

- Essentially, when an application is elevated using the virtual account via EPM, the application doesn't have access to the end user's profile/personalized settings and registry. Thus, documents stored in the user's profile or redirected folders may not be available to the application elevated by the virtual account via EPM.

- Let's say that the end user is a developer who is elevating the Visual Studio application using EPM. Once elevated and launched, if the end user now tries to open any file from the elevated Visual Studio, they won't be able to view any files that were stored in their profile. This is because the elevated Visual Studio is not referencing the end user's profile; it references the virtual account's profile that was used to elevate it. So, in short, the process doesn't easily allow accessing the user's own registry keys under HKCU.

- Also, when the application opens in an elevated context, it uses the customizations and preferences (such as font style/light/dark mode) of the virtual account and not the logged-in user.

As a solution to this problem, Microsoft, with the 2510 service release, announced support for a user account context in EPM elevations. This new option affects how EPM handles elevations. Now we have a new elevation type of **Elevate as current user**, as seen in the following figure:

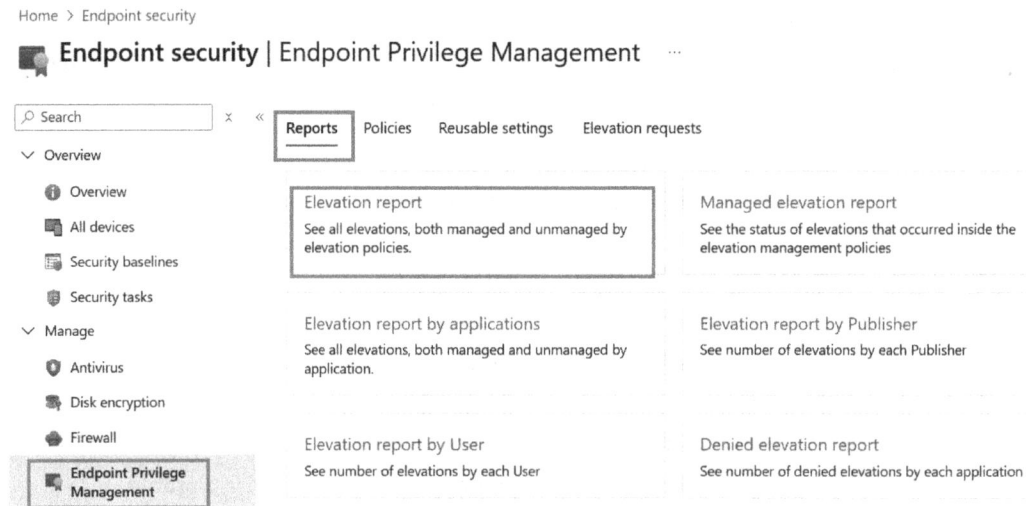

Home > Endpoint security

Endpoint security | Endpoint Privilege Management   ⋯

Reports Policies Reusable settings Elevation requests	
Elevation report See all elevations, both managed and unmanaged by elevation policies.	Managed elevation report See the status of elevations that occurred inside the elevation management policies
Elevation report by applications See all elevations, both managed and unmanaged by application.	Elevation report by Publisher See number of elevations by each Publisher
Elevation report by User See number of elevations by each User	Denied elevation report See number of denied elevations by each application

Left navigation: Overview, Overview, All devices, Security baselines, Security tasks, Manage, Antivirus, Disk encryption, Firewall, **Endpoint Privilege Management**

Figure 2.46: Option to elevate as current user in an EPM elevation rule policy

With this new option, the application, once elevated, can run under the signed-in user's identity instead of the virtual account. When **Elevation type** is set to the current user with authentication required, EPM skips the virtual account approach. It launches the Consent UI as SYSTEM in the user's session, the user verifies their identity, and Windows provides an admin-capable token. EPM duplicates that token and starts the app, so it runs as the signed-in user with full admin rights, thereby preserving HKCU and profile settings. If Windows can't supply an admin token, this path fails and EPM falls back to the virtual account model.

This change finally fixes issues where virtual accounts lost access to user profiles or registry keys and is a welcome addition to EPM's feature capability!

In the next section, we'll look at a workaround that enables the end user to elevate and start/stop a service using EPM functionality.

Elevating via EPM to restart a service

Let's imagine a use case wherein the end user wants to restart a specific service or stop/start a specific service. There could be many reasons behind this; for example, maybe the application is stuck and the service needs a reset. Restarting the service of a specific application is often necessary to restore functionality, apply updates, or resolve performance issues. A standard user on a Windows device cannot restart a service as it requires administrative privileges.

By default, using EPM, there is no option for the end user to request elevation for restarting a specific service from the UI. If the standard user goes to services.msc, the option to restart the service will be grayed out, and if the user tries to restart the service via Command Prompt, they will get an Access is denied error, as shown in the following figure:

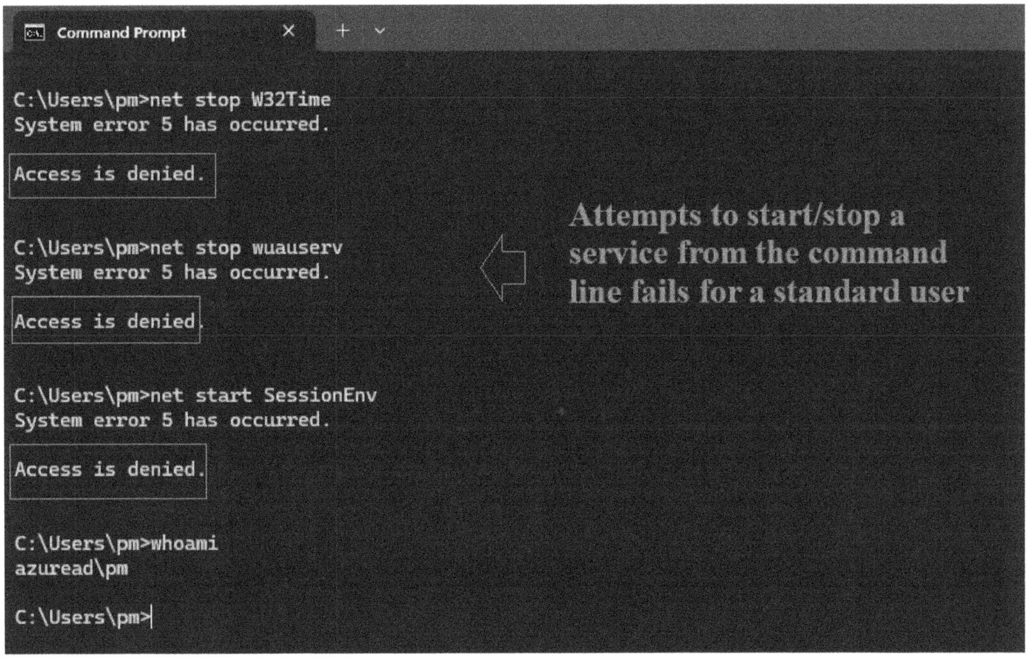

Figure 2.47: Standard user's attempt to restart a service through the command prompt fails

However, there is a workaround that can be implemented by using some tricks in the EPM rule policy by referencing an executable net.exe. The net.exe simplifies and standardizes administrative tasks related to networking and services. It can be used in command prompts, scripts, or batch files and is an essential command-line utility provided by Microsoft as part of the Windows operating system.

We will use the following steps to achieve the use case of allowing end users to elevate and start/restart services via EPM:

1. Create an EPM rule for the net.exe using its certificate.

2. Then, in the argument list, provide a list of commands that the end user can run to start/restart services.

3. Whenever the end user tries to start or stop a service by referencing (elevating) the net.exe and running a command that is whitelisted in the argument list, it is successful.

Let's take a look at the setup in the Intune portal that is needed to achieve this logic.

Setup overview

We need to create an elevation rule policy that creates a rule for net.exe and provides a list of commands (arguments) that the end user is allowed to run in an admin context. Let's take a look at the setup next:

- **Elevation type: Automatic**
- **File name:** net.exe
- **File path:** C:\Windows\System32
- **Signature source:** Upload a certificate file
- **Certificate type: Publisher**
- **File hash** (optional): 2F3D1A52FC7D1DDFAB34B290BCEB31F03E13B658B31C3914E954DBA877009F26
- **Restrict arguments:** Allow
- **Argument list:** Command line for starting/stopping services

Let's take a look at how some of these settings look in the UI:

Rule properties

Elevation rules policy

Rule name * net.exe

Description ⓘ Services

Elevation conditions

Define how EPM handles elevation for this rule. Learn more about these options

Wildcards are not supported for automatic elevation.

Elevation type * Automatic

Child process behavior Require rule to elevate

File information

Using the principle of least privilege, provide properties that apply to the trusted apps you want to let have elevated privileges. If the rule is too broad, there can be unintended elevations. Learn more about elevation rules

File name * net.exe

Using a certificate for elevation rules may allow any signed file to elevate if renamed to match the rule. To mitigate this risk, specify a restricted file path (e.g., C:\Program Files) that standard users cannot modify.

File path C:\Windows\System32

Figure 2.48: Policy settings for elevating net.exe via EPM

We need to export the certificate of net.exe and upload it under the signature source in the EPM rule, as seen in the following figure:

Figure 2.49: Whitelisting net.exe in the EPM policy using its certificate

Now we need to provide a list of commands in the argument list, as seen in the following figure:

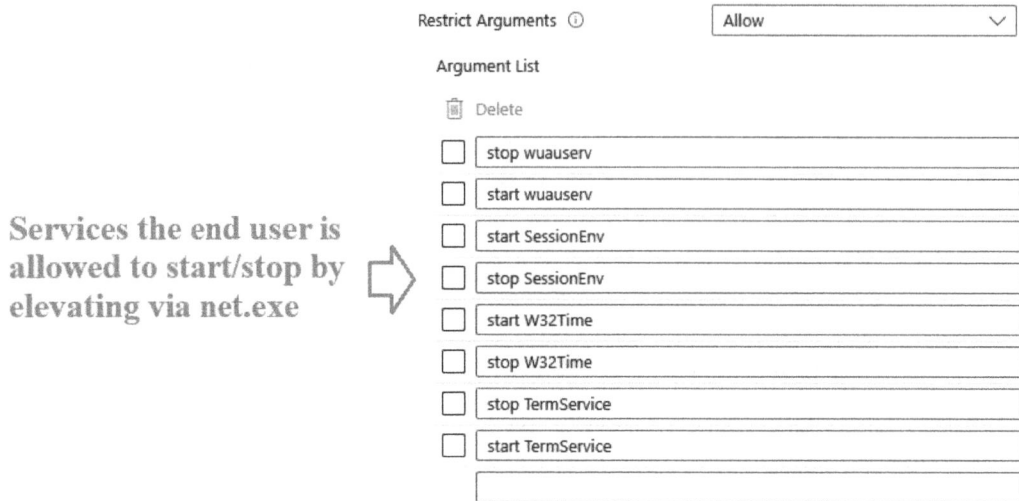

Figure 2.50: Whitelisting services that users can start/stop via an EPM policy argument list

Now, whenever a standard user tries to start/stop a service that is whitelisted in the argument list in an EPM policy by referencing net.exe, it is successful. This is because net.exe gets elevated in the admin context; however, only the whitelisted arguments (commands) run in an elevated context.

After the EPM rule policy is applied, as seen in the following figure, the standard user can elevate themself and stop/restart services that were whitelisted in the policy by referencing net.exe.

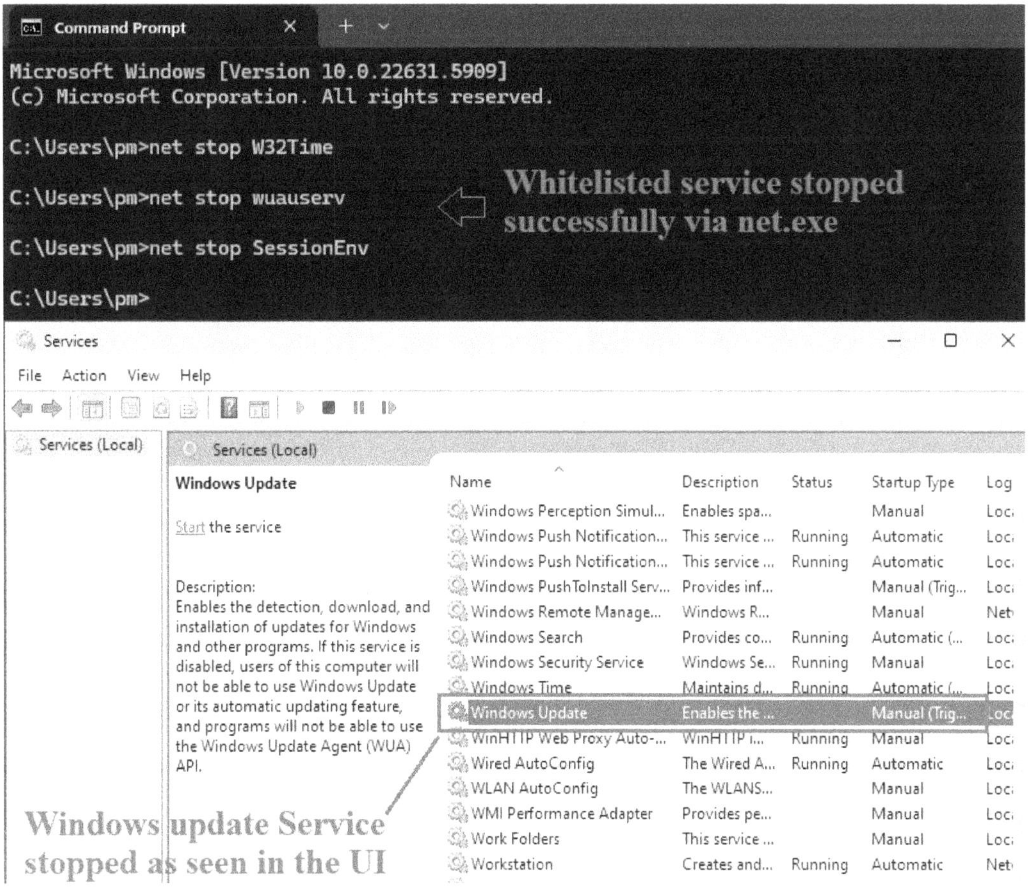

Figure 2.51: Service started/stopped successfully as viewed in the UI

> In this case, we don't need to create a rule for cmd.exe (using which we are running the commands). The user can also run these commands via PowerShell or any other utility.

Creating EPM rules based on reporting

It is possible for us to create EPM rules based on the reporting data that has been collected by the Intune service. The Intune service collects all the elevation requests for unmanaged applications in the reporting. This information also contains the file hash, filename, and all other attributes needed to create an EPM rule for that application. Therefore, the admin doesn't need to fetch any details manually. Thus, this ability of reporting an EPM rule based on the elevation report is a very powerful and quick way to create an EPM rule.

Here are the steps we can take to create an EPM rule based on the report:

1. In the Intune portal, we need to go to **Endpoint Privilege Management**, then **Reports**, and then **Elevation report**:

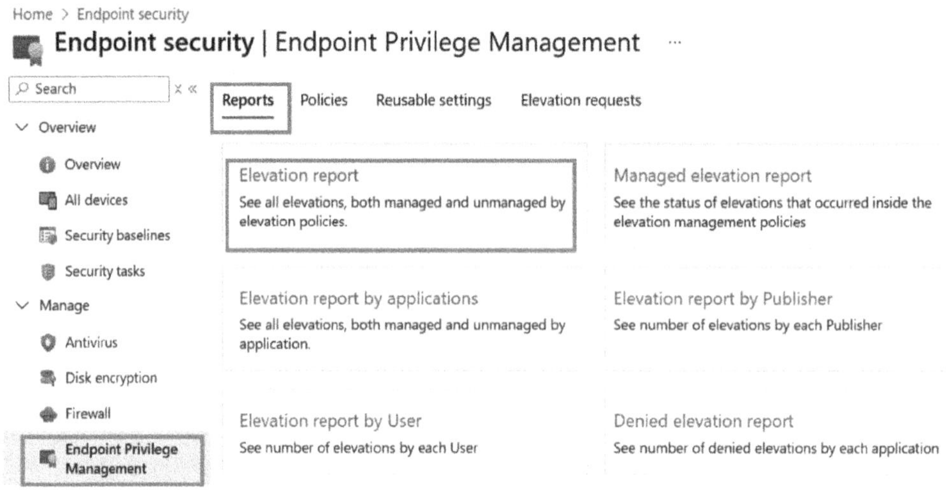

Figure 2.52: Viewing an EPM Elevation report for unmanaged applications in the Intune portal

Here, we can see all the unmanaged elevation requests that have occurred.

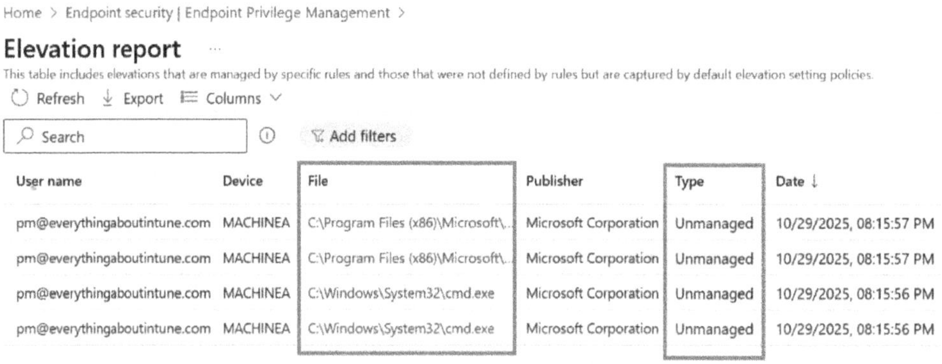

Figure 2.53: Viewing the details of the elevation

2. If we click on any of them, we can see all the details that have been collected for the application, including the filename, file path, and file version. There is also an option to click on **Create a Rule with these file details**. If you click on it, a new elevation rule will be created for the application without needing to extract the app details manually.

Elevation detail ✕

+ Create a rule with these file details

File	C:\Program Files (x86)\Microsoft\EdgeWebView\Application\141.0.3537.9
Publisher	Microsoft Corporation
User	pm@everythingaboutintune.com
Device	MACHINEA
Type	Unmanaged
Result	0 ⓘ
Date and time	10/29/25, 08:15 PM GMT+5:30
Justification	
Process type	Parent
Applicable Rule	Unmanaged Elevation

File information

File path	C:\Program Files (x86)\Microsoft\EdgeWebView\Application\141.0.3537.9
Certificate payload	<Null>
Hash value	02AA85837EBBFF67329D77B3584231C3055DD7ECFA9
File version	141.0.3537.99
File description	Microsoft Edge Installer

Figure 2.54: Creating an EPM rule for unmanaged elevation from a report

3. When we click on **Create a Rule with these file details**, a popup opens that enables us to create an elevation rule from within this screen. We have the option to create this rule as a part of an EPM policy that has already been created in the tenant or to create this as a part of a new policy. We have the option to determine the elevation type and the child process behavior:

Create a rule with these file details

◯ Create a new policy

◉ Add to an existing policy

Select an existing policy	˅

EAI Demo Elevation rule policy

Services policy

Notepad ++

EAI EPM TaskManager

SyncML Viewer

Service Trace Viewer

Universal Switch Finder

Existing policies in the tenant where this rule can be added

Type

User confirmed	˅

User confirmed

Automatic

Deny

Support approved

Elevate as current user

Other options available in this selection

Child process behavior

Require rule to elevate	˅

☑ Require the same file path as this elevation

OK	Cancel

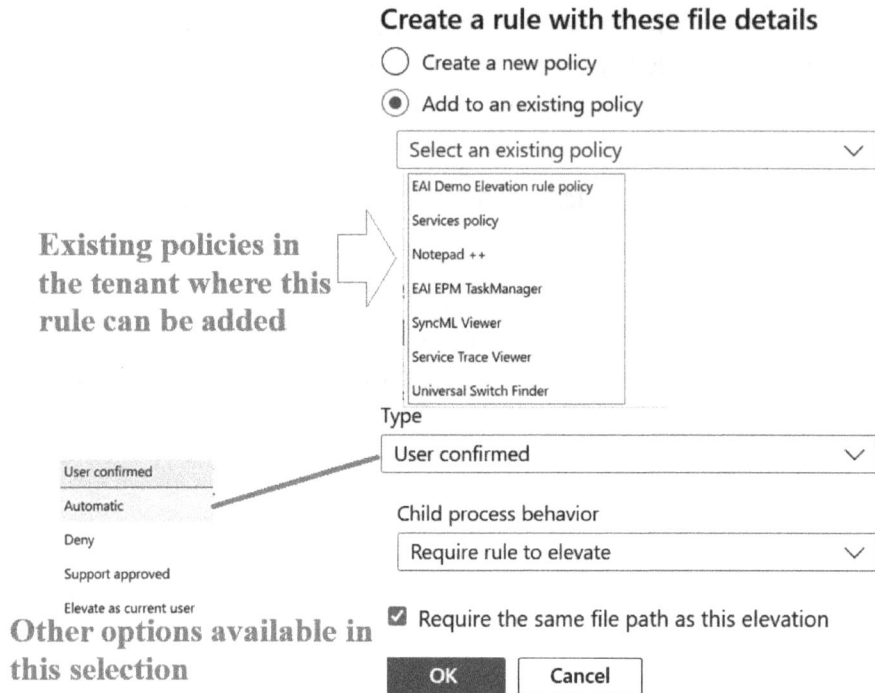

Figure 2.55: Selecting the attributes of the EPM rule policy

4. Once we click on **OK**, and if we have selected to add it to an existing EPM policy, we get the following prompt:

Are you sure?

This will add the details of this elevation to the EAI Demo Elevation rule policy rule. The new rule will apply to the same assignments.

Yes	No

Figure 2.56: Finalizing the EPM policy

5. When you click on **Yes** in the prompt, the EPM rule gets added to an existing policy.

This is how we can add an EPM rule based on the telemetry data that we have received as part of reporting in the Intune portal. This is a very powerful feature as it removes the overhead of finding the attributes of the application (such as filename and certificate) manually.

Now that we've covered the purpose and functionality of EPM, it's important to understand the appropriate scenarios for its use.

When to use EPM and when not to

The preferred method for deploying applications should always be through Microsoft Intune using the **Required** intent, ensuring that essential applications are automatically installed on user devices. If there is uncertainty about whether a user needs a particular application, it should be deployed using the **Available** intent, allowing users to install it on demand via the Company Portal app.

When to use EPM

EPM should be used in specific cases such as the following:

- A user needs to install an application that has not been pre-provisioned and is not commonly used across the organization
- A user requires temporary elevation to run tools in an administrative context for legitimate troubleshooting or diagnostic purposes (e.g., using tools such as ProcMon, Command Prompt, or PowerShell with elevated privileges)

When not to use EPM

EPM is not intended to restrict or block the execution of applications. If the goal is to prevent certain applications from launching, organizations should instead use App Control for Business, which is designed to enforce application allow/block policies at the system level.

Our two cents

Making users administrators on their machines is never advisable. Therefore, we must first ensure that all users in our workforce are standard users.

Does this mean we need to assign EPM licenses to all users so they can elevate themselves to admin status for an application session? The answer is *no*. Our primary method for installing applications on devices should be to push them as required via Intune. If we are unsure whether an end user truly needs an application, we have the option to push those apps as **Available**. This makes the applications accessible in the Company Portal app, allowing users to download and install them as needed without requiring elevation to admin status.

EPM is designed for scenarios where users may need to perform extensive testing and install applications that are not commonly deployed by the admin through the Intune portal. Instead of relying on the admin to deploy the application, the user can request elevation for an application session via EPM. Once approved, the user can install the application. To facilitate this, it is necessary to procure and assign an EPM license for such users. Another use case involves situations where specific users need to run a particular application in an admin context for a specific purpose (e.g., a user wants to launch ProcMon as an admin to gather data). In such cases, assigning an EPM license to the user and using EPM to facilitate the elevation is a sensible approach.

It's also very important to remember that EPM is an elevation control technology (i.e., it decides which app will be elevated for the end user in the admin context), not an app control technology (i.e., it doesn't decide which application will be restricted from being installed/launched in the machine as a standard user).

In summary, EPM should not be treated as a solution for all users to install applications. The primary method for delivering applications should still be through Intune, either as **Available** or **Required**. Only users who need to install specific applications that are not deployed by the admin, or users who genuinely need to elevate an application to admin status while running it, require an EPM license.

Summary

In this chapter, we explored the importance of EPM and its alignment with Microsoft's Zero Trust principles. We examined the underlying processes involved in EPM agent installation and policy deployment. Additionally, we conducted a detailed review of relevant logs and registry entries to establish a structured approach to troubleshooting EPM-related issues. We also introduced the EPM tools at the device level that support diagnostics and validation. The chapter concluded with a discussion on EPM deployment strategies and an overview of supplementary reference resources to support further learning.

In the next chapter, we will delve into **Enterprise App Management** (**EAM**), a key component of the Intune Suite. This chapter will highlight how EAM enhances the efficiency of deploying and updating third-party applications across the organization.

Resources

Apart from official Microsoft docs, I highly recommend exploring the blogs by Rudy Oms (at `https://call4cloud.nl`). He is an exceptionally talented blogger who has authored insightful and technically rich articles on EPM, infused with a touch of humor. His blogs are invaluable resources and should be bookmarked by anyone planning to understand EPM in greater detail.

Join us on Discord

For discussions around the book and to connect with your peers, join us on Discord at `https://discord.gg/dygzddgYCR`

3

Streamlining Application Deployment with EAM

In this chapter, we will explore the importance of **Enterprise Application Management** (**EAM**) and how it can be effectively configured and deployed using Microsoft Intune. The chapter will delve into the underlying processes and logging mechanisms involved in EAM app delivery, correlating each step with relevant registry entries to strengthen troubleshooting skills.

Additionally, we will cover how to integrate EAM with Microsoft Graph to enable automation and discuss potential features that Microsoft may consider introducing in future iterations of EAM. Finally, the chapter will conclude with a brief competitive analysis comparing EAM to similar third-party solutions in the market, along with an objective evaluation of its overall capabilities. By the end of this chapter, you will be equipped with the knowledge and skills required to deploy new EAM solutions, diagnose issues effectively with existing deployments, and have a deeper understanding of the underlying processes.

The following main topics will be covered:

- Why EAM?
- Deploying and updating an EAM app
- Registry
- EAM app inventory
- Key feature updates in EAM around Ignite 2025
- Integrating with Graph APIs
- High-level summary of the flow

- Additional EAM features to consider
- Competitive analysis
- Our two cents

Let's get started!

Why EAM?

A decade ago, IT administrators frequently cited the following as two of their most time-consuming tasks:

- Creating and patching a golden image for device provisioning
- Packaging and deploying the latest versions of applications

Microsoft has addressed these challenges by leveraging the power of the cloud!

The traditional process of creating a golden image has been replaced by Autopilot, eliminating the need to maintain a standard golden image. Devices can now be provisioned over the internet, becoming business-ready with all of the necessary apps and updates.

The task of packaging third-party applications has been simplified with the introduction of EAM, which we will explore further in this chapter.

The need for EAM

IT administrators worldwide spend considerable time replicating the efforts of their industry counterparts by packaging and deploying the same third-party applications. This task is continuous, as IT admins must constantly monitor for updates released by software vendors, which is highly time-consuming. EAM is Microsoft's latest initiative, designed to alleviate the application management burden for IT teams.

According to the Microsoft Digital Defense Report in 2023, 78% of devices remain unpatched 9 months after a critical vulnerability fix is released. Delays in applying patches and updating applications pose a significant vulnerability, exposing organizations to potential cyberattacks.

The following are some of the key challenges IT administrators commonly encounter when ensuring that all third-party applications on end user Windows devices across the organization remain up to date:

- Managing applications from various developers and ensuring each one is up to date is a complex and time-consuming process.
- IT administrators can spend countless hours packaging applications for deployment to ensure end users have reliable access to the necessary tools.

Hence, organizations require a streamlined and efficient method for managing third-party applications, encompassing easy access, discovery, and deployment systems. Addressing these challenges necessitates a comprehensive solution.

Background and basics of EAM

EAM is fundamentally an IT function, crafted to work unobtrusively in the background without the end user's knowledge. It aids IT administrators in simplifying app management and gaining control over the entire app management process. Furthermore, it helps keep systems up to date by allowing the effortless creation of apps for newer versions, thereby offering IT enhanced control over the app life cycle and app security.

The Enterprise App Catalog features Win32 applications that are prepared and hosted by Microsoft. Microsoft handles the packaging of installation files (EXE or MSI) and creates all necessary components to integrate the app as a Win32 application into Microsoft Intune. When an app from the Enterprise App Catalog is added to Microsoft Intune, it includes a comprehensive set of pre-filled installation details, such as install and uninstall commands, installation behavior, return codes, detection rules, and requirements. This greatly simplifies the process of adding apps to Microsoft Intune, minimizing the need for extensive testing and configuration by IT.

Advantages of EAM

EAM enables IT and security operations teams to optimize the life cycle management of both first-party and third-party applications through a secure, prepackaged app catalog. This solution reduces the time and effort IT administrators spend on app packaging and update monitoring. It allows IT teams to efficiently deploy patches to vulnerable applications and ensure all apps remain current via the Intune admin center.

EAM empowers users to seamlessly discover, package, and update an application from the Intune console with just a few clicks.

It ensures that we are regularly updating third-party apps, thereby reducing the risks of vulnerabilities.

Comparison of WinGet with the Win32 app deployment methodology

EAM uses the Win32 app methodology in the background to deploy apps to devices.

Both WinGet and Win32 app deployment are methods used for deploying applications via Microsoft Intune, but they have some key differences.

WinGet deployment via Intune

Let's go over the basics of WinGet and explore its key features.

- **Package manager**: WinGet is a command-line package manager for Windows, similar to package managers on Linux or macOS.

- **Sources**: It can install applications from multiple sources, including the Microsoft Store, GitHub, and other repositories.

- **Ease of use**: WinGet simplifies the process of installing, upgrading, and managing applications programmatically.

- **Deployment methods**: We can deploy WinGet scripts using Intune as PowerShell scripts or as part of proactive remediation.

- **Flexibility**: It supports various package formats, such as EXE, MSIX, APPX, and MS.

Win32 app deployment via Intune

Now let's walk through the basics of Win32 app deployment and its key capabilities.

- **Traditional method**: This method involves packaging Win32 applications (EXE or MSI) and deploying them through Intune.

- **Packaging**: You need to create an `.intunewin` file using the Microsoft Win32 Content Prep Tool.

- **Deployment**: The packaged application is uploaded to Intune and deployed to devices. Intune handles the installation, updates, and uninstallation.

- **Control**: It provides more granular control over installation parameters, detection rules, and dependencies.

Now let's do a comparison between WinGet and the Win32 app deployment methodology.

WinGet versus Win32

The primary focus of this section is to emphasize that app deployment using WinGet is supported via Intune, although it is not utilized within EAM, and to provide a comparison between WinGet and Win32. The following is a brief comparison:

- **Complexity**: WinGet is generally easier to use for simple deployments, while Win32 app deployment offers more control and customization.

- **Sources**: WinGet can pull from multiple repositories, whereas Win32 app deployment typically involves custom-packaged applications.

- **Integration**: Win32 app deployment is more tightly integrated with Intune's management and reporting features.

Now, even though both Win32 app deployment and EAM follow the same background process-ing, which we will discuss later in the chapter, EAM provides some advantages over the Win32 approach, since EAM requires additional licenses. Let's do a quick comparison between Win32 app deployment and EAM app deployment via Intune:

Parameter	EAM	Win32 app
Core concept	Intune Suite add-on with a curated Enterprise App Catalog.	Standard Intune feature for custom Win32 apps.
Packaging	Prepackaged by Microsoft; no manual prep required.	Requires manual packaging using the Intune WinApp utility tool.
Detection rules	Prefilled and editable.	Fully manual configuration. Customers have to test and find the right settings.
Update management	Automated. Self-updating apps also supported.	Need to create manual supersedence for new versions of the app.
Licensing	Requires Intune Suite or EAM license.	Included in standard Intune P1 licensing.
Best-suited use case	Commonly available third-party apps for quick deployment and updates.	For complex apps not in the catalog or when EAM licensing isn't feasible due to budget.

Table 3.1: Table of comparison between EAM and Win32 app deployment methodologies

Now that we have understood how the EAM and Win32 app deployment methodologies compare, in the next section, let's look at the setup needed for deploying EAM apps from the Intune portal.

Deploying and updating an EAM app

In this section, we will walk through the process of initiating a new EAM deployment via the In-tune portal. Additionally, we will cover how to update an existing application that was previously deployed through EAM and now has a pending update released by the vendor.

New deployment of EAM app

Deploying an EAM application from the Intune portal is a straightforward process. Simply select the name and language of the application you wish to deploy from the catalog. The application binaries, along with the install/uninstall commands and detection logic, will be added to your tenant. You always have the option to edit any of these values.

Please note that the option to deploy an app from the EAM catalog is available only if the EAM license/Intune Suite license is present in your tenant and assigned to the end users. Whenever you select any EAM application from the catalog, the wrapped version, along with the binaries of the application, is provided by Microsoft.

The end devices get the application from Microsoft's storage (where the EAM app is wrapped and kept) and not from a third-party location.

The following are the steps that we need to perform in the Intune portal to make a new EAM app deployment:

1. The first step involves selecting **Enterprise App Catalog app** from the dropdown, as shown in the following screenshot.

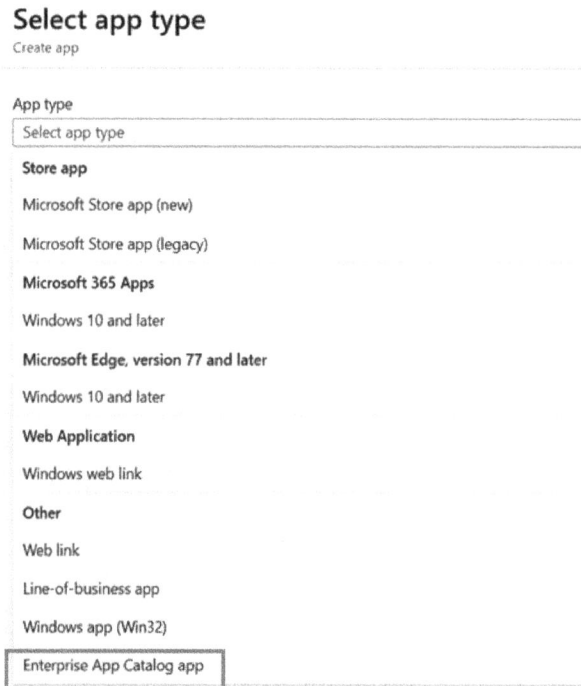

Select app type
Create app

App type

Select app type

Store app

Microsoft Store app (new)

Microsoft Store app (legacy)

Microsoft 365 Apps

Windows 10 and later

Microsoft Edge, version 77 and later

Windows 10 and later

Web Application

Windows web link

Other

Web link

Line-of-business app

Windows app (Win32)

Enterprise App Catalog app

Figure 3.1: Adding the EAM application from the Intune portal

2. Now we need to select the application we wish to deploy, as seen in the following screenshot:

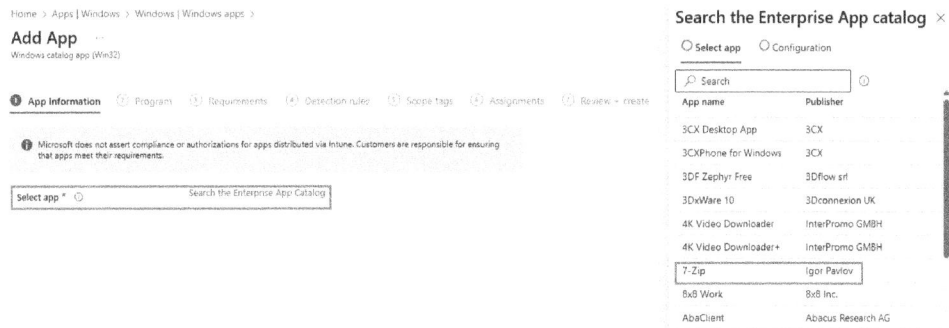

Figure 3.2: Selecting the EAM application from the catalog

3. After selecting the application, its details are automatically pre-populated on the **App information** screen. Here, we can see the **Name**, **Description**, and **Publisher** information pre-filled. As of the time of writing, the logo of the EAM app does not get added automatically; however, it can be added manually here.

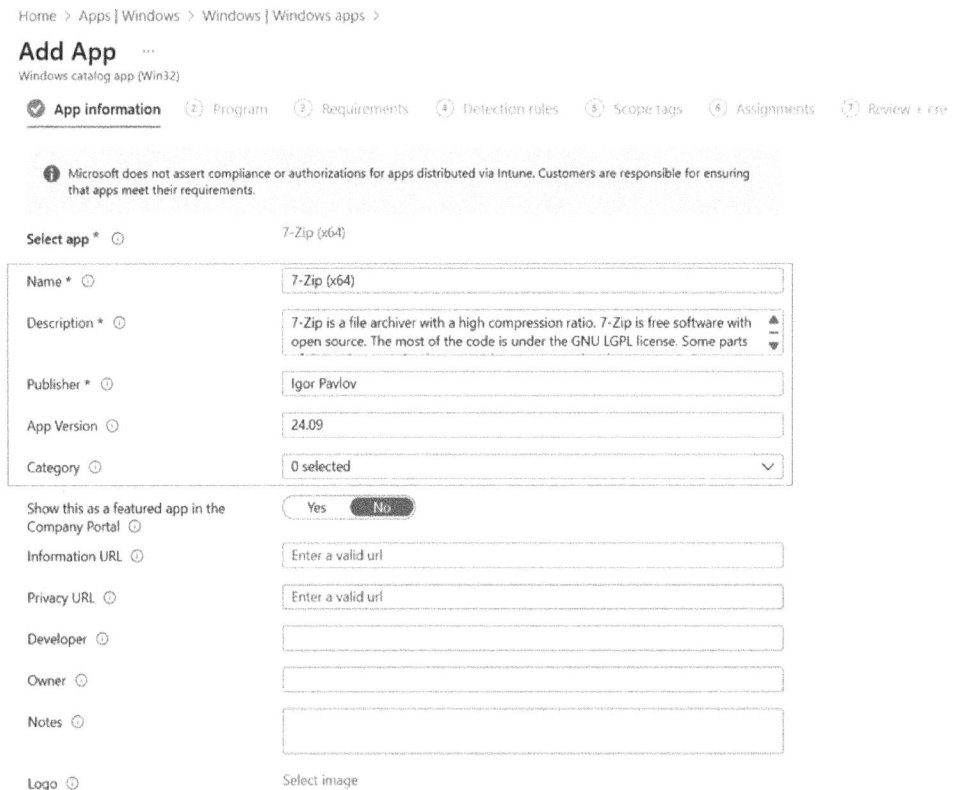

Figure 3.3: App information screen, which is pre-populated while adding the EAM app

4. On the next screen, under **Program**, we can see that the **Install command** and **Uninstall command** fields are automatically populated, along with the relevant return codes. These can be changed if needed; however, it's not recommended as Microsoft adds these parameters after testing them internally.

Figure 3.4: Program section of the EAM app, which is pre-populated with the install/ uninstall commands and exit codes

5. The next page is **Requirements**, which is auto-populated with the minimum version of the operating system that supports this app. We have the option of changing this, as well as adding a custom requirement (based on the file location of the registry), which is optional.

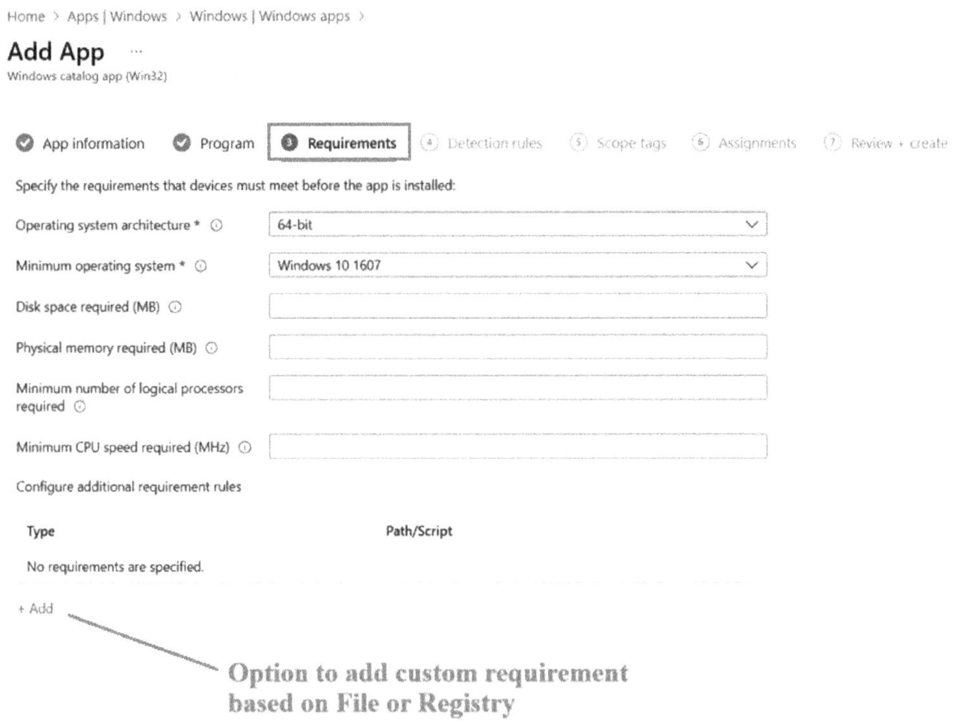

Home > Apps | Windows > Windows | Windows apps >

Add App ...
Windows catalog app (Win32)

✓ App information   ✓ Program   ③ **Requirements**   ④ Detection rules   ⑤ Scope tags   ⑥ Assignments   ⑦ Review + create

Specify the requirements that devices must meet before the app is installed:

Operating system architecture * ⓘ	64-bit ⌄
Minimum operating system * ⓘ	Windows 10 1607 ⌄
Disk space required (MB) ⓘ	
Physical memory required (MB) ⓘ	
Minimum number of logical processors required ⓘ	
Minimum CPU speed required (MHz) ⓘ	

Configure additional requirement rules

Type	Path/Script
No requirements are specified.	

+ Add

Option to add custom requirement based on File or Registry

Figure 3.5: Requirements tab, which is pre-populated with the minimum operating system version

6. The next page, **Detection rules,** is also pre-populated for this application. This determines how the service will detect whether the app was successfully installed on the device or not.

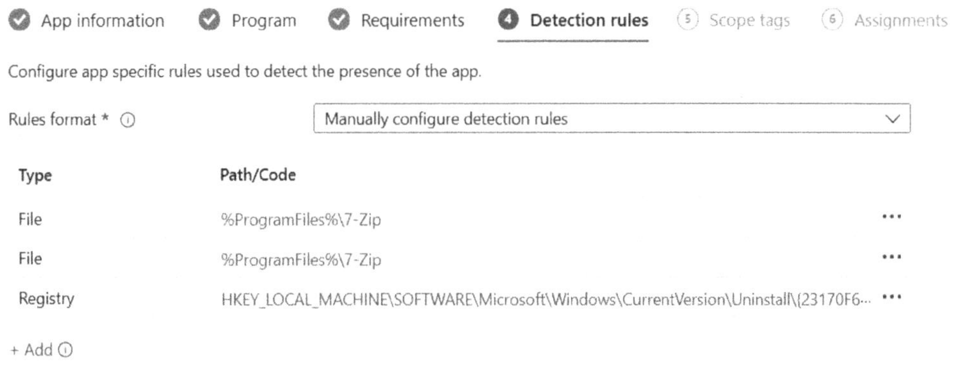

✓ App information   ✓ Program   ✓ Requirements   ④ **Detection rules**   ⑤ Scope tags   ⑥ Assignments

Configure app specific rules used to detect the presence of the app.

Rules format * ⓘ   Manually configure detection rules ⌄

Type	Path/Code	
File	%ProgramFiles%\7-Zip	•••
File	%ProgramFiles%\7-Zip	•••
Registry	HKEY_LOCAL_MACHINE\SOFTWARE\Microsoft\Windows\CurrentVersion\Uninstall\{23170F6···	•••

+ Add ⓘ

Figure 3.6: Detection rules tab, which is pre-populated with file/registry detection logic

The following are a few important pointers to keep in mind when making an EAM app deployment:

- The install and uninstall commands, along with return codes, are provided by the application vendor and tested by Microsoft. We have the option to modify these commands in the portal to alter the installation experience; however, the general recommendation is not to change any of these values unless we have a requirement.

- Currently, the application's logo is not automatically added during deployment.

- EAM applications are always installed in the system context, and this setting cannot be changed from the portal. This means the application installs for all users of the device, and users do not need to be logged in for the EAM app to be installed.

The detection logic used for app deployment varies based on the information provided by the vendor. Some EAM apps may use MSI, file, and registry detection logic (i.e., all three), while others may use only one or two of these methods.

Once the EAM app has been added, it takes a couple of minutes for it to appear in our tenant. Now our EAM application is ready and can be assigned to users or devices as needed. Until now, we have understood how to make a fresh deployment of an EAM application from the Intune portal. In the next section, we will see how we can successfully update an EAM app for which a newer version has been released by the vendor.

Updating an existing EAM app

The steps below outline the process of updating an application deployed from the EAM catalog.

1. When a newer version of any application deployed via EAM becomes available, the admin is notified in the dashboard, as shown in the following screenshot. When we click on this, we will be taken to a list of all EAM apps that have received a new release from the vendor.

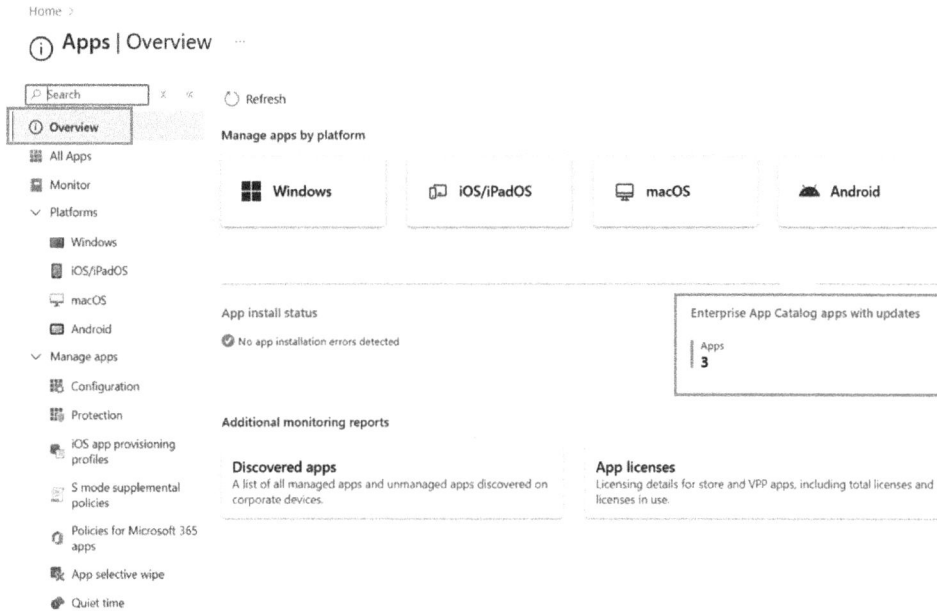

Figure 3.7: Overview tab in the Intune portal notifying the admin of the EAM apps that have updates available

Alternatively, we can also go to **Apps | Monitor | Enterprise App Catalog apps with updates**:

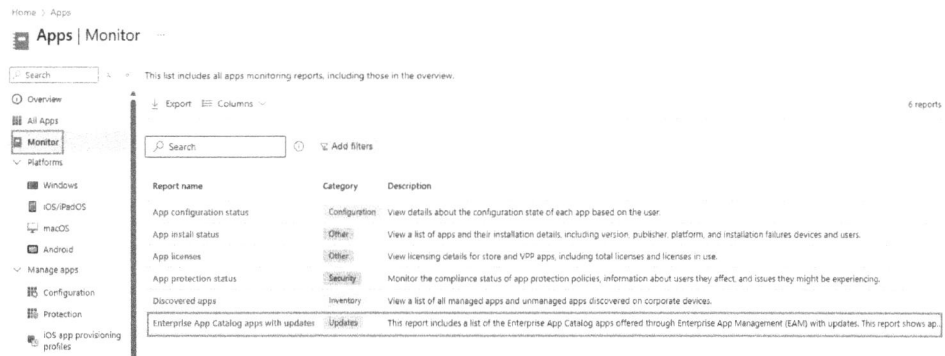

Figure 3.8: Monitor tab in the Intune portal

2. As seen in the following screenshot, we can now get a list of all the EAM apps that have received a newer version:

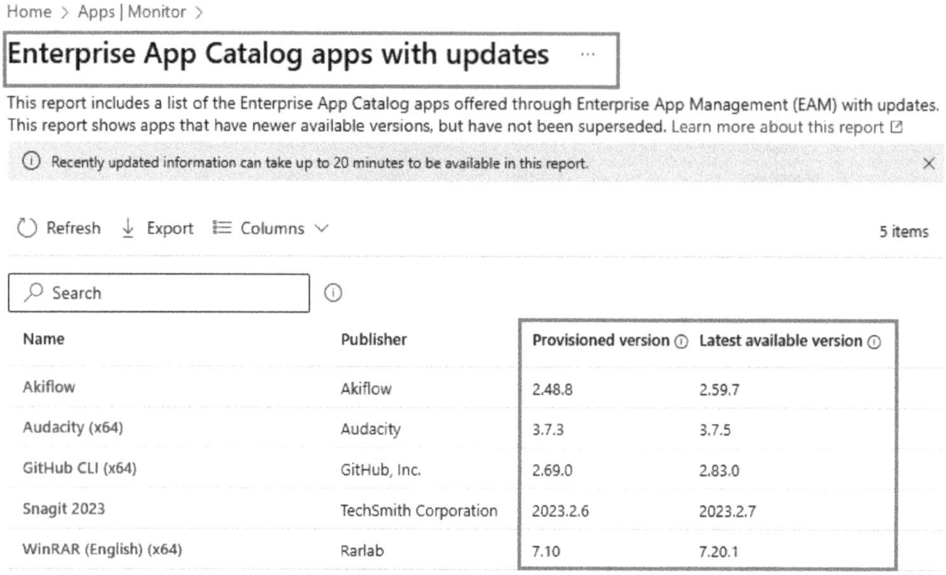

Home > Apps | Monitor >

Enterprise App Catalog apps with updates   ...

This report includes a list of the Enterprise App Catalog apps offered through Enterprise App Management (EAM) with updates. This report shows apps that have newer available versions, but have not been superseded. Learn more about this report ☑

ⓘ Recently updated information can take up to 20 minutes to be available in this report.   ✕

◯ Refresh   ↓ Export   ☰ Columns ∨   5 items

🔍 Search   ⓘ

Name	Publisher	Provisioned version ⓘ	Latest available version ⓘ
Akiflow	Akiflow	2.48.8	2.59.7
Audacity (x64)	Audacity	3.7.3	3.7.5
GitHub CLI (x64)	GitHub, Inc.	2.69.0	2.83.0
Snagit 2023	TechSmith Corporation	2023.2.6	2023.2.7
WinRAR (English) (x64)	Rarlab	7.10	7.20.1

Figure 3.9: Apps under the Monitor blade with their current and latest available version

3. By clicking on the application or navigating to the previously deployed EAM app (which has now received an update), there is an option to deploy its updated version by clicking on **Update**.

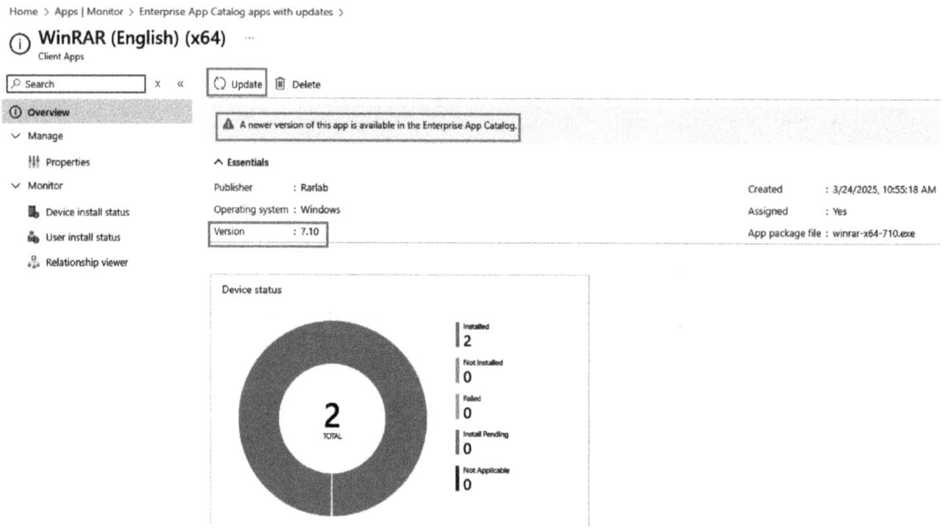

Figure 3.10: Option to update an existing EAM application from the portal

4. Clicking on **Update** initiates a new deployment of the EAM app and supersedes the old app deployment. Superseding creates a new app with the latest app package and establishes the supersedence relationship. Some settings, such as scope tags and assignments, will not be copied to the new app. As explained in the following screenshot, the newer version of the app is automatically packaged and added to the portal, while the older version is moved under **Supersede**.

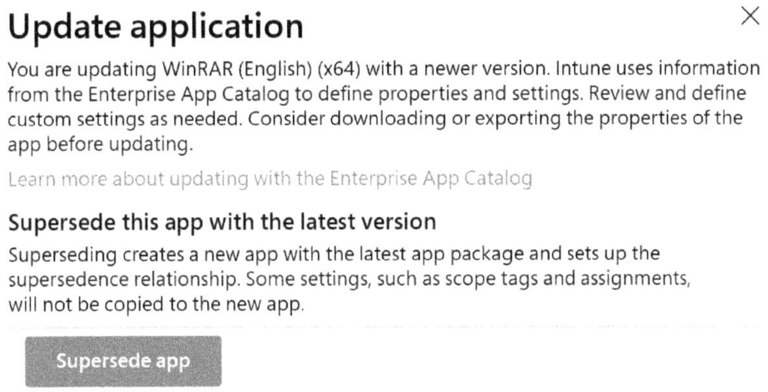

Update application ✕

You are updating WinRAR (English) (x64) with a newer version. Intune uses information from the Enterprise App Catalog to define properties and settings. Review and define custom settings as needed. Consider downloading or exporting the properties of the app before updating.

Learn more about updating with the Enterprise App Catalog

Supersede this app with the latest version

Superseding creates a new app with the latest app package and sets up the supersedence relationship. Some settings, such as scope tags and assignments, will not be copied to the new app.

Supersede app

Figure 3.11: Updating the EAM app by creating supersedence

Some applications require the previous version to be uninstalled before the newer version can be installed.

Conversely, there are applications where both versions (V1 and V2) can coexist on the same machine. During the EAM app update deployment, we have the option to choose whether the older version of the EAM app will be uninstalled or not, as shown in the following screenshot.

Home > Apps | Monitor > Enterprise App Catalog apps with updates > WinRAR (English) (x64) >

Supersede with latest app ⋯
Windows catalog app (Win32)

✅ App information   ✅ Program   ✅ Requirements   ✅ Detection rules   ✅ Scope tags   ⑥ **Supersedence**   ⑦ Assignments

When you supersede an application, you can specify which apps will be directly updated or replaced. To update an app, disable the uninstall previous version option. To replace an app, enable the uninstall previous version option. There is a maximum of 10 updated or replaced apps, including references to other apps outside of this view, forming a graph of apps. The total size of the supersedence app graph is limited to the maximum of 10 plus the parent app (11 total). Learn more

Apps that this app will supersede

Name	Publisher	Version	Uninstall previous version
WinRAR (English) (x64)	Rarlab	WinRAR (English) (x64)	Yes No ⋯

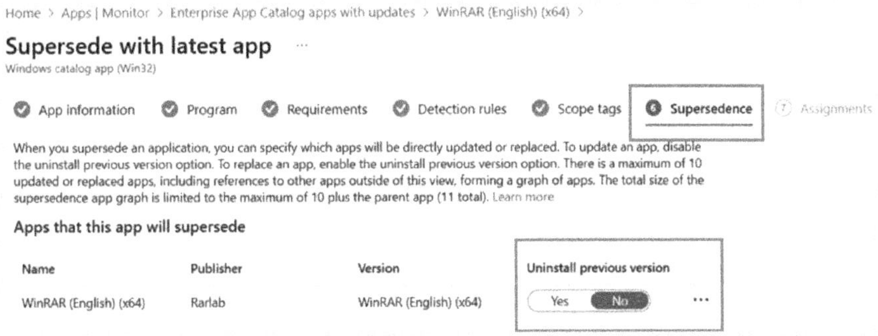

Figure 3.12: Supersedence option available while updating an EAM app from the portal

Self-updating EAM apps

The Enterprise App Catalog includes apps that self-update, for example, Google Chrome, as seen in the following screenshot.

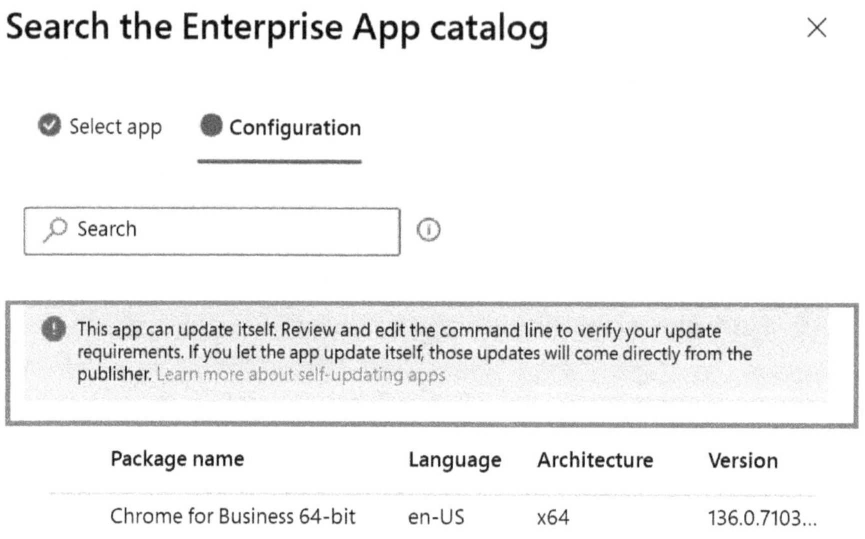

Figure 3.13: Self-updating apps in the EAM catalog

These applications feature a built-in update mechanism, allowing them to automatically update outside of Microsoft Intune or the IT admin's control. The self-update mechanisms download content directly from the vendor. The app selection wizard will notify us when a self-updating app is selected. Self-updating applications update on client devices according to the vendor's update process.

Intune doesn't provide reports on whether the EAM application is being used or not.

At the time of publishing this book, there were approximately 1,100 *unique* applications in the EAM catalog.

End user experience

When the EAM application is deployed to the device with the **Required** intent from the Intune portal, the installation process is seamless and does not require any user interaction. The user will receive a toast notification, as shown in the following screenshot, indicating the status of the app installation as applicable. In case of any errors with the download or installation, this would be reported as a notification.

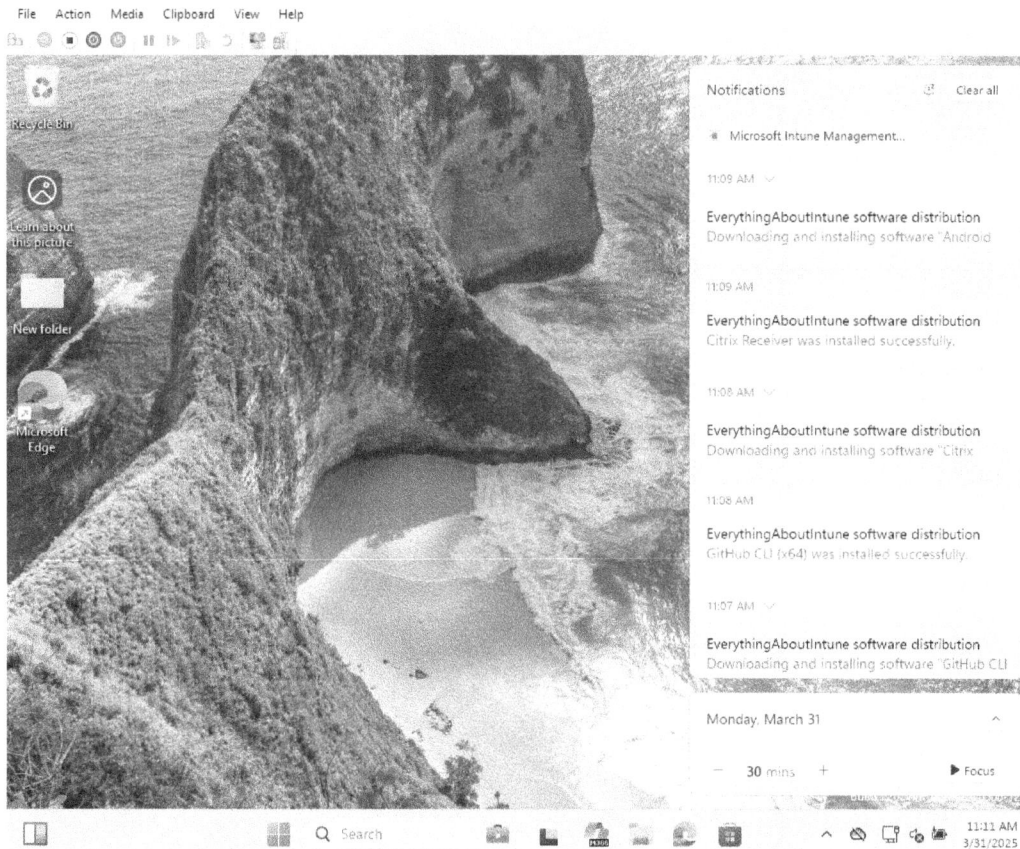

Figure 3.14: End user experience when an EAM app gets installed

All the installed EAM apps will be visible in the control panel app list on the device.

1,000-foot overview: Background flow and logs

In the following section, we will take a detailed look at the flow involved in EAM app delivery and deployment, supported by relevant log data. By analyzing these logs, we can trace each step of the deployment process. Gaining a clear understanding of this flow is essential, as it not only reinforces key concepts but also enhances our ability to troubleshoot effectively in the event of deployment failures.

The **Intune Management Extension** (**IME**) logs, which can help us trace the EAM app deployment, are located in `C:\ProgramData\Microsoft\IntuneManagementExtension\Logs`, as seen in the following figure:

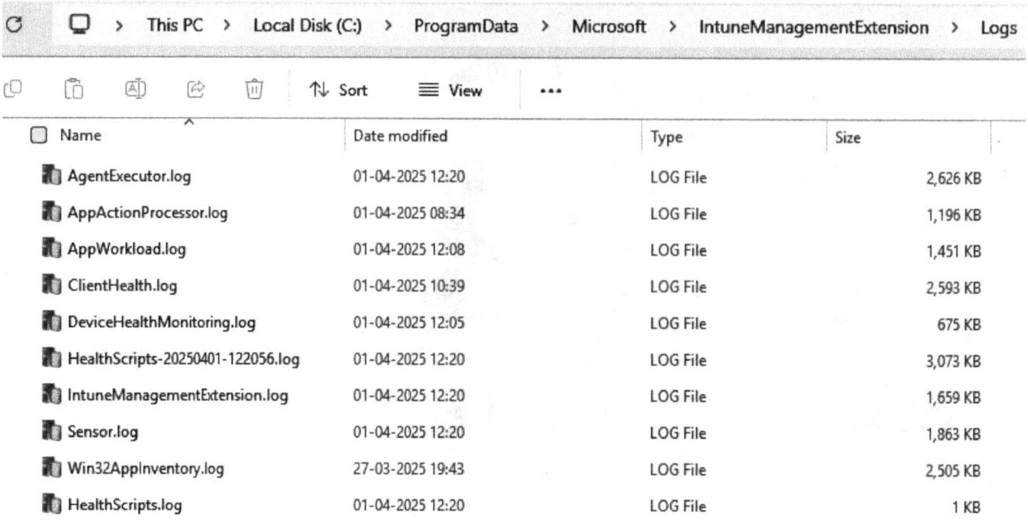

Figure 3.15: IME logs on the device for troubleshooting EAM issues

It is essential to understand the EAM process through the lens of log analysis, as this provides the most critical insights for effective troubleshooting. This is an important concept to understand from an interview standpoint. The following is an extract from the IME logs of a successful EAM app deployment. It highlights the primary processes occurring as indicated by the logs. The flow described remains consistent regardless of the specific EAM application. Also, the flow is the same for any Win32 app deployed from Intune.

	Message in the logs	Explanation
Step 1	IME gets initialized.	EMS agent started.
Step 2	Content manager starts.	
Step 3	Device ID and operating system version are noted.	
Step 4	IME discovers the endpoints of Intune (CDNs).	These endpoints need to be whitelisted in the firewall (if blocked) as per the network prerequisites listed earlier.
Step 5	Impersonation for the user happens and a token is requested/granted.	
Step 6	A PUT request is sent.	

	Message in the logs	Explanation
Step 7	We see a `Get Policies` response, which has the entire policy body. In this case, the policy body will contain the binaries of the EAM app from the catalog that was deployed to the user.	We can check and ensure that the policy received by IME is in accordance with the settings configured in the EAM app.
Step 8	`ExecManager` identifies the app name/ app ID/app installation intent.	
Step 9	Dependency is checked for the apps discovered previously.	If dependencies are discovered, then the dependent app is downloaded and installed first.
Step 10	Detection rules are checked for the apps.	For example: Detection running for policy with ID `d7589f12-bc24-45e0-89b9-c7eb57408217`. Path doesn't exist: `C:\Program Files\WinRAR\WinRAR.exe applicationDetected: False`. If the app is detected in the device at this stage, the download/ installation attempt of the app (in the following step) is skipped.
Step 11	Applicability is checked for the app.	The minimum requirements for operating system version, architecture, and RAM/CPU will be checked. For example: `(requirement and extended requirement)RequiredOSArchitecture: 2,is64BitOperatingSystem: True,isArm64: False` Expected version: `10.0.14393, client version: 10.0.22631, applicability:` `ApplicableRequiredMemory is , skip check` `RequiredCPUSpeed is , skip check`
Step 12	A toast message with `"C:\Program Files (x86)\Microsoft Intune Management Extension\ agentexecutor.exe" -toast "ToastDownloadingMessage"` is displayed.	User can see an intuitive prompt on the device notifying them that the app is downloading.

	Message in the logs	Explanation
Step 13	A download job is created/a timer is set. For example: ``` start creating a new download job, FileId = 225BDA84-AD50-462C-9963- 7B74CFBD5C86_6e831210-f8d2- 52d8-33e3-0c68342672d8_ PE_1742252141, remote URL = https://aam-content-cdn. manage.microsoft.com/ cdncontent/6e831210-f8d2- 52d8-33e3-0c68342672d8.zip ``` For example: ``` Downloading app (id = d7589f12-bc24-45e0-89b9- c7eb57408217, name WinRAR (English) (x64)) via DO, bytes 0/0 for user 3b91c924- 794c-4991-ac6a-2f9d5d684d2f ```	We can see the remote URL from where the EAM app is getting downloaded. We can see that the download is trying to use delivery optimization.
Step 14	Content is downloaded to `C:\Program Files (x86)\Microsoft Intune Management Extension\Content\ Incoming (Staging)`.	
Step 15	Download job completes, time taken is noted, bytes downloaded are noted, and job is closed.	
Step 16	Verifying encrypted hash. Decryption starts.	
Step 17	Unzipping starts from "`Content\ Staging`" to `C:\Windows\ IMECache\`.	
Step 18	Staging content is cleaned up.	
Step 19	`InstallEx` is parsed.	Installer execution starts.
Step 20	`msi cmdline` is prepared for system context.	

	Message in the logs	Explanation
Step 21	Execution of the installation command begins: `winrar-x64-710.exe" /s`. Launch `Win32AppInstaller` in machine session.	Command specified in the EAM app in the portal.
Step 22	Installation completes. Collecting result.	
Step 23	`lpExitCode 0` determines whether it's a success.	
Step 24	`DeviceRestartBehavior: 2` checks device restart behavior. Execution handle is closed.	Device restart action as per the policy defined by the admin in the portal.
Step 25	Now detection rule starts with `SideCarFileDetectionManager`.	The detection rule evaluated in step 10 is evaluated again, post-app installation.

Step 26	Let's look at a couple of log examples below that help clarify how the detection logic is processed:
	
	`Checked filePath: C:\Program Files\WinRAR\WinRAR.exe, Got sizeInBytes:3,311,760.00, compareValue 3,311,760.00`
	
	For example:
	
	`Checked filePath: C:\Program Files\WinRAR\WinRAR.exe, Got versionStr:7.10.0.0, compareValue 7.10.0.0`
	
	For example:
	
	`Got reg value path: HKEY_LOCAL_MACHINE\SOFTWARE\ Microsoft\Windows\ CurrentVersion\Uninstall\ WinRAR archiver, name: DisplayVersion, value: 7.10.0 AppWorkload 24-03-2025 11:20:38 7 (0x0007)`
	
	`actualValue: 7.10.0, DetectionValue: 7.10.0, applicationDetected: True`
		First, the file path is checked (if applicable).
		
		Second, the file version is checked (if applicable).
		
		Lastly, the registry values are checked (if applicable).

	Message in the logs	Explanation
Step 27	A toast message with `"C:\Program Files (x86)\Microsoft Intune Management Extension\ agentexecutor.exe" -toast "ToastSuccessMessage` is displayed.	User is able to see an intuitive prompt in the device notifying them that the app has installed successfully/failed (as applicable).
Step 28	Staged content is cleaned up with `C:\ Windows\IMECache\59f9a567- b92d-4dc2-9c7a-fdb94e29275c_1`.	
Step 29	Reports are sent for the user and app.	The result of the app's successful installation is sent to the Intune service.

Table 3.2: List of all the important logs while processing the EAM application at the device end

The 29 steps outlined in the preceding table give us a clear understanding of the processing we should expect to observe in the IME logs during an EAM app deployment. While troubleshooting, it is important to review the logs mentioned in the table to identify where the process is breaking and pinpoint the source of any errors.

Registry

Understanding the relevant registry locations associated with EAM is critical for effective trouble-shooting. In this section, we will examine the key registry paths and their expected values, which serve as essential reference points when diagnosing issues during EAM deployments.

The primary registry location relevant to EAM app deployment is `Computer\HKEY_LOCAL_MACHINE\ SOFTWARE\Microsoft\IntuneManagementExtension\Win32Apps\{SID}\{App Id GUID}`. Under the `Win32Apps` key, we will find the following:

- `{SID}`: A subkey for each user, where the key name matches the user object ID in Entra ID.
- `{App Id GUID}`: The application ID of the EAM application deployed via Intune.

Example use case

In this example, the user logged in to the device is pm@everythingaboutintune.com, and the user's object ID is 3b91c924-794c-4991-ac6a-2f9d5d684d2f, as seen in the following screenshot.

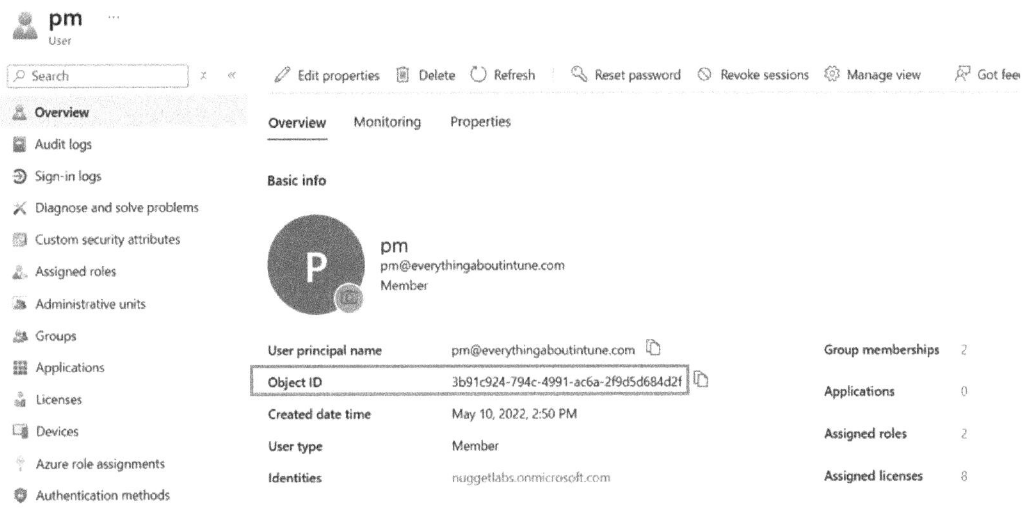

Figure 3.16: User's object ID in the Entra portal

For this user, six EAM applications have been deployed via Intune by following the steps outlined earlier in the chapter under the *New deployment of EAM app* section. These applications are listed in the following figure as they appear in the Intune portal under the **Apps** section.

Name ↑	Platform	Type	Version
Android Studio 4	Windows	Windows catalog app (Win32)	4.2.2.0
AnyDesk	Windows	Windows catalog app (Win32)	9.0.2
Audacity (x64)	Windows	Windows catalog app (Win32)	3.7.3
Citrix Receiver	Windows	Windows catalog app (Win32)	14.12.0.18020
GitHub CLI (x64)	Windows	Windows catalog app (Win32)	2.69.0
WinRAR (English) (x64)	Windows	Windows catalog app (Win32)	7.10

Figure 3.17: EAM applications deployed to the user from Intune

The application IDs can be found in the Intune portal and have been collated in the following table for this example use case:

EAM Application Name	Application ID
Android Studio 4	560a3d57-a114-4ea5-b826-2a4523f6c1ed
AnyDesk	79934a77-c3ca-46b9-8034-59180699a809
Audacity (x64)	599cd13f-75d4-4771-816d-190f843fb5db
Citrix Receiver	3c4e1d36-23b2-4390-afee-43769a21f57e
GitHub CLI (x64)	30141bf0-263d-4e93-9081-565cfe20383d
WinRAR (English) (x64)	d7589f12-bc24-45e0-89b9-c7eb57408217

Table 3.3: List of all the applications deployed to the sample user and their respective app IDs

The preceding application IDs correspond with the app IDs visible in the registry under `Computer\HKEY_LOCAL_MACHINE\SOFTWARE\Microsoft\IntuneManagementExtension\Win32Apps` of the machine, as seen in the following figure:

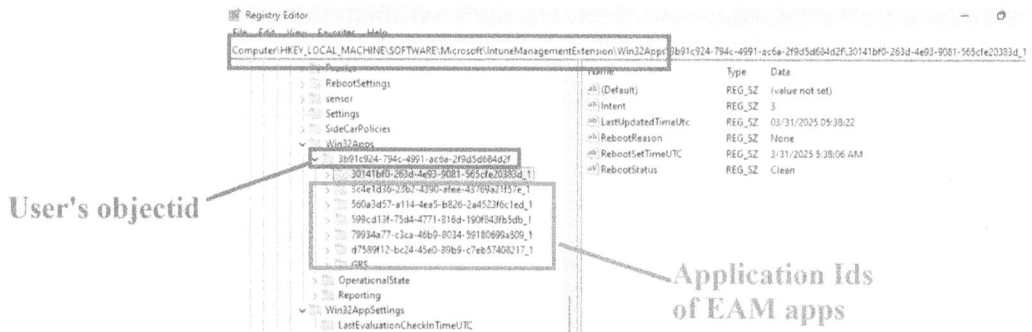

Figure 3.18: Registry from the device

`_1` at the end of each app ID in the registry seen in the preceding screenshot means this is the first version of the application.

If we take a closer look, we will find that under each application ID, there are two subkeys: `ComplianceStateMessage` and `EnforcementStateMessage`. Both of the subkeys contain a `REG_SZ` key with the same name.

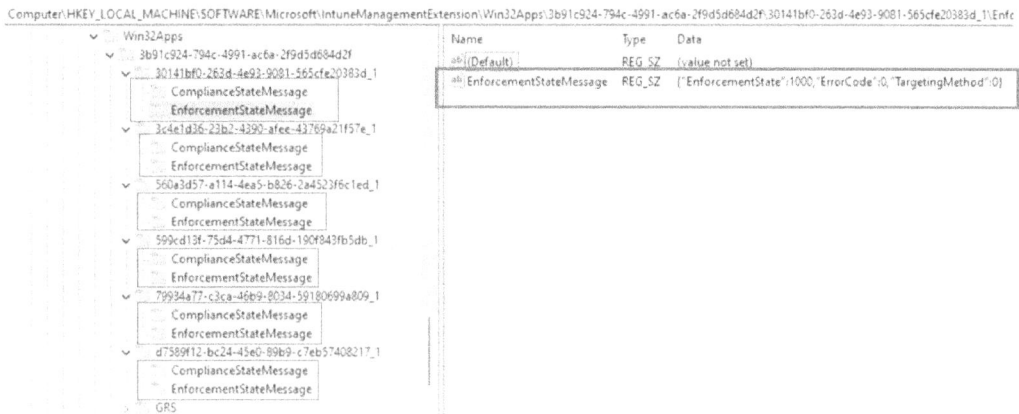

Figure 3.19: Registry from the device

The `ComplianceStateMessage` node contains information on various attributes of the EAM app which has been targeted and its applicability on the device. The information is stored in JSON format in the `ComplianceStateMessage` subkey.

The `EnforcementStateMessage` node provides information on the status of the EAM application, indicating whether it was successfully installed on the device. The results are stored in JSON format within the `EnforcementStateMessage` subkey.

In our example, the relevant values (pasted from `REG_SZ` into Notepad) are as follows for one of the EAM applications:

```
REG_SZ Value Name: ComplianceStateMessage
ValueData:  {"Applicability":0,"ComplianceState":1,"DesiredState":2,
"ErrorCode":null,"TargetingMethod":0,"InstallContext":2,"TargetType":2,
"ProductVersion":null,"AssignmentFilterIds":null}


REG_SZ Value Name: EnforcementStateMessage
Value Data:  {"EnforcementState":1000,"ErrorCode":0,"TargetingMethod":0}
```

These fields contain information on the applicability of the EAM application, whether it has been targeted to a user or device group, the installation context (system or user), and the success of the installation. Each field has a numerical value that needs to be decoded:

- `Applicability`: A value of `0` means `Applicable`
- `ComplianceState`: A value of `1` means `Installed`
- `DesiredState`: A value of `2` means `Present`

- `InstallContext`: A value of 2 means `System` (the only possibility for EAM applications)

- `TargetType`: A value of 1 means `User` (indicating the EAM policy from Intune has been targeted to a user group)

- `EnforcementState`: A value of `1000` means `Success`

In a successful EAM app deployment, the registry values will resemble those mentioned previously.

Using any .NET decompiler, we can view the source code of the IME, which will give us a list of all the state messages and their values, which are as follows:

- Values for applicability:

Value	Translation
0	Applicable
1	RequirementsNotMet
3	HostPlatformNotApplicable
1000	ProcessorArchitectureNotApplicable
1001	MinimumDiskSpaceNotMet
1002	MinimumOSVersionNotMet
1003	MinimumPhysicalMemoryNotMet
1004	MinimumLogicalProcessorCountNotMet
1005	MinimumCPUSpeedNotMet
1006	FileSystemRequirementRuleNotMet
1007	RegistryRequirementRuleNotMet
1008	ScriptRequirementRuleNotMet
1009	NotTargetedAndSupersedingAppsNotApplicable
1010	AssignmentFiltersCriteriaNotMet
1011	AppUnsupportedDueToUnknownReason
1012	UserContextAppNotSupportedDuringDeviceOnlyCheckin

- Values for ComplianceState:

Value	Translation
1	Installed
2	NotInstalled
4	Error
5	Unknown
100	Cleanup

- Values for DesiredState:

Value	Translation
0	None
1	Not Present
2	Present
3	Unknown
4	Available

- Values for InstallContext:

Value	Translation
1	User
2	System

- Values for TargetType:

Value	Translation
0	None
1	User
2	Device
3	Both Device and User

- Values for `EnforcementState`:

Value	Translation
1000	Success
1003	SuccessFastNotify
1004	SuccessButDependencyFailedToInstall
1005	SuccessButDependencyWithRequirementsNotMet
1006	SuccessButDependencyPendingReboot
1007	SuccessButDependencyWithAutoInstallOff
1008	SuccessButIOSAppStoreUpdateFailedToInstall
1009	SuccessVPPAppHasUpdateAvailable
1010	SuccessButUserRejectedUpdate
1011	SuccessUninstallPendingReboot
1012	SuccessSupersededAppUninstallFailed
1013	SuccessSupersededAppUninstallPendingReboot
1014	SuccessSupersedingAppsDetected
1015	SuccessSupersededAppsDetected
1016	SuccessAppRemovedBySupersedence
1017	SuccessButDependencyBlockedByManagedInstallerPolicy
1018	SuccessUninstallingSupersededApps
2000	InProgress
2007	InProgressDependencyInstalling
2008	InProgressPendingReboot
2009	InProgressDownloadCompleted
2010	InProgressPendingUninstallOfSupersededApps
2011	InProgressUninstallPendingReboot
2012	InProgressPendingManagedInstaller

Value	Translation
3000	RequirementsNotMet
4000	Unknown
5000	Error
5003	ErrorDownloadingContent
5006	ErrorConflictsPreventInstallation
5015	ErrorManagedInstallerAppLockerPolicyNotApplied
5999	ErrorWithImmeadiateRetry
6000	NotAttempted
6001	NotAttemptedDependencyWithFailure
6002	NotAttemptedPendingReboot
6003	NotAttemptedDependencyWithRequirementsNotMet
6004	NotAttemptedAutoInstallOff
6005	NotAttemptedDependencyWithAutoInstallOff
6006	NotAttemptedWithManagedAppNoLongerPresent
6007	NotAttemptedBecauseUserRejectedInstall
6008	NotAttemptedBecauseUserIsNotLoggedIntoAppStore
6009	NotAttemptedSupersededAppUninstallFailed
6010	NotAttemptedSupersededAppUninstallPendingReboot
6011	NotAttemptedUntargetedSupersedingAppsDetected
6012	NotAttemptedDependencyBlockedByManagedInstallerPolicy
6013	NotAttemptedUnsupportedOrIndeterminateSupe

These values have been taken from the blog by Ben Whitmore at msendpointmgr.com.

The processing that we have seen for an EAM application via logs and the registry would remain the same if it were a Win32 app deployed via Intune. In this section, we explored the key registry locations relevant to EAM, along with their expected values and corresponding numerical translations. This understanding serves as a valuable reference for effective troubleshooting.

EAM app inventory

Now we are going to understand how the Intune service runs an inventory for the EAM applications on the Windows device.

The Windows app inventory is available in Microsoft Intune, and the information is shown in the **Discovered apps** blade for each device in the portal, as seen in the following screenshot. This blade contains information about all the applications that are present on the device (managed as well as unmanaged).

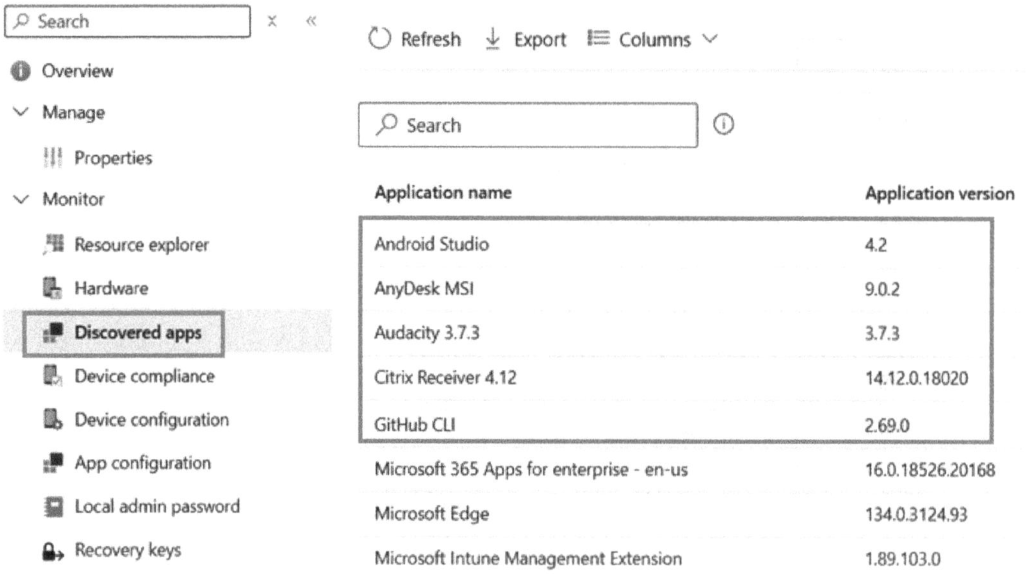

Figure 3.20: Discovered EAM applications for a device from the Intune portal

The process of collecting inventory of all applications (including EAM apps) in an enrolled Windows device is done by the IME.

One of the integral components of the IME is `Win32AppInventoryCollector`. This component's functionality is encapsulated in `Microsoft.Management.Clients.IntuneManagementExtension.Win32AppInventoryCollector.dll`.

The IME leverages the `Win32_InstalledWin32Program` class in WMI to gather the inventory of Win32 applications. The WMI class references the `location-HKLM\SOFTWARE\Microsoft\Windows\CurrentVersion\Uninstall` registry, which contains information about all of the apps (including EAM apps), as seen in the following figure:

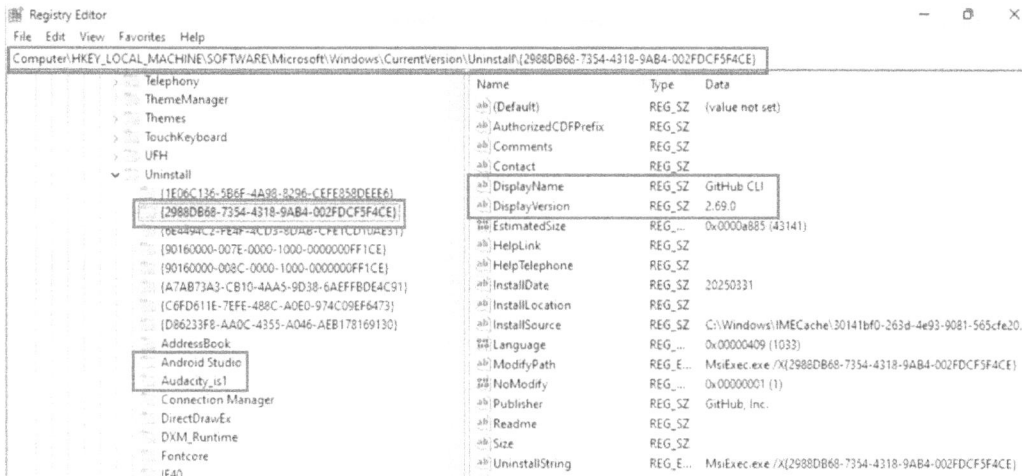

Figure 3.21: Registry from the device highlighting EAM app traces

Another relevant registry for EAM app discovery by the Intune service is `HKLM\SOFTWARE\`
`Microsoft\IntuneManagementExtension\Inventories`. This location will also contain a list of
all the EAM apps and their respective versions present on the device.

Figure 3.22: Registry from the device highlighting EAM app traces for inventory

The `HKLM\SOFTWARE\Microsoft\IntuneManagementExtension\InventorySetting` registry location includes the `LastFullSyncTimeUtc` value, which records the timestamp of the last full inventory run on the device, as shown in the following figure.

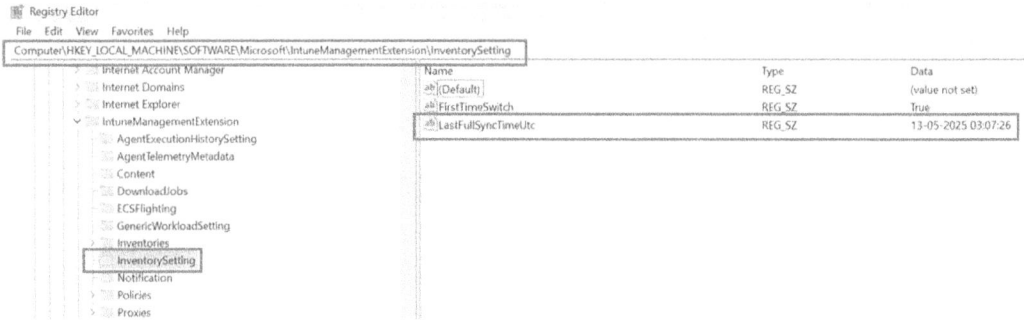

Figure 3.23: Registry from the device highlighting timestamp for inventory run cycle

> The full inventory process initiates upon IME installation and subsequently runs every seven days. In the interim, the delta inventory runs every 24 hours or whenever the IME starts.

In this section, we examined how the Intune service identifies and discovers EAM applications installed on a device, and how this information is utilized for inventory purposes.

Now let's take a look at a few of the latest features that have been added to EAM very recently (around Ignite 2025).

Key feature updates in EAM around Ignite 2025

Microsoft has made a few very important enhancements to the capabilities of EAM around Ignite 2025, which we will spend some time exploring:

- **SLA/SLO for EAM apps**: Microsoft has recently announced that there will be a **Service-Level Objective (SLO)** of 24 hours for application updates. This means we should expect an application version to appear in the catalog within 24 hours of its release by the vendor, which is a welcome improvement for customers who need timely assurance on the availability of newer versions of apps.

- **EAM support during Autopilot device preparation**: With the Intune 2506 release, Autopilot's device preparation takes a big leap forward as it now works seamlessly with apps from the Enterprise App Catalog. This means IT admins can handpick essential apps during setup, ensuring they're installed before the user even reaches the desktop.

- **Auto-updating EAM apps**: In many cases, we would like an application to get updated automatically once it is added to the catalog without the need to go to the portal and approve/deploy the newer release version. This feature enables app rollout to be faster and more streamlined.

- **Using custom PowerShell scripts in install commands for EAM apps**: We can now up-load a PowerShell script to install Enterprise App Catalog apps as an alternative to using a command line. This option gives us more flexibility when deploying apps. However, we should exercise this option with caution as using a custom PowerShell script requires prior testing on a device.

Now that we have understood the basics and all the latest EAM capabilities, in the next section, we will touch base on automation. It is possible to automate the EAM application deployment and update process using Microsoft Graph APIs, as we will discuss.

Integrating with Graph APIs

To automate the deployment and update of EAM apps, we can utilize the exposed Graph APIs. Managing our EAM deployment through Graph APIs makes the flow more seamless and reduces admin intervention.

Next, we will explore a few use cases explaining what can be achieved using Graph APIs. The goal is to understand the fundamentals and then build upon them using PowerShell scripts and automation.

> Beta Microsoft Graph APIs are subject to change, and we should thoroughly check their behavior before using them in production environments.

Use case 1: Getting a list of all the apps available in the EAM catalog

In this use case, we will be installing required PowerShell modules, establishing a connection, and retrieving EAM catalog applications.

To implement this use case, we must first configure the PowerShell execution policy to **Unrestrict-ed**, install the required Microsoft Graph modules, and authenticate using Entra ID credentials. Once authenticated, we can proceed to invoke the EAM endpoint. Here, we'll go through the step-by-step process along with the necessary commands to accomplish this:

1. Firstly, we will run the following commands in PowerShell as an administrator, which will set the execution policy and install the Graph modules:

```
Set-ExecutionPolicy Unrestricted -force
Install-Module Microsoft.Graph
Install-Module Microsoft.Graph.Beta -Force -Verbose
Import-Module Microsoft.Graph.Beta.Devices.CorporateManagement
-Verbose
```

As seen in the following screenshot, once we run the preceding commands, the package and the modules get installed:

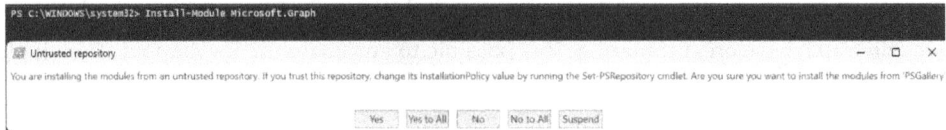

Figure 3.24: PowerShell modules being installed

2. Now we need to run the following commands to connect Graph with our Entra ID tenant:

```
Connect-Graph
Connect-MgGraph
Connect-MgGraph -Scopes "DeviceManagementApps.Read.All"
```

3. After running the preceding commands, we get a pop-up dialog box that requires us to enter our admin credentials and accept the relevant permissions, as seen in the following screenshot:

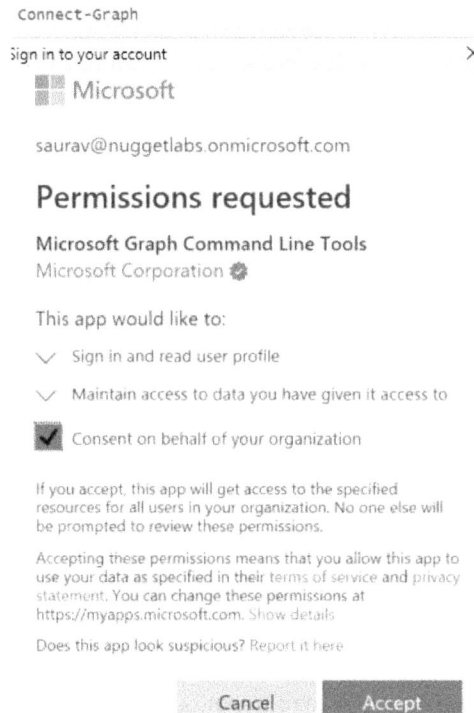

Figure 3.25: Prompt for accepting permissions

4. Now we are successfully authenticated to our tenant. The next step to achieve the use case is running the following commands, which will help us get a list of all the EAM apps in the catalog and display it in the PowerShell output in the form of JSON:

```
Invoke-MgGraphRequest -Method GET https://graph.microsoft.com/beta/
deviceAppManagement/mobileAppCatalogPackages?
$result = Invoke-MgGraphRequest -Method GET -Uri "/beta/
deviceAppManagement/mobileAppCatalogPackages?"
$result.value | convertto-json
```

5. Executing the preceding command will return a list of all EAM applications available in the catalog. The results will be displayed in JSON format within the PowerShell console, as seen in the following figure:

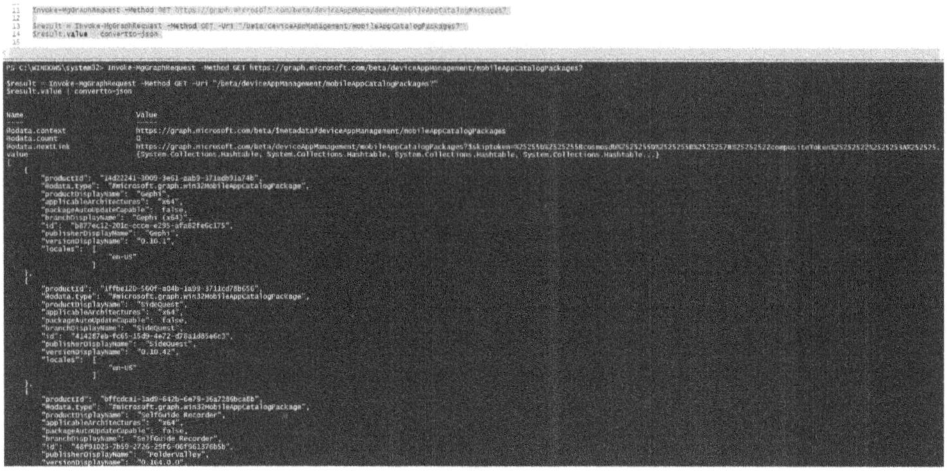

Figure 3.26: PowerShell output: List of EAM apps in JSON

The preceding output is not very readable as it contains more than 1,000 lines with details of various apps.

So, now we will build on the output and export the list of all the EAM apps in the catalog to an Excel file for better visibility/understanding:

1. To achieve this, we will now run the following command to get us a list of all EAM apps in the catalog and export it to a JSON file:

```
Invoke-MgGraphRequest -Method GET -Uri "/beta/deviceAppManagement/
mobileAppCatalogPackages?$select=productId,productDisplayName,
packageAutoUpdateCapable" -OutputFilePath C:\temp\new\filett.json
```

2. Now we will import the JSON file into Excel and filter to get a list of all the application names, IDs, and publishers. For this, let's open an Excel sheet, as seen in the following screenshot, and go to **Get Data | From File | From JSON**:

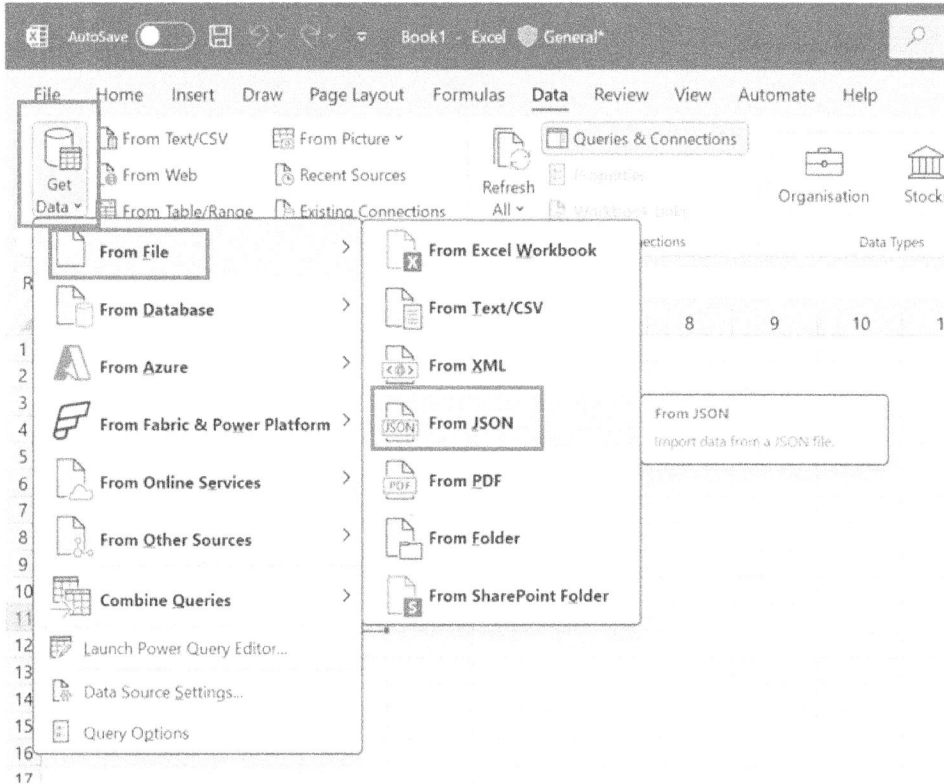

Figure 3.27: Importing the JSON file into Excel

3. After loading the JSON data, we can refine the imported content by selecting **Choose Columns** in Excel. This allows us to include only the relevant fields or exclude any unnecessary columns before finalizing the import. In the following example, I've deselected the first three columns and retained the remaining ones for analysis.

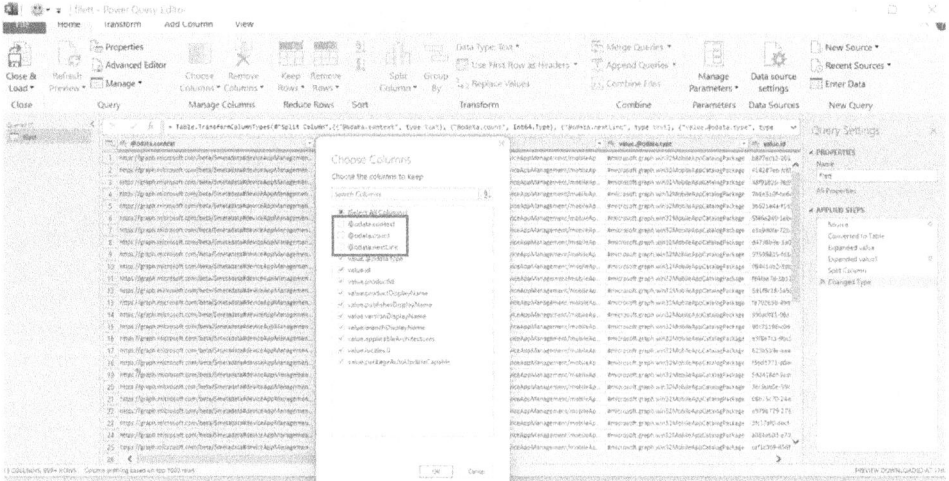

Figure 3.28: Filtering the columns before loading the Excel sheet with JSON data

4. Once the desired columns have been selected, click **OK** to proceed. This action will import the JSON data into Excel, presenting a structured view of all applications available in the EAM catalog, as illustrated in the following screenshot.

Figure 3.29: Final Excel sheet containing all the available EAM apps in the catalog

With the data now available in Excel, we can leverage its full analytical capabilities. For example, we can create pivot tables to filter and summarize the information as needed. Additionally, this process can be automated by scheduling regular calls to the relevant Graph API endpoints, enabling consistent and up-to-date exports. Microsoft also updates its document that contains the list of EAM apps in the catalog at `https://learn.microsoft.com/en-us/intune/intune-service/apps/apps-enterprise-app-management`.

Use case 2: Getting a list of all the EAM apps added to our tenant

As the next use case, if we wish to get a list of the EAM apps that have been added to our tenant, we need to call the following Graph endpoint. Additionally, we can use the `Select-Object` parameter and just filter out the useful details, such as `DisplayName`, `Id`, and `CreatedDateTime`:

```
Get-MgBetaDeviceAppManagementMobileApp -Filter "(isof('microsoft.
graph.win32CatalogApp'))" | Select-Object -Property DisplayName, Id,
CreatedDateTime
```

The output would look like the following, listing all the EAM apps that have been added to the tenant by the admin:

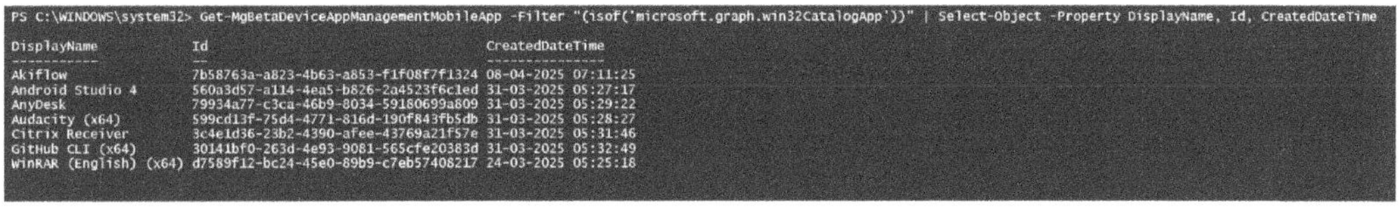

Figure 3.30: PowerShell output showing the list of EAM apps added to the tenant

Lastly, it is also possible to add a new EAM instance from the catalog to our tenant using Graph. To do this, we need to make a `POST` request to the same Graph API endpoint. This request must include a policy body containing key details such as the application ID, display name, description, and other relevant metadata required for the app configuration.

With the preceding three use cases, the primary goal of this section was to understand that, similar to most tasks in the Intune portal, EAM-related tasks can also be managed by administrators through the appropriate Graph APIs. If you have a team that deals with automation, they can do a lot of cool stuff with this!

High-level summary of the flow

The following is a block diagram representation of the flow established from the IME logs in the previous section.

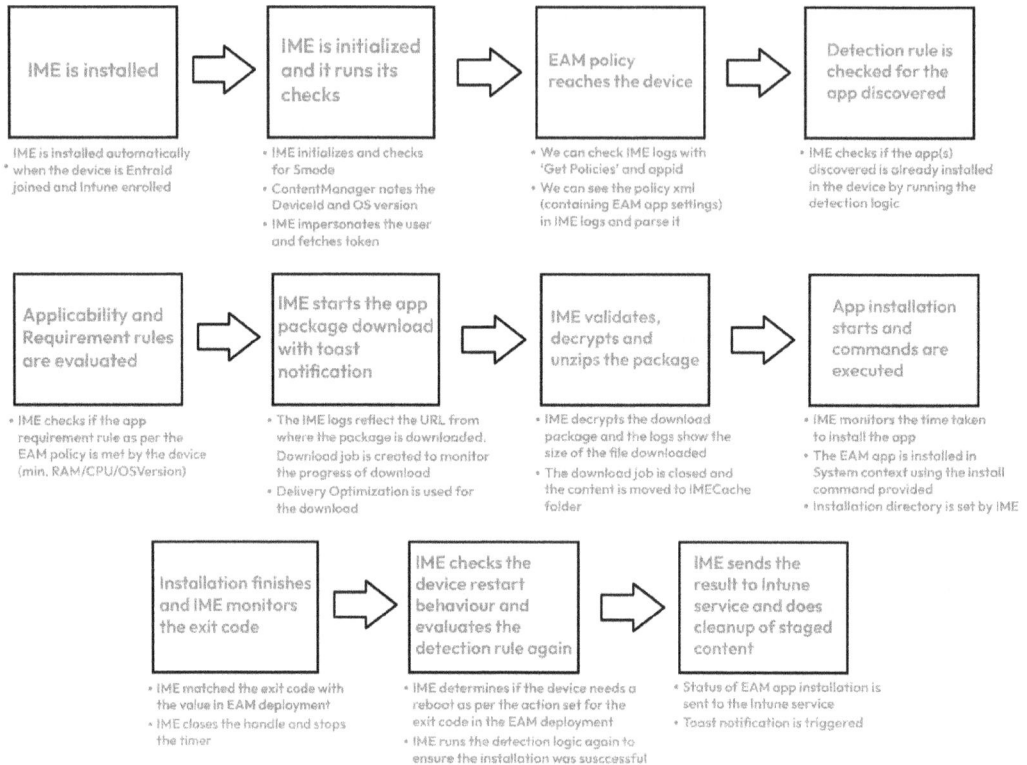

```
┌─────────────────┐      ┌─────────────────┐      ┌─────────────────┐      ┌─────────────────┐
│ IME is installed│  ⇨  │ IME is initialized│  ⇨  │ EAM policy      │  ⇨  │ Detection rule is│
│                 │      │ and it runs its │      │ reaches the device│    │ checked for the │
│                 │      │ checks          │      │                 │      │ app discovered  │
└─────────────────┘      └─────────────────┘      └─────────────────┘      └─────────────────┘
```

- IME is installed automatically when the device is EntraId joined and Intune enrolled

- IME initializes and checks for Smode
- ContentManager notes the DeviceId and OS version
- IME impersonates the user and fetches token

- We can check IME logs with 'Get Policies' and appid
- We can see the policy xml (containing EAM app settings) in IME logs and parse it

- IME checks if the app(s) discovered is already installed in the device by running the detection logic

```
┌─────────────────┐      ┌─────────────────┐      ┌─────────────────┐      ┌─────────────────┐
│ Applicability and│ ⇨  │ IME starts the app│ ⇨  │ IME validates,  │  ⇨  │ App installation│
│ Requirement rules│     │ package download│      │ decrypts and    │      │ starts and      │
│ are evaluated   │      │ with toast      │      │ unzips the package│    │ commands are    │
│                 │      │ notification    │      │                 │      │ executed        │
└─────────────────┘      └─────────────────┘      └─────────────────┘      └─────────────────┘
```

- IME checks if the app requirement rule as per the EAM policy is met by the device (min. RAM/CPU/OSVersion)

- The IME logs reflect the URL from where the package is downloaded. Download job is created to monitor the progress of download
- Delivery Optimization is used for the download

- IME decrypts the download package and the logs show the size of the file downloaded
- The download job is closed and the content is moved to IMECache folder

- IME monitors the time taken to install the app
- The EAM app is installed in System context using the install command provided
- Installation directory is set by IME

```
┌─────────────────┐      ┌─────────────────┐      ┌─────────────────┐
│ Installation    │  ⇨  │ IME checks the  │  ⇨  │ IME sends the   │
│ finishes and IME│      │ device restart  │      │ result to Intune│
│ monitors the    │      │ behaviour and   │      │ service and does│
│ exit code       │      │ evaluates the   │      │ cleanup of staged│
│                 │      │ detection rule again│  │ content         │
└─────────────────┘      └─────────────────┘      └─────────────────┘
```

- IME matched the exit code with the value in EAM deployment
- IME closes the handle and stops the timer

- IME determines if the device needs a reboot as per the action set for the exit code in the EAM deployment
- IME runs the detection logic again to ensure the installation was susccessful

- Status of EAM app installation is sent to the Intune service
- Toast notification is triggered

Figure 3.31: High-level block diagram explaining the flow behind EAM app installation

Our troubleshooting approach must align with the established flow. If there are errors during app installation, the IME log will capture them.

During troubleshooting, we need to ensure that each step of the flow is checked. Various factors can cause EAM app installation failures, such as inaccessible URLs, incorrect detection logic, or unmet device requirements. By tracing the logs, we can pinpoint the cause and work toward a resolution.

Additional EAM features to consider

Microsoft might consider the development of the following capabilities to enhance EAM app deployment based on the feedback received, making the feature even more robust. Currently, there is no ETA for these enhancements:

- **Integration with MDE**: For instance, MDE could detect a vulnerability in a third-party application, and that vulnerability could be addressed through deployment from Intune via the EAM catalog.

- **Updating unmanaged applications**: Extending the ability to push updates to applications that are not currently managed. A scenario could be updating apps that may not have been deployed via the catalog, but an update or security vulnerability has been detected.

- **Support for macOS and Linux**: Expanding EAM capabilities to include macOS and Linux operating systems.

Competitive analysis

PatchMyPC and Robopack are notable competitors in the EAM space, having provided third-party app management for many years with a comprehensive product. In comparison to Intune, they have two key **Unique Selling Points** (**USPs**):

- **Support for server operating system**: PatchMyPC provides the ability to deploy apps to the server operating system as well, and it integrates with `ConfigMgr`. On the other hand, EAM in Intune is focused on the client operating system only.

- **Pricing**: The retail pricing for EAM in Intune is $2 per user per month ($24 annually) with no minimum starting price, allowing for the purchase of a single license for one month. PatchMyPC charges $3.5 per device per year, with a minimum starting price of $2,499.

The pricing for EAM becomes more economical when purchasing the entire Intune Suite at $10 per user per month. Additionally, PatchMyPC's licensing is device-based, meaning costs can add up if a user has multiple devices. In contrast, the EAM license in Intune is user-based, allowing a user to have up to 15 devices under a single license.

We are generally not in favor of deploying third-party agents onto devices unless absolutely necessary. Utilizing a complete solution might require deploying an additional agent onto the device. In contrast, using EAM leverages the IME agent, which is installed by default when a device is Entra ID-joined and enrolled to Intune.

Our two cents

We believe the EAM capability in the Intune Suite is a valuable addition to its features. While pricing may be a consideration, the advantage of having a single pane of glass (i.e., Intune) for all management tasks is highly beneficial from an administrative perspective. Additionally, Microsoft might consider expanding EAM to macOS, which would be a significant enhancement.

Summary

In this chapter, we explored the background, purpose, and key benefits of using EAM. We examined the end-to-end process of EAM app delivery, including the underlying logs and registry interactions that support effective troubleshooting. We also covered how to automate EAM deployments using Microsoft Graph. The chapter concluded with a discussion on potential future enhancements and a competitive analysis comparing EAM with similar third-party solutions.

In the next chapter of this book, we will dive into advanced analytics and understand how we can use it to efficiently query thousands of devices in our organization.

Resource

The Microsoft Digital Defense Report can be found at `https://www.microsoft.com/en-in/security/security-insider/microsoft-digital-defense-report-2023`.

Get This Book's PDF Version and Exclusive Extras

UNLOCK NOW

Scan the QR code (or go to packtpub.com/unlock). Search for this book by name, confirm the edition, and then follow the steps on the page.

Note: Keep your invoice handy. Purchases made directly from Packt don't require an invoice.

4

AI-Driven Insights with Endpoint Analytics and Intune Advanced Analytics

As modern IT ecosystems grow in complexity, the need for actionable insights into device performance and user experience becomes increasingly critical. Microsoft Intune addresses this need through two complementary analytics solutions: **endpoint analytics** and **Advanced Analytics**.

Endpoint analytics delivers a streamlined view of device health and user experience metrics, helping IT teams pinpoint inefficiencies and optimize performance. By analyzing factors such as startup times, application responsiveness, and policy compliance, it enables organizations to proactively enhance productivity and reduce support overhead.

Advanced Analytics takes this a step further by offering customizable, query-driven insights across the entire device fleet. Built on the Intune Data Platform and powered by **Kusto Query Language (KQL)**, it allows administrators to perform deep inventory analysis, monitor hardware trends, and support strategic decision-making. Whether assessing encryption coverage or tracking OS version distribution, Advanced Analytics provides the flexibility and scale needed for enterprise-grade visibility. It also provides deep, data-driven insights into device health and user experience. It helps IT teams proactively detect issues and optimize performance with anomaly detection and advanced reporting.

Together, these tools form the backbone of a data-driven approach to endpoint management, combining real-time diagnostics with historical intelligence to drive efficiency, security, and user satisfaction.

In this chapter, we will begin by exploring endpoint analytics in depth, examining its core components, setup process, and the relevant logs and registry entries found on the device. This foundational understanding will set the stage for our next topic: Advanced Analytics. There, we'll uncover how to extract query-driven insights and transform raw data into actionable intelligence.

The following main topics will be covered in this chapter:

- Endpoint analytics: understanding its background and prerequisites
- Understanding the setup, logs, and registry for EA
- Understanding the scores, insights, and recommendations in EA
- Endpoint analytics versus Advanced Analytics
- Breaking down Advanced Analytics and its components
- Device query (Intune's CMPivot): the game changer!
- Flow behind the working of SDQ
- High-level steps for configuring MDQ and the detailed flow behind its working
- Comparison between SDQ and MDQ and FAQs
- Copilot integration into device query and integrating Intune analytics with Power BI

> Endpoint analytics, although not part of the Intune Suite and available at no additional cost, serves as a critical foundation for understanding Intune's broader analytics capabilities.

Let's start by diving into endpoint analytics and unpacking all the key concepts it encompasses. Gaining a solid grasp of how endpoint analytics works, including its features, setup, and data flow, will make it significantly easier to comprehend Advanced Analytics, as both are tightly integrated and complement each other in delivering actionable insights.

Understanding endpoint analytics

Let's imagine an organization with 100,000 Windows devices distributed globally across various departments: developers, HR, the frontline workforce, and more. Given the diversity of roles, these devices vary in specifications, OEMs, and the applications installed on them.

When these devices are managed through Intune, administrators have some visibility into their performance, as they are responsible for deploying applications and enforcing policies. However, with such a vast fleet, it's impractical for Intune admins to remotely access each device to collect startup logs, monitor resource usage, or manually identify underperforming systems that may require replacement or upgrades.

To address this challenge, it's essential to empower Intune admins with built-in telemetry within the Intune portal. This would allow them to detect patterns of issues, whether hardware-related (such as CPU or RAM bottlenecks) or software-related (such as application crashes or hangs). With access to this data, admins can investigate further and collaborate with relevant teams. For instance, if a specific application version is consistently linked to performance issues, they can coordinate with the application owners. Similarly, if certain hardware configurations are consistently underperforming, those devices can be flagged for upgrades or replacement, or the affected OEM models can be flagged for compatibility issues.

To address this need, endpoint analytics offers a powerful solution. It provides actionable insights into device performance and user experience across the organization. By identifying hardware limitations or policy configurations that degrade performance, endpoint analytics enables IT teams to proactively optimize devices, enhance productivity, and reduce support overhead. With built-in telemetry, it helps detect trends and regressions caused by configuration changes, allowing administrators to deliver a consistently high-quality experience to end users.

The aim of this section is to give you an idea of the key challenges EA is designed to address and understand the value it brings.

Now, let's review the prerequisites of endpoint analytics.

Prerequisites

EA has the following prerequisites, which need to be met:

- Devices must be Intune-enrolled or co-managed, running with Windows 10 version 1903 or later, and the end user should be licensed for Intune:

    - Supported editions are Pro, Pro Education, Enterprise, and Education (Home is not supported)

- Devices must be Microsoft Entra joined or Microsoft Entra hybrid joined
- **Connected User Experiences and Telemetry** should be functional in the device
- The URL `https://*.events.data.microsoft.com` should be accessible from the device, which is used by managed devices to send required functional data to the Intune data
- The Intune **Service Administrator** role is needed for setting up EA and relevant read-only access roles for viewing the data

Now that we have gone through the background and prerequisites of EA, let's delve into how to set it up within our tenant in the next section.

How to set up EA

The first step of the process is enabling endpoint analytics in our tenant. This is very straightforward and is a one-time activity:

1. We need to go to the Intune portal > **Reports** > **Endpoint analytics** > **Settings** (or to `https://aka.ms/endpointanalytics`).

2. Now, we have the option of choosing whether we would like to enable EA for all the devices in the tenant or a selected group of devices. I would suggest selecting **All cloud-managed devices**, as this only collects information from the device but doesn't make any active changes.

Once done, the setup would show **Connected**, as seen here:

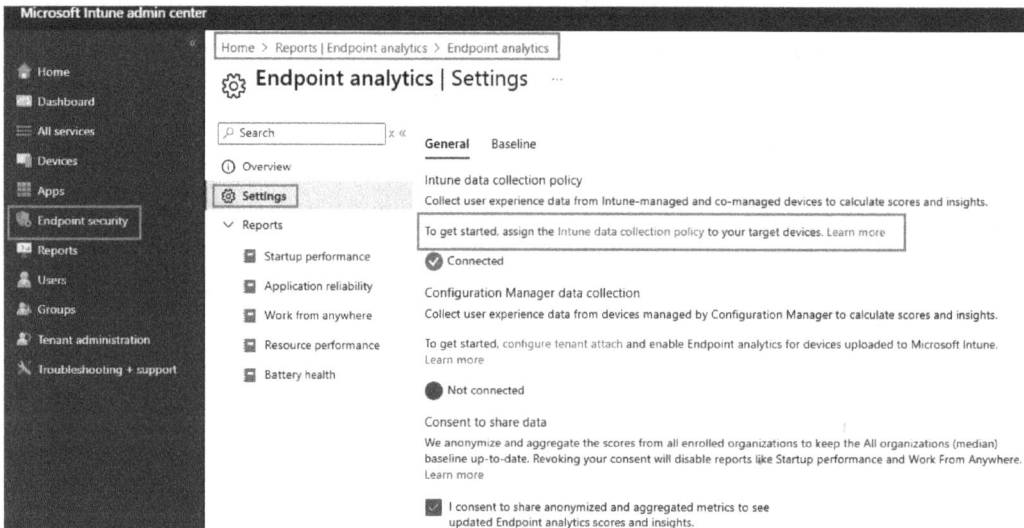

Figure 4.1: Enabling endpoint analytics from the Intune portal

Impact of enabling EA

Just after we enable EA, the portal informs us that the Intune data collection policy has been automatically created, which needs to be assigned, as seen in *Figure 4.1*.

This policy is part of Windows Health Monitoring and is responsible for collecting all the telemetry from the end device. This policy utilizes the `DeviceHealthMonitoring` node in the Policy CSP.

> The preceding **Windows Health Monitoring** policy can also be created as a device configuration policy in Intune (from the template), as shown here:
>
> **Windows 10 and later** > **Template** > **Windows health monitoring** > **Health Monitoring**: Select **Enable** | **Scope**: Select **Endpoint analytics**

Gaining a thorough understanding of the relevant logs and registry entries associated with endpoint analytics is crucial, as it aids in effective troubleshooting. Let's explore these in the next section of this chapter.

Logs and registry

Once the devices have been onboarded to endpoint analytics successfully, the respective registry location is populated, as shown in the following: `Computer\HKEY_LOCAL_MACHINE\SOFTWARE\Microsoft\PolicyManager\providers\xx-yy-zz\default\Device\DeviceHealthMonitoring`

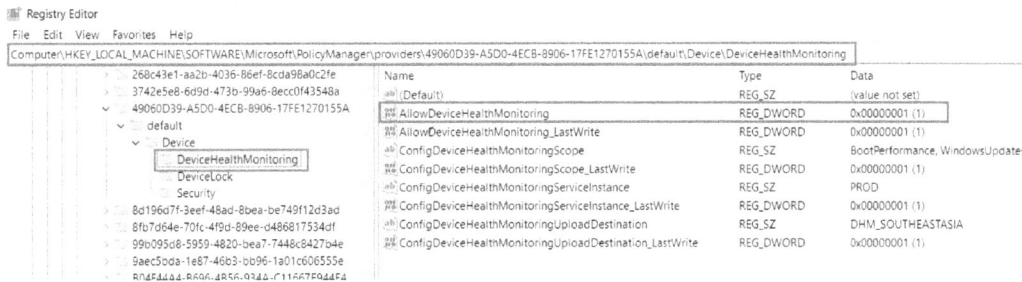

Figure 4.2: Registry location of Device Health Monitoring

As we can see in the preceding screenshot, `REG_SZ` values are created, named as follows:

- `ConfigDeviceHealthMonitoringUploadDestination`
- `ConfigDeviceHealthMonitoringServiceInstance`
- `ConfigDeviceHealthMonitoringScope`

The same is logged in `Microsoft-Windows-DeviceManagement-Enterprise-Diagnostics-Provider/Admin`. The relevant **Event ID** value to check here is **814**.

> The `xx-yy-zz` value is a placeholder for IDs, and its value would be different in each environment. It is referenced throughout this chapter for various registry locations.

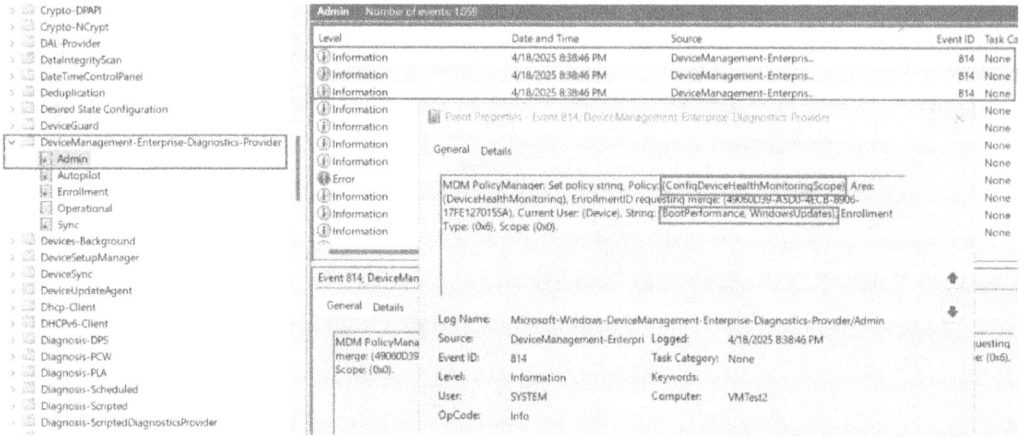

Figure 4.3: Event Viewer logs showing the delivery of the Device Health Monitoring policy

In the event logs, we can see the following settings, which were configured in accordance with the policy that was set by the admin in the portal:

- `ConfigDeviceHealthMonitoringUploadDestination`: In this, the upload destination is set by the service, which is based on the location of the tenant

- `ConfigDeviceHealthMonitoringServiceInstance`: In this, the instance is set (which could be PROD or others)

- `ConfigDeviceHealthMonitoringScope`: In this, the scope of DHM is set, which can be `BootPerformance`, `WindowsUpdates`, `PrivilegeManagement`, or all of these

Sample logs

Let's take a look at a couple of sample Event Viewer logs from a Windows device that is successfully onboarded to endpoint analytics:

- `MDM PolicyManager: Set policy string, Policy: (ConfigDeviceHealthMonitoringScope), Area: (DeviceHealthMonitoring), EnrollmentID requesting merge: (49060D39-A5D0-4ECB-8906-17FE1270155A), Current User: (Device), String: (BootPerformance, WindowsUpdates), Enrollment Type: (0x6), Scope: (0x0).`

- `MDM PolicyManager: Set policy string, Policy: (ConfigDeviceHealthMonitoringServiceInstance), Area: (DeviceHealthMonitoring), EnrollmentID requesting merge: (49060D39-A5D0-4ECB-8906-17FE1270155A), Current User: (Device), String: (PROD), Enrollment Type: (0x6), Scope: (0x0).`

- MDM PolicyManager: Set policy string, Policy: (ConfigDeviceHealthMonitoring UploadDestination), Area: (DeviceHealthMonitoring), EnrollmentID requesting merge: (49060D39-A5D0-4ECB-8906-17FE1270155A), Current User: (Device), String: (DHM_SOUTHEASTASIA), Enrolment Type: (0x6), Scope: (0x0).

In the following section, we will examine the individual components of endpoint analytics and their detailed breakdown.

Breaking down EA

EA basically has three components to it: **scores**, **baselines**, and **recommendations**, as seen here:

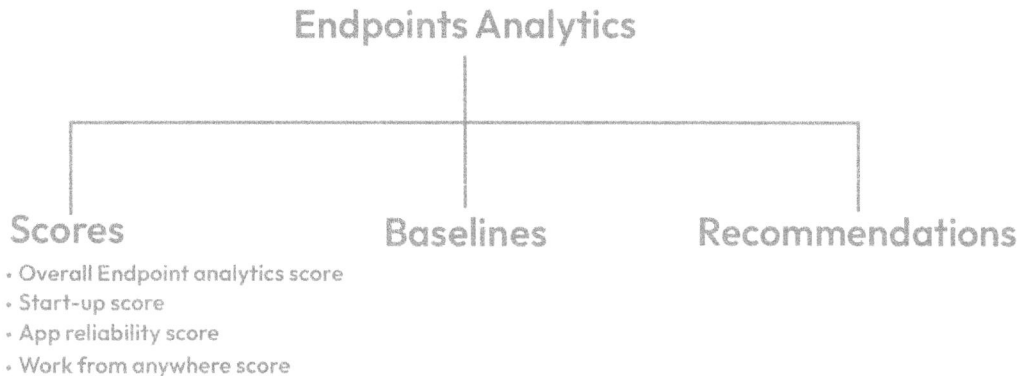

Figure 4.4: Diagram illustrating endpoint analytics components

Let's understand all these components in detail.

Understanding the scores

Let's refer to the following diagram, which illustrates all the scores used in endpoint analytics:

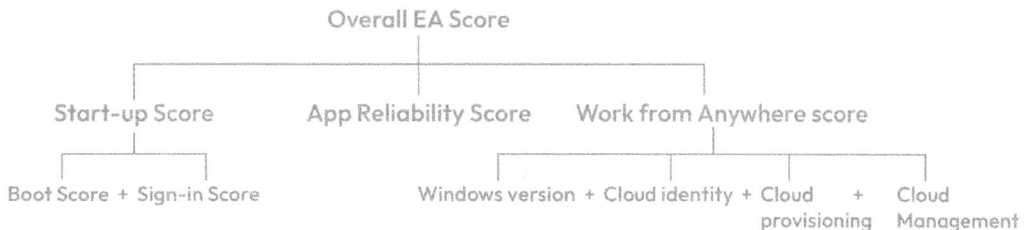

Figure 4.5: Diagram illustrating the scores in endpoint analytics

Overall EA score

This is the average of all sub-report scores on a scale from 0 to 100 (100 is best). Think of this as the overall percentage of a student in a class. The following scores can be considered as the percentage for specific subjects:

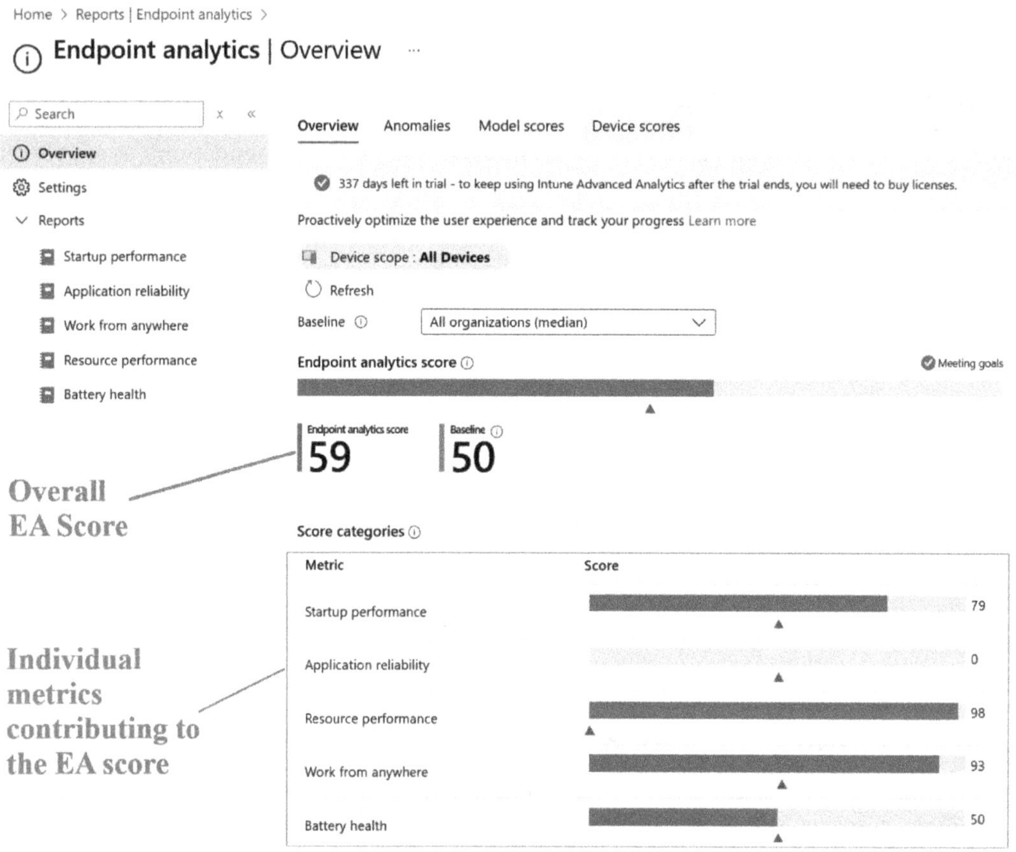

Figure 4.6: Endpoint analytics score in the Intune portal

The overall endpoint analytics score is crucial as it provides a comprehensive view of how Windows devices are performing across our organization based on the collected metrics.

By navigating to the **Device scores** tab, as illustrated next, we can assess the contribution of each individual machine to the overall EA score:

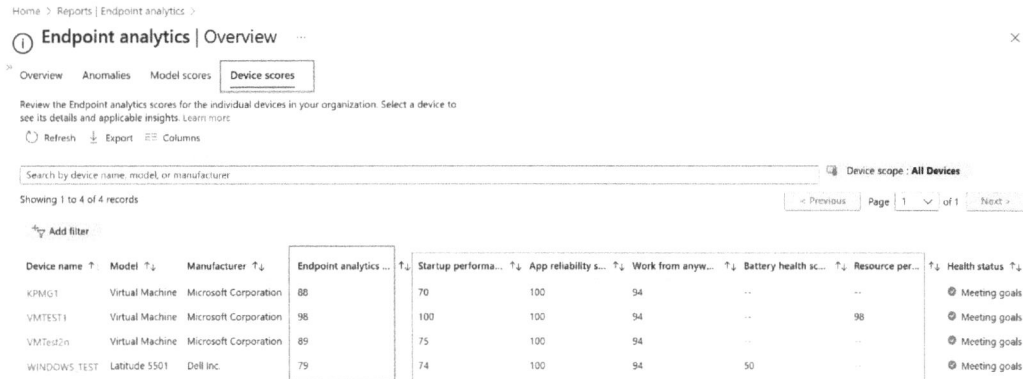

Home > Reports | Endpoint analytics >

ⓘ **Endpoint analytics | Overview**   ···   ✕

» Overview   Anomalies   Model scores   **Device scores**

Review the Endpoint analytics scores for the individual devices in your organization. Select a device to see its details and applicable insights. Learn more

↻ Refresh   ↓ Export   ≣ Columns

| Search by device name, model, or manufacturer | | | | Device scope : **All Devices** | | | | | |

Showing 1 to 4 of 4 records   < Previous   Page 1 ∨ of 1   Next >

+ Add filter

Device name ↑	Model ↑↓	Manufacturer ↑↓	Endpoint analytics ... ↑↓	Startup performa... ↑↓	App reliability s... ↑↓	Work from anyw... ↑↓	Battery health sc... ↑↓	Resource per... ↑↓	Health status ↑↓
KPMG1	Virtual Machine	Microsoft Corporation	88	70	100	94	--	--	⊘ Meeting goals
VMTEST1	Virtual Machine	Microsoft Corporation	98	100	100	94	--	98	⊘ Meeting goals
VMTest2n	Virtual Machine	Microsoft Corporation	89	75	100	94	--	--	⊘ Meeting goals
WINDOWS TEST	Latitude 5501	Dell Inc.	79	74	100	94	50		⊘ Meeting goals

Figure 4.7: Device scores in the Intune portal

Additionally, we can generate and export a comprehensive list of the overall EA scores for all devices within our organization, as well as the scores for each individual contributing metric, using the **Export** option, which can be seen in the previous figure. We can maintain an offline inventory of these reports and build a custom dashboard using Power BI.

Now, we are going to discuss all the metrics (scores) seen in *Figure 4.6* in detail in the following sections.

Startup performance score

The **Startup performance** score is an evaluation of how long it takes for the device to enter a productive state after powering on the machine. This metric indicates whether there are significant delays during the boot and sign-in processes.

The score is an average of the boot score and the sign-in score, calculated as follows:

- **Boot score**: Measures the time from power-on to sign-in. The last boot time from each device is assessed, excluding the update phase.

- **Sign-in score**: Measures the time from credential entry until the user can access a responsive desktop.

We can also see the **Core sign-in** time to a responsive desktop, which is the average time between when the desktop renders and when CPU usage falls below 50%.

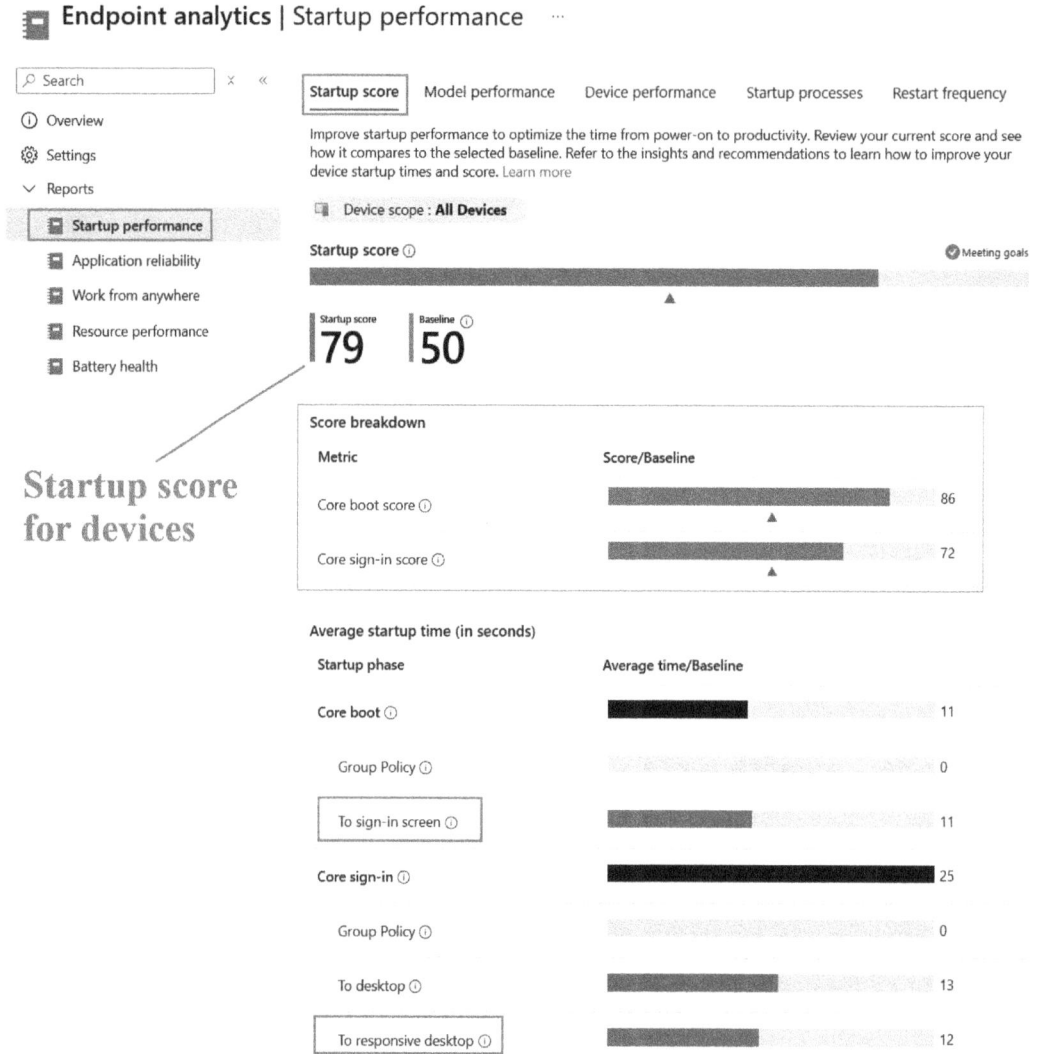

Endpoint analytics | Startup performance   ...

🔍 Search x «	**Startup score** Model performance Device performance Startup processes Restart frequency
ⓘ Overview	Improve startup performance to optimize the time from power-on to productivity. Review your current score and see how it compares to the selected baseline. Refer to the insights and recommendations to learn how to improve your device startup times and score. Learn more
⚙ Settings	
⌄ Reports	🖥 Device scope : **All Devices**
🖼 **Startup performance**	Startup score ⓘ ✓ Meeting goals
🖼 Application reliability	
🖼 Work from anywhere	
🖼 Resource performance	Startup score Baseline ⓘ
🖼 Battery health	**79 50**

Startup score for devices

Score breakdown

Metric	Score/Baseline	
Core boot score ⓘ		86
Core sign-in score ⓘ		72

Average startup time (in seconds)

Startup phase	Average time/Baseline	
Core boot ⓘ		11
Group Policy ⓘ		0
To sign-in screen ⓘ		11
Core sign-in ⓘ		25
Group Policy ⓘ		0
To desktop ⓘ		13
To responsive desktop ⓘ		12

Figure 4.8: The Startup performance score of endpoint analytics in the Intune portal

We can also see a chart that displays trends for the average startup score, boot score, and sign-in score for the devices in our organization over the past 30 days, as shown here:

Score trends

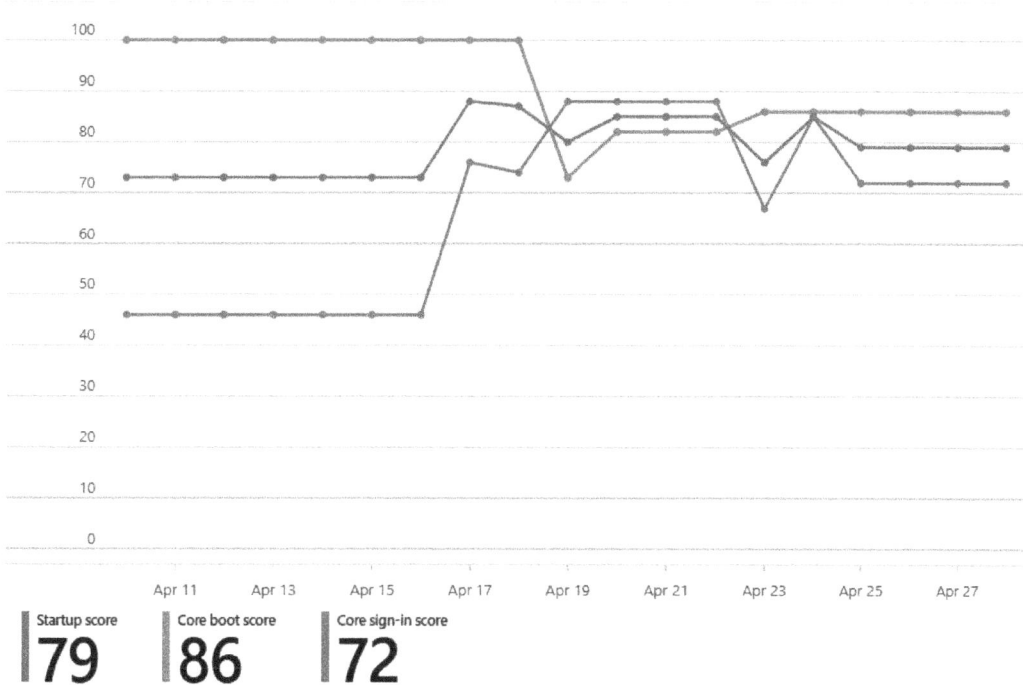

Startup score	Core boot score	Core sign-in score
79	86	72

Figure 4.9: Trends of Startup score, boot score, and sign-in score from the Intune portal

As seen next, by navigating to the **Restart frequency** tab, we can review the restart frequency and types for the devices in our tenant. This allows us to identify trends, such as whether devices are undergoing shutdowns or restarts due to updates, abnormal shutdowns, or user-initiated shutdowns by holding the *power* button.

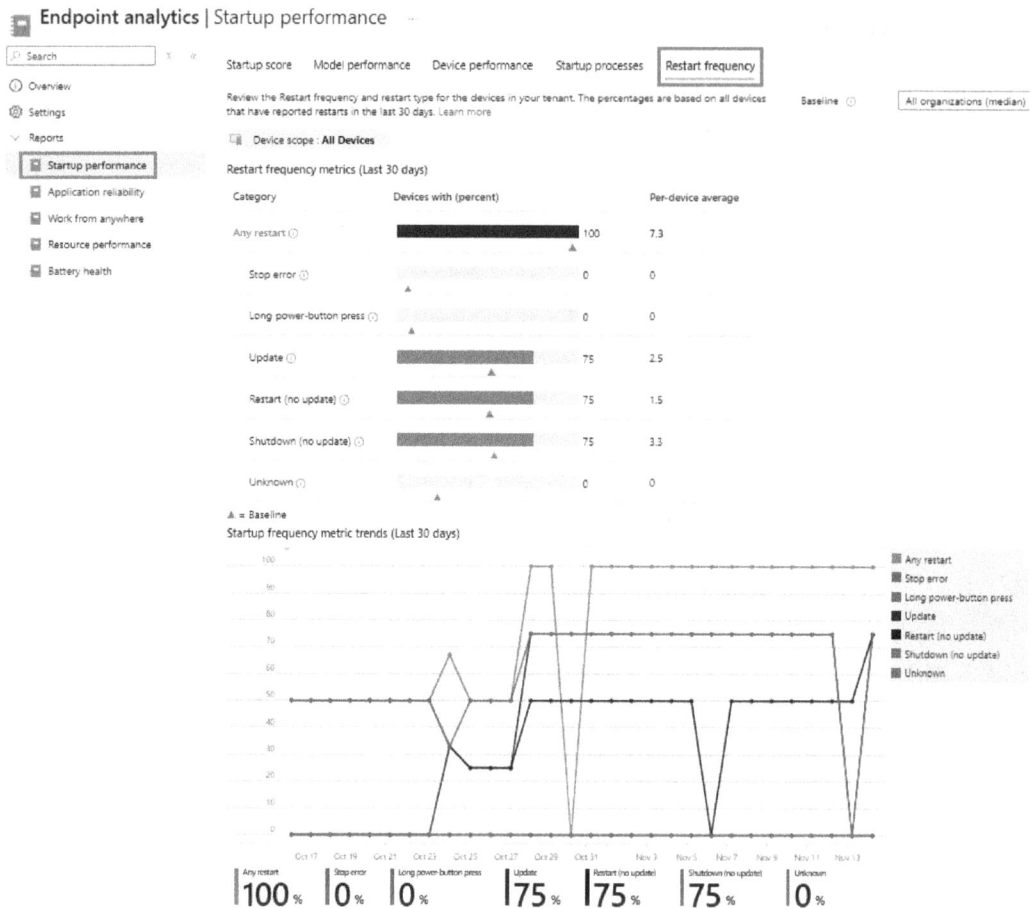

Figure 4.10: Endpoint analytics Startup performance score in the Intune portal

Startup performance is a key metric in endpoint analytics, as it directly reflects the user's experience. In the following section, we'll examine the next metric.

Application reliability score

The **Application reliability** score is an evaluation of the application's performance across the devices in our organization. The score gives us an indication of how often applications are crashing in the devices and provides a high-level view of desktop application robustness across our environment. It also gives us an understanding of app crashes and the OS version in which the crashes are happening, thereby providing us with insights into compatibility issues.

It enables us to drill into specific device data and view a timeline of **Application reliability** events to troubleshoot issues impacting end users. The **Application reliability** score also considers the most frequently used applications, ensuring that they receive greater focus during evaluation.

The following figure shows the **Application reliability** score in an environment:

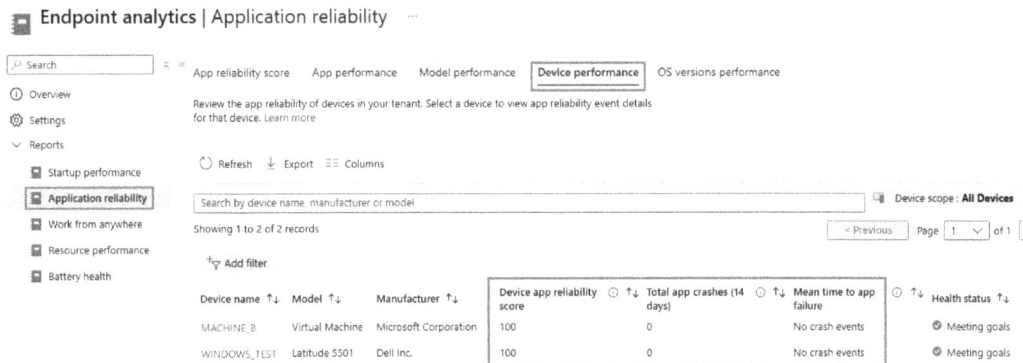

Figure 4.11: The Application reliability score in the Intune portal

The **Application reliability** score is a vital metric in endpoint analytics, as it directly reflects user productivity when working with business applications. The subsequent section will focus on the next metric.

Work from anywhere score

The **Work from anywhere** score is an evaluation of how prepared your workforce is to be productive from anywhere.

The score is an average of the following:

- The **Windows** version: The **Windows** metric measures the percentage of devices on supported/latest versions of Windows. Newer versions of Windows provide a better user experience than older versions of Windows.

- **Cloud identity**: This metric is assigned based on the identity being used in the organization. If users are using Entra ID Premium, they would get a higher score as it has extra features to help protect devices, apps, and data, including dynamic groups, auto-enrollment, and Conditional Access.

- **Cloud provisioning**: This metric measures the percentage of machines that are either Windows 365 Cloud PCs or Windows Intune devices that are both registered and have a deployment profile created for Windows Autopilot.

- **Cloud management**: There are many ways/modes by which a device can be cloud managed, such as via a **cloud management gateway (CMG)**, tenant attach, co-management, and Intune only. The manageability of the device depends on the mode used. **Cloud management** is a metric that is assigned depending on the mode/methodology of cloud management used by the devices in your organization.

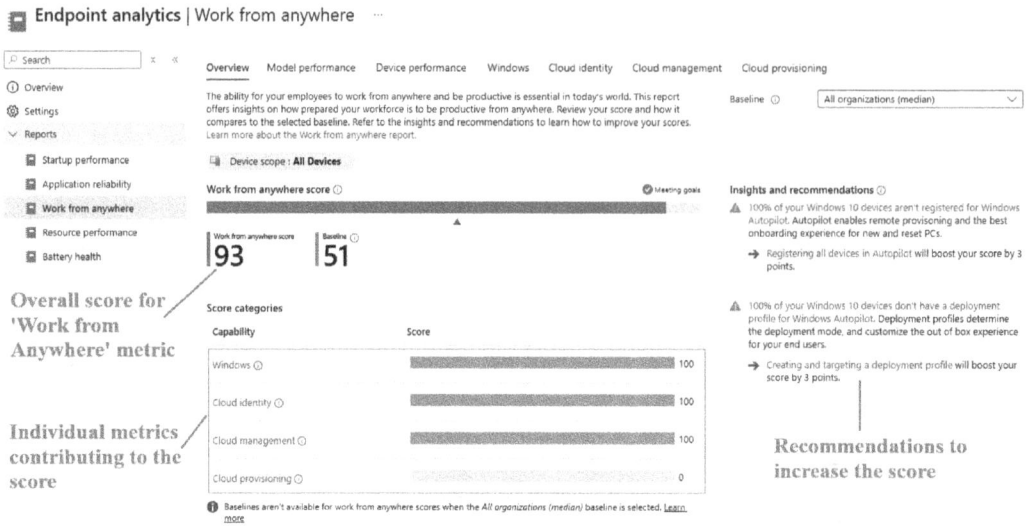

Figure 4.12: The Work from anywhere score in the Intune portal

The **Work from anywhere** score is an important metric in endpoint analytics, as it reflects an organization's readiness to adopt cloud technologies and support a productive remote workforce.

So far, we've gained an understanding of all the scores in endpoint analytics. In the next section, we'll explore baselines and their applications.

Understanding the baselines

We can also see a **Baseline** score (*Figure 4.13*), which is an indication of how other organizations are scored on average for each of the metrics.

Baseline scores are shown on charts as triangle markers. If our current score falls below the baseline and needs attention, the score color changes to red. We can see a **Baseline** score for all the metrics, such as for endpoint analytics overall, for **Startup performance**, for **Application reliability**, and for **Work from anywhere**.

Figure 4.13: Baseline scores in the Intune portal

We can create new baselines, as shown in the following figure, based on our current metrics and use them as a parameter for comparison in the future.

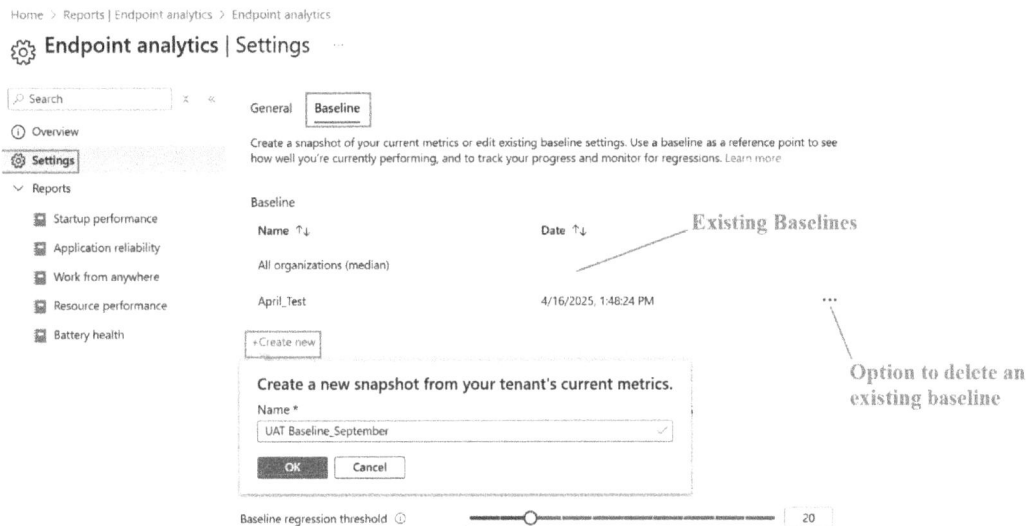

Figure 4.14: Creating a new baseline for endpoint analytics in the Intune portal

Each tenant is limited to 20 baselines. We can remove outdated baselines that are no longer necessary. To delete an existing baseline, we need to click on the three dots right next to it, as highlighted in the preceding figure.

Our current metrics are flagged as regressed and marked in red if they fall below the established baseline. It's normal for metrics to fluctuate daily, so we can set a regression threshold, which defaults to 10%. Metrics are only flagged as regressed if they fall below this threshold by more than 10%.

> Setting up custom baselines in endpoint analytics is optional. Microsoft provides a default baseline in the portal, which serves as a valuable benchmark by showing how other organizations perform across similar parameters. This helps identify deviations and take corrective actions. Additionally, it enables performance comparisons of devices within the organization over time, making it easier to detect significant drops in scores and respond accordingly.

In the next section of this chapter, we'll explore the insights and recommendations that endpoint analytics provides based on our scores.

Understanding the insights and recommendations

The **Insights and recommendations** section provides a prioritized list aimed at enhancing our score. Each recommendation is associated with an insight detailing how to improve the score and specifies the points gained upon completion.

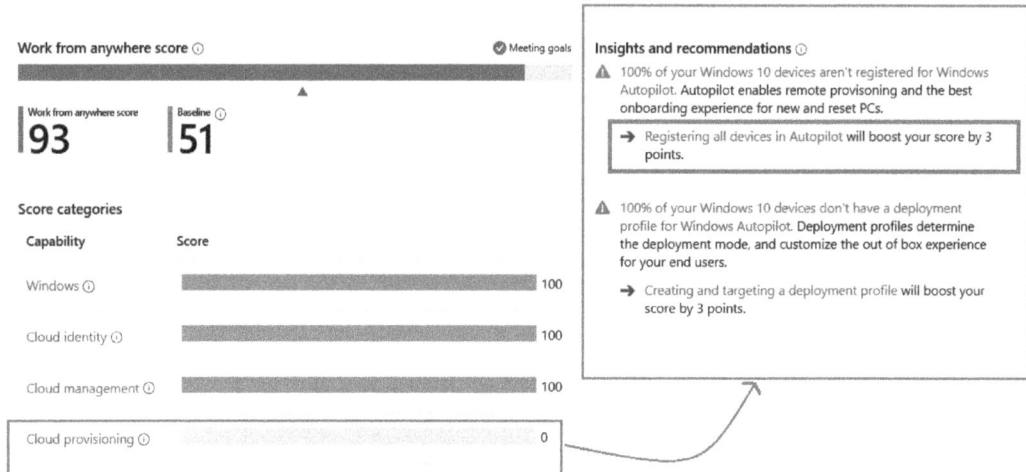

Figure 4.15: Recommendations for increasing the score in the Intune portal

In the preceding example, none of the Windows devices in the tenant are registered with Autopilot or provisioned via Windows 365. Consequently, the score for the **Cloud provisioning** metric is zero. The recommendations suggest targeting an Autopilot profile to these devices.

Endpoint analytics versus Advanced Analytics

Endpoint analytics is a powerful and cost-free feature; hence, implementing it is a no-brainer. I strongly encourage everyone to onboard their devices to endpoint analytics as soon as possible to fully leverage its capabilities and drive better insights across your environment.

Before exploring the full capabilities of Advanced Analytics, let's take a moment to compare it with endpoint analytics. This quick comparison will help clarify their distinct purposes, feature sets, and licensing requirements, providing a clearer understanding of how each tool fits into our endpoint management strategy.

The following table provides a side-by-side comparison of endpoint analytics and Advanced Analytics, highlighting their key differences:

Criteria	Endpoint Analytics	Intune Advanced Analytics
Purpose/ scope	Provides baseline insights into device performance, startup times, and user experience.	Builds on endpoint analytics with deeper, real-time diagnostics and proactive remediation capabilities.
	Used by IT admins/leadership looking for general health and performance metrics.	Used by IT admins and support teams needing advanced troubleshooting, anomaly detection, and device-level insights.
Capabilities	Provides basic capabilities such as insights into Startup performance, Application reliability, Work from anywhere (cloud readiness), baselines, and recommendations.	Provides advanced capabilities such as insights into Battery health, Enhanced device timeline, Anomaly detection, Resource performance, Device scopes, and Device query.
Cost/ licensing	No additional licensing is required for this feature. The device needs to be Intune-enrolled.	Microsoft Intune Suite/add-on license for Advanced Analytics is needed.

Table 4.1: Comparison between endpoint analytics and Advanced Analytics

Until now, we've explored endpoint analytics in depth, covering its features, onboarding process, relevant logs and registries, scoring system, and significance. We also compared endpoint analytics with Advanced Analytics, highlighting their distinct use cases.

We're now ready to dive into Advanced Analytics in the next section to explore its capabilities and insights.

Breaking down Intune Advanced Analytics

To better relate to the use case of Advanced Analytics, let's first explore the following two scenarios:

- **Scenario 1**: Let's imagine an admin needing to assess the available C:\ drive space across 100,000 Windows devices to ensure readiness for deploying a storage-intensive application. Following the installation, there's a security requirement to verify that all physical drives on these devices are encrypted with BitLocker. Manually checking each device is clearly impractical, and while deploying PowerShell scripts via Intune might seem like a solution, it comes with limitations. These scripts run only once per deployment, may fail silently, and often produce outdated results by the time data is aggregated. Troubleshooting failures involves digging through IME logs, adding further complexity.

This is where Advanced Analytics and its **Device query for multiple devices** feature offer a scalable alternative. With this capability, admins can instantly query all devices to retrieve real-time data on disk space and encryption status without deploying scripts, managing outputs, or worrying about failures. It streamlines the process, reduces overhead, and ensures timely, accurate insights for both operational and security decisions.

- **Scenario 2**: Another practical scenario involves device refresh cycles and enabling users for remote work. Suppose an organization with 100,000 Windows devices wants to identify systems with degraded battery performance, which could hinder productivity for mobile users. To support remote work, the organization sets a baseline requirement: each device must deliver at least two hours of battery backup.

Manually checking battery health across all devices is impractical, and Advanced Analytics effectively solves this challenge with scalable, real-time insights. It enables visibility into battery performance across all physical devices, including estimated backup duration and identification of OEM models needing battery replacement. This empowers admins to target underperforming devices during refresh cycles, improving user mobility and productivity. Additionally, it allows proactive hardware replacement while devices are still under warranty, reducing long-term maintenance costs and enhancing operational efficiency.

Advanced Analytics builds upon the existing endpoint analytics experience, offering deeper insights and expanded functionality for device monitoring across the organization. The following diagram shows the different features of Advanced analytics:

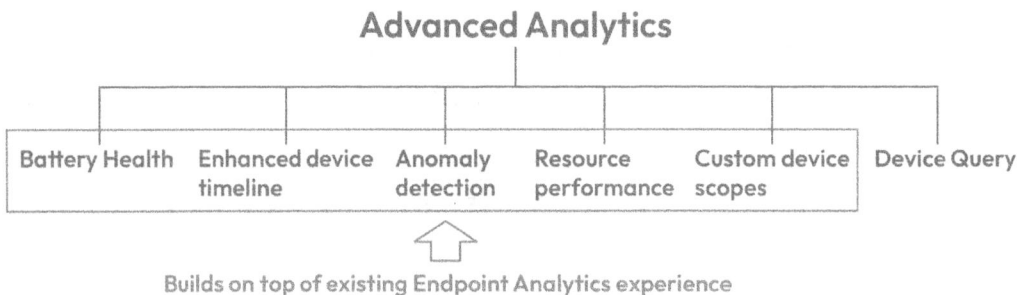

Figure 4.16: The breakdown of Advanced Analytics components

With Advanced Analytics enabled, we gain access to additional data and features such as **Battery health**, **Enhanced device timeline**, **Anomaly detection**, **Resource performance**, and **Device scopes**, as shown in the preceding diagram. Initially, these sections will appear empty, but once Advanced Analytics is in use, they will populate with rich, actionable information.

The **Device query** capability is also provided as a part of Advanced Analytics, which we will delve into next.

Now, let's understand each component of Advanced Analytics in detail. In the next section, we'll dive into one of the most powerful features of Advanced Analytics: **Device query**.

Device query (Intune's CMPivot)

Microsoft Intune is constantly evolving, and one of the most exciting additions to the Intune Suite is the new **Device query** feature, which is part of Advanced Analytics. It includes both **single-device query (SDQ)** and **multi-device query (MDQ)**, and it's a big step forward in cloud-native endpoint management. This long-awaited capability brings real-time diagnostics and fleet-wide insights right into the Intune experience, similar to what many admins loved about CMPivot in Configuration Manager.

With SDQ, IT admins can run live queries on individual devices to pull volatile data such as running services or active applications. It's incredibly useful for quick, targeted troubleshooting. On the other hand, MDQ lets teams analyze inventory data across multiple devices, helping them spot trends, check compliance, and evaluate hardware readiness across their entire environment.

In our opinion, the **Device query** feature in Intune is shaping up to be a must-have tool in every Intune admin's toolkit. Let's begin by exploring SDQ, including its practical applications, the underlying workflow, and how it operates, as detailed in the upcoming section.

Single-device query

Device Query empowers IT administrators to instantly retrieve live data from managed devices using KQL. By executing real-time queries on selected endpoints, administrators can gain immediate visibility into device status, enabling rapid response to security incidents. Let's look at a scenario to understand this topic better.

Let's imagine a Windows device enrolled in Intune, used by a senior executive. The user reports that the device becomes extremely slow during a specific time of day, affecting productivity. A few possible causes come to mind: maybe Windows Update kicks in during that window, or a scheduled task or antivirus scan is consuming high CPU or RAM.

Since the user is often remote or traveling, it's not feasible for IT to physically inspect the device, and because the issue is time-bound and resolves on its own, capturing the right data at the right moment becomes tricky, especially when dealing with volatile information that isn't stored historically.

This is where SDQ comes in. It allows IT admins to pull real-time data from the device during the affected window without needing any action from the user. For instance, the admin can run an SDQ to fetch the top 10 processes by CPU and RAM usage, giving instant visibility into what's running and potentially causing the slowdown. They can also query specific Event Viewer logs to investigate further.

In short, SDQ empowers IT teams to troubleshoot quickly and efficiently, even when the user is halfway across the world.

Let's take a look at the following diagram, which provides us with insights into the background flow while running SDQ:

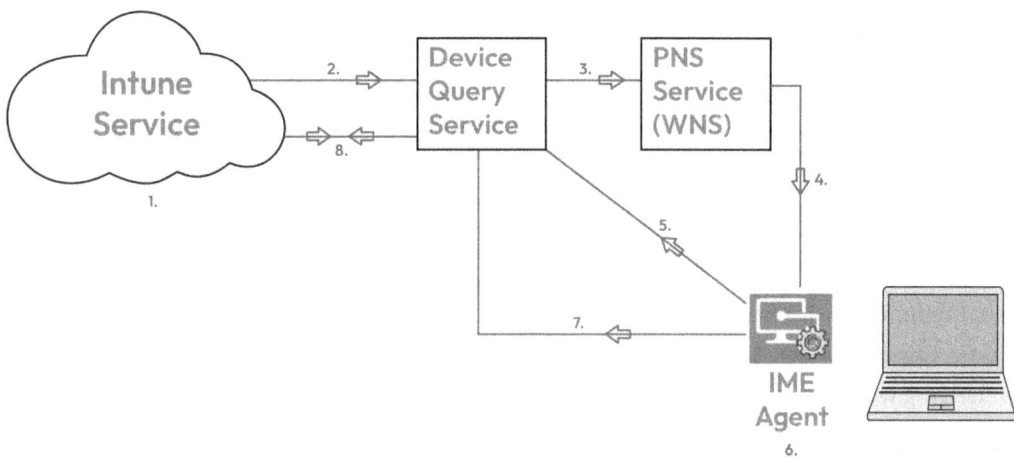

Figure 4.17: The flow behind SDQ

Let's go through the eight steps in the flow, referring to the preceding diagram:

1. The Intune admin runs the query for a specific device in the Intune portal. The admin can write the query in KQL format or use Security Copilot, which translates a natural language query to KQL.

2. The backend **Device query** service is notified of this ask.

3. The request is sent to the **Push Notification Service** (**PNS**), which utilizes the **Windows Push Notification Service** (**WNS**).

4. WNS sends a notification to the device. WNS is a cloud-based service that plays a key role in delivering push notifications to Windows devices in a power-efficient and reliable manner. WNS in the device must be running, and the URL `*.wns.windows.com` should be accessible.

This step is recorded in the device's Event Viewer logs under `Microsoft-Windows-PushNotifications-Platform/Operational`, with **Event ID** values of **1268** and **1010**, as shown here:

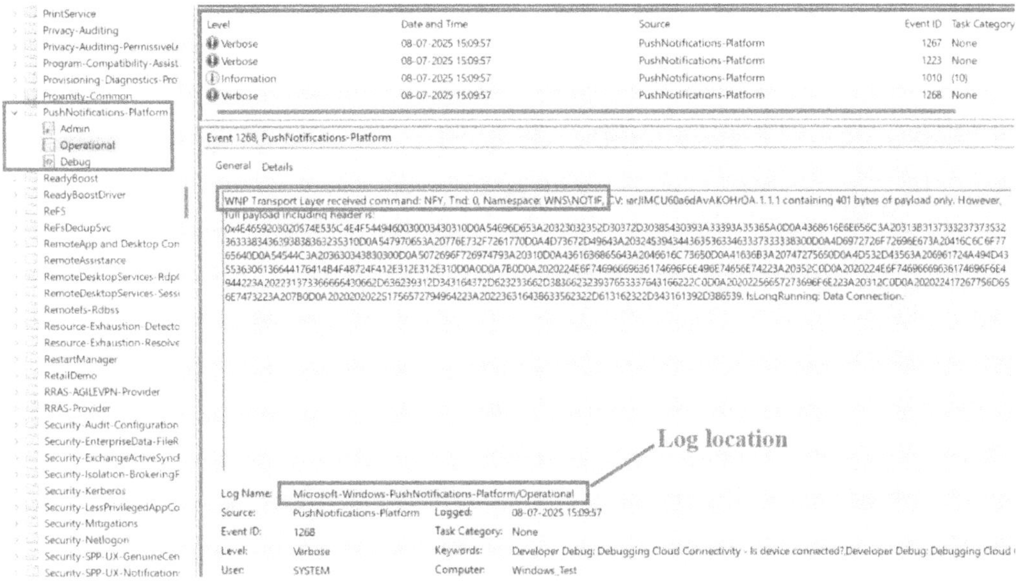

Figure 4.18: The Event Viewer logs of a WNS notification from the device

5. The sidecar agent (IME) in the device reaches out to the **Device query** service and fetches the query. The **Intune Management Extension (IME)** agent gets installed automatically when a device is onboarded to endpoint analytics. The installation of the IME agent is triggered by the Intune service using its CSP, and after its installation, it can be checked in the registry: `'HKEY_LOCAL_MACHINE\SOFTWARE\Microsoft\EnterpriseDesktopAppManagement\S-0-0-00-0000000000-0000000000-000000000-000\MSI\guid\'`

The service for this agent in the device is **Microsoft Intune Management Extension**, which should be running.

6. The relevant WMI provider is loaded in the device, and the query is executed.

7. The sidecar agent sends the result of the query back to the **Device query** service.

8.   The Intune service communicates with the **Device query** service and fetches the result, which is displayed in the Intune portal.

> Access to the **Device query** service is not exposed via Graph APIs to ensure that the service is not flooded with an unreasonable number of calls originating from a tenant.
>
> The query sent by the Intune service and its results are end-to-end encrypted.
>
> The maximum query timeout period for SDQ is 20 minutes. There is a 10-query submission per minute limit.

In the next section, we'll explore the SDQ-related flow by debugging the IME logs.

Decoding the IME logs behind SDQ

Let's refer to the following block diagram, which outlines the eight high-level steps involved in processing an SDQ:

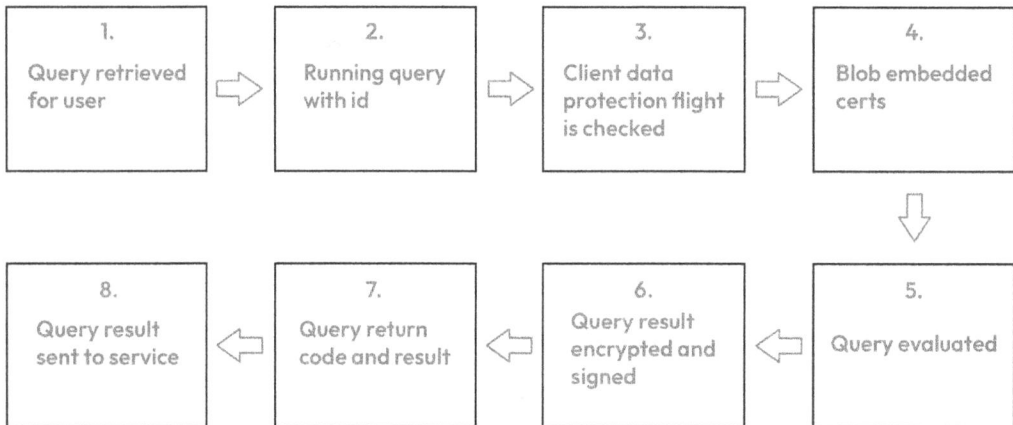

Figure 4.19: The important steps of SDQ as viewed in the IME logs

Now, let's break down each of the eight steps and correlate them with relevant excerpts from the IME logs:

1.   In this step, the query is received for the user. The user would be the Entra ID UPN who has enrolled and is using the device against which the SDQ has been run. In the following sample log, located at `C:\ProgramData\Microsoft\IntuneManagementExtension\Logs`, we can see the user ID, which will be the object ID of the user.

[IntunePivot] Query retrieved for user **250e0e1b-e562-4c32-a7f1-5e629a6fec26** in session 5, raw payload truncated:

```
[{"PolicyType":13,"PolicyPayload":"{\"QueryId\":\"ce127ff2-dd50-
4b0d-8a36-3a61ca44c338\",\"QueryAsS        IntuneManagementExtension
07-07-2025 12:59:01 54 (0x0036)
```

The user ID from the preceding IME logs matches the object ID of the user who has enrolled the device and is logged in.

Figure 4.20: The user's object ID as viewed in the Intune/Entra portal

2. Now, the query is executed. Each query is assigned a unique query ID along with a timestamp, as illustrated in the following log excerpt:

```
[IntunePivot] Running query with id: ce127ff2-dd50-4b0d-8a36-
3a61ca44c338 IntuneManagementExtension    07-07-2025 12:59:01   54
(0x0036)
```

3. Client data protection is checked, which secures the query process and logs it:

```
[IntunePivot] Client data protection flight is: True. Query
input b64 encoding is: False. Data protection is: True.
IntuneManagementExtension  07-07-2025 12:59:01   54 (0x0036)
```

4. The certificates from DigiCert and Microsoft Azure RSA are embedded, which will be used for signing later:

```
[IntunePivot] Blob embedded certs:DigiCert Global Root
G2:DigiCert Global Root G2|01-08-2013 17:30:00|15-01-
2038 17:30:00|DF3C24F9BFD666761B268073FE06D1CC8D4F82A4
||| Microsoft Azure RSA TLS Issuing CA 07:DigiCert
Global Root G2|08-06-2023 05:30:00|26-08-2026
05:29:59|3382517058A0C20228D598EE7501B61256A76442
```

5. The query evaluation is finished, and the timestamp is logged:

```
[IntunePivot] Finished evaluating Query    IntuneManagementExtension
07-07-2025 12:59:15 54 (0x0036)
```

6. The result of the query is encrypted and signed:

```
[IntunePivot] Encrypting and signing query result for QueryId =
ce127ff2-dd50-4b0d-8a36-3a61ca44c338        IntuneManagementExtension
07-07-2025 12:59:15 54 (0x0036)
```

7. The query return code is logged. A return code of 0 signifies the successful running of the query on the device:

```
[IntunePivot] Completed getting results, return code: 0
IntuneManagementExtension    07-07-2025 12:59:15    54 (0x0036)
[IntunePivot] Ran query complete, query result: QueryId =
ce127ff2-dd50-4b0d-8a36-3a61ca44c338; QueryReturnCode=0;
QueryErrorMessage={"Summary":{"ReturnedRowCount":"7",
"TruncatedRowCount":"0"},"ErrorMessage":null}; QueryResultAsString.
Length=16409 IntuneManagementExtension    07-07-2025 12:59:15    54
(0x0036)
```

> While we can't view the exact query or its output on the device's logs, the log shows a ReturnRowCount value, indicating how many values the query returned.

In the preceding sample logs, the `ReturnedRowCount` value of 7 signifies that there were 7 values returned, which corresponds with the 7 output items we see as the query result in the Intune portal, as seen here:

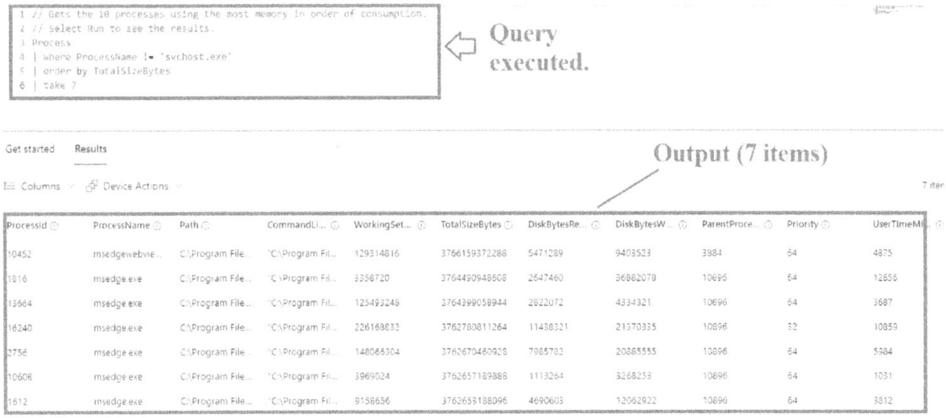

Figure 4.21: The output of the SDQ in the Intune portal

8. The result of the query is sent to the Intune service and displayed in the portal:

```
[IntunePivot] Sending query result with GW session id 66aafbad-3e1e-
4d15-a730-76725f9eeefb ... IntuneManagementExtension    07-07-2025
12:59:16    54 (0x0036)
```

In this section, we learned how to correlate the SDQ flow with IME logs on the device, providing clearer insight into the query processing at the device level.

When executing an SDQ, it must be targeted at a specific property or category, such as CPU, process, registry, and so on. In the next section, we'll delve deeper into these properties and review the list of available properties in the schema that can be queried.

What SDQ queries can we run from the Intune portal?

The Intune data platform schema outlines the structure and scope of data accessible through **Device query**. It defines how device and inventory data is structured, queried, and consumed across Microsoft Intune. Each of the access points in the data platform supports a set of entities (tables) and properties (columns) that can be queried using KQL.

The following is a list of properties that are supported to be queried from the Intune data platform using SDQ:

Category	Details
BiosInfo	Retrieves basic information about the BIOS of the device
Certificate	Retrieves information about the installed certificates for the computer
Cpu	Retrieves information about the CPU of the device
DiskDrive	Retrieves information about the physical disks of the device
EncryptableVolume	Retrieves information about the encryptable volume status of the device
FileInfo	Retrieves information about the specified file or files under the specified directory on the device
LocalGroup	Retrieves information about the local groups on the device
LocalUserAccount	Retrieves information about the local user accounts on the device
LogicalDrive	Retrieves information about the logical drives of the device
MemoryInfo	Retrieves information about the memory of the device
OsVersion	Retrieves information about the operating system version of the device, such as Android, iOS, iPadOS, or Windows
Process	Retrieves information about the running process on the device
SystemEnclosure	Retrieves information about the chassis and security status of the device
SystemInfo	Retrieves system information of the device
Tpm	Retrieves information about the TPM of the device
WindowsAppCrashEvent	Retrieves information about app crashes from the Application log on the device
WindowsDriver	Retrieves information about in-use Windows device drivers on the device
WindowsEvent	Retrieves information from the specified information from a specified log on the device
WindowsQfe	Retrieves information about security updates on the device
WindowsRegistry	Retrieves information about the registry under the specified registry key
WindowsService	Retrieves information about the installed Windows services on the device

Table 4.2: List of available properties for SDQ

Device query serves as an essential tool for real-time troubleshooting, offering immediate insights into individual devices. Whether you're verifying TPM configurations, reviewing CPU specifications/memory utilization, or exploring other system attributes, it delivers precise answers on demand. The following screenshot highlights the UI categories against which SDQs can be performed:

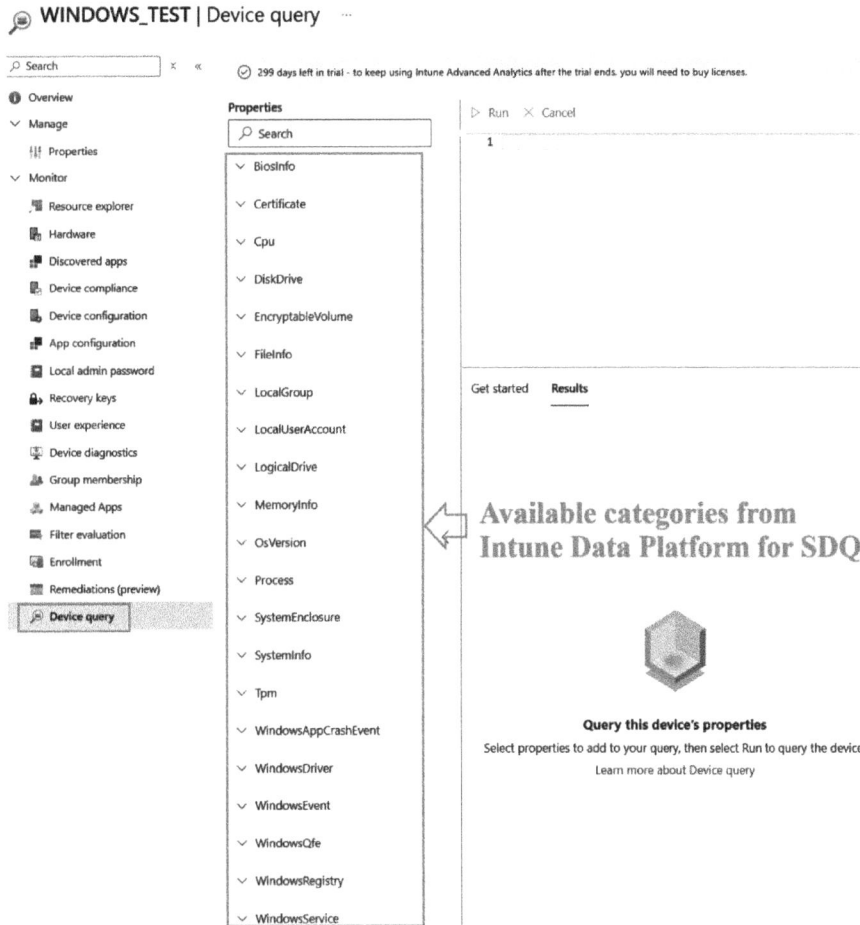

Figure 4.22: The available properties/categories for SDQ in the portal

During the writing of the book, there are 21 distinct categories against which we can fetch information from the Intune data platform using SDQ. This list of categories is expected to increase with time, based on feedback.

Let's take a look at a couple of sample queries, referencing these categories:

- **Scenario 1:** Get the 10 processes using the most memory in order of consumption. Here is the query:

```
Process
| where ProcessName != 'svchost.exe'
| order by TotalSizeBytes
| take 10
```

- **Scenario 2**: Get the registry keys and values under the Run registry key to identify the list of apps that are set to run automatically at startup. Here is the query:

```
WindowsRegistry('HKEY_LOCAL_MACHINE\Software\Microsoft\Windows\
CurrentVersion\Run') | project RegistryKey, ValueName, ValueType,
ValueData
```

Next, let's briefly go through a couple of frequently asked questions about SDQ to enhance understanding and provide better clarity:

- **Data source**: Where is the SDQ data response coming from?

  The response to the SDQ comes directly from the device. The end device needs to be powered on and connected to the internet in order to generate and send the response. The IME agent needs to be installed in the device, and the device should be marked as **Corporate**.

- **Data freshness**: How old is the SDQ response data?

  The response to the SDQ is in real time, as established in the previous section.

Up to this point, we've understood the importance and benefits of running SDQs, particularly for troubleshooting specific scenarios and accessing volatile device data.

SDQ is optimized for real-time diagnostics on individual endpoints, making it effective for focused troubleshooting. However, its scope is limited—it doesn't provide visibility across the broader device ecosystem. As a result, it falls short in identifying fleet-wide trends, enforcing compliance, or conducting large-scale analysis. Without the ability to aggregate or correlate data across multiple devices, SDQ becomes inefficient and time-consuming for enterprise-level insights.

In the next section, we'll explore how MDQ addresses gaps and walk through its configuration process within the Intune portal.

Multi-device query

MDQ overcomes SDQ limitations by enabling holistic analysis across your entire device fleet. It's designed to surface patterns, detect compliance gaps, and highlight misconfigurations at scale. With MDQ, IT teams can shift from reactive troubleshooting to proactive device management, driving operational efficiency and a stronger security posture.

MDQ empowers IT administrators to efficiently identify devices that meet specific criteria—such as all Windows machines experiencing a particular application crash—or to generate summaries, such as counting devices with a certain CPU type. These queries operate on pre-collected inventory data rather than executing in real time on the devices themselves, ensuring performance efficiency while providing valuable insights across the device fleet!

> MDQ also utilizes the same Intune data platform schema as used in the SDQ scenario, meaning the query structure remains consistent. However, MDQ extends this schema with additional categories, offering a broader range of data points to query against

High-level steps for configuring MDQ

The following is a high-level view of the steps needed in order to make use of MDQ in our tenant:

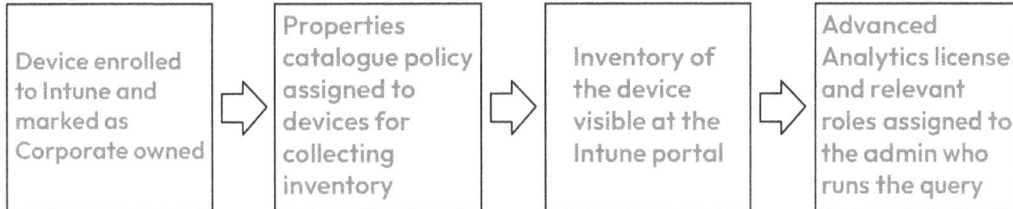

Figure 4.23: Block diagram explaining steps for configuring MDQ

Let's now break down the preceding four blocks into four distinct steps and examine each one in detail:

1. The first step involves enrolling the device in Intune. The enrolled device must be marked as **Corporate** and not personally owned.

    Intune automatically marks the following devices as **Corporate** post-enrollment:

    - Devices enrolled via DEM account
    - iOS/iPadOS/macOS devices enrolled via ABM/ASM
    - Devices enrolled via Autopilot
    - Co-managed devices enrolled via the ConfigMgr agent

- Hybrid Windows devices enrolled using GPO
- AVDs
- Windows devices enrolled using .ppkg (provisioning packages)
- Android devices enrolled via KME or Google ZTE
- Android fully managed and dedicated devices
- Corporate-owned userless devices and corporate-owned devices with a work profile
- AOSP devices

> If we enroll devices in our tenant using any other methodology from the ones listed, we can add the corporate identifier of those devices ahead of time in the Intune portal. Adding the corporate identifier will mark the device as **Corporate**, irrespective of the mode/methodology of enrollment. Intune supports IMEI, serial number, and manufacturer/model (Windows only) as corporate identifiers. Windows corporate identifiers only apply at enrollment time, and they don't determine ownership type in Intune after enrollment.
>
> It is also possible to change device ownership from **Personal** to **Corporate** manually post-enrollment by going into the device's properties in the Intune portal.

2. The second step involves collecting Device Inventory from the Windows devices in our organization using Properties catalogue. After the Device Inventory is collected, we will be able to perform MDQ from the portal against the inventory.

As seen here, under **Profile type**, select **Properties catalog**:

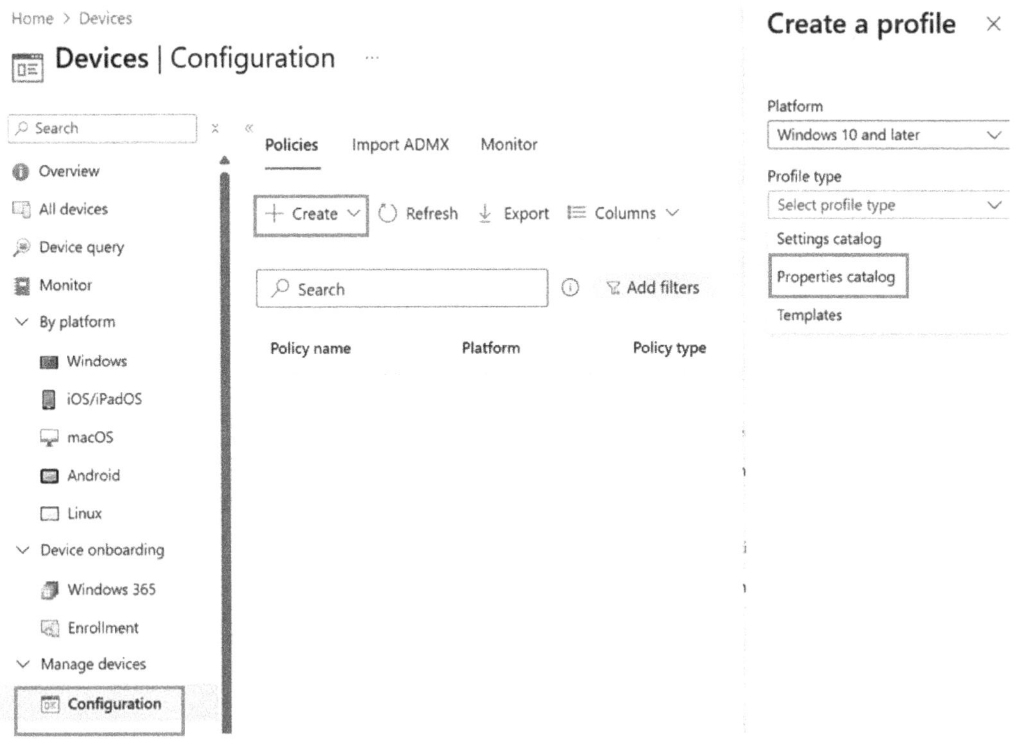

Home > Devices

Devices | Configuration   ...

Create a profile   ×

Platform

Windows 10 and later   ∨

Profile type

Select profile type   ∨

Settings catalog

Properties catalog

Templates

Policies   Import ADMX   Monitor

+ Create ∨   ○ Refresh   ↓ Export   ☰ Columns ∨

🔍 Search   ⓘ   ☶ Add filters

Policy name   Platform   Policy type

Search   ×   «
ⓘ Overview
🖳 All devices
🖉 Device query
🖵 Monitor
∨ By platform
   🪟 Windows
   📱 iOS/iPadOS
   🖥 macOS
   📱 Android
   ☐ Linux
∨ Device onboarding
   🖳 Windows 365
   🖾 Enrollment
∨ Manage devices
   🗔 **Configuration**

Figure 4.24: The steps for creating a Properties catalog profile for a Windows device in the portal

Now, we need to select **+ Add properties**. Expand the categories to view individual properties and then select the properties you would like to collect from the Properties picker.

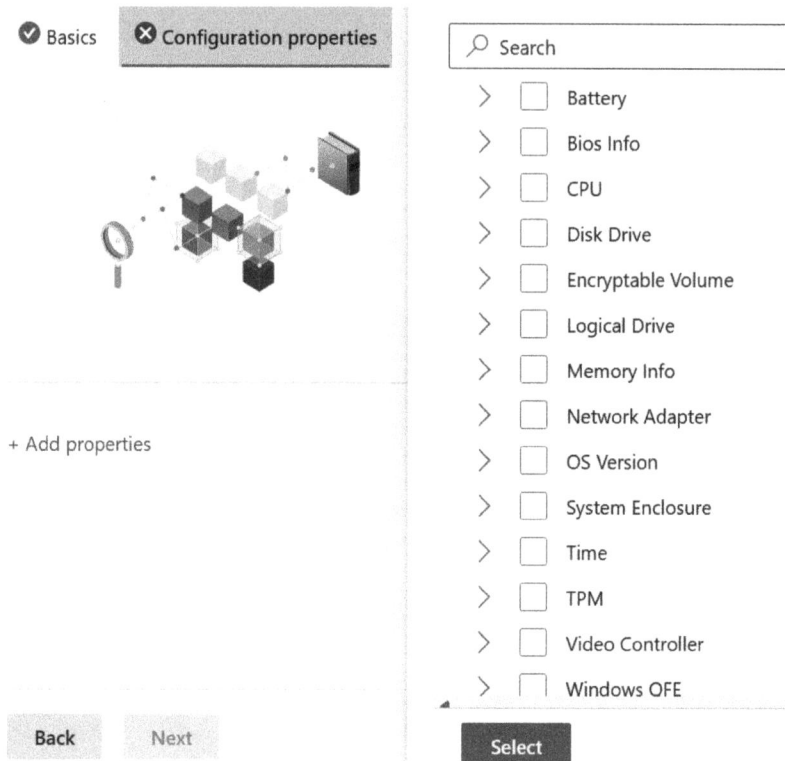

Figure 4.25: The attributes that can be collected from the device by the profile

This profile basically allows us to select which properties we would like to collect from our devices. Once done, the policy can then be assigned to a scoped group.

> Microsoft has renamed the **Resource explorer** blade in the Intune portal to **Device inventory** around Ignite 2025. This is only a name change; the functionality remains the same. In this chapter, you will see images referring to both versions from the Intune portal.

3. After 24 hours, the inventory of the device that has been collected using the preceding policy is visible in the Intune portal. There is a new tab for each device named **Resource explorer**, wherein the collected inventory is made visible:

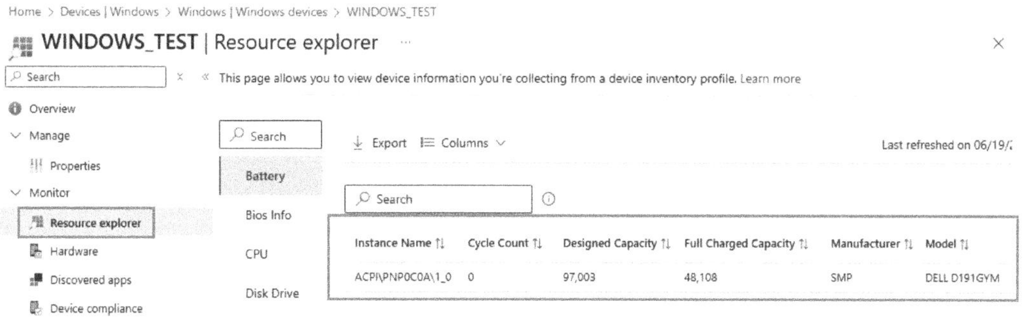

Figure 4.26: The collected values from a device by the Properties catalog profile

Data collected by the preceding profile is referred to as **Enhanced Device Inventory**. This data is refreshed every 24 hours and is stored for 28 days

Microsoft recommends using Device Inventory and Resource Explorer for the most up-to-date and comprehensive data about our devices.

4. Now that the device has sent its data to the Intune service and it's available under **Resource explorer** (now known as **Device inventory**), the data can now be queried using MDQ. The admin making the query should be licensed for Advanced Analytics/Intune Suite. If the admin is not a Global admin/Intune admin, we need to assign the permission at **Managed devices > Query and Organization > Read permissions**.

A maximum of 10 queries can be submitted per minute, and 1,000 queries can be submitted per month.

So far, we've explored the high-level steps involved in configuring inventory collection and executing MDQ. In the upcoming section, we'll dive deeper into the behind-the-scenes workflow that takes place during inventory collection and MDQ execution.

Detailed workflow behind MDQ

We will break down the flow of MDQ into two parts:

- The data collection for facilitating the MDQ
- Execution of the MDQ

Data collection for facilitating the MDQ

Let's first start with taking a closer look at the process behind the collection of data against which the MDQ operates:

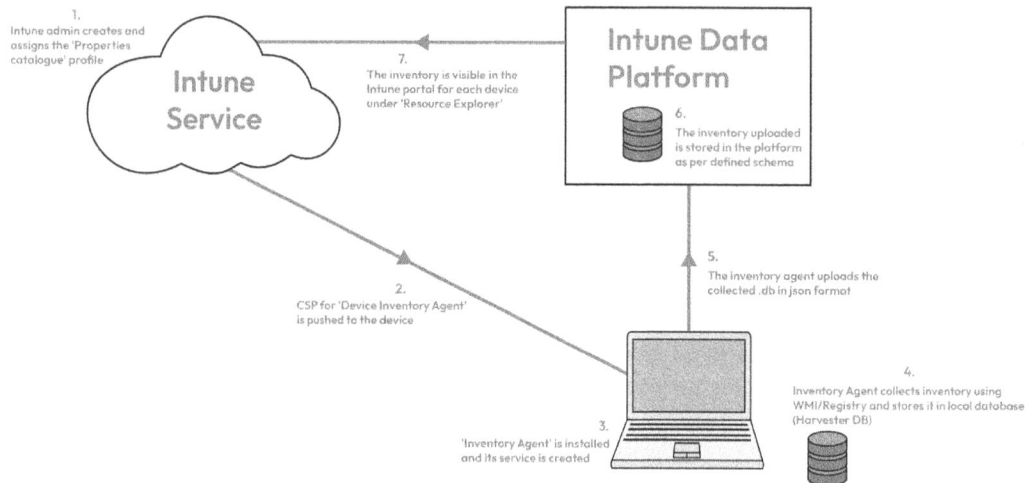

Figure 4.27: The flow behind data collection for MDQ/Resource explorer

Referencing the preceding diagram, let's break down the seven steps in detail and examine the corresponding logs and registry entries at each stage:

1. In the first step, the Intune admin creates and assigns the **Properties catalog** profile to a user/group. This profile only needs to be created for Windows devices. We don't need to create any profile explicitly for Android/iOS devices.

2. The CSP for the device inventory agent gets pushed to the device as seen by the following SyncML trace:

```
<Item>
  <Source>
    <LocURI>./Device/Vendor/MSFT/DeviceManageability/Provider/Microsoft%20Device%20Management/PayloadTransfer</LocURI>
  </Source>
  <Data>EnterpriseModernAppManagementHostedInstall;ExtensibilitySetting;ExtensibilityAdapter;DeviceAction;
    DeviceInventory;OpenExtensibilitySettings</Data>
</Item>
```

Figure 4.28: SyncML trace from a device

3. The **configuration service provider (CSP)** facilitates the deployment of a new enterprise desktop application on the device—namely, the inventory agent— ensuring its associated service is properly instantiated. The agent retrieves its configuration through linked or dual enrollment mechanisms tightly integrated with the MMP-C infrastructure. The relevant registry location is Computer\HKEY_LOCAL_MACHINE\SOFTWARE\Microsoft\

`EnterpriseDesktopAppManagement\S-0-0-00-0000000000-0000000000-000000000-0`
`00\MSI`, as seen here:

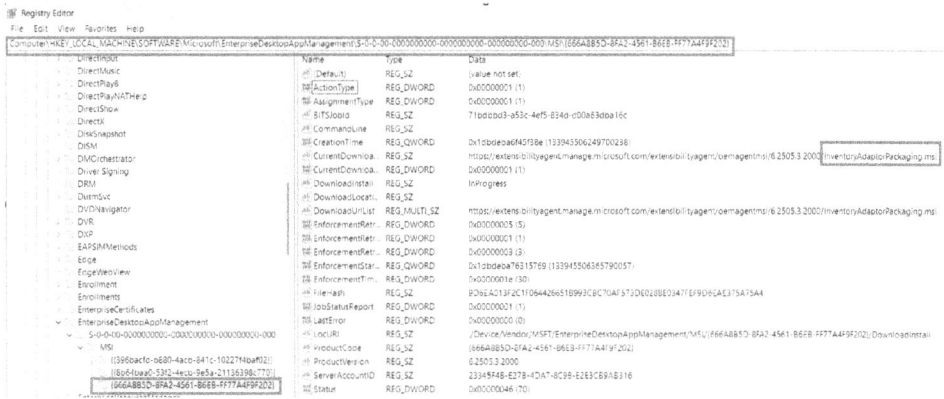

Figure 4.29: Registry from a device illustrating the Inventory agent MSI

There is a folder structure that gets created for the inventory agent, as shown here:

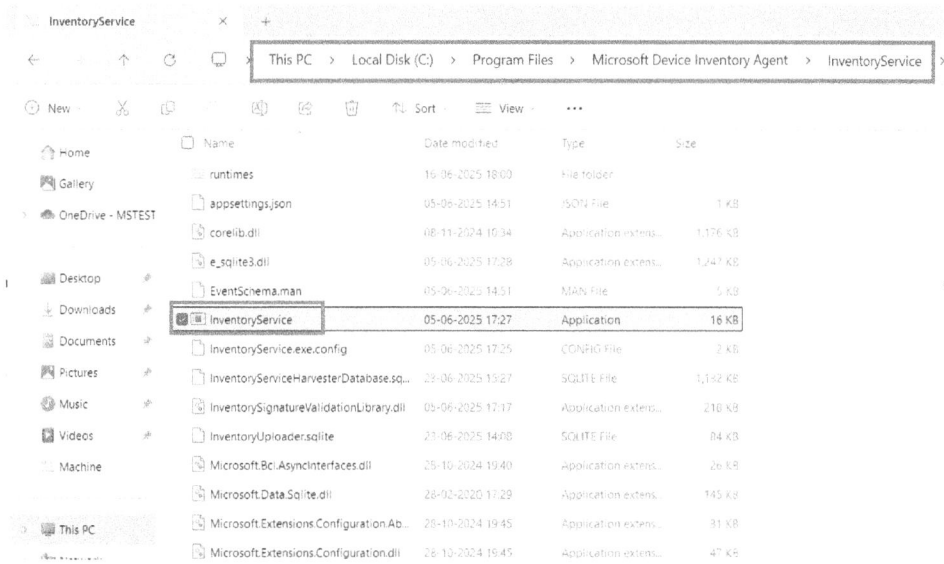

Figure 4.30: Folder structure of the Inventory agent from a device

A new inventory service is also created, which is responsible for inventory collection in the device, as shown here:

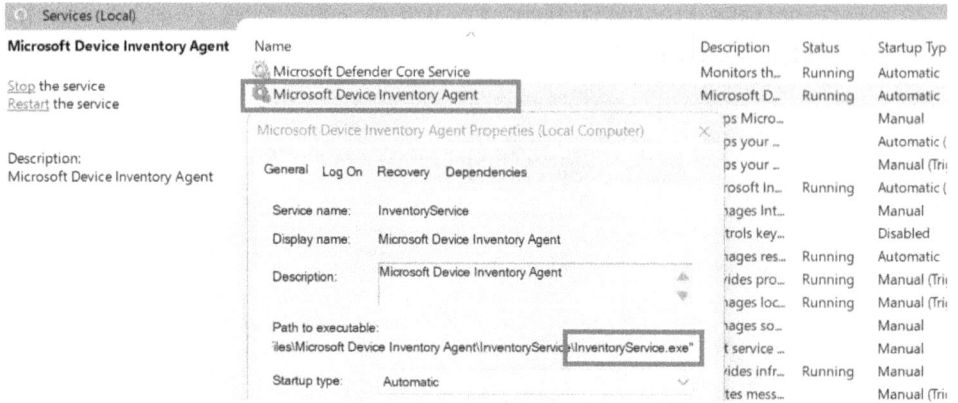

Figure 4.31: The inventory agent service

The relevant registry location for the device inventory agent is Computer\HKEY_LOCAL_MACHINE\SOFTWARE\Microsoft\DeviceInventory:

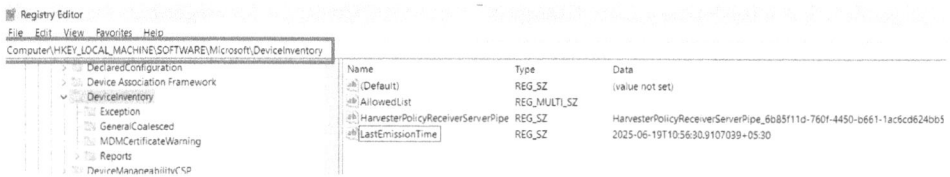

Figure 4.32: Relevant registry location for the DeviceInventory agent

A dedicated configuration document gets established for the Microsoft Device Inventory Agent. Similar to **Endpoint Privilege Management (EPM)**, which also utilizes declared configuration documents, the device inventory now follows this standardized approach. These documents depend on the **Windows Declared Configuration Service (dcsvc)** to fetch and update their configurations dynamically. The relevant registry location for the same is Computer\HKEY_LOCAL_MACHINE\SOFTWARE\Microsoft\DeclaredConfiguration\HostOS\Config\enrollments\xxx-xxx-xxxx\Device\state, as shown here:

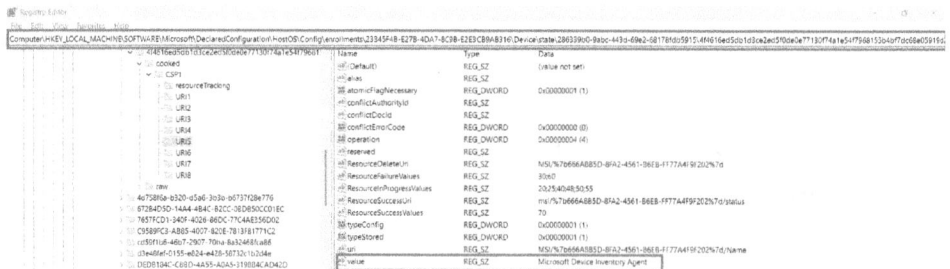

Figure 4.33: Relevant registry location for Device Inventory Agent

4. The Device Inventory Agent leverages **Windows Management Instrumentation (WMI)** to extract detailed hardware and system attributes, such as TPM status, processor specifications, and so on. Throughout the data collection life cycle, the inventory service meticulously logs each operation—capturing initiation and completion timestamps, along with any encountered errors—in the harvested status report.

The Device Inventory Agent collects system attributes and stores them locally in a dedicated database known as the **Harvester DB**. The Harvester DB is a SQLite-based repository that resides on each managed device and serves as the central store for inventory data. The inventory service uses it primarily for the following important functions:

- To log collected device information
- Monitor the application of inventory policies
- Identify data that needs to be uploaded to Intune

5. Upon completion of data collection, the Device Inventory agent initiates the data preparation phase by structuring the information into a standardized JSON format. This formatted data is then securely transmitted to the data platform service using an encrypted HTTP protocol. Concurrently, the agent updates the registry with the latest upload timestamp and logs the successful completion of the transfer process.

6. The inventory collected from the device is uploaded to the Intune data platform and structured and labeled there as per the predefined schema.

7. The Intune service queries the Intune data platform, and the collected inventory is now made visible in the Intune portal (per device basis) under the **Device inventory** tab, as shown here:

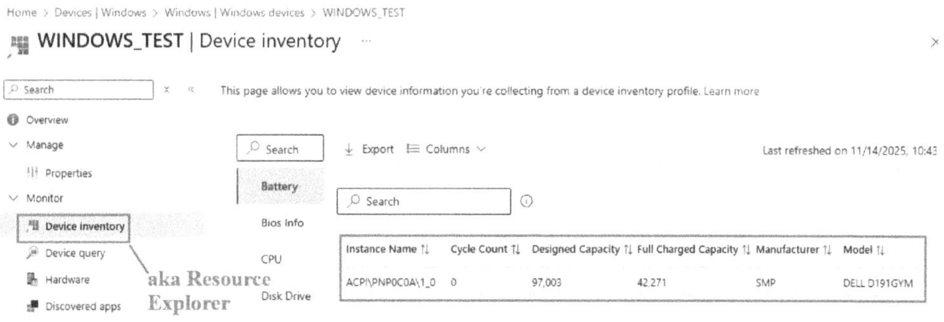

Figure 4.34: Data collected by the inventory agent

Until now, we have understood how device inventory data is collected and ingested into the Intune data platform, making it accessible to administrators via the Intune portal. Now the administrators can leverage this data to execute multi-device queries, enabling broader insights and more efficient device management.

In the next section, we will understand the flow behind running an MDQ from the Intune portal.

Execution of the MDQ

Now, let's reference a new diagram to understand the next sequence of steps that happen during an MDQ:

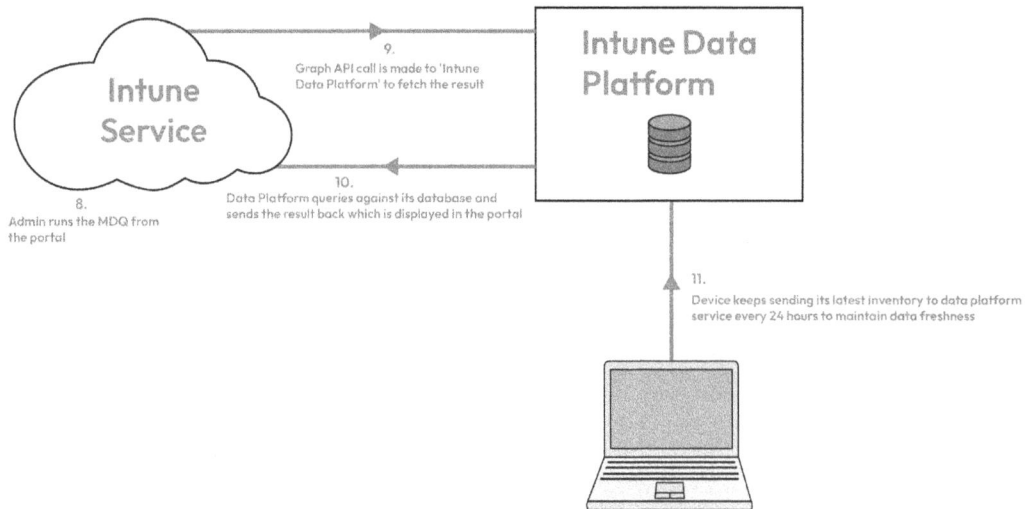

Figure 4.35: The flow behind the execution of an MDQ

8. The Intune administrator can now initiate an MDQ directly from the Intune portal. To do this, we need to navigate to **Devices** > **Device query**. Here, we can construct queries using any of the device properties that have already been collected. A searchable list of all available properties is provided, allowing admins to easily select the criteria they wish to query against, as shown here:

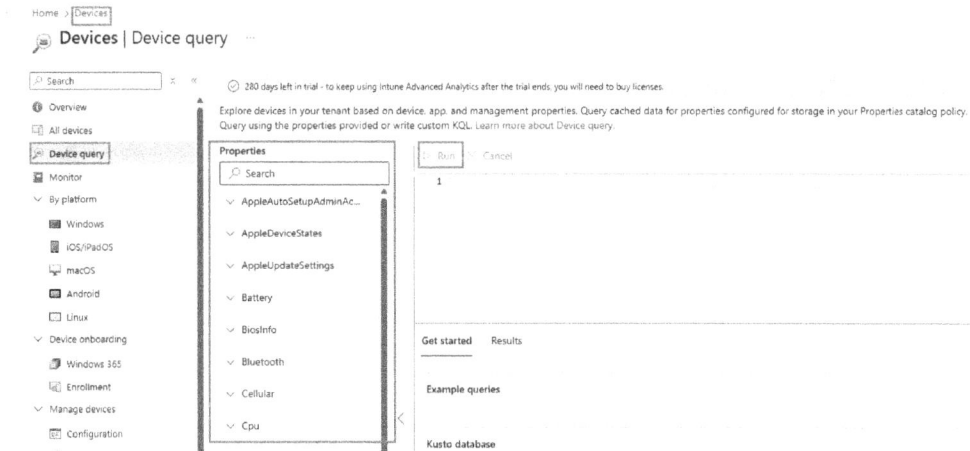

Figure 4.36: The execution of the MDQ from the Intune portal

9. Once the query is executed, the Intune portal—via the browser session—triggers a Graph API request to the Intune data platform. This request includes both the endpoint of the data platform and the specific query parameters defined by the administrator.

10. The Intune data platform processes the incoming query by scanning its dataset for matching records. Once the query execution is complete, the resulting data is returned to the Intune portal's browser session, where it is rendered and displayed to the administrator.

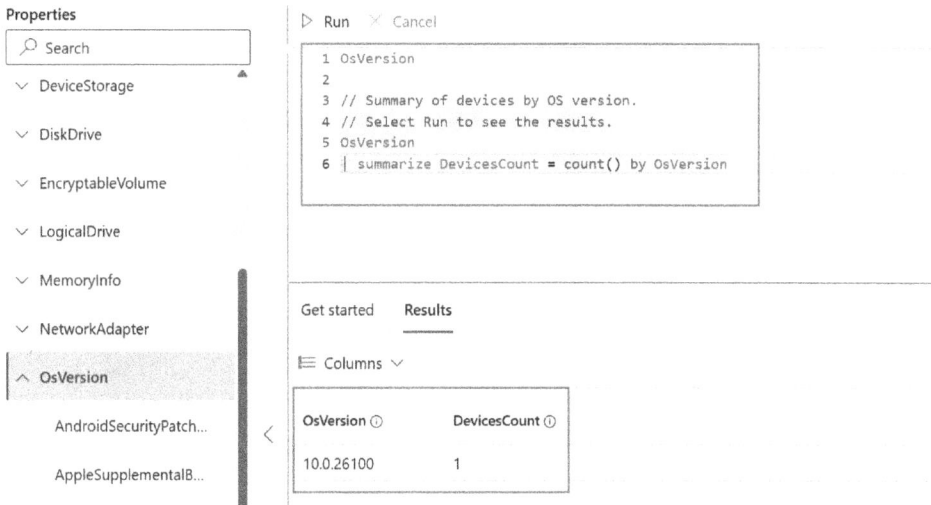

Figure 4.37: The output of MDQ

By taking an *F12* browser trace, we can establish that there are three Graph API calls that are being made by the browser. Two of them are POST calls, and one of them is a GET call, as shown here:

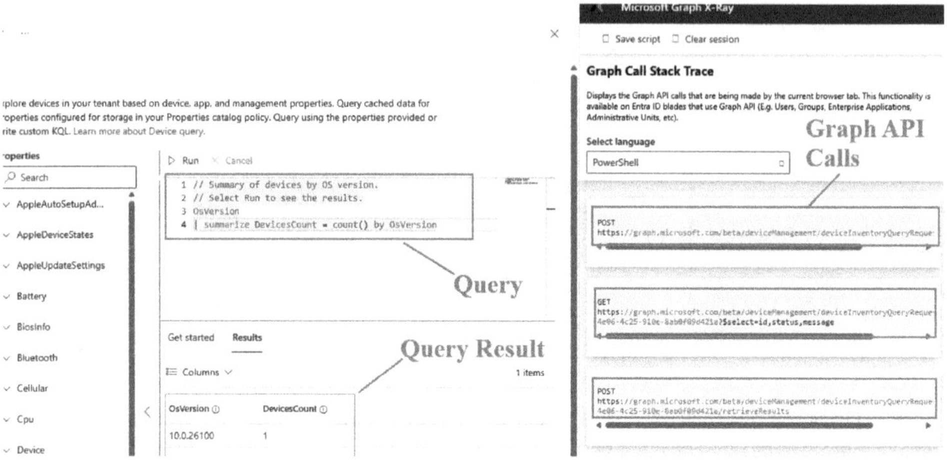

Figure 4.38: The API calls made by the browser during the execution of the MDQ

As seen in the screenshot of the browser session, these are the API calls that are made during an MDQ:

- POST:

```
https://graph.microsoft.com/beta/deviceManagement/
deviceInventoryQueryRequests/initiateQuery
```

- GET:

```
https://graph.microsoft.com/beta/deviceManagement/
deviceInventoryQueryRequests/fba97671-4e06-4c25-910e-8ab0f09d
421a?$select=id,status,message
```

- POST:

```
https://graph.microsoft.com/beta/deviceManagement/
deviceInventoryQueryRequests/fba97671-4e06-4c25-910e-
8ab0f09d421a/retrieveResults
```

11. All the devices keep sending their inventory data periodically (usually every 24 hours) to ensure that the information in the Intune data platform is up to date.

> Inventory uploads occur once every 24 hours; hence, changes made in the device won't be reflected in the portal in real time.
>
> As discussed previously, an MDQ pulls data from the uploaded inventory, not from the device directly; hence, we get query results even if the devices are not powered on/connected to the internet.

Usage of Device query

We should use an SDQ when we need to perform live troubleshooting and retrieve volatile data—information that can change frequently and reflects the device's current state. Examples include checking which services are actively running or identifying applications consuming memory or CPU at a specific moment.

We should use an MDQ when analyzing non-volatile data—details that remain relatively stable over short periods and are suitable for fleet-wide assessments. This includes attributes such as BitLocker encryption status, operating system version, or available disk space.

Now, let's do a quick side-by-side comparison of SDQ and MDQ to see when to use each and where they pull their data from:

	SDQ	MDQ
Data freshness	Queries are executed in real time on the selected device	Queries run against collected inventory data, not live data
Use case	Ideal for troubleshooting individual devices, such as checking registry keys, file existence, event logs, or installed applications	Best for fleet-wide insights, such as identifying all devices missing a patch, running a specific OS version, or lacking disk encryption
Data scope	21 items	Limited to what's collected via the Properties catalog

Table 4.3: Comparison between single- and multi-device queries

We will now take a look at a couple of sample queries and scenarios, pertaining to MDQ, to better understand its usage:

- **Scenario 1**: Due to a security audit requirement, we need to get a list of all the Windows devices that are not encrypted via BitLocker. For these devices, we also need to get the TPM version and manufacturer. Here is the query:

```
EncryptableVolume
| where Device.OsDescription contains 'Windows'
| where ProtectionStatus != 'PROTECTED' or EncryptionPercentage == 0
| join (Tpm)
| project Device.DeviceId, Device.DeviceName, ManufacturerVersion,
Manufacturer, Activated, Enabled, Owned, Device.Encrypted
```

- **Scenario 2**: We need to install a heavy application, such as AutoCAD, on the device. Before this, we need to make sure the device has sufficient resources to run the app. Hence, we need to get a list of Windows devices that have at least 8 GB of RAM and more than 50 GB of storage space, and at least 1 volume encrypted. Here is the query:

```
MemoryInfo
| where PhysicalMemoryTotalBytes >= 8589934592
| join (LogicalDrive | where DiskSizeBytes > 53687091200)
| join (EncryptableVolume | where EncryptionPercentage > 0)
| where Device.OsDescription contains 'Windows'
| project Device.DeviceId, Device.DeviceName,
PhysicalMemoryTotalBytes, DiskSizeBytes, EncryptionPercentage
```

MDQ can be used in so many ways, and the two examples given are just a glimpse of its potential. They show how simple it is to run queries and pull data from a large set of devices without much effort.

Now, let's explore a couple of FAQs to deepen our understanding and build upon the insights we've covered so far:

- **What is the purpose of Resource explorer in Microsoft Intune?**

  Resource explorer in Microsoft Intune is a powerful feature that empowers IT administrators with granular visibility into device hardware inventory. Accessible via the Intune portal, it presents detailed insights into individual device attributes such as TPM configuration, CPU specifications, disk health, and more.

This functionality is powered by the Device Inventory Agent, which utilizes WMI to collect system data every 24 hours. The collected data remains available in **Resource explorer** for up to 28 days, enabling historical analysis and informed decision-making.

To activate this capability, administrators must deploy a **Properties catalog** policy that defines which hardware attributes to gather. Once configured, the agent begins automated data collection, which is then surfaced per device within the **Resource explorer** interface. This new set of inventories is also referred to as *Enhanced Device Inventory* in Microsoft Intune.

Importantly, **Resource explorer** is included at no extra cost with Intune Plan 1, requiring no additional licensing, making it a cost-effective solution for scalable device inventory management.

- **Explain the relationship between MDQ, Resource explorer, and Enhanced Device Inventory within Intune:**

MDQ, **Resource explorer**, and Enhanced Device Inventory are interconnected components within Microsoft Intune that together provide a comprehensive device data management and troubleshooting ecosystem. Here's how they relate:

  - **Enhanced Device Inventory, the foundation**: Automatically collects detailed hardware data (e.g., TPM, CPU, and disk health) from managed Windows devices every 24 hours using the Device Inventory Agent. This data is uploaded to the Intune data platform, a centralized repository. Admins define what data to collect via a **Properties catalog** policy.
  - **Resource explorer, the viewer**: Displays the inventory data collected by the Device Inventory Agent for each device.
  - **MDQ, the analyzer**: Allows admins to run KQL queries across multiple devices using the data stored in the Intune data platform.

> To summarize, the **Properties catalog** profile collects Enhanced Device Inventory. The Enhanced device Inventory is made visible in the portal under the **Resource explorer** view/tab. Admins can query the data collected across multiple devices using MDQ.

So far, we've explored how SDQ and MDQ can be effectively leveraged by administrators to tackle a variety of troubleshooting scenarios. However, not everyone is proficient in crafting KQL queries. In the next section, we'll look at how natural language can be used to generate KQL queries more efficiently with the assistance of Security Copilot.

Copilot integration into Device query

Microsoft Security Copilot (which includes Microsoft Intune) empowers IT admins and security professionals to perform real-time device queries using natural language prompts. This eliminates the need for deep knowledge of KQL, making Advanced Analytics and troubleshooting accessible to a broader audience.

Let's look at the following four sample use cases, each demonstrating how a natural language prompt can be used to generate a KQL query for different scenarios:

- **Use case 1, SDQ**: Verifying installation of a specific security KB on a device.

  Suppose we want to check whether a particular device has a specific security-related KB installed. We only have the KB number and need help structuring the KQL query.

  We can use a natural language prompt in Security Copilot to generate the KQL query. Here is an example prompt: `Was KB5044030 installed on this device?`

  Here is the generated KQL query:

  ```
  WindowsQfe
  | where HotFixId == 'KB5050575'
  | project HotFixId, InstalledDate, ComputerName
  ```

  The following is a screenshot from the Intune portal showing the same information for reference:

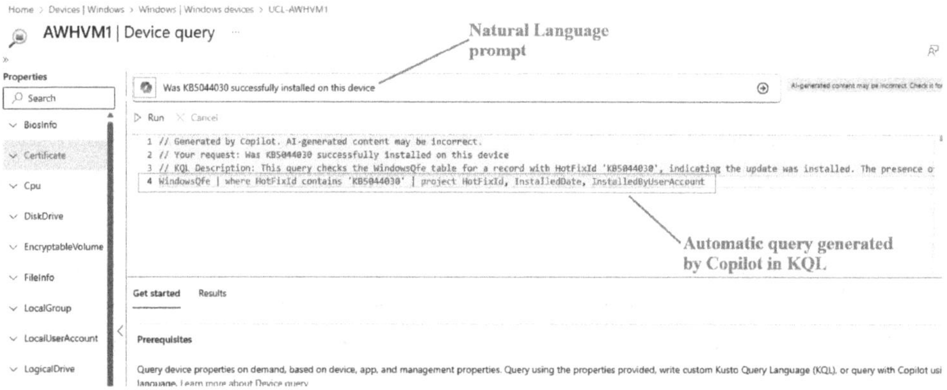

Figure 4.39: The generation of a device query using Security Copilot

The query output, shown next, displays the KB name and the corresponding computer name—confirming that the KB was successfully installed on the device:

```
▷ Run   ✕ Cancel

  1 WindowsQfe | where HotFixId =='KB5050575' | project HotFixId,ComputerName


Get started    Results

☰ Columns ∨    🖵 Device Actions ∨

⟨   HotFixId ⓘ              ComputerName ⓘ
```

Figure 4.40: Image illustrating the output of device query which was generated by Security Copilot

- **Use case 2, SDQ**: Validating the port set for RDP in the device's registry.

  We can use a natural language prompt in Security Copilot to generate the KQL query. Here is an example prompt: Show me the RDP port configured in the relevant registry in the device

  Here is the generated KQL query:

  ```
  WindowsRegistry('HKLM:\\SYSTEM\\CurrentControlSet\\Control\\Terminal
  Server\\WinStations\\RDP-Tcp') | where ValueName == 'PortNumber'
  ```

  Here is a screenshot from the Intune portal showing the same information for reference:

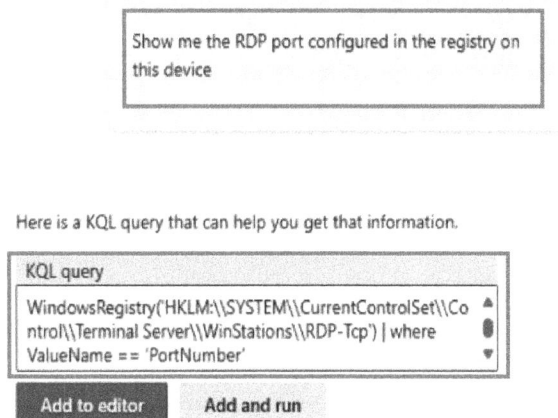

  Show me the RDP port configured in the registry on this device

  Here is a KQL query that can help you get that information.

  ```
  KQL query
  WindowsRegistry('HKLM:\\SYSTEM\\CurrentControlSet\\Co
  ntrol\\Terminal Server\\WinStations\\RDP-Tcp') | where
  ValueName == 'PortNumber'
  ```

  Add to editor   Add and run

Figure 4.41: The prompt and generation of a device query using Security Copilot

The query output, shown next, displays the value set in the REG_DWORD key PortNumber:

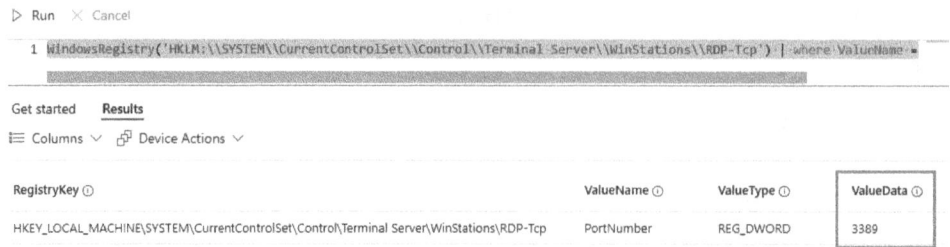

Figure 4.42: The output of the device query generated by Security Copilot

For reference, the following is the registry the query is referring to for this sample use case:

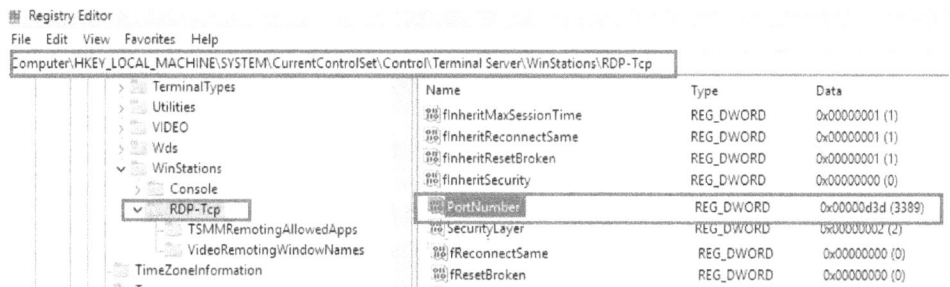

Figure 4.43: The relevant registry for RDP port

- **Use case 3, MDQ:** Validating how many Windows 11 24H2 devices in the organization have not been patched in the past 20 days.

We can use a natural language prompt in Security Copilot to generate the KQL query. Here is an example prompt: Show me how many devices running the windows version 10.0.26100 have not patched in last 20 days. Summarize the update counts. Display the Device name, OS version and architecture for those devices.

Here is the generated KQL query:

```
OsVersion
| where OsVersion == '10.0.26100' | join kind=leftouter (WindowsQfe)
| where isnull( InstalledDate) or InstalledDate <= ago(20d)
```

The following is a screenshot from the Intune portal showing the same information for reference:

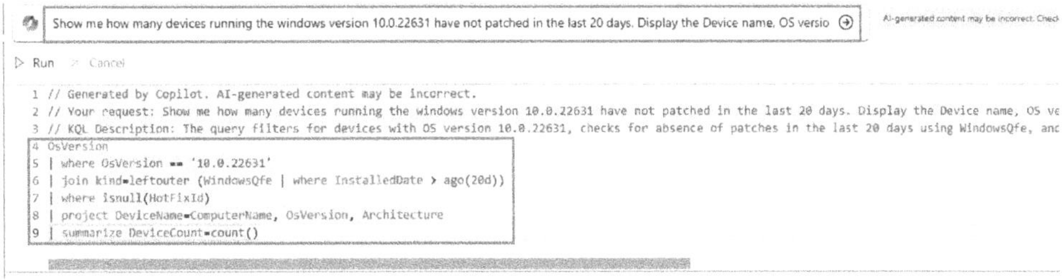

Figure 4.44: The prompt and the query generated by Security Copilot

The following query output shows the device name along with the date the patch was last installed:

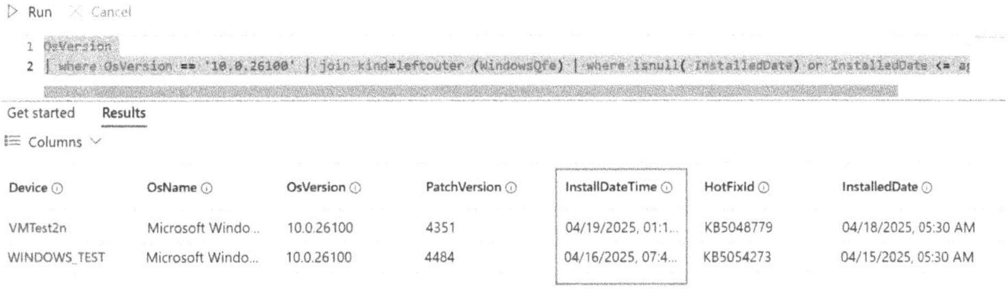

Figure 4.45: The output for the query, which was generated by Security Copilot

- **Use case 4, MDQ:** Validating how many Windows 11 24H2 devices in the organization have more than 50 GB of free space available.

We can use a natural language prompt in Security Copilot to generate the KQL query. Here is an example prompt: `Generate a report of all windows 11 devices running with OS version 10.0.26100 with more than 50gb storage`

Here is the generated KQL query:

```
OsVersion
| where OsName contains "Windows 11" and OsVersion contains
"10.0.26100" | join (LogicalDrive | where DiskSizeBytes >
53687091200)
```

The following is a screenshot from the Intune portal showing the same information for reference:

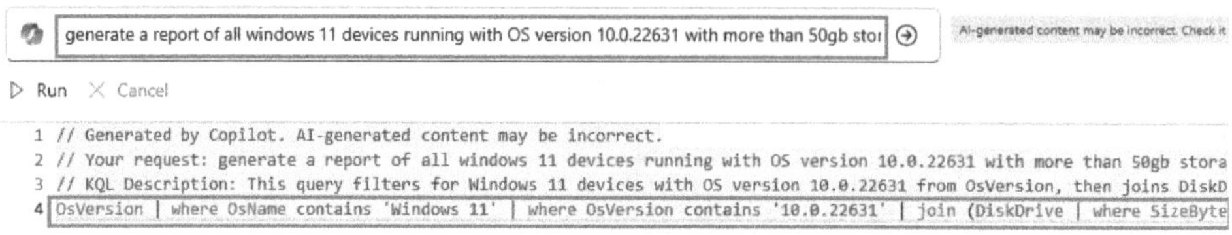

Figure 4.46: The prompt and the query generated by Security Copilot

The following query output shows the respective devices and the free space available in each of them, along with the relevant filesystem and the drive letter:

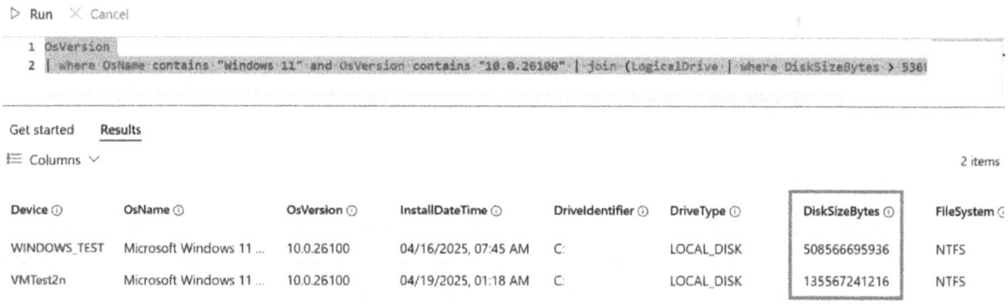

Figure 4.47: The output of the query, which was generated by Security Copilot

Now that we've learned how to efficiently write single- and multi-device queries using the power of Copilot and AI, in the next section, let's explore the **Battery health** feature of Advanced Analytics.

Battery health

The **Battery health** report offers comprehensive insights into the condition of device batteries across your organization and their impact on end user experience. By analyzing this data, you can proactively detect early signs of hardware degradation that may affect productivity—enabling you to take corrective action before users encounter issues or raise support requests.

The report also quantifies the potential improvement in overall device performance by replacing underperforming batteries. Additionally, it helps identify rapidly deteriorating batteries that may still be eligible for warranty replacement, allowing for timely intervention and cost savings.

The following screenshot highlights the **Battery health** scores using Advanced Analytics:

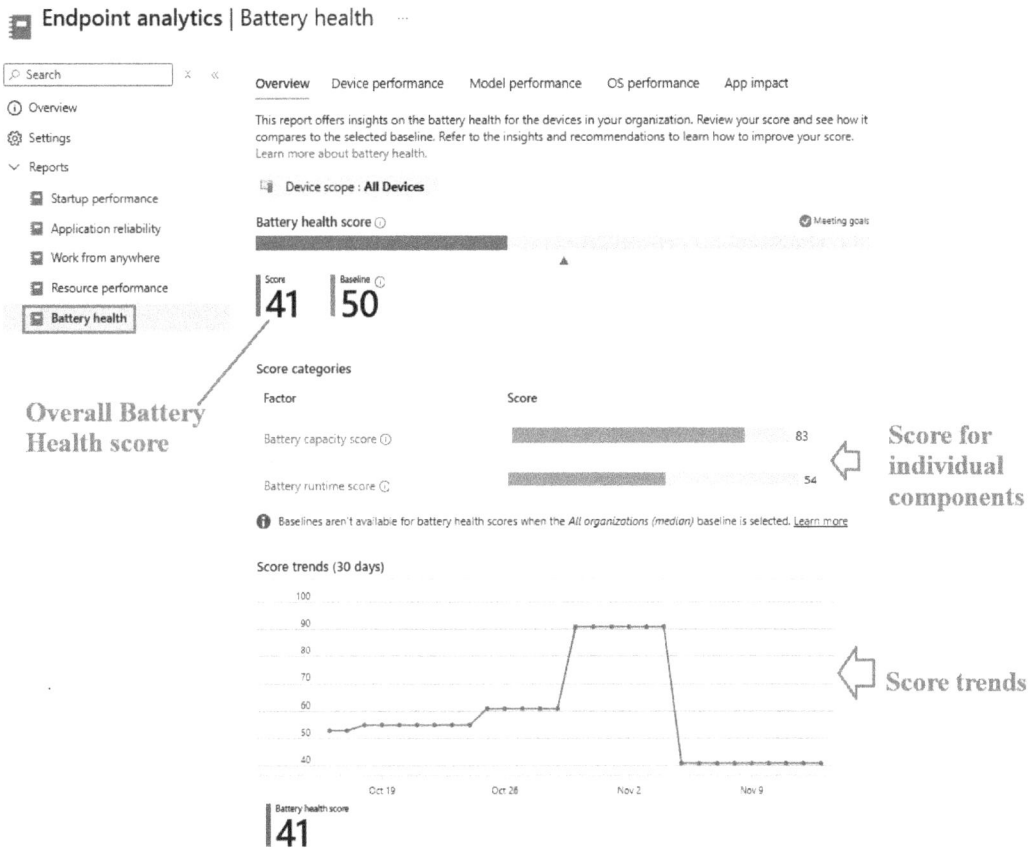

Figure 4.48: The Battery health score in the Intune portal

The following is a breakdown of the different metrics related to the **Battery health** score that is visible in the portal:

- The overall **Battery health** score gives an overview of laptop battery health, helping you identify batteries that need replacement. This score is essentially an average of the scores of two components—**Battery capacity score** and **Battery runtime score**:

  - **Battery capacity score:** This metric reflects the current battery capacity as a percentage compared to when it was new (with the original design capacity). A lower score indicates that the battery retains significantly less charge than when it was new. Devices with battery capacities below 60% are flagged as highly impacted, as they are likely to experience reduced performance and shorter operational time.

- **Battery runtime score:** This score estimates how long a device can operate on a full charge. Devices with an estimated runtime of less than 3 hours are considered critically impacted. Reduced runtime is often a consequence of diminished battery capacity. Such devices typically lead to suboptimal user experience, as they require frequent charging and limit mobility.

- If we go to the **Device performance** tab, we can see and export a list of all the physical Windows devices in the organization with their respective manufacturer/model details and estimated runtime on battery, as shown here:

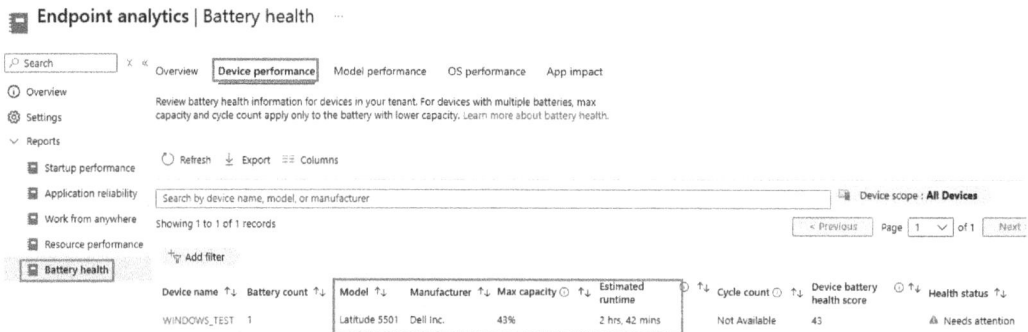

Figure 4.49: The battery health of each device in the Intune portal

This information also lets us identify whether a specific model of an OEM is having consistent battery issues across the environment.

In some cases, devices may report healthy battery capacity while still exhibiting low estimated runtimes. This discrepancy often arises when applications running on the device consume power at an accelerated rate.

Such scenarios typically indicate that users are relying on high-power or inefficient applications that may require optimization. The insights provided in this context help identify affected devices and suggest reviewing the **App impact** tab. This can reveal whether the short runtime is due to the necessary usage of resource-intensive apps or whether certain applications are consuming more power than expected due to inefficiencies.

It might take up to 48 hours (after license assignment) to see the **Battery health** data in our tenant.

The battery health is only captured for Windows devices that are Intune-only enrolled or co-managed.

So far, we've explored **Battery health** and its associated scores, which help proactively identify hardware issues that may require replacement. Now, let's move on to see how Advanced Analytics helps with detecting anomalies.

Anomaly detection

Anomaly detection is a vital capability for proactively identifying system irregularities, such as device restarts, application hangs, or crashes, before they evolve into critical disruptions. By harnessing real-time data and actionable insights, IT administrators can continuously monitor device health, swiftly troubleshoot issues, and maintain a seamless user experience and high productivity levels.

This technology plays a pivotal role in tracking the operational health of devices across an organization, especially in the wake of configuration changes. When anomalies are detected, the system intelligently correlates relevant deployment components, enabling rapid root cause analysis and suggesting targeted remediation steps.

Rather than relying solely on traditional support channels—which often surface only a fraction of the actual issues—**Anomaly detection** empowers administrators to uncover user-impacting problems early. Its initial focus includes detecting application failures and stopping error restarts, areas that frequently degrade user satisfaction and operational efficiency.

Historically, IT support teams have operated with limited visibility, responding reactively to reported incidents. **Anomaly detection** transforms this paradigm by offering a comprehensive, data-driven view of system behavior, allowing teams to address emerging issues before they escalate, ultimately fostering a more resilient and responsive IT environment.

In addition to detecting anomalies, Advanced Analytics also creates device correlation groups to explore potential root causes for anomalies. These groups allow us to view patterns identified among devices. We'll explore these correlation groups in greater detail in the next section.

As seen in the following figure, there are four levels of anomaly severity: **High**, **Medium**, **Low**, and **Informational**.

Home > Reports | Endpoint analytics >

ⓘ **Endpoint analytics** | Overview   ...

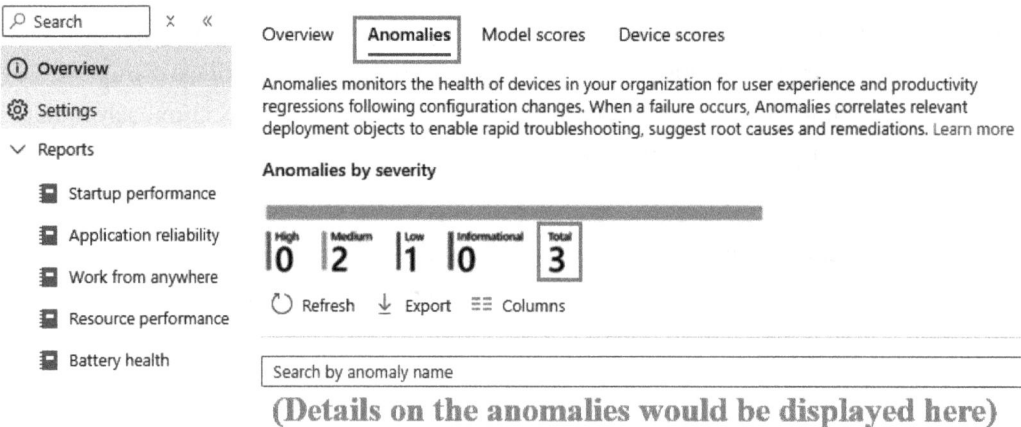

🔍 Search   ✕   «

ⓘ **Overview**

⚙ Settings

∨ Reports

    🖥 Startup performance

    🖥 Application reliability

    🖥 Work from anywhere

    🖥 Resource performance

    🖥 Battery health

Overview   **Anomalies**   Model scores   Device scores

Anomalies monitors the health of devices in your organization for user experience and productivity regressions following configuration changes. When a failure occurs, Anomalies correlates relevant deployment objects to enable rapid troubleshooting, suggest root causes and remediations. Learn more

Anomalies by severity

High	Medium	Low	Informational	Total
0	2	1	0	3

◯ Refresh   ↓ Export   ☰☰ Columns

Search by anomaly name

(Details on the anomalies would be displayed here)

Figure 4.50: The Anomalies score in the Intune portal

Advanced Analytics uses different statistical models (such as threshold-based heuristic models, paired t-tests models, time series Z-score model, etc.) for detecting and calculating anomalies.

In the next section, we'll explore **Device correlation groups**, another intelligent feature offered by Advanced Analytics.

Device correlation groups

When multiple devices experience the same anomaly, Advanced Analytics intelligently groups them based on shared characteristics such as application version, driver update, operating system version, or device model. This grouping enables IT administrators to pinpoint patterns and isolate root causes more effectively.

For instance, consider a scenario where five devices encounter a crash involving chrome.exe. If three of those devices are running the same version of Chrome—say, version 136.0.7103.93—Advanced Analytics will automatically cluster these devices together. This correlation highlights that this specific version may be more susceptible to the issue, offering a granular view into version-specific vulnerabilities.

Similarly, if four of the five affected devices are Dell Latitude 5400 laptops, the system will group them accordingly. This allows administrators to quickly identify that the anomaly may be linked to a particular hardware model, streamlining the troubleshooting process and informing targeted remediation strategies.

By surfacing these contextual groupings, **Anomaly detection** not only accelerates root cause analysis but also enhances the precision of IT operations.

In the following screenshot, we can see that devices that are showing an anomaly are intelligently grouped into two groups: based on application version and based on drivers.

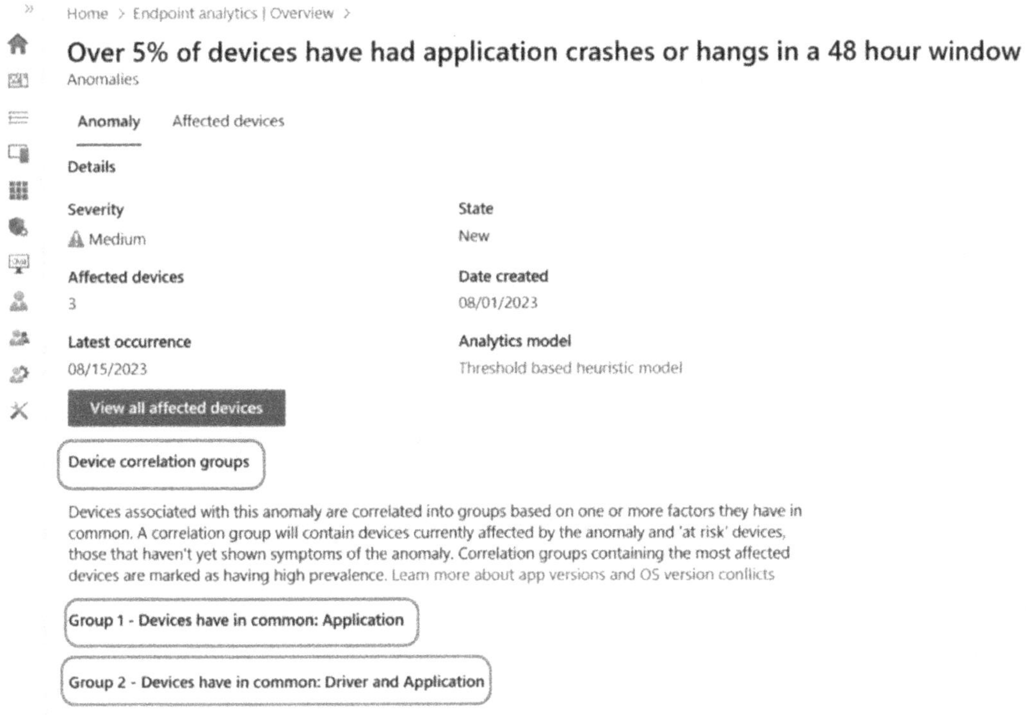

Figure 4.51: Correlation groups in the Intune portal

If we expand **Group 1** (which contains faulty devices grouped together on application version), we can see the name, publisher, and version of the application, as shown here:

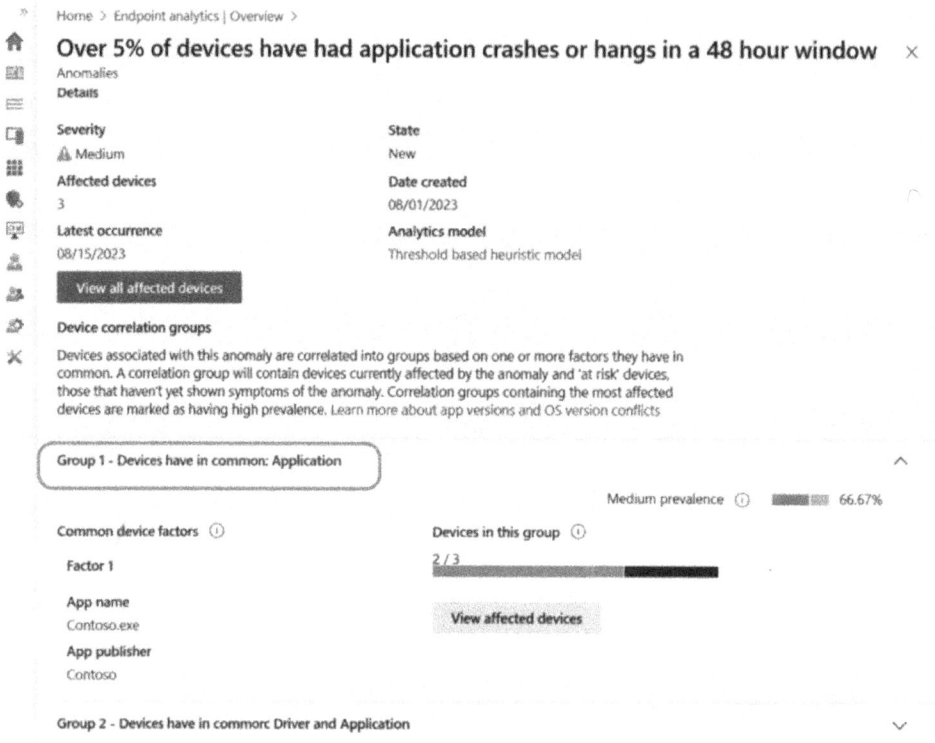

Figure 4.52: Correlation groups with application details in the Intune portal

In this section, we've explored how **Device correlation groups** within Advanced Analytics stream-lines troubleshooting by clustering similar or affected devices, enabling IT administrators to identify issues more accurately and resolve them efficiently.

In the next section, let's explore **Resource performance** scores and the insights they provide within Advanced Analytics.

Resource performance

The **Resource performance** report offers insights into CPU and RAM performance across cloud-managed Windows devices, highlighting how hardware efficiency impacts end-user experience.

The **Resource performance** score, ranging from 0 to 100, provides an overall rating of device performance within your organization, including both physical Windows devices and Cloud PCs. This score is calculated as a weighted average of two key metrics: **CPU spike time score** and **RAM spike time score**.

By monitoring this score, organizations can proactively detect emerging hardware issues that may affect user productivity, enabling action before support tickets are raised.

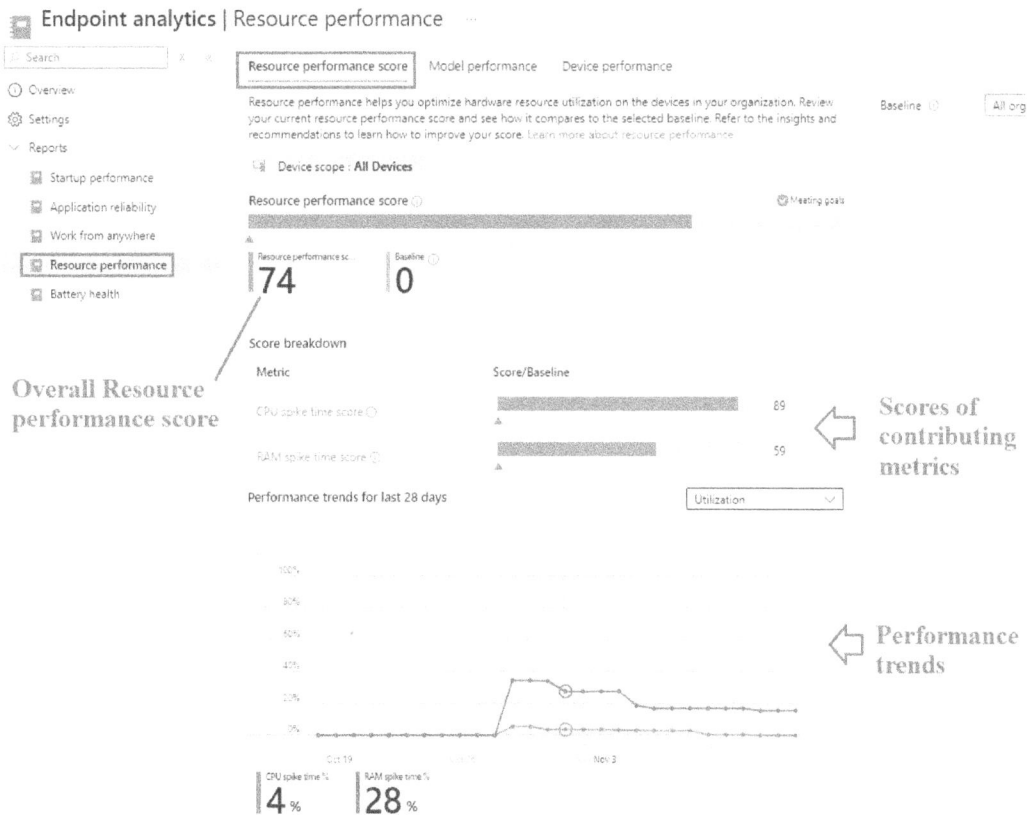

Figure 4.53: The Resource performance score in the Intune portal

As seen in the preceding figure, the **Resource performance** score is an average of the CPU spike time score and RAM spike time scores:

- **CPU spike time score**: This is a performance metric reflecting the percentage of time the CPU experiences high usage while the device is actively in use. Elevated spike times typically indicate degraded device responsiveness and contribute to a lower score, signaling a suboptimal user experience. A CPU usage exceeding 50% is classified as a spike:

  - **For Windows physical devices**: In the case of spikes, we can enhance performance by upgrading to processors with higher core counts or faster clock speeds. Additionally, we can optimize the operating system and adjust power management settings to reduce unnecessary CPU load.

- **For Cloud PCs**: In the case of spikes, we can enhance performance by transitioning to a higher-tier Cloud PC configuration that offers more robust CPU resources.

- **RAM spike time score**: This is a performance metric that measures the percentage of time a device's memory (RAM) operates under high usage while actively in use. Elevated RAM usage, particularly when it exceeds 75%, is classified as a spike and typically correlates with reduced system responsiveness and a lower overall score:

  - **For Windows physical devices**: In the case of spikes, we can enhance performance by increasing RAM capacity, upgrading to higher-speed modules, or fine-tuning UEFI/BIOS settings to enhance memory efficiency.

  - **For Cloud PCs**: In the case of spikes, we can enhance performance by upgrading to a higher-spec Cloud PC configuration to ensure sufficient memory resources for user workloads.

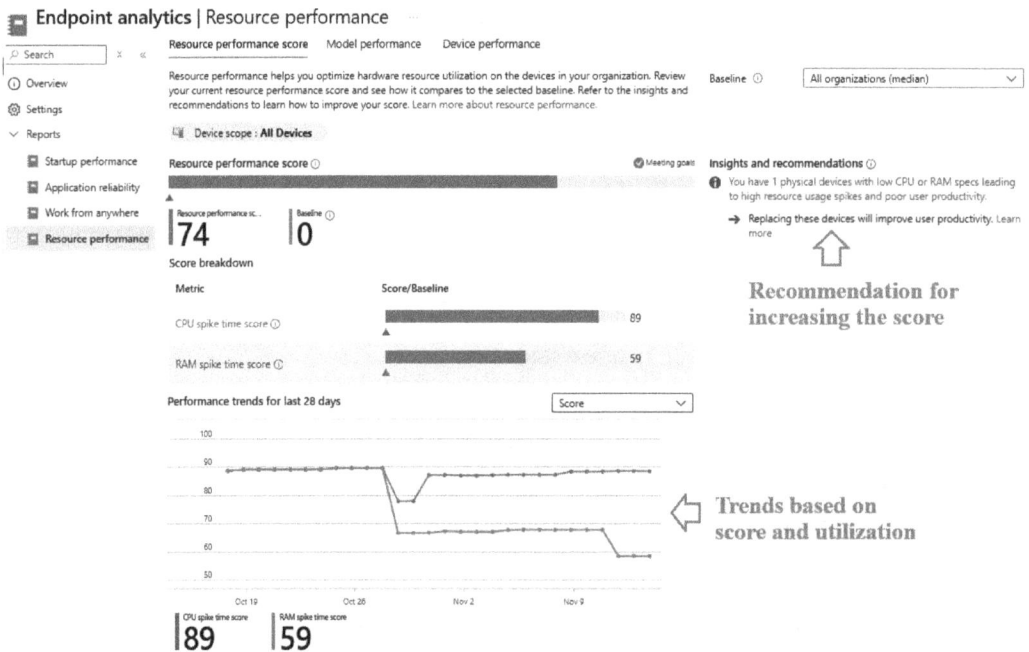

Figure 4.54: The Resource performance score and relevant recommendations

By navigating to the **Model performance** tab, you can view the CPU spike time score and RAM spike time score segmented by device model. This breakdown provides valuable insight into whether specific device models or OEMs are consistently exhibiting performance issues, enabling targeted investigation and remediation.

Home > Reports | Endpoint analytics > Endpoint analytics

Endpoint analytics | Resource performance ...

Resource performance score | Model performance | Device performance

View the resource performance for the device models in your organization. Select model devices to view their performance details. Learn more

○ Refresh   ↓ Export   ≡≡ Columns

Search by model or manufacturer   Device scope : **All Devices**

Showing 1 to 2 of 2 records   < Previous   Page 1 ∨ of 1

⁺ᵧ Add filter

Model ↑↓	Device count ↑↓	Manufacturer ↑↓	Resource performan... ↑↓	CPU spike time score ↑↓	RAM spike time score ↑↓	CPU spike time % ○ ↑↓	RAM spike time % ○ ↑↓	Health status ↑↓
Latitude 5501	1	Dell Inc.	88	88	88	0	0	⊘ Meeting goals
Virtual Machine	1	Microsoft Corporation	58	88	28	0	31	⊘ Meeting goals

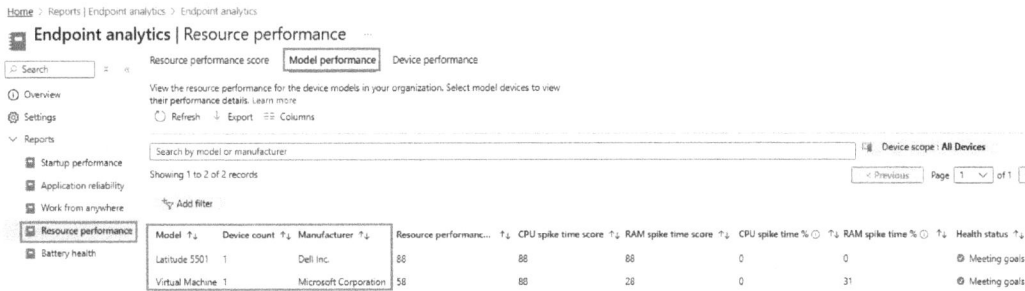

Figure 4.55: Resource performance based on device models

So far, we've explored how the **Resource performance** report helps proactively identify potential productivity issues caused by device slowdowns due to CPU or RAM spikes, and how corrective actions can be taken to address them. Now, let's move on to the next section to explore how Intune analytics data can be integrated with Power BI, making the data more visually engaging and easier to interpret.

Integrating Intune analytics with Power BI

The new Advanced Analytics feature offers deep, data-rich insights into device health, enabling IT teams to monitor and assess performance with a high degree of granularity. To unlock the full potential of this data, organizations can integrate it with tools such as Power BI to build more advanced, customizable dashboards and reports, enhancing visibility and enabling more strategic decision-making.

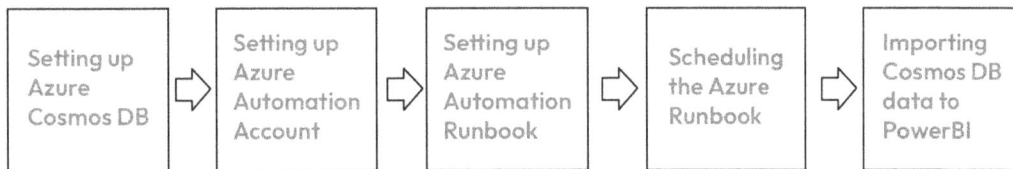

| Setting up Azure Cosmos DB | ⇨ | Setting up Azure Automation Account | ⇨ | Setting up Azure Automation Runbook | ⇨ | Scheduling the Azure Runbook | ⇨ | Importing Cosmos DB data to PowerBI |

Figure 4.56: The steps for integrating Advanced Analytics data with Power BI

Now, let's split the preceding block diagram into five steps and go through each one in detail:

1. This step involves setting up Azure Cosmos DB, which will serve as the storage layer for the data currently visible in the Intune portal. By centralizing this information, it becomes possible to seamlessly import it into Power BI, enabling richer and more customizable visualizations for deeper analysis.

2. The second step involves creating an Azure Automation account, which will later be used to execute a script that retrieves data from the Intune service. This data will then be programmatically transferred and stored in Azure Cosmos DB, enabling further analysis/visualization.

3. In this step, we need to set up an Azure runbook, which contains the script responsible for retrieving data from the Intune service. This script runs through the previously configured Azure Automation account and transfers the collected data into Azure Cosmos DB.

4. Once we've confirmed that the Azure runbook executes successfully without errors and accurately retrieves the required data, the next step is to schedule the runbook. This allows the script to run automatically at defined intervals, ensuring consistent data collection and seamless updates to Cosmos DB.

5. In the final step, we'll import the data stored in Azure Cosmos DB into Power BI to enable rich, interactive report visualizations. Cosmos DB acts as the data source, having been configured earlier to ingest information from the Intune service. To establish the connection, we'll need the access credentials found under the **Keys** section of our Cosmos DB instance. Once the data is successfully imported, Power BI's built-in filters and visualization tools can be used to create dynamic, user-friendly dashboards that bring your device insights to life.

Having access to rich data within Intune is incredibly powerful, but interpreting raw numbers alone can be challenging and limiting. To unlock the true value of this data, visualizing it through tools such as Power BI can make a significant difference. By transforming complex datasets into interactive dashboards and intuitive reports, we can turn raw metrics into meaningful insights that drive smarter decisions and more effective endpoint management.

> For more details and the script for the Azure runbook, please refer to the *Resources* section at the end of this chapter.

Our two cents

Onboarding devices to endpoint analytics is a no-brainer. As we mentioned earlier, it's a free feature, and we highly recommend enabling it. Once onboarded, it gives us valuable insights into device boot times, sign-in experiences, app performance, and overall readiness for cloud adoption.

On top of that, if we really want to take things to the next level, Advanced Analytics is where the magic happens. It brings in powerful metrics such as **Battery health** and **Resource performance**, which are incredibly useful for spotting hardware issues before they become a problem. And then there's SDQ and MDQ, which are absolute game changers.

Back in the on-premises world, tools such as ConfigMgr gave us the flexibility to run custom queries and pull device-specific data. Now, as we shift to cloud-first environments and move away from maintaining on-premises infrastructure, having similar capabilities in Intune is essential.

If we think about it, with **Device query**, we can remotely check a registry value on any device; no physical access is needed. And if something needs to be changed, we can push a PowerShell script to update it. That kind of end-to-end visibility and control makes life so much easier for Intune admins.

Summary

In this chapter, we took a closer look at endpoint analytics, breaking down its core components and walking through the setup process. We also explored the key logs and registry entries that come in handy when troubleshooting common issues.

To help put things in perspective, we compared endpoint analytics with Advanced Analytics, highlighting what makes the latter stand out, especially its ability to deliver deeper, data-driven insights.

A major focus of the chapter was on SDQ and MDQ, two powerful features within Advanced Analytics. We covered how they work, when to use each, and shared practical examples to show their impact in real-world scenarios.

We also looked at how Copilot can be used to simplify writing custom queries, making the process more intuitive and efficient. Finally, we wrapped up with tips on using Power BI to turn Intune's analytics data into clear, actionable visuals.

The key takeaway from this chapter is understanding how analytics can empower IT admins to be proactive, whether it's planning hardware upgrades, spotting app compatibility issues, or troubleshooting performance problems in real time using SDQ and MDQ. It's a game-changer for modern endpoint management.

In the upcoming chapter, we will explore Microsoft Tunnel for Mobile Application Management, which enables users to securely access on-premises apps and resources from a non-Intune-enrolled device.

Resources

If you prefer not to write KQL queries manually and don't have access to Microsoft Security Co-pilot, which can generate queries from natural language prompts, please check out `https://www.kqlsearch.com/devicequery`. It offers a well-organized collection of pre-built KQL queries tailored for Intune's **Device query** feature, making it easier to get started and accelerate your analysis.

For reference, I highly recommend checking out Rudy Ooms' insightful blogs on this topic at `https://call4cloud.nl`.

For a deeper dive into integrating Intune analytics with Power BI and to access a reference script that can be used within an Azure runbook to extract data from the Intune service and load it into Azure Cosmos DB, we recommend checking out Michael Meier's blog post: `https://mikemdm.de/2024/07/07/power-bi-intune-endpoint-analytics-reporting-series-part-7/`. His guide provides step-by-step instructions along with the necessary script, making it easier to automate data flows and enhance reporting capabilities using Power BI.

Join us on Discord

For discussions around the book and to connect with your peers, join us on Discord at `https://discord.gg/dygzddgYCR`

5

Enabling Secure Connectivity with Microsoft Tunnel for MAM

In this chapter, we will start by exploring the background and the rationale behind Microsoft Tunnel for MAM. We'll examine its prerequisites and compare its functionality with the MDM Tunnel offered by Intune. We will also understand common scenarios where MAM Tunnel is used by an organization. Additionally, we'll walk through the detailed setup and configuration steps required for implementing MAM Tunnel. This information will enable us to roll out MAM in situations where employees are using their personal Android or iOS devices and need secure access to on-prem resources over the internet. It's especially useful when users prefer not to enroll their devices in MDM, as it allows them to stay productive without handing over control or visibility of their devices to IT admins.

The key topics covered in this chapter include the following:

- Background and overview of MAM Tunnel
- Comparison between MDM Tunnel and MAM Tunnel
- Typical use cases and scenarios leveraging MAM Tunnel
- Architecture of MAM Tunnel
- Pre-reqs of MAM Tunnel
- MAM Tunnel setup and configuration
- End device experience

Now, let's get started with exploring all these topics in detail!

Understanding the basics of MAM Tunnel

Microsoft Tunnel for MAM is a VPN gateway extension of Microsoft Intune that enables secure access to on-premises resources from iOS/iPadOS and Android Enterprise devices, without requiring device enrollment. Designed for unmanaged or BYOD scenarios, Tunnel for MAM empowers users to access corporate apps and internal websites from personal devices, without handing over control to IT. This flexibility allows organizations to deliver secure, policy-driven access to sensitive resources without compromising user autonomy.

By extending Microsoft Tunnel's capabilities to **mobile app management** (**MAM**), IT teams can now support secure access to internal resources on personally owned devices, maintaining compliance and security standards. This chapter highlights how Microsoft Edge can be used to access an on-premises website via Tunnel for MAM.

Now that we have understood the significance of MAM Tunnel, let's perform a comparative analysis of the MDM Tunnel and MAM Tunnel functionalities within Microsoft Intune.

MDM Tunnel (Microsoft Tunnel for Intune) versus MAM Tunnel

Both MDM and MAM Tunnel serve the same core purpose, which is providing a secure channel for mobile devices to access on-prem resources over the internet. That's why it's important to understand where they overlap, how they differ, and the specific use cases where each one is better suited. We'll begin by examining the similarities between the two solutions, followed by a review of their key differences, to provide a clearer understanding of their respective use cases and capabilities. MDM Tunnel is used in scenarios where the device is corporate-owned and enrolled in Intune. On the contrary, MAM Tunnel is used in scenarios where the end device is BYOD and not enrolled in Intune. Both these devices (MDM-enrolled and MAM) using the Tunnel offering are able to access on-prem hosted resources over the internet.

Feature	MDM Tunnel (Microsoft Tunnel for Intune)	MAM Tunnel
Purpose	Secure access to on-premises resources via VPN	Secure access to on-premises resources via VPN
Technology	Uses Microsoft Tunnel Gateway and containerized Linux infrastructure	Same underlying Tunnel infrastructure

Feature	MDM Tunnel (Microsoft Tunnel for Intune)	MAM Tunnel
Security	Encrypted traffic, certificate-based authentication	Same security standards and encryption
Monitoring	Managed and monitored through Intune	Same monitoring capabilities via Intune
Scalability	Supports multiple sites and servers	Same scalability model

Table 5.1: Similarities between MDM and MAM Tunnel in Intune

Let's go over the differences next. This will help us understand when we should use MAM Tunnel and when we should use MDM Tunnel, respectively, based on the intended use case:

Feature	MDM Tunnel (Microsoft Tunnel for Intune)	MAM Tunnel
Device Management Requirement	Requires full device enrollment in Intune (MDM)	Does not require device enrollment; works with app protection policies (MAM)
Use Case	Ideal for corporate-owned or fully managed devices	Designed for Bring Your Own Device (BYOD) scenarios
VPN Scope	Device-wide VPN or per-app VPN	Strictly per-app VPN (only managed apps use Tunnel)
User Experience	VPN may affect all device traffic, depending on the configuration	VPN is invisible to the user and only applies to protected apps
Deployment Complexity	Requires device enrollment, certificates, and compliance policies	Simpler setup for end users; no enrollment or compliance checks needed
Supported Platforms	iOS, Android, Windows (via full device management)	Currently supported on iOS and Android (for apps with MAM policies)

Table 5.2: Differences between MDM and MAM Tunnel in Intune

Now that we've explored the similarities and differences between MAM and MDM Tunnels, let's move on to the next section to understand the scenarios where organizations can efficiently leverage MAM Tunnel features.

Typical use cases and scenarios leveraging MAM Tunnel

Let's understand the use case of MAM Tunnel in any organization using the following scenarios. The following three scenarios are actual use cases of MAM Tunnel by customers we have worked with in their organization:

- **Scenario 1: Secure access from personal devices (BYOD)**

  Let's say, as an organization, we want to allow the use of personal mobile devices (iOS and Android) for work purposes. The use case involves allowing end users to access intranet sites and LOB apps (for example, an app developed by an organization for fulfilling their custom needs, such as billing, etc.), which are hosted on-prem, without enrolling the device. MAM Tunnel can be efficiently used here, which preserves user privacy while enforcing corporate security policies and access.

  Example: An employee uses their personal iPhone to access an internal HR portal via Microsoft Edge. MAM Tunnel automatically launches a secure VPN connection when the app is opened, without requiring full device management.

- **Scenario 2: Contractor or temporary staff access**

  Contractors or temporary workers often need access to internal resources but cannot be enrolled in MDM due to policy or technical constraints. MAM Tunnel enables secure, policy-driven access to corporate apps without compromising device ownership or autonomy.

  Example: A freelance developer accesses internal APIs and documentation from an Android device using Microsoft Defender and Edge, with a VPN triggered only for work-related apps.

- **Scenario 3: Remote work enablement for emergencies**

  MAM Tunnel supports the "work from anywhere" model by allowing employees to connect securely to corporate resources from any location, using personal devices. This can be particularly valuable in situations where end users urgently need to access internal websites—such as those related to Mediclaim or policy information—while away from the office during an emergency, and only have their personal device available.

These scenarios are crucial for understanding how organizations apply MAM Tunnel in real-world use cases and implementation contexts. Now that we've established the importance of MAM Tunnel for organizations, let's take a closer look at its backend architecture and explore how its internal components work together in the following section.

In the following section, we'll build upon the foundational concepts to explore the architectural flow that powers the functioning of MAM Tunnel.

Architectural flow of MAM Tunnel

Let's understand the background flow behind the working of MAM Tunnel by referencing the following diagram.

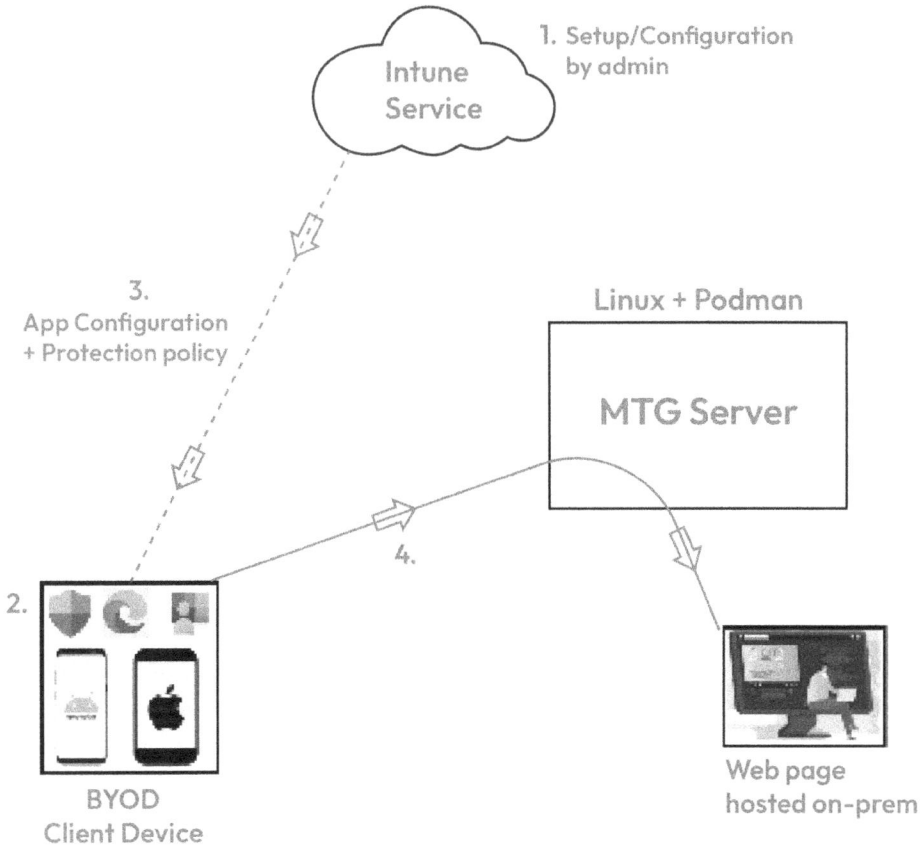

Figure 5.1: Background flow during the working of MAM Tunnel

As seen in the preceding diagram, we primarily have the following main components involved in the MAM Tunnel setup:

- Intune service where app protection and configuration policies have been created
- Personal Android/iOS mobile device (not enrolled)
- Linux RHEL server with Podman
- **Microsoft Tunnel Gateway (MTG)**
- Web page/on-prem resource

So, what's MTG?

MTG is deployed within a container running on a Linux server, which can be either a physical machine in an on-premises setup or a virtual machine hosted locally or in the cloud; MTG is a component responsible for functioning for MAM Tunnel. To configure Tunnel, Microsoft Defender for Endpoint is installed as the Tunnel client app, and Intune VPN profiles are assigned to iOS and Android devices. These components work together to enable secure device connectivity to corporate resources through Tunnel.

Later in this chapter, in the *Configuration on the server/on-premises, Step 4*, section, we'll explore how MTG functions in detail and walk through the setup process for all the components required to get it up and running.

Now, let's go through the flow behind MAM Tunnel:

1. **Setup/configuration by the admin:** The first step is where the admin does all the setup and configuration in the Intune portal. They need to install and configure the MTG server. Additionally, the admin needs to create app protection and configuration profiles and deploy them to the end user. These profiles will help establish the VPN connection. The steps have been explained later in this chapter, in the *MAM Tunnel setup and configuration* section.

2. **Download of the apps by the end user:** The next step involves the end user downloading the needed applications on the device. Since this is an MAM Tunnel scenario and the device is not managed via Intune, the apps cannot be pushed by the admin. The end user can go to the App Store/Play Store and install the apps. In this case, the user needs to install the Microsoft Defender and Microsoft Edge applications on the device.

3. **Deployment of the app configuration payload:** Now the end user needs to log in to both applications. The apps are now going to receive the app protection and configuration policy, pushed by the Intune admin, which is signified by the flow in the diagram. This policy will contain the required trusted root certificate, along with the VPN related settings of the MTG server, such as the connection name and the site.

4. **Session establishment with the on-prem URL/resource via MTG:** The device will now utilize the settings received, and it will reach out to the MTG server, thereby establishing a connection session. The traffic from MTG for this session will then be sent to the on-prem resource/URL, which was defined in the MAM Tunnel settings.

In this way, the end device (Android/iOS) would establish a successful connection to the on-prem hosted resource over the internet via the MTG server

Tunnel Gateway maintains two communication channels with the client. Initially, it establishes a control channel over TCP secured with TLS, which also functions as a backup data channel. It then attempts to set up a primary data channel using UDP with **Datagram TLS (DTLS)**, a protocol that enables TLS over UDP. If the UDP channel cannot be established or becomes temporarily unavailable, the system automatically falls back to the TCP/TLS channel to maintain connectivity. By default, both channels use port 443, although this can be customized based on network requirements.

In the following section of this chapter, we will explore the process for configuring MAM Tunnel, including the detailed steps required for the setup of each of the components we discussed earlier.

MAM Tunnel setup and configuration

Before discussing the configuration, let's quickly take a look at the prerequisites of setting up MAM Tunnel:

- An Azure subscription
- Intune P1 license + Intune Suite license/add-on license for MAM Tunnel/Intune Plan 2 license
- **Other requirements:** (which we will set up later in this chapter)
    - A Linux server that runs containers: Podman for **Red Hat Enterprise Linux (RHEL)** and Docker for all other Linux distributions
    - A **Transport Layer Security (TLS)** certificate for the Linux server to secure connections from devices to the Tunnel Gateway server

The setup process for MAM Tunnel can be divided into two distinct phases:

- The first phase involves server-side (on-premises) configuration, which includes provisioning the RHEL server, installing MTG, and performing necessary system-level setups.
- The second phase focuses on configurations within the Microsoft Intune portal, such as creating the MTG server configuration, setting up a site, and deploying the Tunnel client application to user devices.

Let's now refer to the following block diagram, which outlines the two key phases of, and the steps involved in, setting up MAM Tunnel. Throughout this chapter, we'll follow the sequence presented in the diagram as we walk through the configuration process.

Setting up MAM Tunnel

```
                              Setting up MAM Tunnel
                                        |
            ┌───────────────────────────┴───────────────────────────┐
    Configuration at the                                    Configuration at
    Server/On-premise                                       the Intune portal
            ⇩                                                       ⇩
```

| Generating the TLS certificate | Provisioning and configuring Red Hat Linux | Configuring Podman and checking Readiness for MTG | Installing and Configuring MS Tunnel Gateway | Network and Proxy configuration of the MTG server | | Creating MTG server configuration | Creating a Site | Deploying MS Tunnel Client App + App configurations |

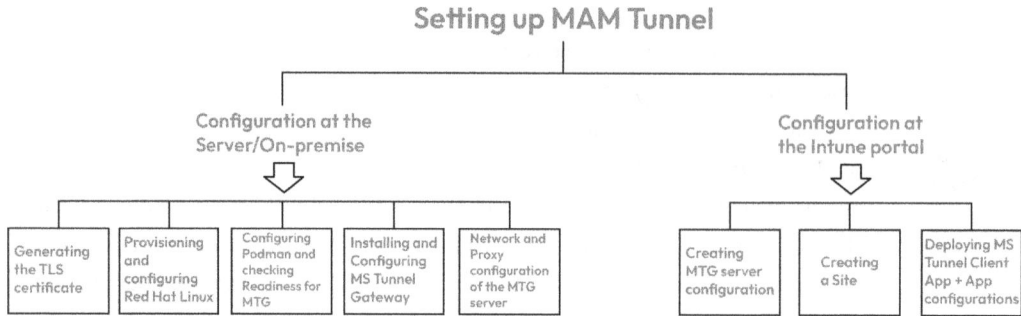

Figure 5.2: Block diagram illustrating the steps for setting up MAM Tunnel

Let's begin by reviewing the server-side configuration steps required for the on-premises environment.

Configuration on the server/on-premises

There are five key configurations required on the server (on-premises) side for setting up MTG:

1. **Generating the TLS certificate**: This certificate is used to encrypt communication between the client devices and the MTG server, ensuring secure data transmission.

2. **Provisioning and configuring the RHEL server**: The RHEL server serves as the host environment for Tunnel Gateway.

3. **Configuring Podman and checking readiness for MTG**: Podman is configured as the container runtime, and a readiness script is executed to validate that the server meets all prerequisites for MTG installation.

4. **Installing and configuring MTG**: The MTG software is deployed within a container and configured to act as the secure gateway between client devices and on-premises resources.

5. **Network and proxy configuration for MTG**: This step ensures that any existing proxy settings are properly integrated, allowing network traffic to be routed through the designated proxy infrastructure.

> MTG acts as the bridge between mobile devices and your internal network. The MTG software runs inside a container on the RHEL server. This container encapsulates the MTG service and its dependencies, making deployment and updates easier and more consistent. Podman, the container engine used to run the MTG container, is daemonless, rootless, and secure for enterprise environments.

It's essential to understand each component involved in the setup of MAM Tunnel and its respective role. The following table outlines each component, along with its corresponding function.

Component	Role
RHEL Server	Hosts the MTG container and provides the OS environment
MTG	Tunnel Gateway software that routes VPN traffic
Podman	Container engine that runs the MTG container

Table 5.3: Table illustrating the MAM Tunnel components and their function (role)

Now, let's review the five steps outlined earlier that are essential for configuring the server/on-premises environment for the MAM Tunnel setup.

Step 1: Generating the TLS certificate

A trusted TLS certificate in PFX format is required on the Linux server to secure communication between mobile clients (iOS, Android) and MTG. This certificate must include the complete trusted certificate chain and be installed during MTG setup. The TLS certificate can be issued by a public or private **Certificate Authority (CA)**.

The certificate must include the **Fully Qualified Domain Name (FQDN)** of the MTG server in the **Subject Alternative Name (SAN)** field. The **Subject Name (SN)** of the certificate should ideally also contain the FQDN and be of type DNS, which we will see in detail in *Step 10*. A minimum key size of 2,048 bits is recommended.

During MTG installation, the entire trusted certificate chain must be copied to the Linux server. The certificate should have a validity period of at least 2 years.

If using a certificate from a private CA, the full trust chain must be deployed to client devices via an Intune trusted certificate profile to ensure trust.

Let's go through the following steps, which the admin needs to follow in the on-prem CA in order to generate the TLS certificate needed:

1. Go to the on-prem CA and run `certsrv.msc` to open the **Certification Authority** console.
2. Now right-click on **Certificate Templates** and select **Manage**. The **Certificate Templates** console will open. Right-click on the **Web Server** template and select **Duplicate Template**.

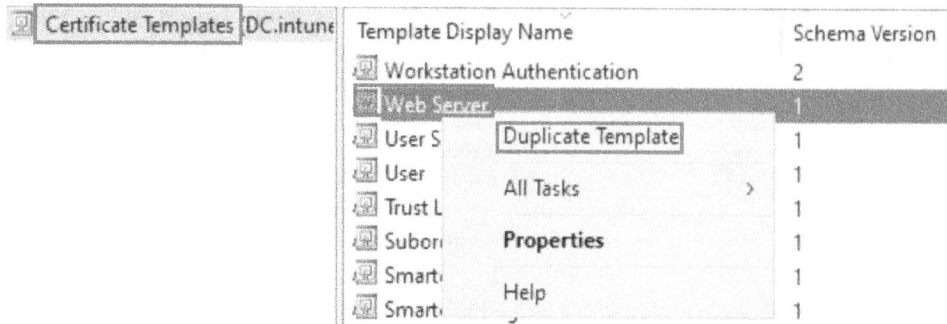

Figure 5.3: Creation of a new certificate template in the CA

3. In the **General** tab, update **Template display name** to MS Tunnel Gateway and set the
    certificate validity to 2 years, as seen here:

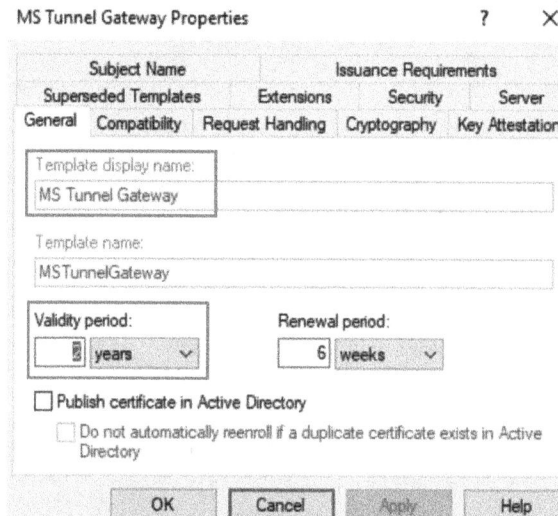

Figure 5.4: Configuring the validity of the certificate template

4. Navigate to the **Subject Name** tab and ensure **Supply in the request** is enabled. This al-
    lows custom values for both the SN and SAN to be specified during certificate enrollment.

5. Under the **Request Handling** tab, enable **Allow private key to be exported.**

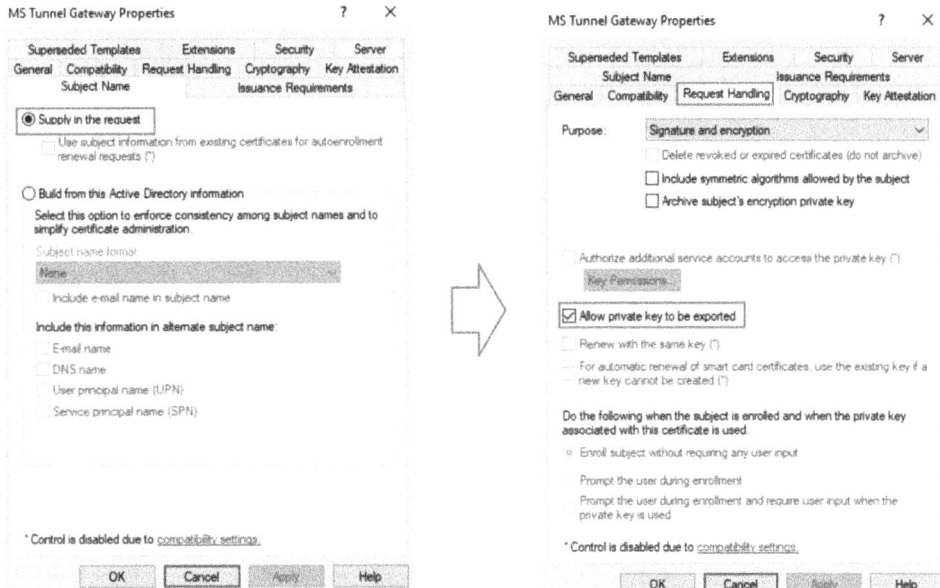

Figure 5.5: Configuring properties of the certificate template

6. Now, in the **Extensions** tab, verify that **Application Policies** include **Server Authentication** to ensure the certificate is valid for server-side TLS.

7. In the **Security** tab, grant **Enroll permissions** to the server or desktop that will be used to request and export the certificate for deployment to the Linux server. Once the certificate template is configured, publish it to make it available for enrollment. Open the **Certificate Authority** console, right-click on **Certificate Templates**, then select **New → Certificate Template to Issue**.

We can leave all the other tabs of the certificate template to their default values.

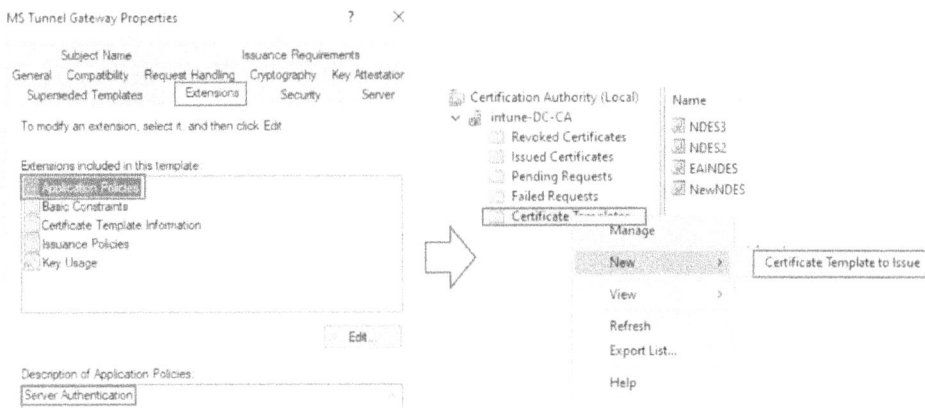

Figure 5.6: Issuing the certificate template

With the certificate template successfully created and published, the setup phase is complete. The next step is to initiate a certificate request using the configured template.

> This certificate template will not be used by the VPN clients/end devices.
>
> When utilizing a TLS certificate issued by an on-premises CA, it is essential to provision the complete certificate chain—including the trusted root and any intermediate CA certificates—onto mobile devices via Microsoft Intune. This step ensures that mobile endpoints recognize and trust the certificate used to establish secure VPN connections.

8. Now that the certificate template has been issued by the CA, the next step involves going to a device and requesting the TLS certificate by referencing the respective template. We will now go to the computer with permissions to request the certificate. We will run `certlm.msc` and go to **Personal** -> **Certificates**. Right-click on **Certificates** -> **All Tasks** -> **Request New Certificate....**

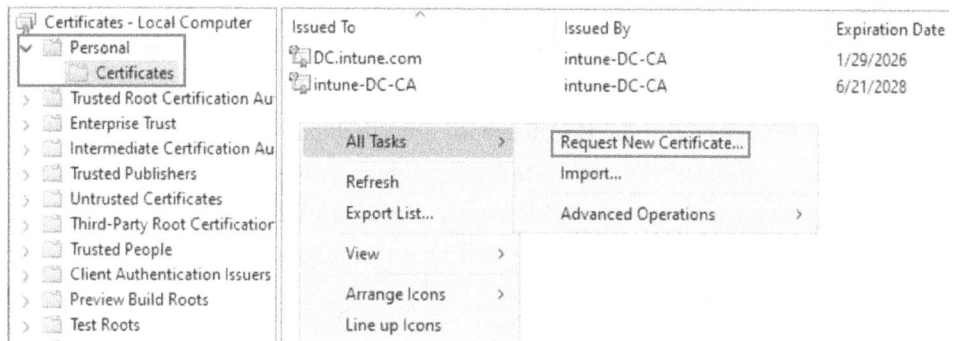

Figure 5.7: Requesting a TLS certificate from the CA

9. Select the **MS Tunnel Gateway** certificate template and click **More information is required to enroll for this certificate** to begin defining the certificate identity. If the template is not visible, verify that security permissions are correctly configured by checking the permissions of the certificate template.

10. Under **Subject name**, choose **Common name** and enter the public hostname portion of the server's FQDN (e.g., `mtg1.intune.com`). In the **Alternative name** section, select **DNS** and enter the same FQDN value (`mtg1.intune.com`). Ensure you click **Add** after each entry to apply the configuration.

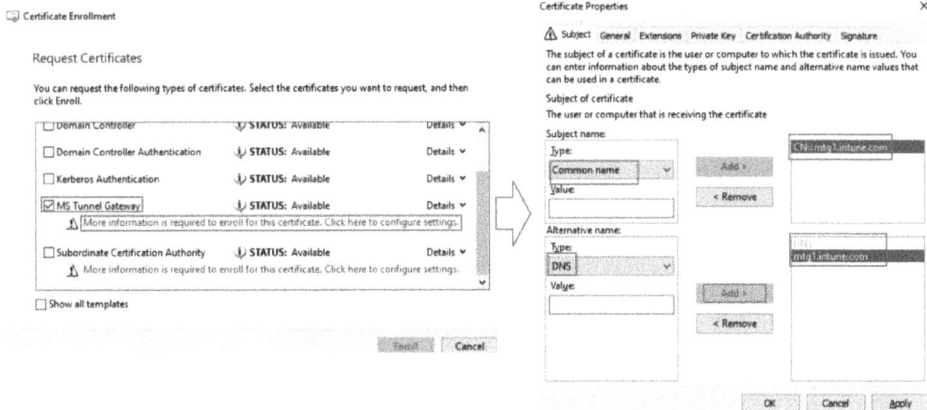

Figure 5.8: Populating values while requesting a certificate from the CA

11. Now we need to click **Apply**, then **Finish**:

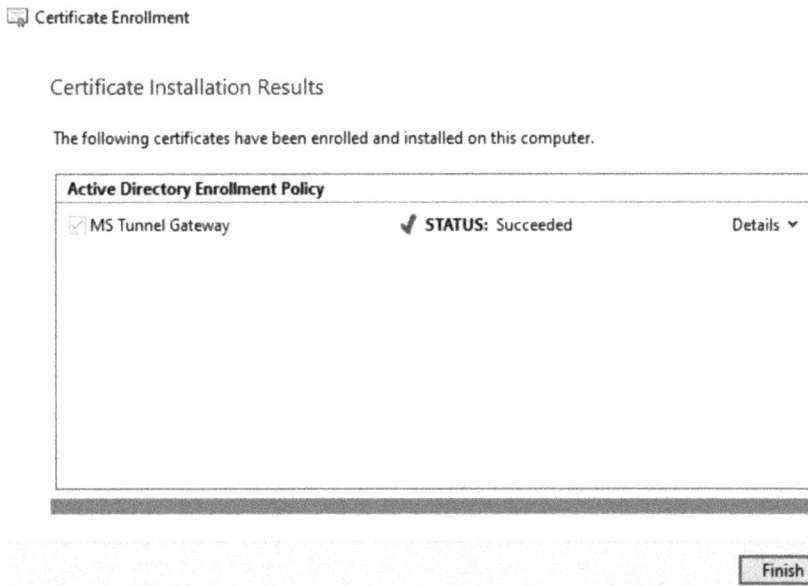

Figure 5.9: Successful request of a certificate from the template

12. Now, we will export the certificate along with its private key. From a Windows machine, we will go to certlm.msc. Go to **Personal** -> **Certificates**. Locate the certificate by its common name, which should be the Linux server name (i.e., mtg1.intune.com). We will right-click on the certificate > **All Tasks** -> **Export….**

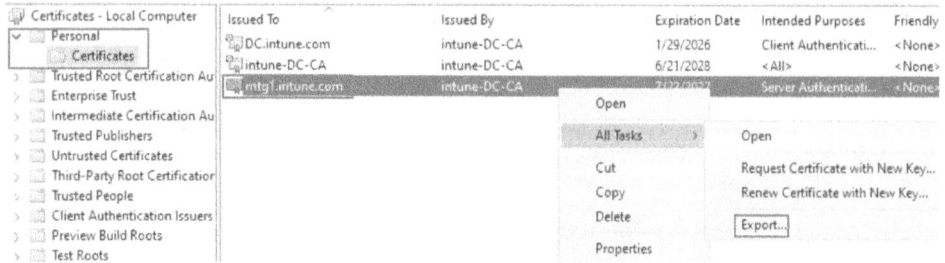

Figure 5.10: Exporting the TLS certificate

13. In **Certificate Export Wizard**, begin by selecting the **Yes, export the private key** option and proceed to the next step. In the **Personal Information Exchange – PKCS #12 (.PFX)** format settings, ensure the following options are selected:

   - **Include all certificates in the certification path if possible**, to maintain the full trust chain.

   - **Delete the private key if the export is successful**, to enhance security by removing the key from the source system.

   - **Export all extended properties**, to preserve all certificate metadata.

   These settings ensure a secure and complete export suitable for deployment on the Linux server.

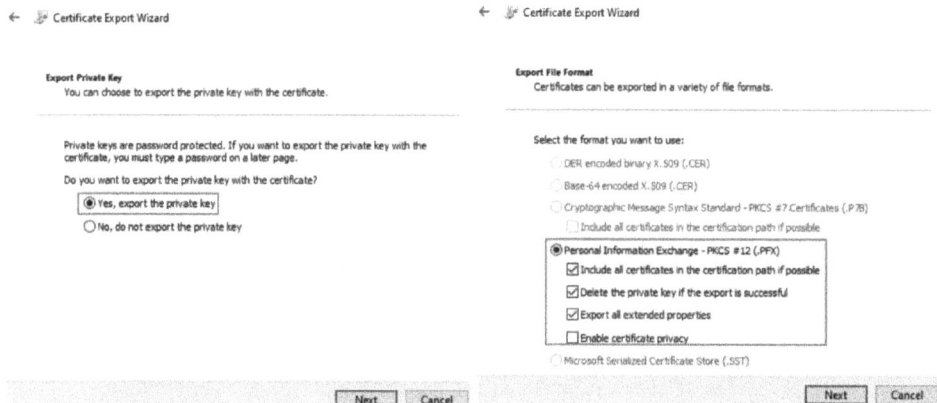

Figure 5.11: Selecting appropriate values while exporting the TLS certificate

14. In the security configuration step, select the **Password** option and enter a strong password to protect the certificate's private key. This password is essential for securing the exported certificate and will be required during the installation of the MTG server. It is important to securely store or document this password, as it will be needed later to complete the deployment process.

Figure 5.12: Successful export of the TLS certificate

Now that we have successfully exported the TLS certificate, in the next section, we will understand how to set up the RHEL server and utilize the TLS cert.

Step 2: Provisioning and configuring the RHEL server

In this step, we will create and configure the virtual machine that will run the RHEL server by following these steps:

1. The **virtual machine (VM)** is configured with the name MTG1 and stored at the location D:\Machines\MTG1 Server.

2. It is set up as a Generation 1 VM with 4,096 MB of startup memory, and dynamic memory is enabled to optimize resource usage.

3. Networking is configured using the default switch to ensure basic connectivity.

4. A new virtual hard disk named MTG1.vhdx is created with a total size of 127 GB.

5. For installation, the VM is configured to boot from a CD/DVD-ROM using an ISO image file, specifically rhel-9.6_x86_x64.iso, to install the operating system.

6. Once the VM boots, the ISO image will automatically load and display the RHEL installation interface. At this stage, select **Install Red Hat Enterprise Linux 9.6** to begin the operating system setup process.

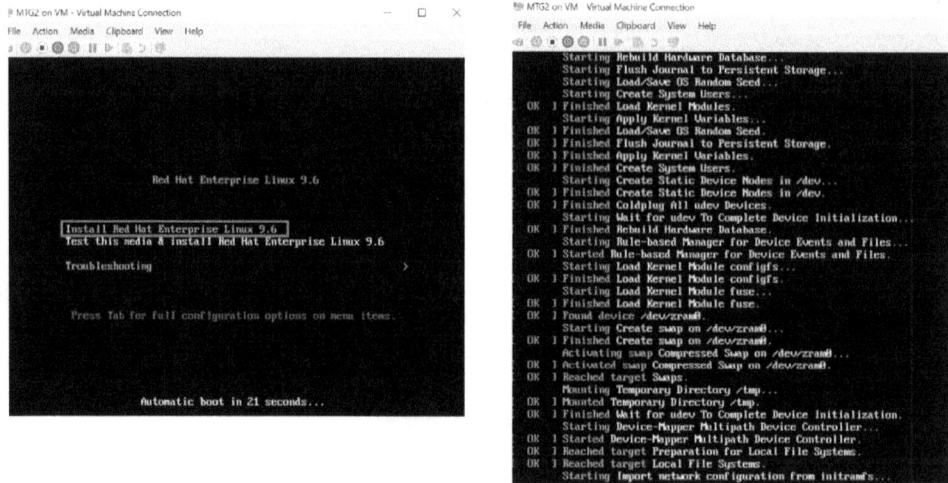

Figure 5.13: Installation of RHEL in VM

7. We will select the language and region that applies and proceed. On the **INSTALLATION SUMMARY** screen, we will select/confirm the installation destination partition. We can also configure the hostname of the server and configure it with a static or dynamic IP. We can also set the root's password and create an additional user if needed.

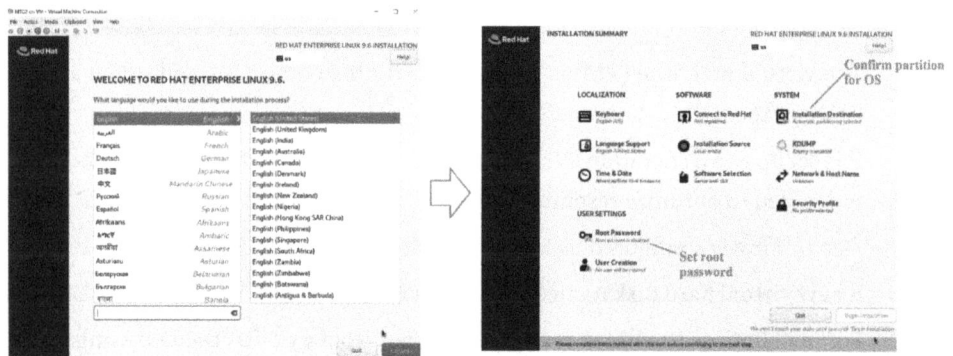

Figure 5.14: Configuring the RHEL in VM

8. Once all installation prerequisites are fulfilled, click **Begin Installation** to initiate the setup process. After the installation is completed successfully, finalize the setup by selecting **Reboot System**, which will restart the server and complete the Red Hat Enterprise Linux 9.6 deployment.

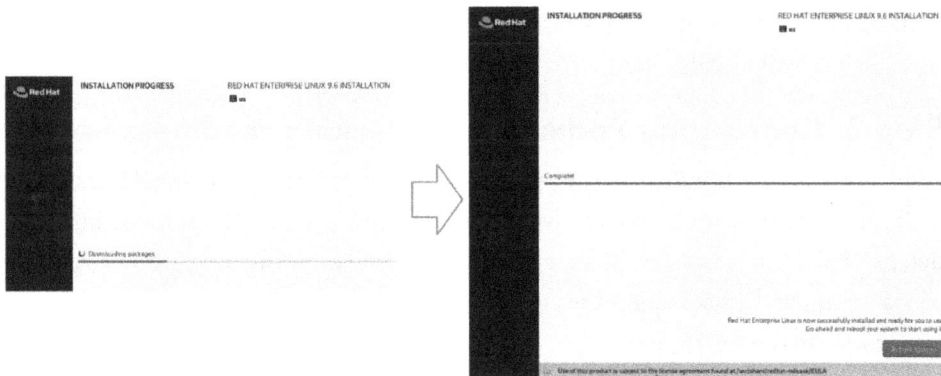

Figure 5.15: Finishing the installation of RHEL in VM

When the server boots up, we will get a welcome screen and the option to log in.

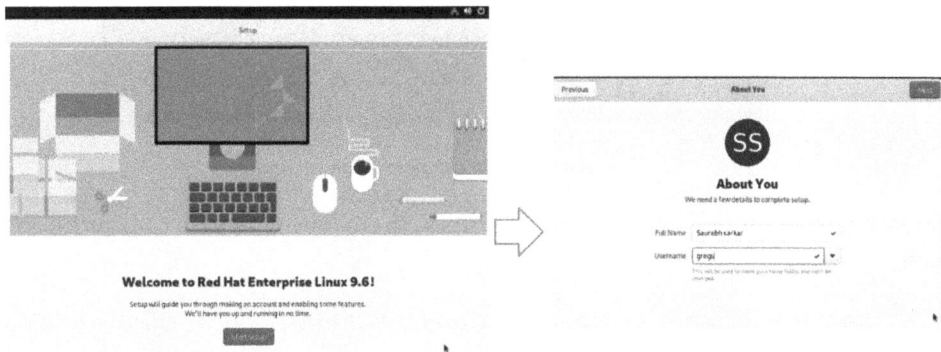

Figure 5.16: Logging into the RHEL server

Post login, we will go to the desktop screen, as seen in the following screenshot:

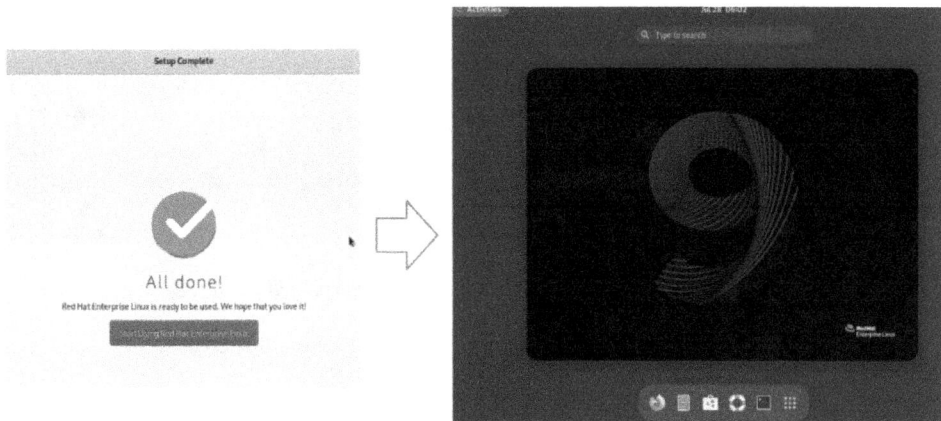

Figure 5.17: Successful creation and login to the RHEL server

In this section, we were able to successfully install a RHEL server. In the next section, we will go through its configuration, along with the installation of MTG.

Step 3: Configuring Podman and checking readiness for MTG

Podman comes pre-installed on the server, eliminating the need for manual installation. To verify its presence, execute the `podman version` command, which will return the installed version details. If, for any reason, Podman is not available, it can be installed using the `dnf install podman` command. This ensures the container engine is properly set up for managing containerized workloads on the system.

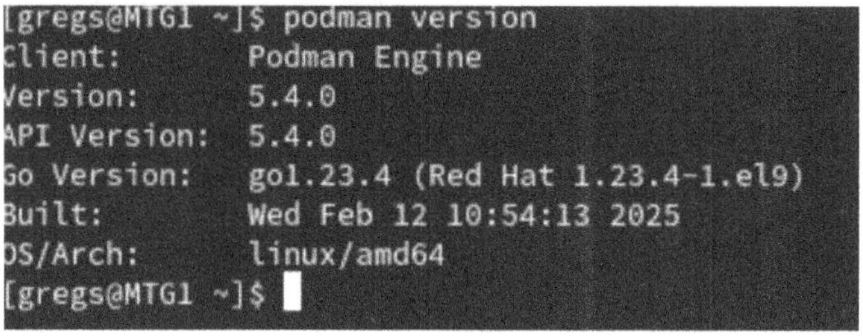

```
[gregs@MTG1 ~]$ podman version
Client:        Podman Engine
Version:       5.4.0
API Version:   5.4.0
Go Version:    go1.23.4 (Red Hat 1.23.4-1.el9)
Built:         Wed Feb 12 10:54:13 2025
OS/Arch:       linux/amd64
[gregs@MTG1 ~]$
```

Figure 5.18: Checking Podman version

After Podman is successfully installed, we will use the following steps to configure it and review MTG readiness:

1. Now that the server is ready, we need to enable IP forwarding (so that the traffic is routed (forwarded) to the correct IPs). We need to run the `nano /etc/sysctl.conf` command:

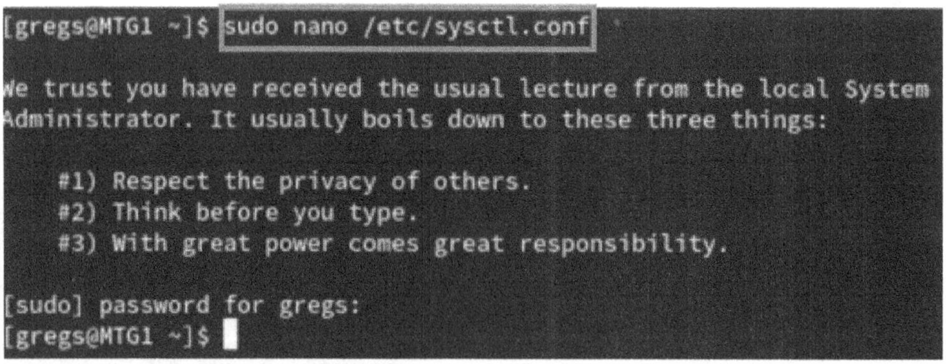

```
[gregs@MTG1 ~]$ sudo nano /etc/sysctl.conf

We trust you have received the usual lecture from the local System
Administrator. It usually boils down to these three things:

    #1) Respect the privacy of others.
    #2) Think before you type.
    #3) With great power comes great responsibility.

[sudo] password for gregs:
[gregs@MTG1 ~]$
```

Figure 5.19: Enabling IP forwarding in the server

2. We will now edit this file and add `net.ipv4.ip_forward=1` to it.

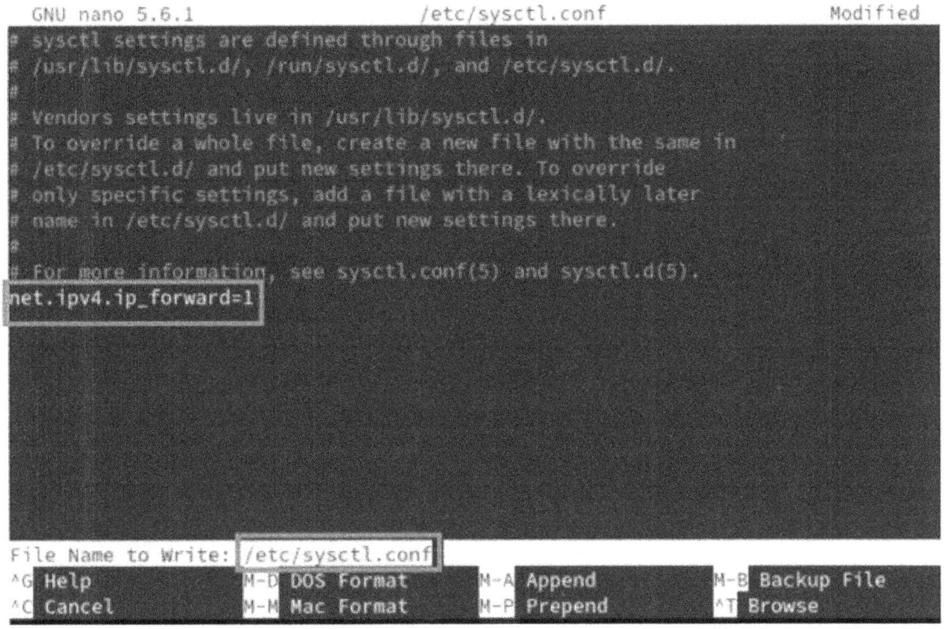

Figure 5.20: Enabling IP forwarding in the server

We can go to the nano /etc/ location and open the sysctl.conf file in the editor to make sure that the IP forwarding is added, as shown in the following screenshot:

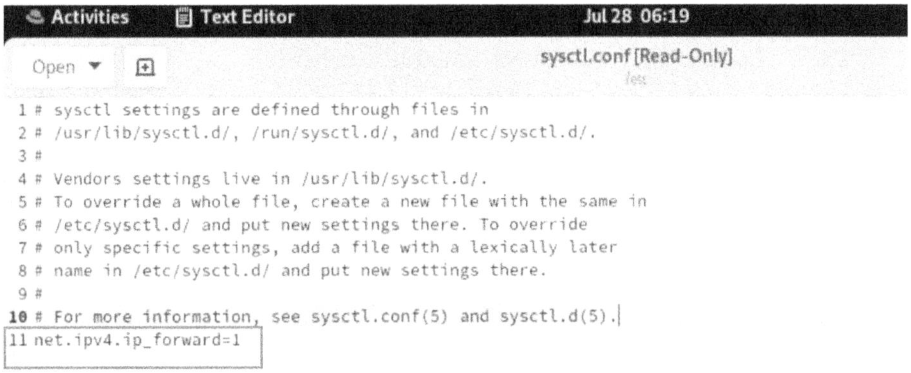

Figure 5.21: Verifying IP forwarding in the server

3. Now we need to load ip_tables during boot time by running echo ip_tables > /etc/modules-load.d/mstunnel_iptables.conf and load tun into the kernel by running echo tun > /etc/modules-load.d/mstunnel_tun.conf. Once done, we need to reboot the server as seen here:

```
[root@MTG1 ~]# echo ip_tables > /etc/modules-load.d/mstunnel_iptables.conf
[root@MTG1 ~]# echo tun > /etc/modules-load.d/mstunnel_tun.conf
[root@MTG1 ~]# reboot
```

Figure 5.22: Loading IP tables in the server

4. Now we need to use the `mst-readiness` script to validate whether the network and authentication prerequisites are in place. We can use `wget` or `curl` to open the `https://aka.ms/microsofttunneldownload` link, which contains the readiness script. In this case, we will have to run `wget --output-document=mstunnel-setup https://aka.ms/microsofttunneldownload` as seen here:

```
[gregs@MTG1 ~]$ sudo wget --output-document=mst-readiness https://aka.ms/microsofttunnelready
[sudo] password for gregs:
--2025-07-28 06:40:12--  https://aka.ms/microsofttunnelready
Resolving aka.ms (aka.ms)... 23.45.41.245
Connecting to aka.ms (aka.ms)|23.45.41.245|:443... connected.
HTTP request sent, awaiting response... 301 Moved Permanently
Location: https://download.microsoft.com/download/7/3/0/730915ab-f8e5-4cdc-9600-2b007731cb9a/mst-readiness.sh [following
--2025-07-28 06:40:13--  https://download.microsoft.com/download/7/3/0/730915ab-f8e5-4cdc-9600-2b007731cb9a/mst-readines
sh
Resolving download.microsoft.com (download.microsoft.com)... 204.79.197.219
Connecting to download.microsoft.com (download.microsoft.com)|204.79.197.219|:443... connected.
HTTP request sent, awaiting response... 200 OK
Length: 30502 (30K) [application/octet-stream]
Saving to: 'mst-readiness'

mst-readiness        100%[====================>]  29.79K  --.-KB/s    in 0.001s

2025-07-28 06:40:13 (26.3 MB/s) - 'mst-readiness' saved [30502/30502]

[gregs@MTG1 ~]$
```

Figure 5.23: Downloading the readiness script on the server before MTG installation

The readiness script will be downloaded as seen here.

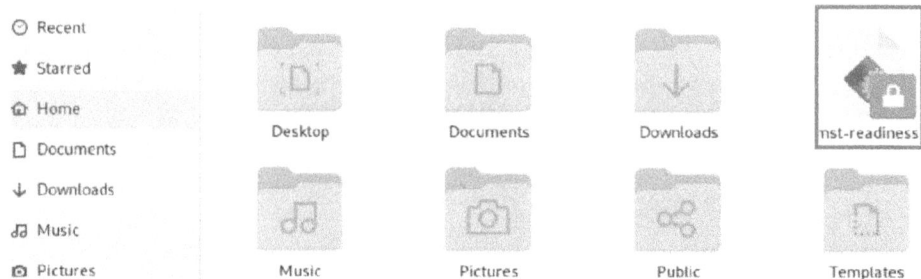

Figure 5.24: Locating the readiness script on the server

To continue the setup, we need to follow these steps:

1. Firstly, we need to make the script executable using the `chmod +x mstunnel-setup` command:

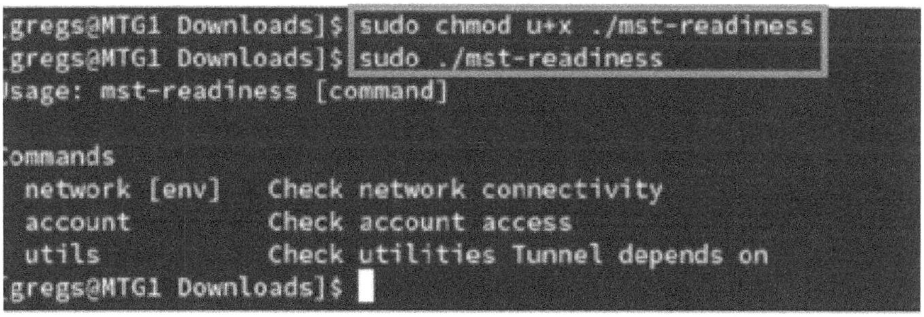

```
gregs@MTG1 Downloads]$ sudo chmod u+x ./mst-readiness
gregs@MTG1 Downloads]$ sudo ./mst-readiness
Usage: mst-readiness [command]

Commands
  network [env]    Check network connectivity
  account          Check account access
  utils            Check utilities Tunnel depends on
gregs@MTG1 Downloads]$ ▮
```

Figure 5.25: Running the MTG readiness script

2. Next, we need to validate network connectivity to Microsoft Intune service endpoints by running mst-readiness network. This ensures the server can successfully communicate with the required cloud services.

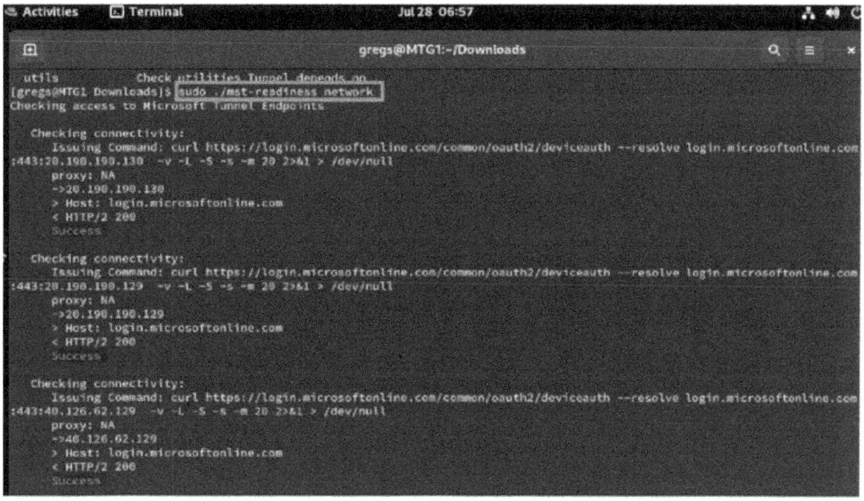

Figure 5.26: Running the MTG readiness script

3. Now we need to execute mst-readiness utils to confirm that all system prerequisites are properly configured.

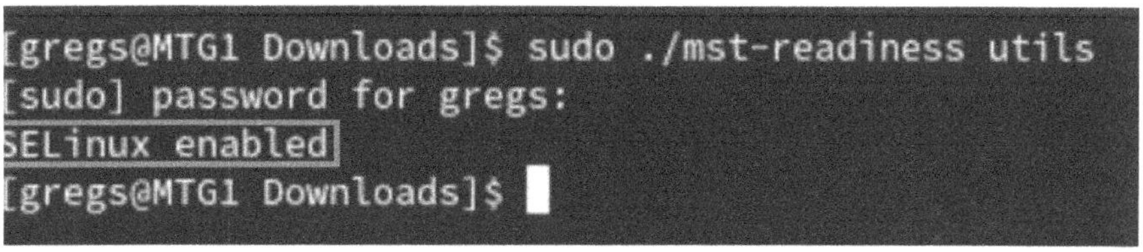

```
[gregs@MTG1 Downloads]$ sudo ./mst-readiness utils
[sudo] password for gregs:
SELinux enabled
[gregs@MTG1 Downloads]$ ▮
```

Figure 5.27: Running the readiness script

4. Finally, we need to run `mst-readiness account` to verify that the server is eligible for Intune enrollment. This step requires an account with either Global Administrator or Intune Service Administrator privileges, and the account must have an active Intune license assigned.

Now that we've confirmed readiness for the MTG installation, we can move ahead with setting up MTG in the next step.

Step 4: Installing and configuring MTG

MTG is installed in a container on a Linux server. The end devices reach out to this gateway over the internet and then are redirected to the on-premises hosted resource.

We need to follow these steps in order to install and configure MTG:

1. To install MTG, we need to run `wget --output-document=mstunnel-setup https://aka.ms/microsofttunneldownload` to download the setup file and make it executable by running `chmod +x mstunnel-setup`. The following screenshot shows the command output.

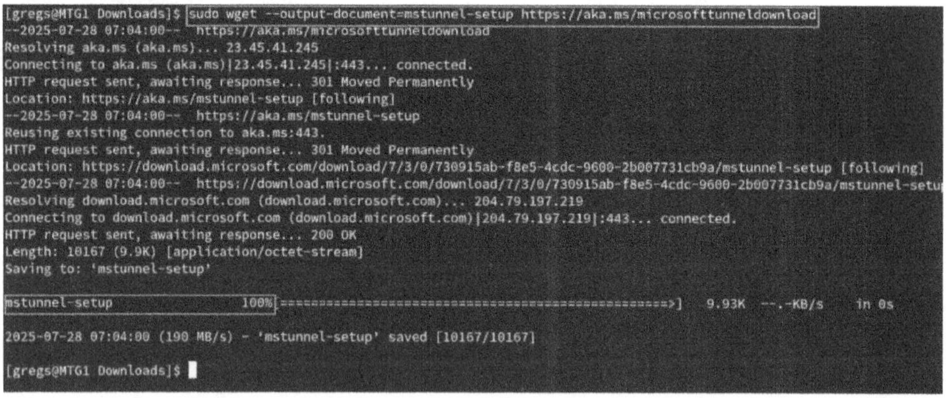

Figure 5.28: Downloading the setup file for MTG installation

2. Now we need to start the installation process by running `./mstunnel-setup`. The binaries will be downloaded, and the EULA prompt will appear, which we need to accept by typing yes:

```
[gregs@MTG1 Downloads]$ sudo ./mstunnel-setup
[sudo] password for gregs:
Trying to pull mcr.microsoft.com/tunnel/gateway/agent@sha256:5ded906dbfe63a7920e817939b83ebf38917b3317162438180038ad
5eddae...
Getting image source signatures
Copying blob e1ec5e0a8678 done   |
Copying blob e1ec5e0a8678 done   |
Copying blob e1ec5e0a8678 done   |
Copying blob 99608f49c530 done   |
Copying blob 6d70cbcabffc done   |
Copying blob e1ec5e0a8678 done   |
Copying blob e1ec5e0a8678 done   |
Copying blob e1ec5e0a8678 done   |
Copying blob e1ec5e0a8678 done   |
Copying blob e1ec5e0a8678 done   |
Copying blob e1ec5e0a8678 done   |
Copying blob e1ec5e0a8678 done   |
Copying blob e1ec5e0a8678 done   |
Copying blob e1ec5e0a8678 done   |
Copying blob e1ec5e0a8678 done   |
Copying blob e1ec5e0a8678 done   |
Copying blob ffe7c890d10c done   |
Copying config e8e8f9f66e done   |
Writing manifest to image destination
e8e8f9f66e3cc93ab0bd698b3bd14c524bcf78401341130d63f8529086f940f5
Do you accept the terms of the license? (yes/no) :  |
```

Figure 5.29: Prompts during MTG installation

To enable detailed console output during the Microsoft Tunnel and installation agent enrollment process, initiate verbose logging by executing export mst_verbose_log="true" prior to running the ./mstunnel-setup script. We can verify that verbose mode is active by running the export command. Once setup is complete, enhance persistent logging by editing the environment configuration file located at /etc/mstunnel/env.sh and appending the line mst_verbose_log="true". After making this change, restart the server using mst-cli server restart to apply the updated logging settings.

If we stop the installation and script, we can restart it by running the command line again. Installation continues from where you left off. When we start the script, it downloads container images from MTG container images from the Intune service and creates necessary folders and files on the server. During setup, the script prompts you to complete several admin tasks, such as editing the environment variable, copying the TLS certificate, accepting the EULA, and so on, which we will see in the next section.

3. After accepting the EULA, the admin needs to perform two tasks to proceed, which are displayed on the screen, as shown in the following screenshot:

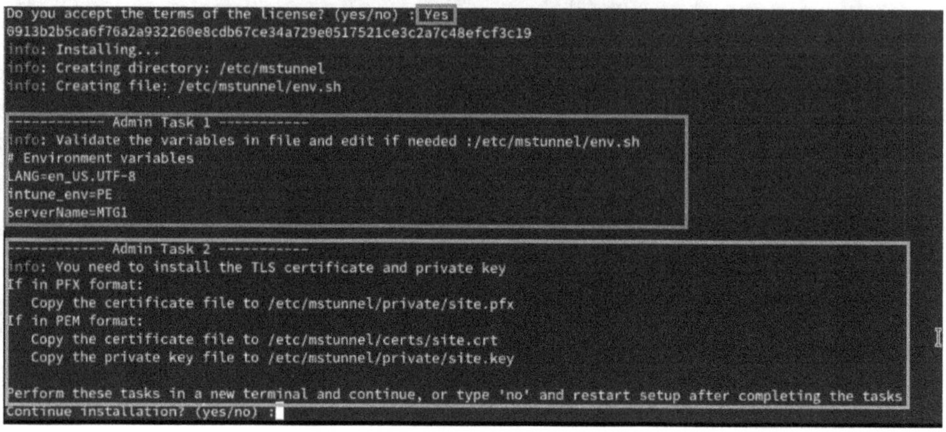

Figure 5.30: Prompts showing admin tasks during MTG installation

We will now understand both of these admin tasks:

- **Admin Task 1**: In this task, we need to ensure that the contents of the env.sh file are correct and edit it if needed. We need to open a new terminal and run the etc/mstunnel/env.sh command. This will show the contents of the env.sh file. We can also browse to etc/mstunnel using File Explorer and view the contents of the file.

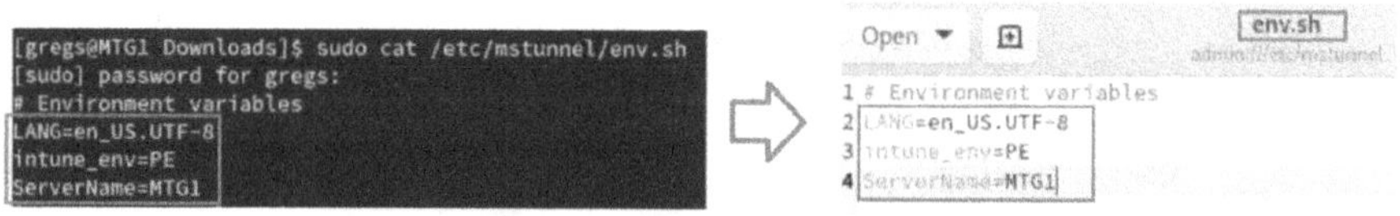

Figure 5.31: Configuring the environment variables

- **Admin Task 2**: In this step, the TLS certificate generated on the Windows machine needs to be securely transferred to the Linux server hosting the MTG. To perform this operation, open Command Prompt on the Windows machine and use the **Secure Copy Protocol (SCP)** tool to initiate the transfer. In this example, the command used to copy the file is scp c:\users\administrator\desktop\ site.pfx gregs@192.168.100.91:/tmp/site.pfx.

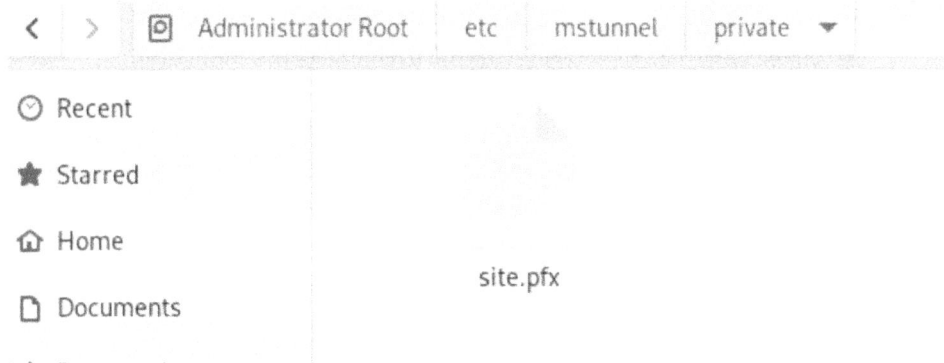

```
C:\>scp C:\Users\Administrator\Desktop\site.pfx gregs@192.168.100.91: /temp
        1 file(s) copied.
The authenticity of host '192.168.100.91 (192.168.100.91)' can't be established.
ECDSA key fingerprint is SHA256:AarPhn/LotmrS5CHjpkbp5PoxPFKU8MbXSDP82T0GnU.
Are you sure you want to continue connecting (yes/no/[fingerprint])?
Warning: Permanently added '192.168.100.91' (ECDSA) to the list of known hosts.
gregs@192.168.100.91's password:
```

Figure 5.32: Copying the TLS file to the server

Once the file is moved, we should be able to view it using File Explorer as well, as seen here:

Figure 5.33: Locating the TLS file in the server once copied successfully

The TLS certificate used with Microsoft Tunnel can be in .pfx or .pem format. If you use a public CA like DigiCert, we can download the full certificate chain (root, intermediate, and end-entity) as a single .pem file named site.crt.

We also need to place the full chain certificate at /etc/mstunnel/certs/ site.crt. Use either cp [path] /etc/mstunnel/certs/site.crt or create a symbolic link with ln -s – for example: ln -s [full path to cert] /etc/mstunnel/certs/site.crt.

We need to place the unencrypted private key at /etc/mstunnel/private/ site.key – for example, cp [full path to key] /etc/mstunnel/ private/site.key. Again, use cp or ln -s as needed – for example: ln -s [full path to key file] etc/mstunnel/private/site.key.

We must ensure both files are named exactly site.crt and site.key for the tunnel to function correctly.

4. Now we will return to the old terminal where the MTG setup was being done. Since we have completed Admin task 1 and 2, we will proceed by typing yes:

```
Perform these tasks in a new terminal and continue, or type 'no' and restart setup after completing the tasks
Continue installation? (yes/no) [yes]
```

Figure 5.34: Setting up MTG in the terminal window

5. During this phase, the required payload is automatically downloaded from Microsoft service endpoints and placed in the designated directory at /etc/mstunnel. As part of the setup process, the agent service is created, and we will be prompted to enter the password associated with the TLS server certificate to complete the configuration.

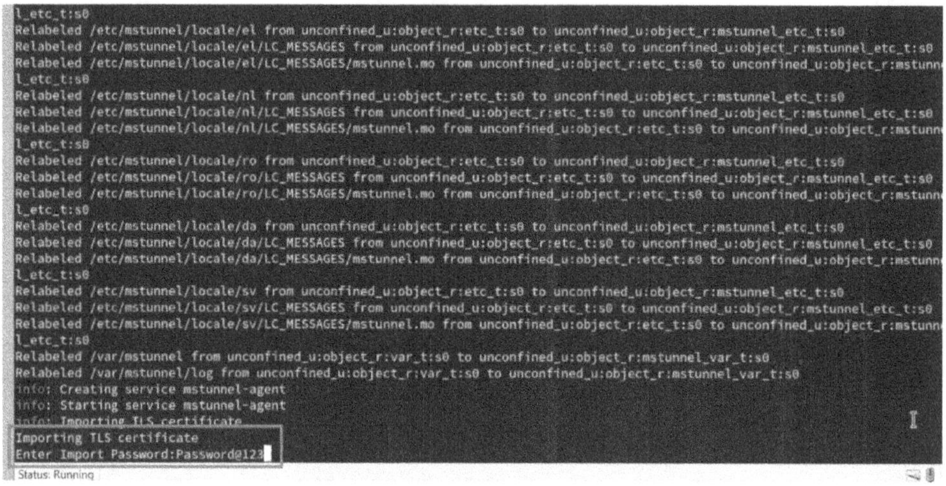

```
l_etc_t:s0
Relabeled /etc/mstunnel/locale/el from unconfined_u:object_r:etc_t:s0 to unconfined_u:object_r:mstunnel_etc_t:s0
Relabeled /etc/mstunnel/locale/el/LC_MESSAGES from unconfined_u:object_r:etc_t:s0 to unconfined_u:object_r:mstunnel_etc_t:s0
Relabeled /etc/mstunnel/locale/el/LC_MESSAGES/mstunnel.mo from unconfined_u:object_r:etc_t:s0 to unconfined_u:object_r:mstunn
l_etc_t:s0
Relabeled /etc/mstunnel/locale/nl from unconfined_u:object_r:etc_t:s0 to unconfined_u:object_r:mstunnel_etc_t:s0
Relabeled /etc/mstunnel/locale/nl/LC_MESSAGES from unconfined_u:object_r:etc_t:s0 to unconfined_u:object_r:mstunnel_etc_t:s0
Relabeled /etc/mstunnel/locale/nl/LC_MESSAGES/mstunnel.mo from unconfined_u:object_r:etc_t:s0 to unconfined_u:object_r:mstunn
l_etc_t:s0
Relabeled /etc/mstunnel/locale/ro from unconfined_u:object_r:etc_t:s0 to unconfined_u:object_r:mstunnel_etc_t:s0
Relabeled /etc/mstunnel/locale/ro/LC_MESSAGES from unconfined_u:object_r:etc_t:s0 to unconfined_u:object_r:mstunnel_etc_t:s0
Relabeled /etc/mstunnel/locale/ro/LC_MESSAGES/mstunnel.mo from unconfined_u:object_r:etc_t:s0 to unconfined_u:object_r:mstunn
l_etc_t:s0
Relabeled /etc/mstunnel/locale/da from unconfined_u:object_r:etc_t:s0 to unconfined_u:object_r:mstunnel_etc_t:s0
Relabeled /etc/mstunnel/locale/da/LC_MESSAGES from unconfined_u:object_r:etc_t:s0 to unconfined_u:object_r:mstunnel_etc_t:s0
Relabeled /etc/mstunnel/locale/da/LC_MESSAGES/mstunnel.mo from unconfined_u:object_r:etc_t:s0 to unconfined_u:object_r:mstunn
l_etc_t:s0
Relabeled /etc/mstunnel/locale/sv from unconfined_u:object_r:etc_t:s0 to unconfined_u:object_r:mstunnel_etc_t:s0
Relabeled /etc/mstunnel/locale/sv/LC_MESSAGES from unconfined_u:object_r:etc_t:s0 to unconfined_u:object_r:mstunnel_etc_t:s0
Relabeled /etc/mstunnel/locale/sv/LC_MESSAGES/mstunnel.mo from unconfined_u:object_r:etc_t:s0 to unconfined_u:object_r:mstunn
l_etc_t:s0
Relabeled /var/mstunnel from unconfined_u:object_r:var_t:s0 to unconfined_u:object_r:mstunnel_var_t:s0
Relabeled /var/mstunnel/log from unconfined_u:object_r:var_t:s0 to unconfined_u:object_r:mstunnel_var_t:s0
info: Creating service mstunnel-agent
info: Starting service mstunnel-agent
info: Importing TLS certificate
Importing TLS certificate
Enter Import Password:Password@123
Status: Running
```

Figure 5.35: Importing the TLS certificate during MTG installation

6. After entering the password, the TLS certificate is installed. Once the certificate is successfully installed, the system will initiate a sign-in request to enroll the server into your Intune tenant. A unique authentication code will be displayed, which must be entered by visiting https://microsoft.com/devicelogin from any device with internet access. This step securely links the server to our organization's Intune environment.

The following screenshot shows what the administrator views in the terminal window and the instructions provided to them:

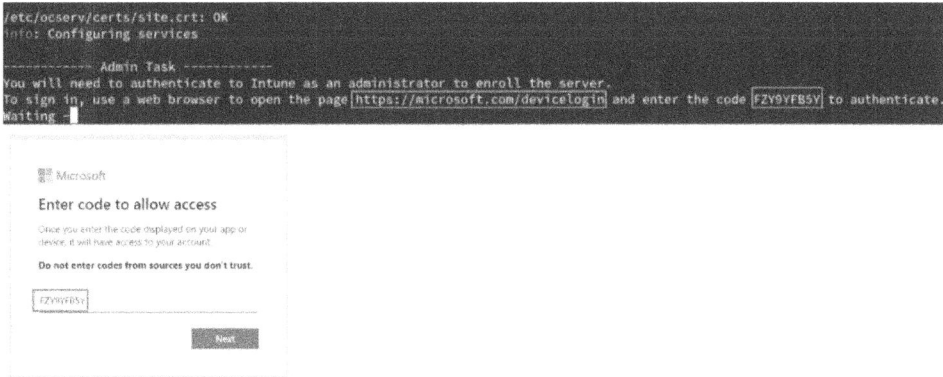

Figure 5.36: Steps during MTG configuration (installation)

7. After the setup installs the certificate and creates the Tunnel Gateway services, we'll be prompted to enter the username of an account that holds either Global Administrator or Intune Service Administrator privileges and has an active Intune license assigned. After entering the username, click **Next**, then provide the corresponding password and select **Sign in**. A confirmation prompt will appear asking whether you are attempting to sign in to the Microsoft Tunnel Gateway agent. Click **Continue** to proceed with the enrollment.

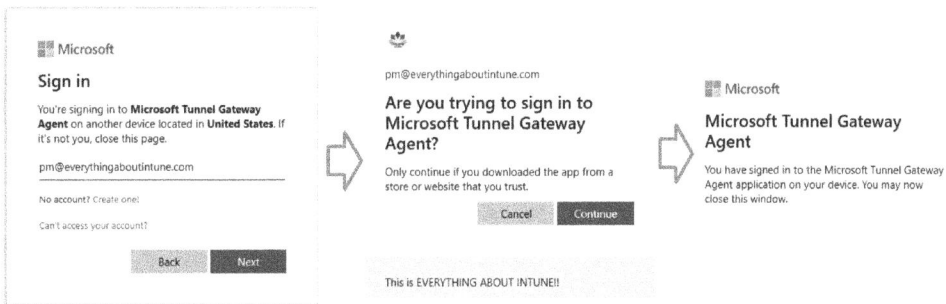

Figure 5.37: Steps during MTG configuration (installation)

The admin credentials are used only for the initial Microsoft Entra ID sign-in. After successful authentication, secure communication between Tunnel Gateway and Entra is handled using Azure app IDs and secret keys. This authentication successfully registers Tunnel Gateway with Microsoft Intune and our Intune tenant.

8. Now the relevant configuration is downloaded to the MTG server. The server then creates the mstunnel-server container and restarts it to apply the configuration. This completes the installation process.

The following screenshot displays the prompts and messages received by the admin in the terminal window.

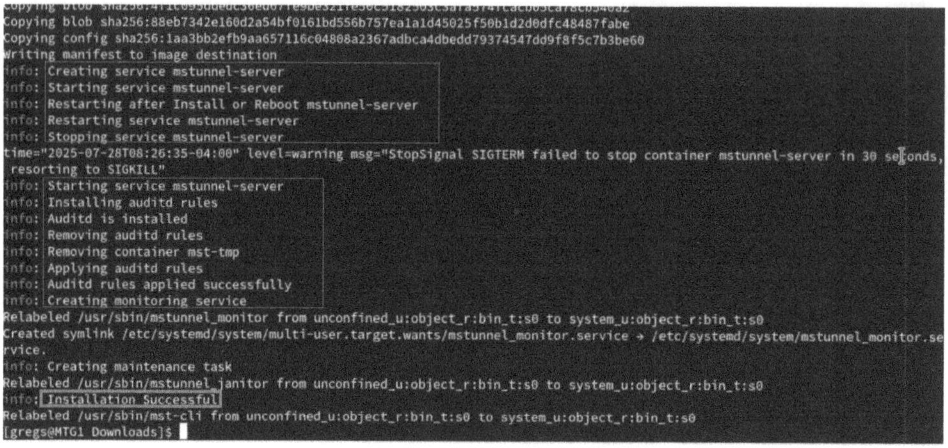

Figure 5.38: Successful installation of the MTG server in the VM

The MTG server will now appear in the Microsoft Intune admin center as healthy:

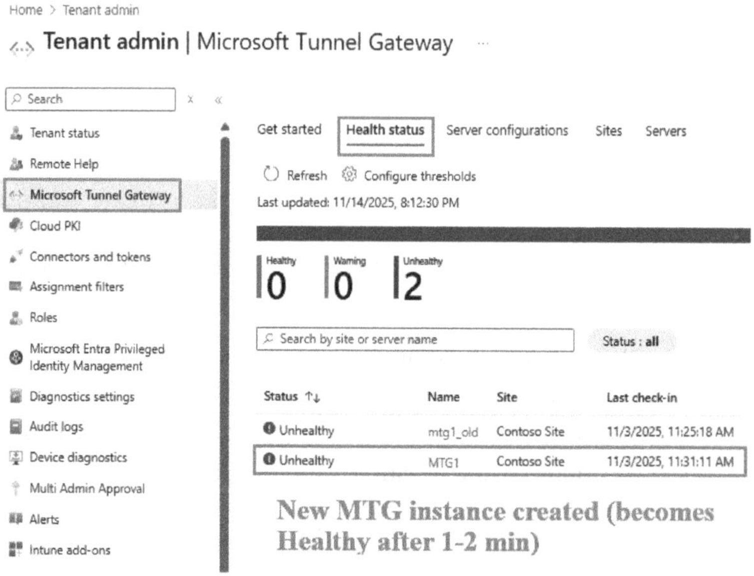

Figure 5.39: Viewing the MTG server in the Intune portal

Step 5: Network configuration on the MTG server

To enable external connectivity to the MTG server, it is critical to configure the network firewall to permit inbound traffic directed at the VPN server's IP address and forward it to the MTG server on ports 443/TCP and 443/UDP. While the exact setup may vary depending on the firewall solution in use, this configuration is a foundational requirement for successful deployment. Additionally, if outbound traffic from the MTG server to the internet is managed by a firewall or proxy, it must be explicitly configured to allow access to the necessary Microsoft Intune service endpoints. We won't go into the specifics of this configuration, as it depends on the third-party proxy or firewall in use and falls outside the scope of this book. In a nutshell, we just need to ensure that inbound traffic over port 443 is allowed on the server.

(Optional): Configuring proxy for Podman image updates on Microsoft Tunnel Gateway

After installing the MTG server, configure Podman to use a proxy for pulling updated container images, essential for future upgrades. We need to follow these four steps to configure that.

1. On the Tunnel Gateway server, launch a command prompt and run `systemctl edit --force mstunnel_monitor` to open the override configuration editor for the Microsoft Tunnel service.

2. Next, we will be replacing `address` with our proxy's IP and port. To do so, add the following two lines to the file. Replace each instance of `address` with your proxy DN or address and then save the file. For example, if the address of your proxy is `10.10.10.1` and available on port 3128, the next two lines after `[Service]` should appear as follows:

    *   `Environment="http_proxy=http//10.10.10.1:3128"`
    *   `Environment="https_proxy=http//10.10.10.1:3128"`

3. Next, run the following at the command prompt to restart the service:

    ```
    systemctl restart mstunnel_monitor
    ```

4. Finally, run the following at the command prompt to confirm the configuration is successful:

    ```
    systemctl show mstunnel_monitor | grep http_proxy
    ```

To change the proxy server configuration that is in use by the Linux host of the tunnel server, on the tunnel server, edit /etc/mstunnel/env.sh and specify the new proxy server. Then we need to run `mst-cli install`.

This command rebuilds the containers with updated proxy settings. During the process, we'll be prompted to verify the contents of /etc/mstunnel/env.sh and confirm that the certificate—already configured from the previous proxy setup—is present. To proceed and finalize the configuration, enter yes when prompted.

This concludes the primary configuration and setup tasks required on the server side. In the following section, we'll walk through the configuration steps required in the Intune portal to complete the MTG setup.

Configuration in the Intune portal

There are three key configurations required in the Intune portal to set up MTG:

1. Creating MTG server configuration
2. Creating a site
3. Deploying the root certificate/tunnel app/app configurations and app protection policy

Let's take a look at each of these steps in detail:

Step 1: Creating MTG server configuration

This configuration specifies the VPN parameters that the client will use to establish a connection with the service. As seen in the following screenshot, we need to go to the Microsoft Intune admin center and navigate to **Tenant admin -> Microsoft Tunnel Gateway -> Server configurations -> + Create new**:

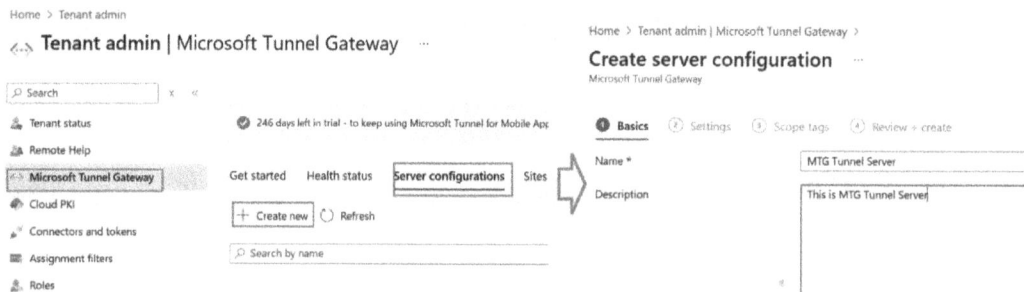

Figure 5.40: Creating an MTG server in the Intune portal

In the **Security** section, we need to configure the following settings:

- **IP address range**: We can leave this as the default. This IP is only used between the VPN client and the VPN server. We need to ensure the Tunnel client IP range does not overlap with on-premises networks. Using the APIPA range (169.254.0.0/16) helps avoid conflicts. Overlapping ranges may cause the client to break VPN connectivity.

- **Server port**: By default, the port is 443/TCP. This is the port on which the MTG server is listening for incoming traffic

- **DNS servers**: This is the IP address of the DNS server the VPN tunnel will use.

- **Split tunnelling rules**: In case we want some of the traffic to go via the VPN tunnel and some not to, we can use split tunnelling and specify the IP address to include and exclude from the tunnel.

The following screenshot shows what the configuration looks like in the Intune portal:

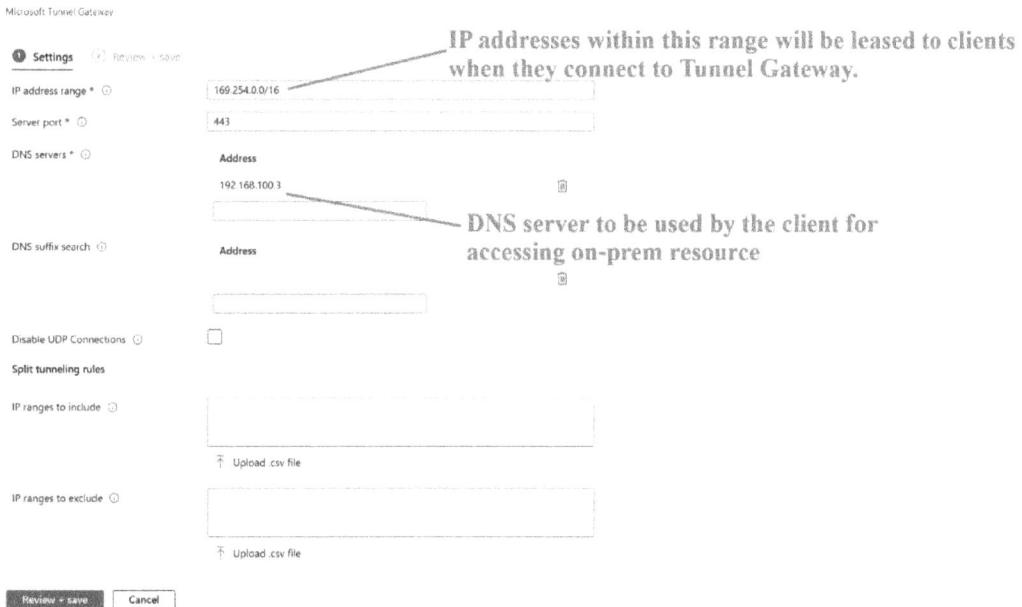

Figure 5.41: Configuring the MTG server in the Intune portal

We can click on **Review + save** and then create the profile. This finalizes the server configuration in the Intune portal.

Now that the MTG server is created, the next step involves creating a Site.

Step 2: Creating a Site

Next, we will create the Site for this configuration. The Site configuration specifies the VPN public name that clients use to access the VPN server, outlines the server upgrade methodology, and defines the internal URL used for validating network access.

In Microsoft Tunnel deployments, Sites function as logical groupings that organize Tunnel-hosting servers. Each Site is linked to a designated server configuration, which is uniformly applied to all servers that are added to that Site.

As seen in the following figure, we need to go to Microsoft Intune admin center -> **Tenant admin > Microsoft Tunnel Gateway** -> **Sites**, then **+ Create**:

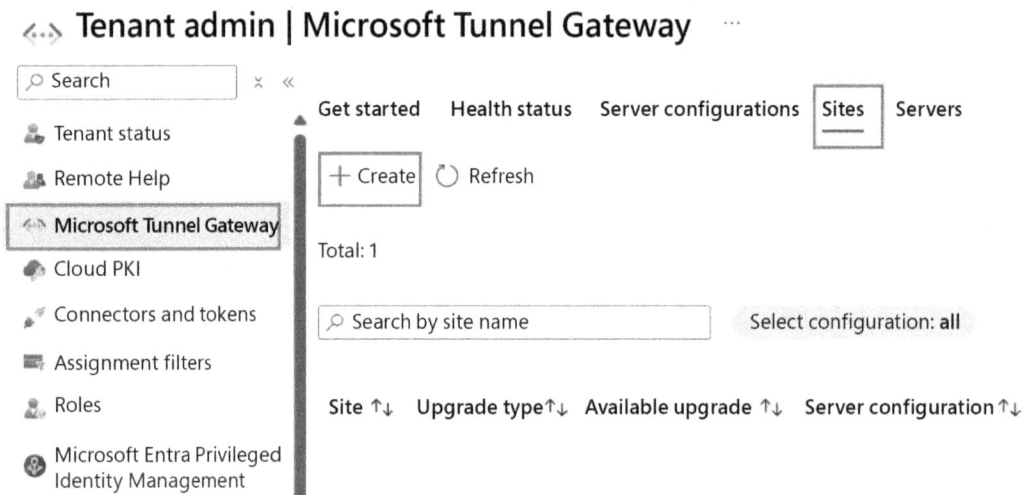

Figure 5.42: Creating a Site for the MTG server in the Intune portal

In the **Security** section, we need to configure the following settings:

- **Public IP address or FQDN**: This is the public/external IP address of the MTG server that the clients will reach out to.

- **Server configuration**: This specifies the server configuration that VPN servers linked to this site will use. In this step, we will enter the name of the server configuration previously created.

- **URL for internal network access check**: Over here, we need to specify a health check URL that is accessible within the internal corporate network. The MTG server uses this URL to confirm connectivity to internal/on-prem resources. If the server can reach it, client devices should be able to access it.

- **Automatically upgrade servers at this site**: If this is configured to **Yes**, the MTG server will upgrade once an upgrade is available.
- **Limit server upgrades to maintenance window**: This setting allows us to configure a maintenance window for the automatic server upgrade.

The following screenshot shows what the configuration looks like in the Intune portal:

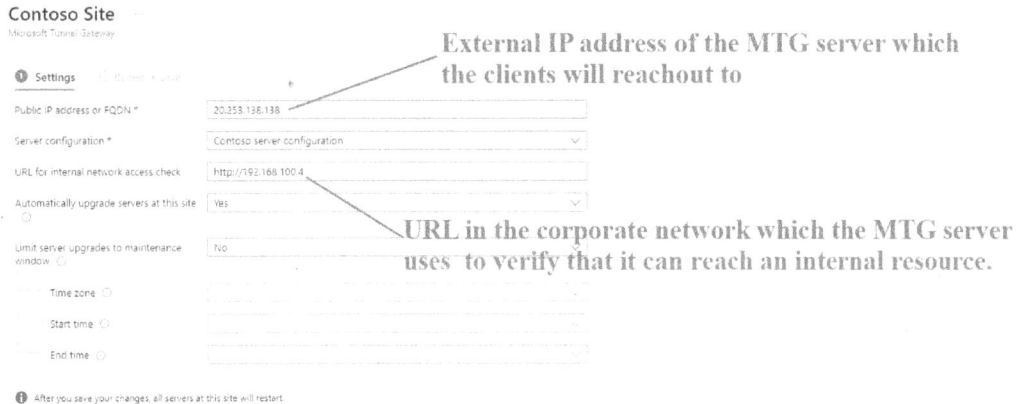

Figure 5.43: Configuring the Site created in the Intune portal

After completing the configuration, we click **Next**, leave **Scope tags** unchanged, and proceed. On the **Review + create** screen, we need to verify the settings and click **Create** to finalize the site configuration.

Since we've already reviewed a couple of settings related to the MTG server's automatic upgrade options in the Intune portal in the previous section, let's now explore the Tunnel upgrade process in greater detail in the following section.

Understanding the Microsoft Tunnel upgrade process

Microsoft Tunnel, the VPN gateway solution integrated with Microsoft Intune, receives periodic software updates to maintain support and security compliance. To remain supported, Tunnel servers must run the latest available release. Intune automates the upgrade process for servers assigned to each Tunnel Site. When an upgrade is initiated, servers within the Site are updated sequentially—this is known as an **upgrade cycle**. During the upgrade of a server, its tunnel service becomes temporarily unavailable. Sequential upgrades help reduce service disruption, especially in multi-server environments.

The upgrade begins with one server and may start as early as 10 minutes after the new release is published. If a server is offline, its upgrade is deferred until it powers on. Once a server is successfully updated, Intune waits briefly before proceeding to the next server in the Site.

To manage when Intune initiates the upgrade cycle for Microsoft Tunnel servers, configure the following Site-level settings:

- Automatically upgrade servers at this Site
- Limit server upgrades to the maintenance window

These options can be set during Site creation or by editing an existing Site's properties. If automatic upgrades are enabled (**Yes**), Intune begins updating servers shortly after a new tunnel version is released—without requiring admin action. If a maintenance window is defined, upgrades occur within that time frame. Without a window, upgrades start as soon as possible.

If automatic upgrades are disabled (**No**), Intune waits for an admin to manually trigger the upgrade. In this case, regularly check the **Health Check** tab to identify available updates and determine whether the current Tunnel version is out of support. For Sites using automatic upgrades, the process runs only during the configured window. For Sites requiring manual approval, the upgrade begins during the next scheduled maintenance window after approval is granted.

The current Microsoft Tunnel version isn't displayed in the Intune UI. To retrieve version details, run the following command on the Linux server hosting the tunnel:

```
cat /etc/mstunnel/images_configured
```

This will output the hash values for `agentImageDigest` and `serverImageDigest`, which identify the deployed container images.

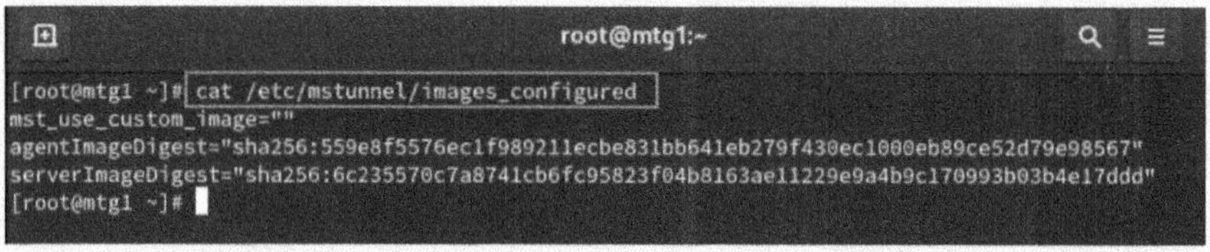

```
 ⊞                                    root@mtg1:~                                    Q    ≡

[root@mtg1 ~]# cat /etc/mstunnel/images_configured
mst_use_custom_image=""
agentImageDigest="sha256:559e8f5576ec1f989211ecbe831bb641eb279f430ec1000eb89ce52d79e98567"
serverImageDigest="sha256:6c235570c7a8741cb6fc95823f04b8163ae11229e9a4b9c170993b03b4e17ddd"
[root@mtg1 ~]# █
```

Figure 5.44: Viewing the MS Tunnel version from the terminal window

The next step is to create a trusted root certificate profile for client devices within the Intune portal, along with the needed app configuration and protection policies. We'll explore this process and its importance in the following section.

Step 3: Deploying the root certificate/app configurations and app protection policy

First, let's walk through the steps to deploy the trusted root certificate from the Intune portal, as outlined in the following section.

Step 3.1: Deploying the trusted root certificate

We used a TLS certificate from our on-prem CA during the setup of MTG in the RHEL server. This TLS certificate is for securing Tunnel-based connection between the client and the MTG server. However, by default, the client is not going to trust the TLS certificate that MTG has to offer. Hence, we need to push the root certificate of the CA that issued the TLS certificate to the end device. This will ensure that the end device can recognize the legitimacy of our on-prem CA and the TLS certificate. This certificate would be pushed as .cer via a trusted root certificate profile from the Intune portal.

> When devices are enrolled in Intune, the trusted root certificate must be assigned to a user or device group to ensure it is pushed to the device. However, for MAM Tunnel setups—where devices are not enrolled in Intune—we only need to create the trusted root certificate. There's no need to assign it, as it will be automatically deployed through the app channel, as we will be linking this certificate to the app configuration policy in the next section.

As seen in the following screenshot, we have the option of creating a **Trusted certificate** profile for Android BYOD devices. The same approach applies to iOS as well. We need to ensure that we have the .cer certificate file ready when creating the profile.

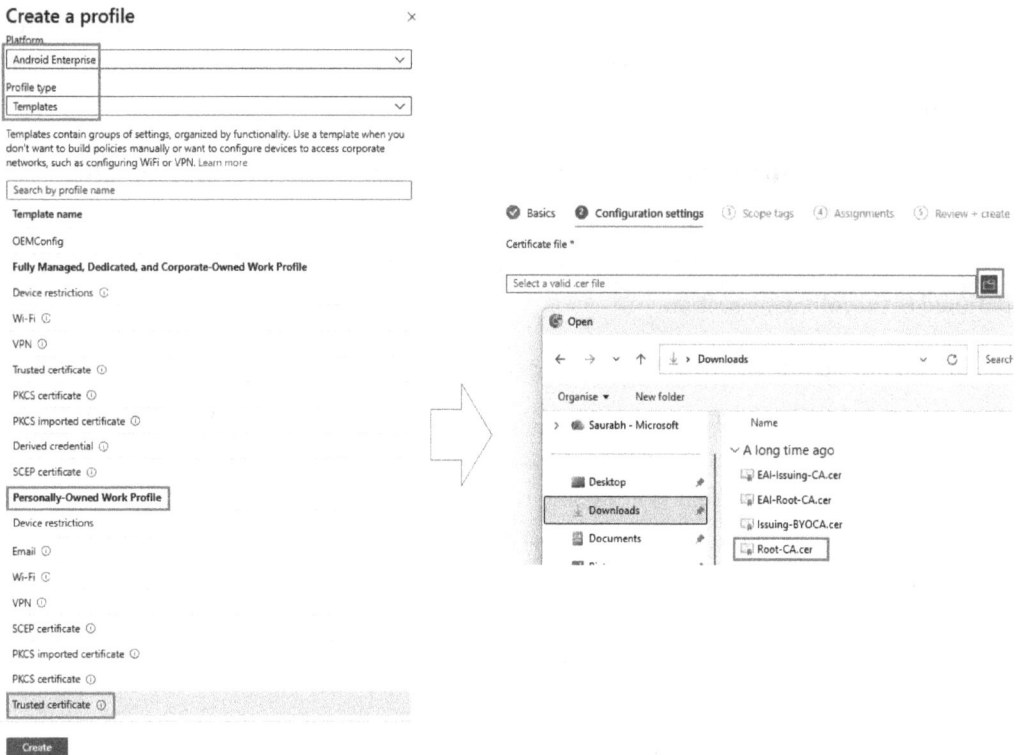

Figure 5.45: Creating a trusted root certificate profile for a MAM Tunnel scenario

The next step of the MAM Tunnel setup involves deploying the app configuration profile, which we will discuss in the next section.

Step 3.2: Deploying the app configuration policy

This app configuration profile deploys VPN settings to the Microsoft Edge app. Let's take a look at the settings of this profile.

We need to go to the Microsoft Intune admin center -> **Apps** -> **Manage apps** -> **Configuration** -> **+ Create** -> **Managed apps**

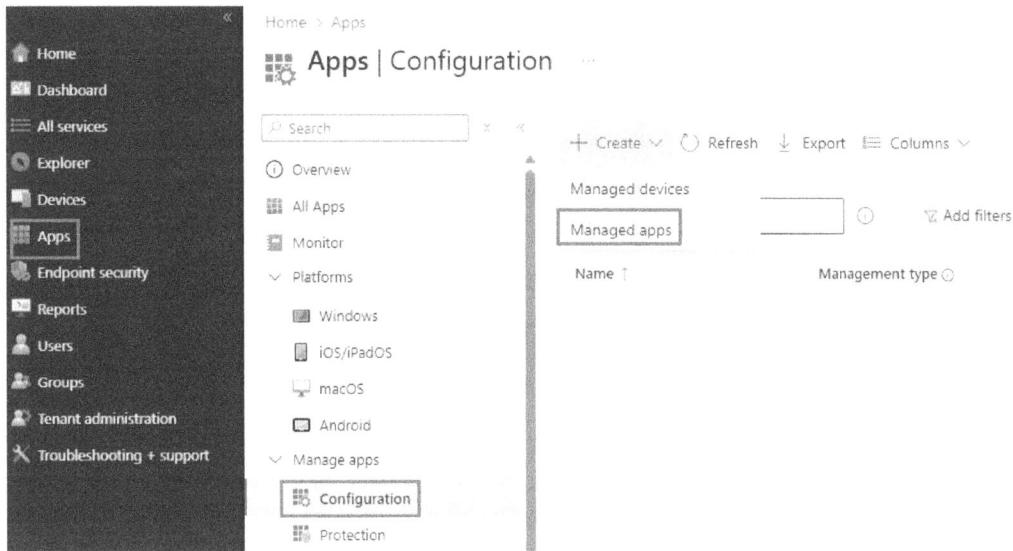

Figure 5.46: Creating an app configuration policy in the Intune portal

On the next screen, under **Target policy to**, select the **Selected apps** option from the dropdown, and under **Select public apps**, add **Microsoft Edge: iOS/iPadOS**, and then click on **Next**:

Home > Apps | Configuration > Targeted App Config | Properties >

Edit app configuration policy   ...

1 Basics   (2) Review + save

Name *	Microsoft Tunnel_App Config_iOS
Description	Microsoft Tunnel_App Config_iOS

Device enrollment type	Managed apps ∨
Target policy to	Selected apps ∨

Public apps	Platform	Remove
Microsoft Edge	iOS/iPadOS	Remove

+ Select public apps

Custom apps	Platform	Remove
No custom apps selected		

+ Select custom apps

Figure 5.47: Settings of the app configuration policy

On the next screen, we need to configure the VPN settings for the app with the following values:

- **General configuration settings:**

    - `com.microsoft.intune.mam.managedbrowser.TunnelAvailable.IntuneMAMOnly` = True

    - `com.microsoft.intune.mam.managedbrowser.StrictTunnelMode` = True

- **Microsoft Tunnel for Mobile Application Management settings:**

    - **Use Microsoft Tunnel for MAM: Yes**

    - **Connection name:** `contoso vpn`

    - **Select a Site: Contoso Site**

    - **Root Certificate:** We need to include the trusted certificate profiles here, which were created in the previous section, under *Step 3.1.*

The following screenshot shows what these settings look like in the Intune portal:

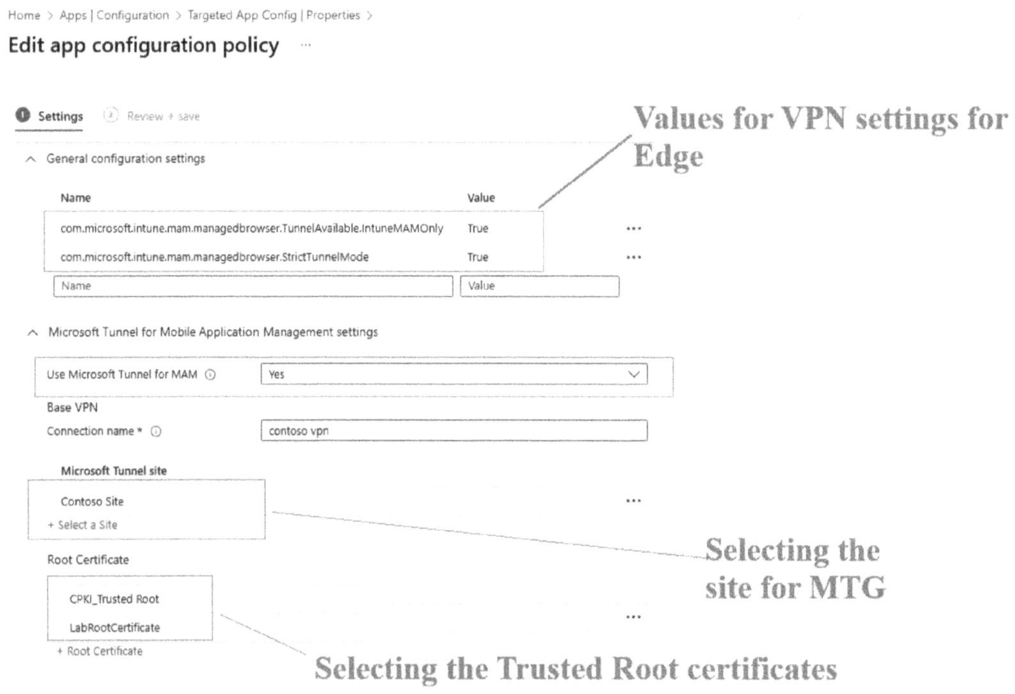

Figure 5.48: Settings (values) of the app configuration policy

The preceding app configuration policy is now ready, and it needs to be assigned to the necessary user group. In the next section, we will create an app protection policy for the Edge application from the Intune portal.

Step 3.3: Deploying an app protection policy

This app protection policy safeguards data and also delivers app configuration settings to supported apps. It ensures that the MAM tunnel automatically connects when Microsoft Edge is launched.

As seen in the following screenshot, we will go to Microsoft Intune admin center -> **Apps** -> **Protection** -> **+ Create** -> **iOS/iPadOS**.

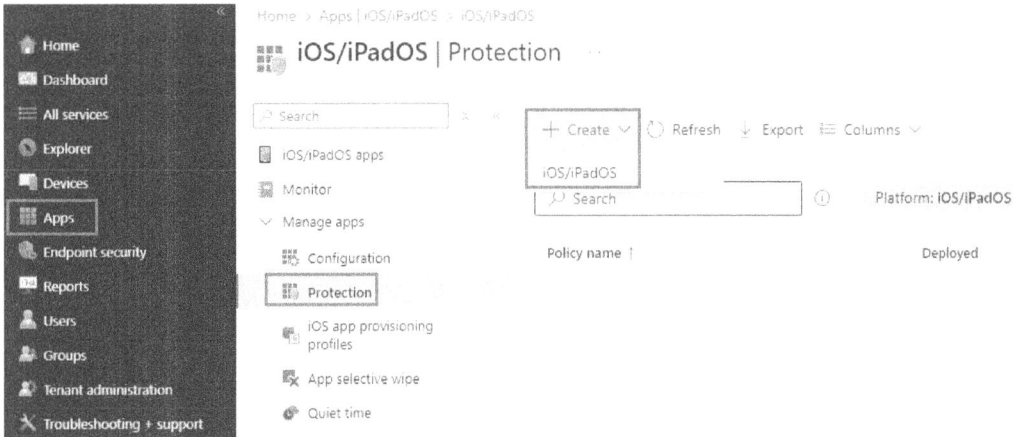

Figure 5.49: Creating an app protection policy in the Intune portal

Next, we need to configure the MAM policy with the following values:

- **Target policy to: Selected apps**
- Under **Public apps**, add **Microsoft Edge**
- Under **Data protection**, **Access requirements**, and **Conditional launch:** We can leave the values as either the default or configure them as per our organization's requirements.

The following screenshot shows how these settings appear in the Intune portal:

Home > Apps | iOS/iPadOS > iOS/iPadOS | Protection > Intune App Protection | Properties >

Edit policy   ...

MAM Tunnel_App Protection_iOS

---

① Apps   ② Review + save

> ℹ️ If you apply assignment filters to this policy, the 'Device Management Type' property will apply in addition to the values specified for 'Target to apps on all device types' and 'Device types' on the 'Apps' page.
>
> To edit device management type targeting, reset 'Target to apps on all device types' = 'Yes'. Then create a MAM assignment filter with the desired values for 'Device Management Type'. <u>Learn more about assigning App Protection Policies</u>

Choose how you want to apply this policy to apps on different devices. Then add at least one app.

Target to apps on all device types ⓘ   [**Yes**   No]

   └──── Device types ⓘ   [0 selected   ⌄]

Target policy to   [Selected apps   ⌄]

Public apps	**Remove**
Microsoft Edge	Remove

+ Select public apps

Custom apps	**Remove**
No custom apps selected	

+ Select custom apps

[Review + save]   [Cancel]

Figure 5.50: Setting the values in the app configuration policy

We can now click on **Review + save** and assign the profile to the required user group. With this step, we've successfully completed all the necessary configurations for MAM Tunnel within the Intune portal.

> This chapter primarily focuses on the MAM Tunnel scenario, which applies when end-user devices are not enrolled in Intune (i.e., not MDM-managed). MAM Tunnel is typically used in BYOD cases, allowing users to access corporate or on-premises resources from their personal devices without requiring MDM enrollment. This feature is part of the Intune Suite and requires additional licensing.
>
> Intune also supports a similar feature called MDM Tunnel, which is used when devices are enrolled in Intune. The underlying logic and functionality remain consistent with MAM Tunnel—both require setting up the MTG server as described in this chapter. The next two sections are relevant only for MDM-enrolled devices and do not apply to MAM Tunnel setups. These sections are therefore labelled as *Optional/only for MDM scenarios.*

Optional/only for MDM scenarios: deploying app configurations/VPN profiles

In MDM Tunnel scenarios, since the device is enrolled in Intune, we have the option to deploy a VPN profile directly to the device. The configurations in the VPN profile will be used for connecting the application to the MTG server and then, in turn, to the on-prem hosted resource. Let's take a look at the following configurations for the profile:

As seen in the following screenshot, the profile would be **VPN** under the **Personally-Owned Work Profile** category:

Home > Devices | Android > Android

▦ Android | Configuration ⋯

🔍 Search ✕ «

☐ Android devices

▣ Monitor

∨ Device onboarding

   🖥 Enrollment

∨ Manage devices

   ▦ **Configuration**

   📄 Compliance

∨ Manage updates

   📱 Android FOTA deployments

∨ Organize devices

   📑 Device clean-up rules

   ▦ Assignment filters

Policies
_____

➕ Create ∨   ↻ Refresh   ↧ Export   ☰ Columns ∨

🔍 Search   ⓘ   ▽ Add filters

Policy name   Platform

Create a profile

Platform

| Android Enterprise |

Profile type

| Templates |

Templates contain groups of settings, organized by functionality. Use
don't want to build policies manually or want to configure devices to
networks, such as configuring WiFi or VPN. Learn more

| Search by profile name |

Template name

OEMConfig

Fully Managed, Dedicated, and Corporate-Owned Work Profile

Device restrictions ⓒ

Wi-Fi ⓒ

VPN ⓘ

Trusted certificate ⓘ

PKCS certificate ⓘ

PKCS imported certificate ⓘ

Derived credential ⓘ

SCEP certificate ⓘ

| **Personally-Owned Work Profile** |

Device restrictions

Email ⓘ

Wi-Fi ⓒ

| VPN ⓘ |

SCEP certificate ⓘ

Figure 5.51: Creating an app configuration policy in the Intune portal for an MDM Tunnel scenario

On the next screen, we need to configure the following settings in the policy:

- **Connection type: Microsoft Tunnel**: This VPN profile would be used for establishing MAM Tunnel with the MTG server and, in turn, with the on-premise hosted application

- **Base VPN > Connection Name**: We can name this anything, as per our liking

- **Microsoft Tunnel Site:** Select the Site created during MTG configuration

- **Per-app VPN**: Add the Microsoft Edge browser

- **Custom settings**: We need to add a key-value pair, as follows:

Configuration key	Configuration value
Vpn	1
antiphishing	0
defendertoggle	0

Table 5.4: Values to be used in the app configuration policy for MDM Tunnel

The following screenshot illustrates how these settings appear in the Intune portal:

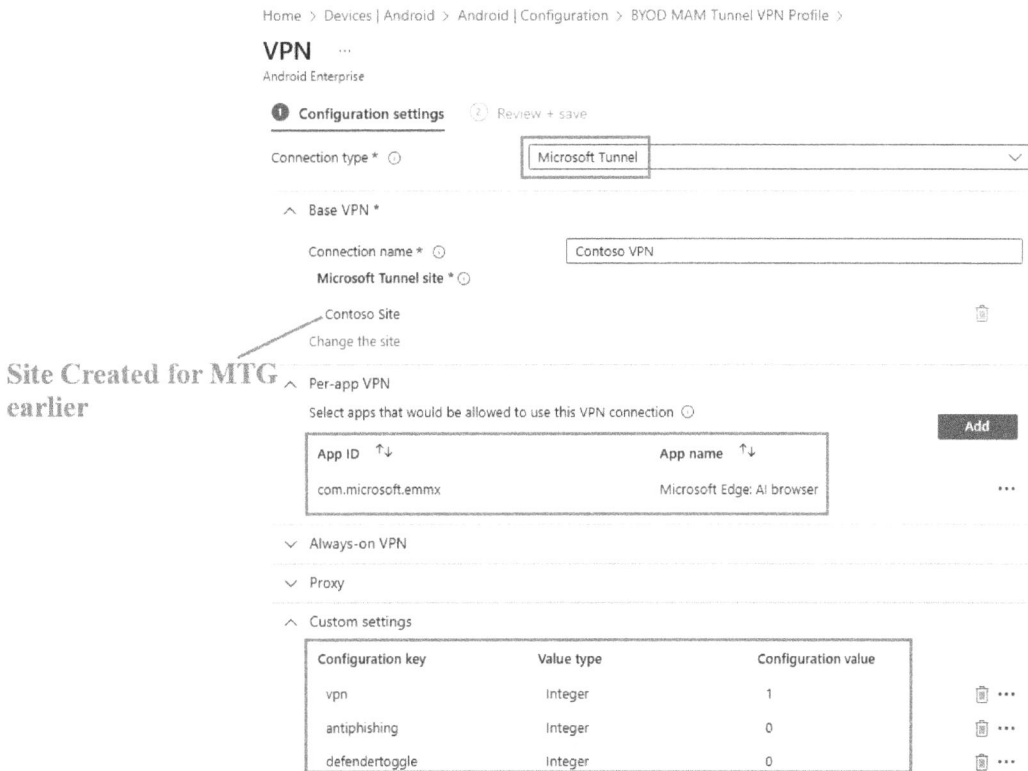

Figure 5.52: Image showing the configuration/settings of the app configuration policy for MDM Tunnel

With the VPN profile and app configuration settings now in place, the next step is to deploy the application that will utilize these configurations. In the next section, we'll walk through the deployment process of these apps within the Intune portal.

Optional/only for MDM scenarios: deploying an MS Tunnel client app to Android/iOS devices

Since the device is enrolled in Intune, we can deploy applications as **Required**, which ensures automatic installation on the device. We need to deploy two applications as the next step of the MDM tunnel setup:

- We need to deploy the **Microsoft Defender for Endpoint** application. This app manages the VPN connection from the device.

- We need to deploy **Microsoft Edge**. This browser will utilize the tunnel as per the per-app VPN configuration done earlier, and it will access the on-premise hosted resource – in this case, a URL.

As seen in the following screenshot, both apps need to be deployed as **Managed Google Play app** from the Intune portal.

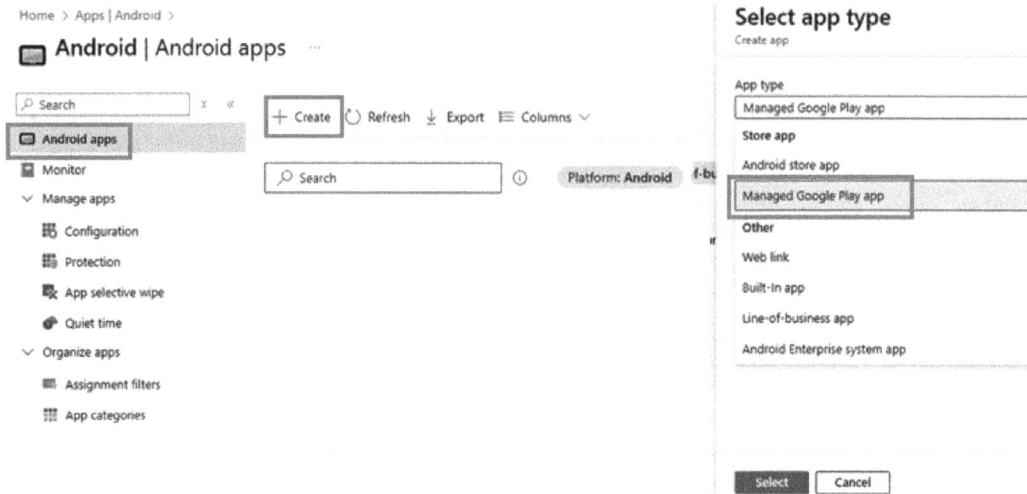

Figure 5.53: Deploying applications to MDM devices (Android- BYOD) from the Intune portal

For reference, the store URLs for the applications are as follows:

- Playstore URL for Microsoft Edge Browser: `https://play.google.com/store/apps/details?id=com.microsoft.emmx&hl=en_IN`

- Playstore URL for Microsoft Defender: `https://play.google.com/store/apps/details?id=com.microsoft.scmx&hl=en_IN`

On the **Managed Google Play** screen in the portal, we have to approve both the applications – Microsoft Defender and Microsoft Edge.

Home > Apps | Android > Android | Android apps >

Managed Google Play   ...

◯ Sync

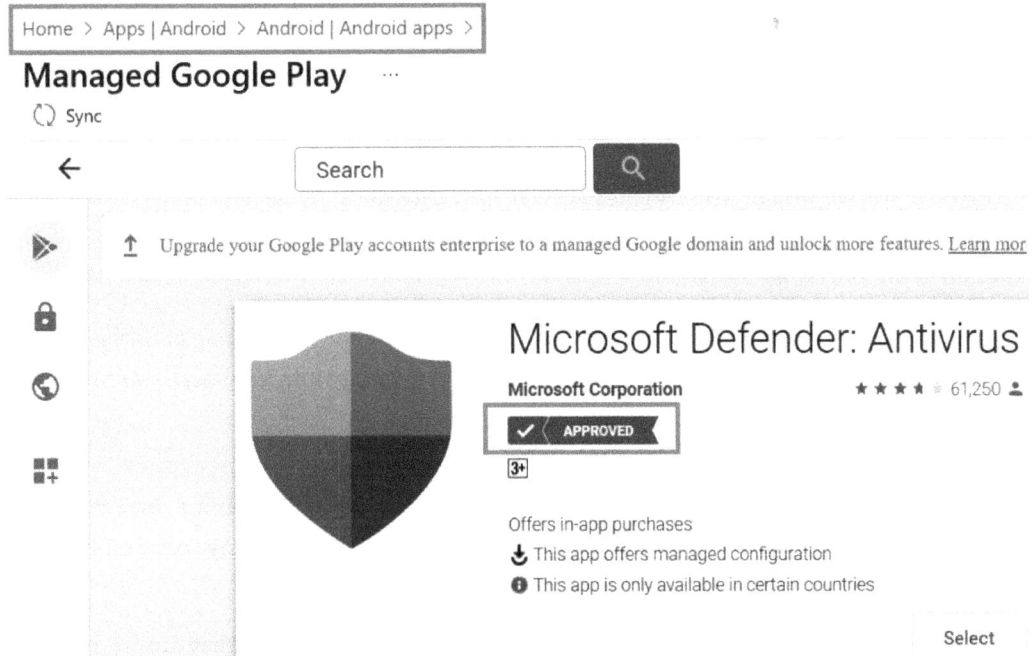

Figure 5.54: Adding/approving apps for Android from the Managed Google Play store in the
Intune portal

Once approved, both applications will be listed under the **All Apps** section as seen in the following
screenshot. Now these apps have to be deployed to the relevant user group as **Required** so that
they get installed automatically.

Home > Apps | Android >

Android | Android apps   ...

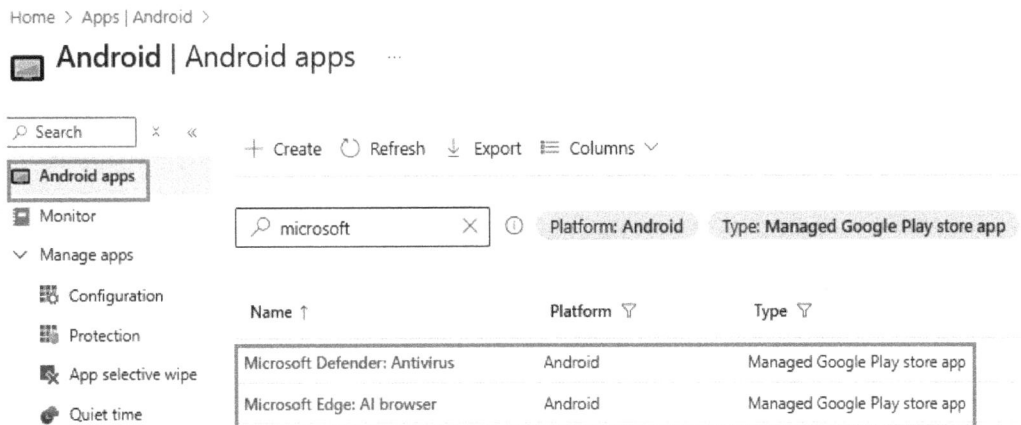

Figure 5.55: Android apps added to the Intune portal for BYOD devices

It is important to remember that while an Intune-enrolled device could receive the VPN for a MAM scenario, it is not supported to have both MDM and MAM scenarios applied to the same device.

Up to this point, we've completed all the necessary setup for the MTG server—both on the server/on-premises side and within the Intune portal. We also reviewed the optional configuration steps relevant to MDM Tunnel scenarios.

In the next section, we are going to see the end user's experience while using both these applications, and we are going to understand how the user can successfully connect to MAM Tunnel.

End user experience on the device

As mentioned earlier, in the case of a MAM Tunnel scenario, users' devices are not enrolled in Intune; they must install Microsoft Defender, Microsoft Edge, and Company Portal on their Android/iOS device before they can use Tunnel for an MAM scenario.

Following is the end user's experience while launching the Defender app. They are prompted to sign in and accept the EULA.

The following screens/UI are subject to change with the release of newer versions of the operating system.

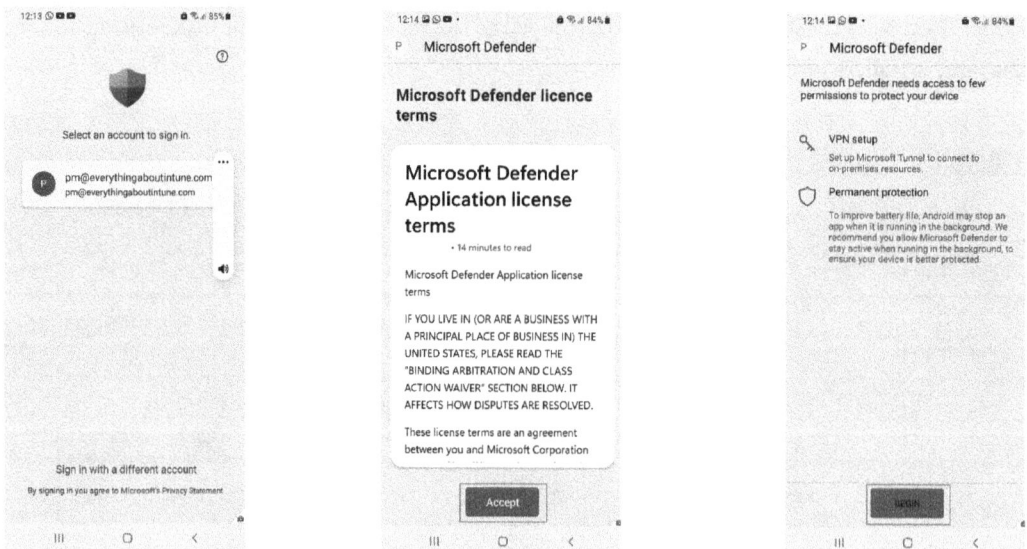

Figure 5.56: Initial screens while signing in to the Defender app on an Android device for an MDM Tunnel scenario

There is a toggle for the user to connect to MAM Tunnel:

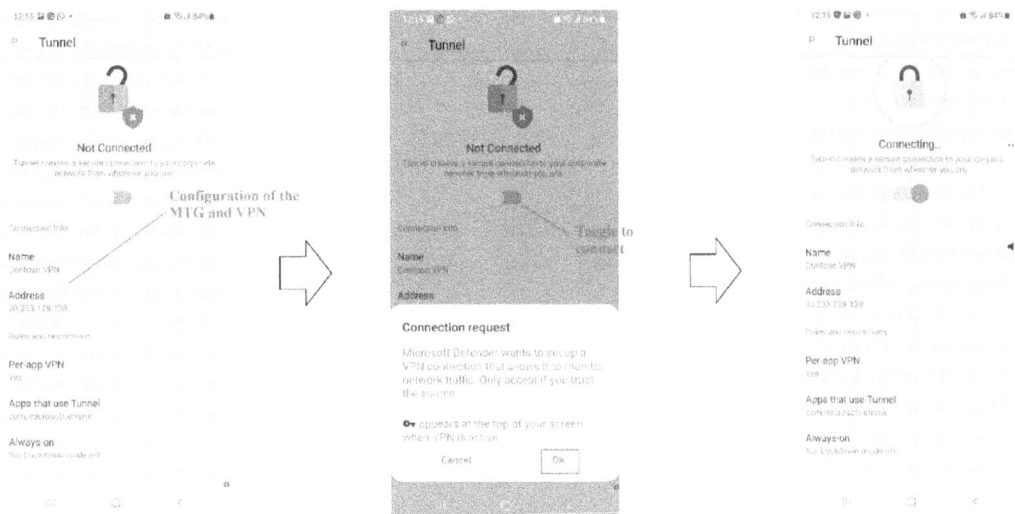

Figure 5.57: Connecting to MDM Tunnel on an Android BYOD device

Similarly, the user also needs to launch Microsoft Edge and sign in to it. Once they do, the app protection and configuration policy will automatically trigger Tunnel to connect to the VPN whenever Microsoft Edge is launched:

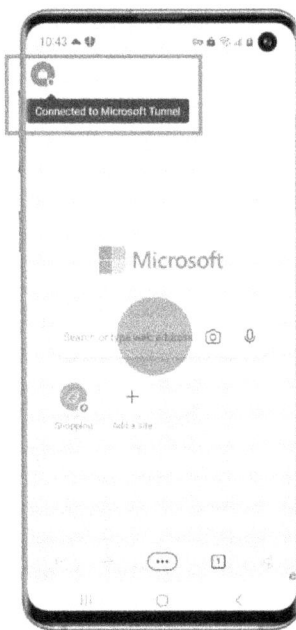

Figure 5.58: Experience using Microsoft Edge on an Android device with MAM Tunnel

The end user can browse to the intranet site, which is protected by a TLS certificate, and get successfully connected:

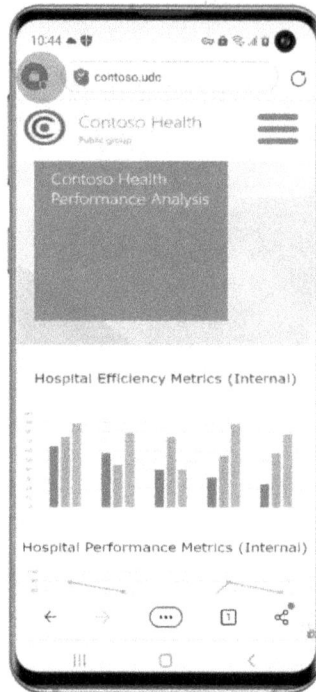

Figure 5.59: Intranet site accessible using Microsoft Edge via MAM Tunnel

If the end user changes profiles in Edge, they will no longer have access to company resources, and the Tunnel connection will automatically be disabled.

The Company Portal app must be installed on the device, even though users won't need to sign in to the app or enroll their device with Intune.

Figure 5.60: Experience when the user switches the profile in Microsoft Edge

In that case, the intranet website becomes inaccessible:

Figure 5.61: Internal site becomes inaccessible via MAM Tunnel when the user switches Edge profiles

Edge only connects to MAM Tunnel when signed in with an org account in order to protect privacy, as well as to use application policies for data protection.

As seen in the preceding user experience section, MAM Tunnel enhances enterprise security by enabling protected access to sensitive corporate resources from personal devices. It ensures a privacy-respecting experience for end users, empowering them to securely interact with company data without compromising personal boundaries.

We can also explore the following websites, which feature a UI-based mock-up of various MAM Tunnel scenarios. It provides an interactive, click-through experience that simulates policy setup and the end-user journey—allowing us to visualize both the admin and user perspectives without needing to configure everything manually!

- End User Experience: `https://regale.cloud/microsoft/play/1896/microsoft-tunnel-for-mobile-application-management-for-android#/4/1`

- Setting up the App Configuration Policy (Edge): `https://regale.cloud/microsoft/play/1896/microsoft-tunnel-for-mobile-application-management-for-android#/2/0`

- Setting up App Configuration Policy to Defender/LOB App: `https://regale.cloud/microsoft/play/1896/microsoft-tunnel-for-mobile-application-management-for-android#/1/17`

- Setting up App Protection Policy (Edge): `https://regale.cloud/microsoft/play/1896/microsoft-tunnel-for-mobile-application-management-for-android#/3/0`

MTG containers can run on RHEL servers using a non-root user for added security. Rootless mode reduces container escape risks but must be chosen before installation, as switching later requires reinstallation.

If we're installing Tunnel on a rootless Podman container, use the following modified command-line to start the script:

```
mst_rootless_mode=1 ./mstunnel-setup
```

If we don't have access to a test tenant or end-user devices, we recommend exploring the interactive demos in the preceding repository. They offer a hands-on preview of the MAM Tunnel setup and the end-user experience, helping us understand the look and feel without needing a full deployment.

This wraps up the steps the end user needs to follow to use the MAM Tunnel feature via Intune. The steps mostly remain the same for both Android and iOS devices. In the following section, we'll explore common troubleshooting methods and the key tools available to help diagnose MTG-related issues.

Troubleshooting

We'll explore troubleshooting options for the MTG setup from two perspectives: server-side diagnostics and troubleshooting from the Intune portal. The most common issues that we might have to troubleshoot involve scenarios wherein the MTG server shows **Unhealthy** in the Intune portal, or even when the server is functional, the Tunnel sessions don't get established. The troubleshooting approach discussed next will cater to both those scenarios.

Server-side troubleshooting

We can use the `mst-cli` command-line tool to retrieve information about the Microsoft Tunnel server. This tool is installed on the Linux server as part of the Microsoft Tunnel setup and is located at `/usr/sbin/mst-cli`:

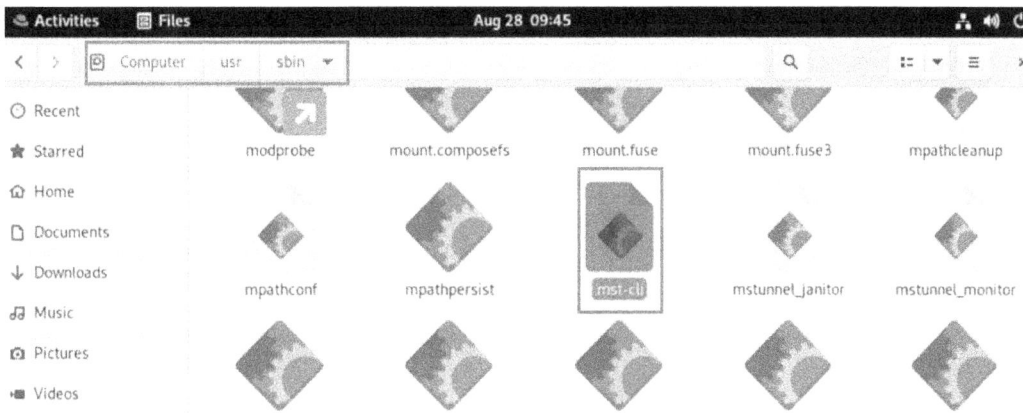

Figure 5.62: Command-line tool in the RHEL server

Microsoft Tunnel logs are written to the Linux system logs in standard syslog format.

We can use this tool to perform tasks such as the following:

- Retrieve detailed information about the Tunnel server
- Configure or update Tunnel server settings
- Restart the Tunnel server
- Remove the Tunnel server from the system

The following is a list of commonly used commands that can be used to troubleshoot any issues with the MTG server:

Command	Use
`mst-cli uninstall`	Uninstall Microsoft Tunnel
`mst-cli import_cert`	Import or update the TLS certificate
`mst-cli agent status`	Show the agent status
`mst-cli agent restart`	Restart the agent service
`mst-cli server show status`	Show the server status
`journalctl -t ocserv`	Display server logs
`journalctl -t ocserv-access`	Display access logs
`journalctl -t mstunnel-agent`	Display agent logs
`sudo podman images`	List of all running containers
`sudo podman port mstunnel-server`	List the port mappings from the Tunnel server to the local Linux host

Table 5.5: List of commonly used commands for MTG troubleshooting

Next, let's review a few key commands, along with their expected output in a working scenario for reference:

- We can run the `mst-cli diagnose` command to validate the MTG server's status. This command verifies that all prerequisites and critical configurations necessary for the solution to function correctly are in place.

  The following screenshot displays a partial output of the command:

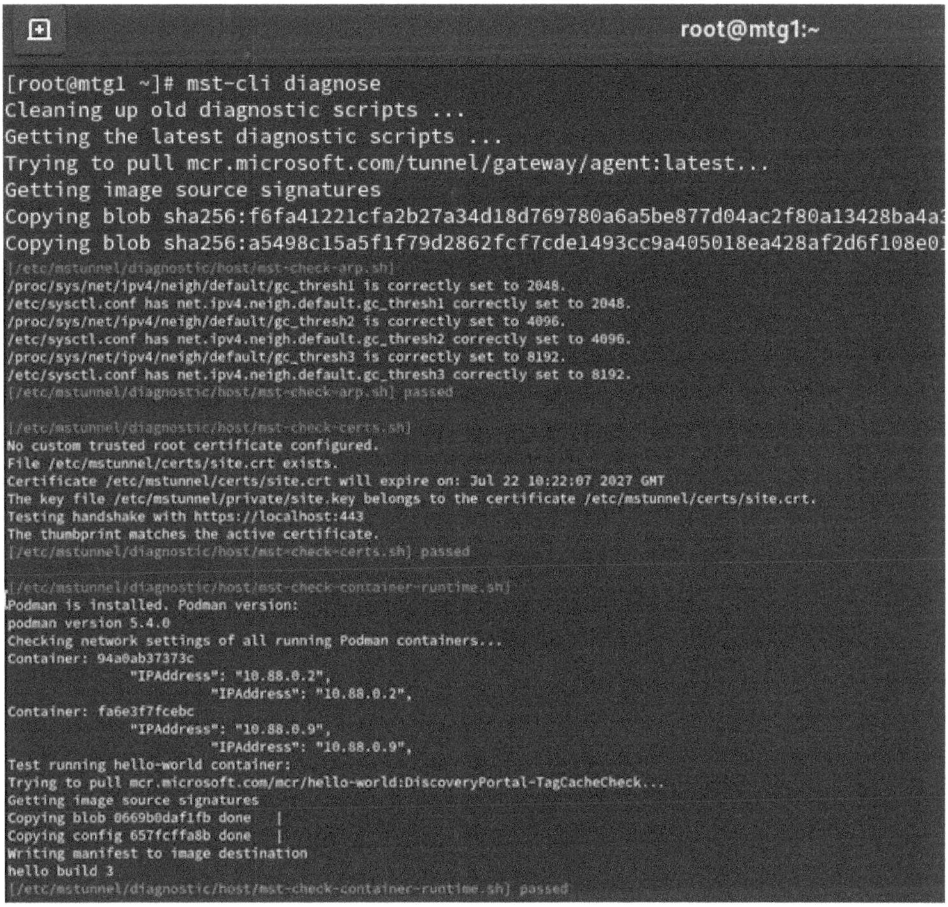

Figure 5.63: Sample output of troubleshooting commands for MTG

A report named `diagnosticReport.txt` under `/etc/mstunnel/diagnostic` is created, as seen in the following screenshot, which can be analyzed in case of any errors.

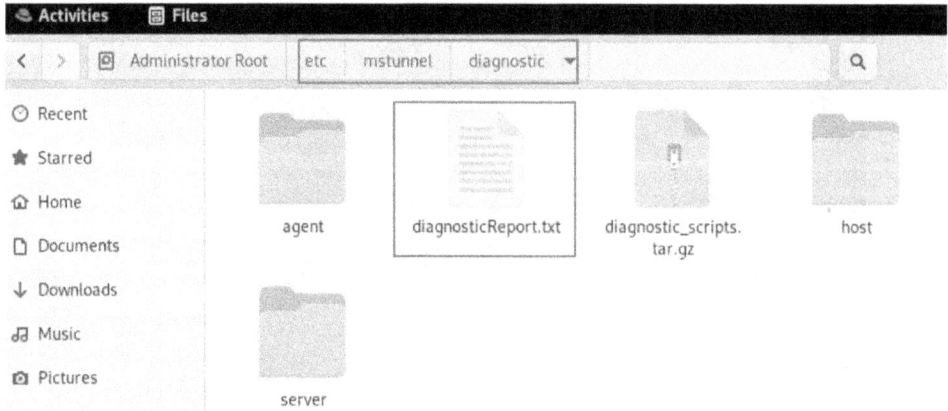

Figure 5.64: Diagnostic report after running command for troubleshooting in the server

- We can also get a list of the users connected to the VPN via the MTG server by executing the `mst-cli server show users` command:

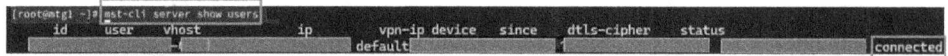

Figure 5.65: Viewing users connected to MTG via terminal

This can be very helpful when our MTG site operates multiple servers behind a load balancer, and we need to pinpoint which server is managing a specific connection. Running this command will identify the responsible server. If no user appears in the output, it means the current server isn't handling the connection—try running the query on the next server. We can also list all running containers using the `sudo podman images` command and view the port mappings from `mstunnel-server` to the local Linux host by running `sudo podman port mstunnel-server`.

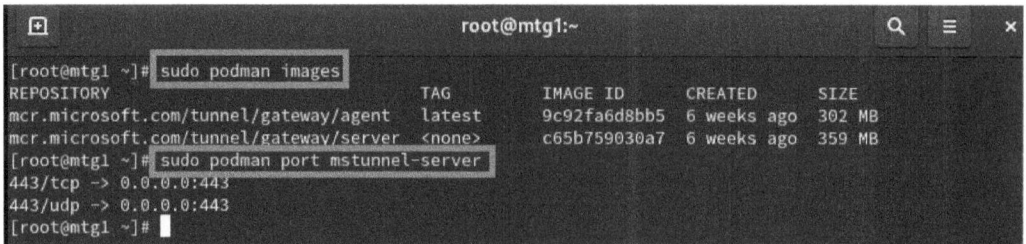

Figure 5.66: Viewing all the containers in the server via the terminal

So far, we've reviewed the commands that can be executed, explored the available troubleshooting options on the MTG side, and examined how working operational logs are expected to appear. In the next section, let's explore the troubleshooting options and available logs within the Intune portal that can help diagnose issues related to MAM Tunnel.

Troubleshooting from the Intune portal

In this section, we'll review the logs available for download and the troubleshooting actions that can be performed directly from the Intune portal.

If the MTG server is offline or any of its components are malfunctioning, you can check its health status in the Intune portal by navigating to **Microsoft Tunnel Gateway > Health status**. If the service detects any common errors, the server will be marked as **Unhealthy**, as shown in the following screenshot.

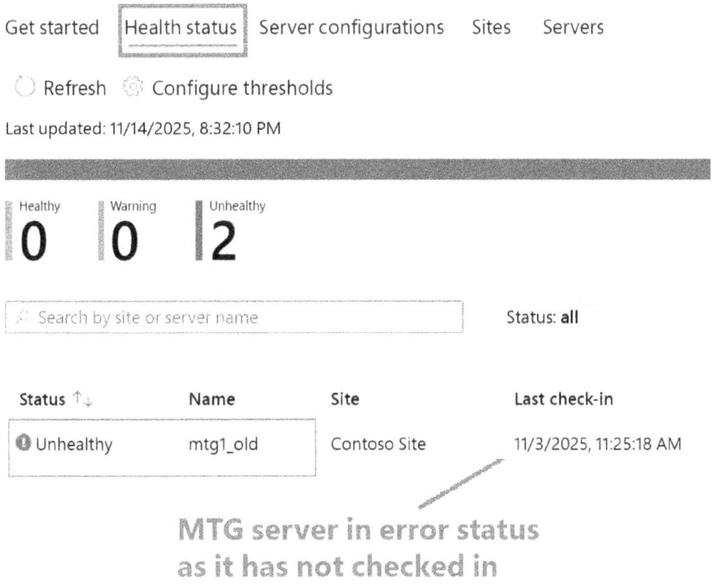

Figure 5.67: Viewing the MTG server's error in the Intune portal

We can download error-related logs via the Intune admin center, by going to **Tenant admin ->
Microsoft Tunnel Gateway -> Health status ->** Select the server and then select the **Logs** tab. We
need to select the timeframe the logs should be collected for, and then select **Generate**.

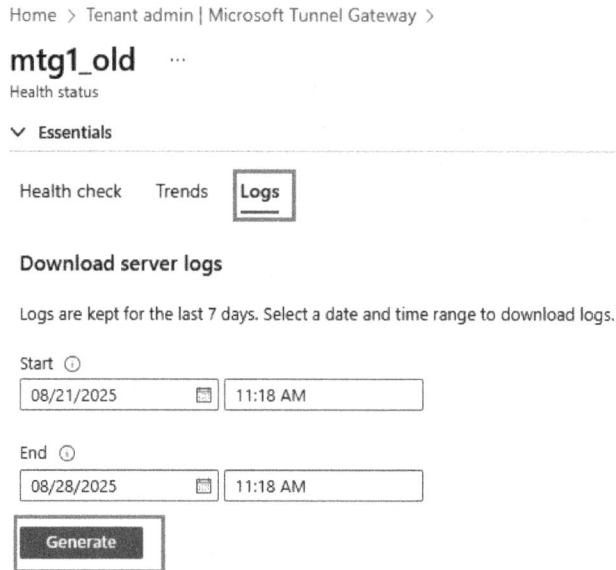

Home > Tenant admin | Microsoft Tunnel Gateway >

mtg1_old   ⋯
Health status

∨ Essentials

Health check   Trends   Logs

Download server logs

Logs are kept for the last 7 days. Select a date and time range to download logs.

Start ⓘ

| 08/21/2025 📅 | 11:18 AM |

End ⓘ

| 08/28/2025 📅 | 11:18 AM |

Generate

Figure 5.68: Generating logs for MTG from the Intune portal

Once the log is generated for a specific timeframe, we have the option of downloading it from
the portal:

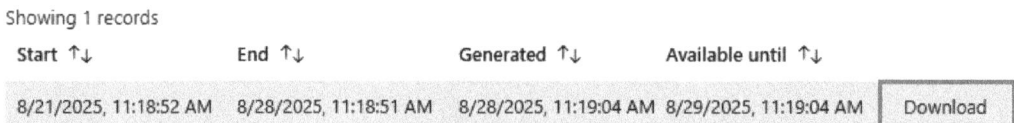

Showing 1 records

Start ↑↓	End ↑↓	Generated ↑↓	Available until ↑↓	
8/21/2025, 11:18:52 AM	8/28/2025, 11:18:51 AM	8/28/2025, 11:19:04 AM	8/29/2025, 11:19:04 AM	Download

Figure 5.69: Option to download the MTG log from the Intune portal

The following snippet shows a sample log that indicates whether there are any errors preventing
the server from successfully communicating with the Microsoft Intune endpoint.

```
20250821-05mtg1_old.txt          x    +
File   Edit   View                                          H1 v   ≡ v   B   I   ∞   Aᵥ
8/26/2025 4:25:20 AM Error main: main-sec-mod-cmd.c:107: command socket for sec-mod closed
8/26/2025 4:25:20 AM Error main: main.c:1242: error in command from sec-mod
8/26/2025 4:25:20 AM Error main: main.c:832: ocserv-secmod died unexpectedly
8/26/2025 4:25:54 AM Error ocserv-oidc: failed to download JSON document: URI https://sts.windows.net/5412af29-72aa-4e87-b5e4-8861b19a2674/v2.0/.well-known/openid-
configuration, CURLcode 6
8/26/2025 4:25:54 AM Error ocserv-oidc: Unable to fetch config doc from https://sts.windows.net/5412af29-72aa-4e87-b5e4-8861b19a2674/v2.0/.well-known/openid-configuration
8/26/2025 4:25:54 AM Error ocserv-oidc: failed to load jwks
8/26/2025 4:25:54 AM Error main: main-sec-mod-cmd.c:107: command socket for sec-mod closed
8/26/2025 4:25:54 AM Error main: main.c:1242: error in command from sec-mod
8/26/2025 4:25:54 AM Error main: main.c:832: ocserv-secmod died unexpectedly
8/26/2025 4:26:28 AM Error ocserv-oidc: failed to download JSON document: URI https://sts.windows.net/5412af29-72aa-4e87-b5e4-8861b19a2674/v2.0/.well-known/openid-
configuration, CURLcode 6
8/26/2025 4:26:28 AM Error ocserv-oidc: Unable to fetch config doc from https://sts.windows.net/5412af29-72aa-4e87-b5e4-8861b19a2674/v2.0/.well-known/openid-configuration
8/26/2025 4:26:28 AM Error ocserv-oidc: failed to load jwks
8/26/2025 4:26:28 AM Error main: main-sec-mod-cmd.c:107: command socket for sec-mod closed
8/26/2025 4:26:28 AM Error main: main.c:1242: error in command from sec-mod
8/26/2025 4:26:28 AM Error main: main.c:832: ocserv-secmod died unexpectedly
8/26/2025 4:27:01 AM Error ocserv-oidc: failed to download JSON document: URI https://sts.windows.net/5412af29-72aa-4e87-b5e4-8861b19a2674/v2.0/.well-known/openid-
configuration, CURLcode 6
8/26/2025 4:27:01 AM Error ocserv-oidc: Unable to fetch config doc from https://sts.windows.net/5412af29-72aa-4e87-b5e4-8861b19a2674/v2.0/.well-known/openid-configuration
8/26/2025 4:27:01 AM Error ocserv-oidc: failed to load jwks
8/26/2025 4:27:01 AM Error main: main-sec-mod-cmd.c:107: command socket for sec-mod closed
8/26/2025 4:27:01 AM Error main: main.c:1242: error in command from sec-mod
8/26/2025 4:27:01 AM Error main: main.c:832: ocserv-secmod died unexpectedly
8/26/2025 4:27:35 AM Error ocserv-oidc: failed to download JSON document: URI https://sts.windows.net/5412af29-72aa-4e87-b5e4-8861b19a2674/v2.0/.well-known/openid-
configuration, CURLcode 6
8/26/2025 4:27:35 AM Error ocserv-oidc: Unable to fetch config doc from https://sts.windows.net/5412af29-72aa-4e87-b5e4-8861b19a2674/v2.0/.well-known/openid-configuration
8/26/2025 4:27:35 AM Error ocserv-oidc: failed to load jwks
8/26/2025 4:27:35 AM Error main: main-sec-mod-cmd.c:107: command socket for sec-mod closed
8/26/2025 4:27:35 AM Error main: main.c:1242: error in command from sec-mod
8/26/2025 4:27:35 AM Error main: main.c:832: ocserv-secmod died unexpectedly
8/26/2025 4:28:09 AM Error ocserv-oidc: failed to download JSON document: URI https://sts.windows.net/5412af29-72aa-4e87-b5e4-8861b19a2674/v2.0/.well-known/openid-
configuration, CURLcode 6
8/26/2025 4:28:09 AM Error ocserv-oidc: Unable to fetch config doc from https://sts.windows.net/5412af29-72aa-4e87-b5e4-8861b19a2674/v2.0/.well-known/openid-configuration
8/26/2025 4:28:09 AM Error ocserv-oidc: failed to load jwks
8/26/2025 4:28:09 AM Error main: main-sec-mod-cmd.c:107: command socket for sec-mod closed
8/26/2025 4:28:09 AM Error main: main.c:1242: error in command from sec-mod
8/26/2025 4:28:09 AM Error main: main.c:832: ocserv-secmod died unexpectedly
8/26/2025 4:28:42 AM Error ocserv-oidc: failed to download JSON document: URI https://sts.windows.net/5412af29-72aa-4e87-b5e4-8861b19a2674/v2.0/.well-known/openid-
configuration, CURLcode 6
8/26/2025 4:28:42 AM Error ocserv-oidc: Unable to fetch config doc from https://sts.windows.net/5412af29-72aa-4e87-b5e4-8861b19a2674/v2.0/.well-known/openid-configuration
```

Figure 5.70: Viewing the MTG log generated from the Intune portal

Additionally, as a diagnostic tool, the Intune admin center allows us to initiate verbose logging from a Tunnel Gateway server with a single click, as seen in the following screenshot. This action enables, collects, and submits detailed logs directly to Microsoft. These logs become immediately accessible to Microsoft support when assisting you in identifying or resolving Tunnel server issues.

Send verbose server logs

When you select Send logs, current logs with default verbosity (level 0) are sent immediately to Microsoft and verbose logging (level 4) starts. Once you send the logs, you have 8 hours to reproduce the reported issue. After 8 hours the verbosity goes back to default. Learn more about Tunnel Server logs ⬀

Send logs

Figure 5.71: Option for sending logs for diagnosis to Microsoft from the Intune portal

We can also see the status of the MTG server and its various components by going into the **Health check** tab in the Intune portal. This view will highlight any warnings and the health status of each of the MTG server's components.

Home > Tenant admin | Microsoft Tunnel Gateway >

mtg1_old ...
Health status
∨ Essentials

| Health check | Trends | Logs |
Snapshot

Last check-in: Healthy ⓘ   Current connections ⓘ   Throughput ⓘ
2 minutes ago   **0**   **0.00** kbps

CPU usage ⓘ	✔ Healthy	4%
CPU cores ⓘ	⚠ Warning	1 core
Memory usage ⓘ	✔ Healthy	22%
Disk space usage ⓘ	✔ Healthy	67.65 GB available of 73.33 GB
Latency ⓘ	✔ Healthy	0 ms
Management agent certificate ⓘ	✔ Healthy	Certificate expires in 248 days
TLS certificate expiration ⓘ	✔ Healthy	Certificate expires in 693 days
TLS certificate revocation ⓘ	⚠ Warning	Unable to check if the TLS certificate is revoked.
Internal network accessibility ⓘ	✔ Healthy	Internal resource is reachable.
Upgradeability ⓘ	✔ Healthy	Server can contact the Microsoft Container Repository.
Server version ⓘ	✔ Healthy	Up to date
Server container ⓘ	✔ Healthy	The server container status is healthy.
Server configuration ⓘ	✔ Healthy	The server configuration was successfully applied.
Server logs ⓘ	✔ Healthy	Server logs have been uploaded in the last 60 minutes.

Figure 5.72: Viewing options for the MTG server's health check from the Intune portal

These troubleshooting tools and logs can be very useful for the diagnosis of any MTG-related issues.

Just as MAM Tunnel can be used for accessing on-premise applications from a mobile device that is not enrolled in Intune, to some extent, an app proxy also provides a similar functionality. Let's do a quick comparison between the two in order to understand their relevant use cases.

MAM Tunnel and app proxy

The following table compares the relevant features and use cases of MAM Tunnel in the Intune Suite with app proxy.

Parameter	MAM Tunnel (Intune Suite)	Microsoft Entra/Web Application Proxy
Primary Use case	Securing access for mobile apps (iOS/Android) to on-premises resources via per-app VPN	Securing access to on-premises web apps through an external URL
Device Enrollment	Not required (works on unenrolled BYOD devices)	Not required
Access method	Per app VPN tunnel	No VPN needed. Connection via a published external URL that translates to an internal URL
Supported platform	iOS, iPadOS, and Android	Works on any device with a browser
Network dependency	Need to set up inbound and outbound connectivity to Microsoft Tunnel Gateway (MTG)	No gateway is needed. A lightweight connector needs to be installed. Required ports to be allowed.
Best-suited scenario	Mobile apps needing access to internal resources from an unenrolled device	Web-based apps (SharePoint, LOB portals) accessed remotely over the internet

Table 5.6: Comparison between MAM Tunnel and app proxy use cases

Our two cents

MAM Tunnel is a very valuable enhancement to Intune. It allows BYOD (un-enrolled) devices to securely access on-prem resources and stay productive—just like managed devices. That said, its use is typically seen in organizations with Android or iOS users who are permitted to use personal devices for work. In more tightly controlled environments, access to corporate resources from personal devices may be restricted through Conditional Access policies. In our opinion, we don't see the need for MAM Tunnel to be rolled out across the entire organization. It's best to assess which users actually have a valid use case and would benefit from it. Typically, users on Windows, macOS, or company-owned mobile devices don't require MAM Tunnel. It's mainly intended for employees using personal devices for work. We've seen it used effectively in setups where companies have outsourced teams, vendors, or contractors who need access to corporate data over the internet but don't have company-issued mobile devices.

Summary

In this chapter, we explored the importance of MAM Tunnel and identified key scenarios where its implementation proves invaluable for organizations. We walked through the complete setup and configuration steps required for deploying MAM Tunnel. Additionally, we examined the end-user experience when accessing corporate resources through this approach. The chapter concluded with a troubleshooting guide to address potential issues related to the MTG server or the MAM Tunnel setup. This knowledge will help us better support our mobile workforce, enabling them to work more efficiently from their personal BYOD devices over the internet using MAM Tunnel.

In the next chapter, we'll explore Remote Help—another highly valuable feature within the Intune Suite.

Get This Book's PDF Version and Exclusive Extras

UNLOCK NOW

Scan the QR code (or go to `packtpub.com/unlock`). Search for this book by name, confirm the edition, and then follow the steps on the page.

Note: Keep your invoice handy. Purchases made directly from Packt don't require an invoice.

6

Empowering Support from Anywhere with Remote Help

In this chapter, we'll explore all the important concepts related to **Remote Help**. We'll start by understanding why Remote Help is important, along with its prerequisites and privacy considerations. From there, we'll dive into the architecture and background flow of the Remote Help app to give us a clear picture of how it works behind the scenes.

Once the foundation is set, we'll walk through the setup process of Remote Help in the Intune portal. We'll also dive into how Remote Help behaves across different operating systems (i.e., Windows, Android, and macOS) so that we can support a variety of devices in the environments. The chapter also covers all the session logs available in the Intune portal and how they can help with troubleshooting for compliance. By the end of this chapter, you'll have the knowledge and practical skills to configure and deploy Remote Help in your tenant for all supported platforms, as well as a deep understanding of Remote Help's architecture.

The following main topics will be covered in this chapter in the following sequence:

- Need for Remote Help in today's hybrid workplace world
- Architecture and background flow during a Remote Help session
- Setting up Remote Help in the tenant
- Detailed analysis of Remote Help for Windows, Android, macOS, and Linux
- Monitoring remote sessions from the portal
- Key considerations before rolling out Remote Help and current gaps
- Our two cents

We will start with understanding the background and need for a tool such as Remote Help, which is especially relevant in today's hybrid workplace scenario.

Need for Remote Help in today's hybrid workplace world

As IT admins, one of our biggest responsibilities is providing remote support to end users. We often manage a large workforce using corporate devices, and it's common for them to reach out when something goes wrong, such as when a configuration change is needed, or an application needs to be installed, or one of many other issues that might hinder their productivity. Many times, we need direct access to the user's device to troubleshoot effectively. It could be to see what the user is experiencing, capture details, reproduce an issue, or collect logs. There are also situations where help desk admins, who provide the first line of IT support, might need view-only access to a user's device just to gather information. Another common scenario is when we have user-less or kiosk devices deployed in stores without any local IT presence. In such cases, if we need to check settings or make configuration changes, the ability to remotely connect and diagnose the device becomes important. The need for a remote tool has become more critical than ever in today's world, where we have a hybrid workforce and end users may not be in the office for us to physically check their devices.

In all these scenarios, having a way to securely access the user's machine is essential. Sure, we could use screen sharing through Teams or Quick Assist, but those options aren't really enterprise-ready for this purpose. In an enterprise environment, we need a solution that not only enables remote sessions but also logs every session and enforces RBAC controls and compliance notifications, and that's exactly what Remote Help enables us to achieve!

Remote Help is a cloud-based solution that is integrated with Microsoft Intune, and it helps the admin to connect with the end user's devices securely. The new Remote Help tool is essentially an evolved version of Quick Assist. It still relies on the **Remote Desktop Protocol** (**RDP**) for session connectivity, but now everything runs over HTTPS, with traffic secured using TLS 1.2 encryption. As this Remote Help feature is natively a part of the Intune console, we don't need to go through any complex setup steps as we did earlier with Intune-TeamViewer integration. We will delve into the functionality of Remote Help through various sections in this chapter.

Firstly, let's do a quick comparison between Remote Help and other tools that provide similar functionality, such as Quick Assist and TeamViewer. The following comparison will better help us understand the scenarios in which Remote Help has an edge over other solutions. Once we have established that, we will understand the intricacies of the Remote Help tool.

Feature/Aspect	Remote Help	Quick Assist	TeamViewer
Use case	For enterprise	For standalone/ personal user	For enterprise
Integration	Integrated with Intune by default	No integration with MDMs	Can be integrated with MDMs such as Intune and WS1 via a connector
Authentication	Requires an organizational account for sign-in (Entra ID)	Only session code is used; no enterprise identity	Account-based and session code-based with MFA support
OS support	Multi-platform	Only Windows	Multi-platform
Security	TLS 1.2 encryption, RBAC, and CA controls	TLS 1.2 encryption with no other control	RSA and bit encryption
Admin privileges	Supports elevation/ UAC	No support for elevation	Supports elevation/ UAC
Reporting	Yes, session details are logged centrally in the Intune console	No	Yes
File transfer	No	No	Yes
Session recording	No	No	Yes
Pricing	Paid	Free	Paid
Installation	Needs to be installed, or a web view can be used via a browser	Built into Windows	Needs to be installed

Table 6.1: Comparison between TeamViewer, Remote Help, and Quick Assist

Using the preceding comparison, the advantages and the added value of Remote Help are very clear! Now, throughout this chapter, we will explore most of the capabilities of Remote Help that have been highlighted in this comparison.

Before we dive into Remote Help's capabilities and the setup process, let's first take a look at the data privacy aspect of the tool in the following section.

Privacy of Remote Help session data

Microsoft captures some session data to monitor the health of the Remote Help service and to maintain visibility into which admins are accessing which devices. This data is retained for 30 days and includes the following:

- The start and end times of each session
- Details of the helper and the sharer, along with the device information where assistance was provided
- Features used during the session, such as view-only or elevation

Microsoft doesn't store any chat details or recordings of the screen during the session at its end.

Remote Help records session details in the Windows event logs on both the helper's and the sharer's devices. Microsoft has no access to the session itself and cannot see any actions or keystrokes performed during it.

Now, in the next section, let's take a look at the background architecture and flow behind a Remote Help session, as it is essential to understand what happens under the hood.

Architecture and background flow

Before we talk about the detailed flow, let's first understand the different components and their roles using the following diagram. Then, we will see how each component contributes to the Remote Help session flow.

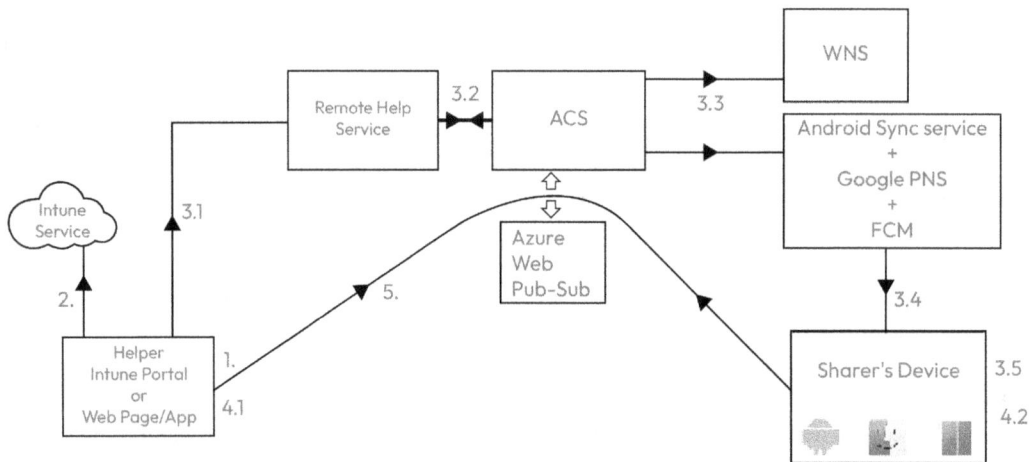

Figure 6.1: Background flow during a Remote Help session

As seen in the diagram, there are five main components involved here:

- **The Intune portal (the helper)**: The Intune admin initiates the Remote Help session from here.

- **Remote assistance cloud service (Intune service)**: This service facilitates the API calls for session creation and establishes the communication channel between helper and sharer. It's also responsible for ending a Remote Help session.

- **Azure Communication Services (ACS)**: This is a cloud service and is responsible for issuing all the tokens needed for establishing a Remote Help session. It is also used for streaming the screen capture content that was captured by the Remote Help app in the sharer's device to the helper.

- **Azure Web PubSub**: This is a cloud service responsible for facilitating real-time data exchange. This service maintains the command channel and is responsible for carrying all the commands that the helper is sending, such as clicking on the home button, volume up/down keys, and so on, to the sharer's device.

- **Notification service**: The notification service is responsible for notifying the sharer that an admin wishes to take a remote session of their device. Depending on the OS, we have different services involved. **Windows Notification Service (WNS)** is used for Windows, while the Android sync service, along with the Google push notification service and **Firebase Cloud Messaging (FCM)**, is used in the case of Android devices.

Now that we understand all the components involved during a Remote Help session, let's break down the flow during a Remote Help session into the following steps by referencing the diagram:

1. In the first step, the helper (admin) goes to the Intune portal, selects the device, and clicks on **New Remote Assistance Request**. They can also go to aka.ms/rhh and authenticate using their credentials.

2. Now, the request goes to the Intune service, and the helper's RBAC is checked. This check is to verify the level of access the admin has to devices.

3.1. Next, the request goes to the Remote Help cloud service, which generates a code and displays it to the helper. The helper needs to share this code with the sharer (end user).

3.2. At the same time, the request from the Remote Help service goes to ACS, which generates the needed tokens for the helper and sharer that will be used by them to join the session. The token is sent to the helper.

3.3. In the case of Android devices, the request is now sent to the Android sync service,

Google push notification service, and FCM in the cloud. These notification services work together to send a notification down to the end device. In the case of Windows, WNS is utilized to send the notification to the end device.

3.4. The notification is received by the Intune app (in the case of Android), and is processed and then sent to the Remote Help app on the device. The notification informs the end user that an admin is trying to take control of their device, and they need to launch the Remote Help app in order to continue.

3.5. If the end user (sharer) is launching the Remote Help app on the device for the first time, they must sign in and accept a privacy prompt on the device, which is applicable for all operating systems.

4.1. Now, both the helper and sharer join the session using the session codes. The helper gets prompted to choose the kind of control they would like to take (screen sharing/full control).

4.2. The sharer gets a prompt to share their screen, along with prompts to allow access to the microphone and screen during the screen-sharing session. The profile (name, photograph, etc.) of both the helper and sharer is made visible to each other for security before the session starts.

5. Now, a session is established between the helper and the sharer. The data is transferred via the ACS and Azure Web PubSub channel. The keyboard events, mouse events, and scrolls by the helper are captured as inputs by the browser and are sent by ACS to the sharer, where they are implemented using the Remote Help app. This allows the helper to control the device via a browser.

6. The helper and sharer can end the Remote Help session at any time from their end.

This architectural diagram is meant to give us a clear picture of the key components working behind the scenes during a Remote Help session. Throughout this chapter, we'll see how these pieces fit together to make a session successful. In the next section, we'll walk through the steps to set up Remote Help in the Intune portal so that it can be used across our organization.

Setting up Remote Help

In this section, we will see how we can set up and activate the Remote Help feature in the tenant. This is a one-time activity that needs to be performed by the tenant admin.

Prerequisites

Let's look at the requirements to have ready before proceeding with the setup:

- **Intune subscription**: There needs to be an Intune tenant, and the Remote Help feature needs to be turned on there.

- **Remote Help license**: Both the sharer and the helper need to be licensed for Remote Help (via an add-on or the Intune Suite).

- **Supported devices**: Intune enrolment of the end user's (sharer's) device is not mandatory. You can take remote sessions of unenrolled devices as well.

- **Network endpoints**: Port 443 must be open as it's used by the Remote Help service. The following URLs need to be allowed for the session to establish successfully:

Domain	Usage

Default URLs	`*.support.services.microsoft.com`
	`remoteassistance.support.services.microsoft.com`
	`teams.microsoft.com`
	`remoteassistanceprodacs.communication.azure.com`
	`edge.skype.com`
	`aadcdn.msftauth.net`
	`aadcdn.msauth.net`
	`alcdn.msauth.net`
	`wcpstatic.microsoft.com`
	`*.aria.microsoft.com`
	`browser.pipe.aria.microsoft.com`
	`.events.data.microsoft.com`
	`v10c.events.data.microsoft.com`
	`*.monitor.azure.com`
	`js.monitor.azure.com`
	`edge.microsoft.com`
	`*.trouter.communication.microsoft.com`
	`*.trouter.teams.microsoft.com`
	`api.flightproxy.skype.com`
	`ecs.communication.microsoft.com`
	`remotehelp.microsoft.com`
	`remoteassistanceprodacseu.communication.azure.com`

Domain	Usage
Remote Help Web PubSub	`*.webpubsub.azure.com` `AMSUA0101-RemoteAssistService-pubsub.webpubsub.azure.com`

Used by ACS for signaling, call automation, media traffic, and telemetry	`*.skype.com`
	`*.microsoft.com`
	`*.azure.net`
	`*.azure.com`
	`.office.com`
	`.lync.com`
	`*.teams.cloud.microsoft`
	`*.teams.microsoft.com`

Table 6.2: Network endpoints for using the Remote Help service

Microsoft recommends whitelisting the preceding URLs instead of IP addresses wherever applicable, since the IPs are subject to change at any moment.

Configuring Remote Help from Intune

To configure Remote Help, go to the Intune portal and then navigate to **Tenant administration -> Remote Help**. Now, go to the **Settings** tab, as seen in the following figure, and click on **Configure**. Here, we will have three options:

- **Enable Remote Help**: This needs to be enabled, and it's a tenant-wide setting.
- **Allow Remote Help to unenrolled devices**: This setting controls whether the helper can initiate a remote session when the sharer's device is not enrolled in Intune. We can allow/disallow the same here as per need.
- **Disable Chat**: This setting determines whether the chat option is enabled during the session.

The following screenshot shows these settings in the Intune portal:

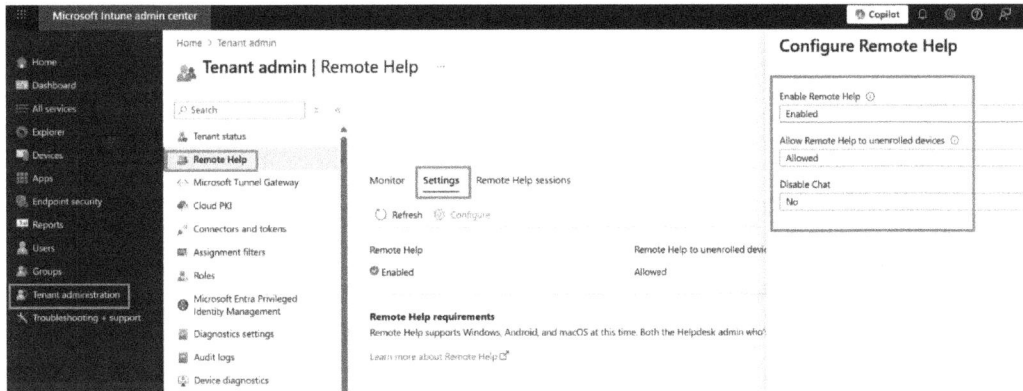

Figure 6.2: Enabling Remote Help in the Intune portal

Once Remote Help has been enabled for the tenant, any Global admin or Intune admin in the tenant who is licensed for Remote Help will be able to initiate sessions. If, additionally, we wish to delegate permission to other staff, such as help desks and so on, we also have the option of creating RBAC permissions for them, which we will discuss in the next section.

Setting up RBAC options for Remote help

Let's say that we have some helpdesk admins or L1 admins who need to take remote control of devices to perform the preliminary troubleshooting. One option is to provide them with Intune admin access. However, that's not the best practice, as by making them Intune admins, they would be able to create and delete all configuration items in the Intune portal. As a solution, we can create and assign them custom RBAC permissions with the relevant permission for Remote Help. This will ensure that they are able to perform Remote Help-related tasks without having any admin privileges in the portal. Let's discuss the steps to create the custom RBAC role for Remote Help from the Intune portal:

1. First, navigate to **Tenant administration -> Manage -> Roles -> All roles -> + Create**, as seen here:

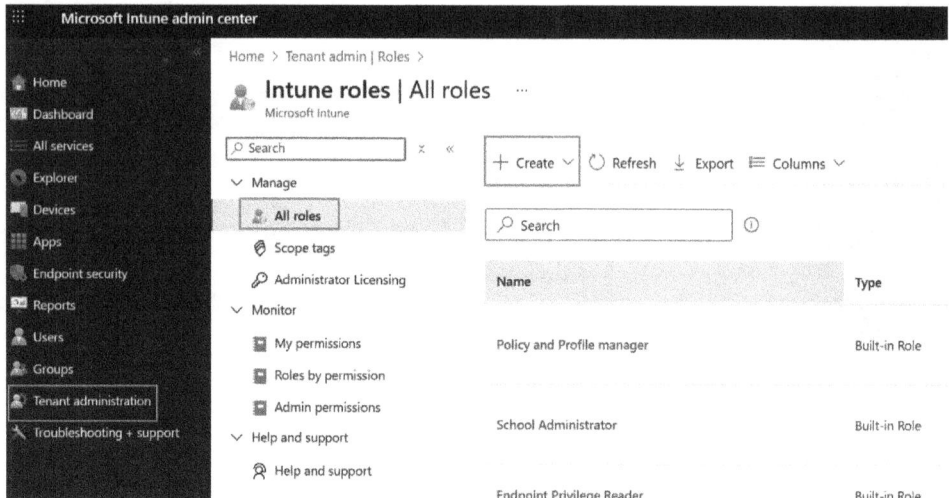

Figure 6.3: Creating a new RBAC role for Remote Help in the Intune portal

2. After clicking on **+ Create**, we will now have the option to choose the permission/level of access that we wish to grant. In this case, we will grant the options needed under the **Remote Help app** section, as seen here:

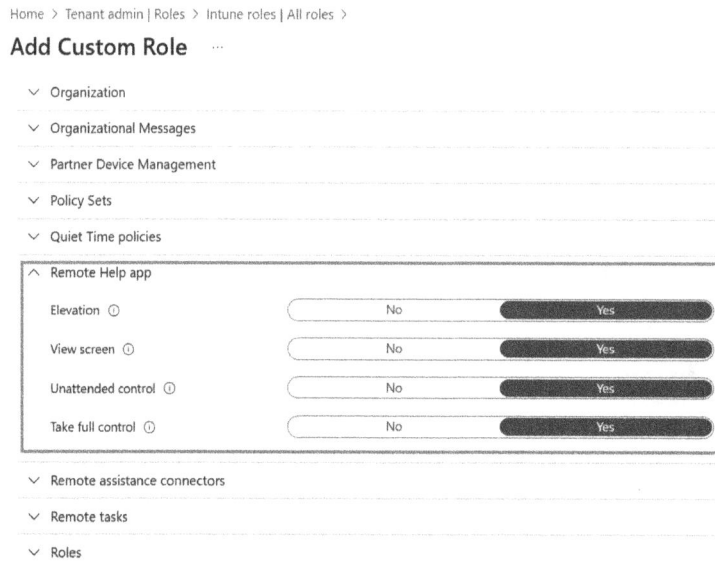

Figure 6.4: RBAC permissions related to Remote Help

The settings will determine the level of control the admin will get, such as the ability to view the screen, the ability to take unattended control of devices, the ability to take full control of the devices, and so on.

3. Once we have selected the settings and clicked on **Create**, the RBAC role will be ready, and it will be visible under **All roles**, as seen here:

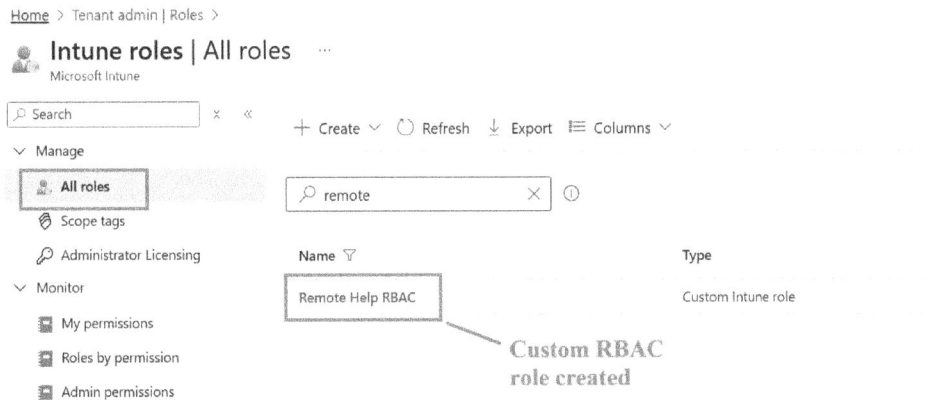

Figure 6.5: Custom RBAC for Remote Help

4. In the next step, all we must do is assign this RBAC role to a group containing users. To do the same, click on the role, go to the **Assignments** tab, and click **+ Assign**, as seen here:

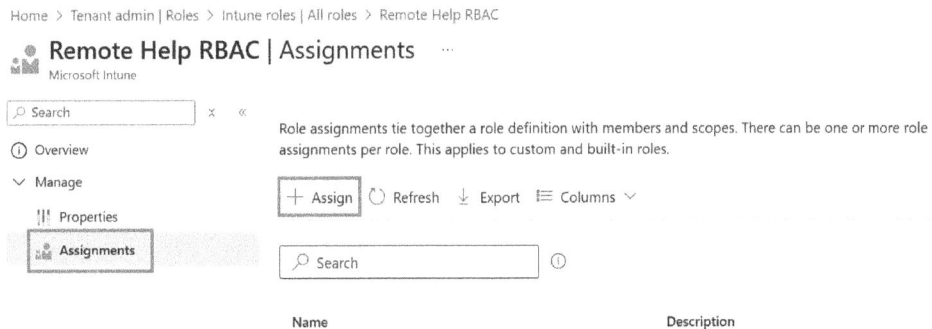

Figure 6.6: Assigning RBAC from the Intune portal

The assignment has to be done for a user group. The users who are part of this group will get the RBAC settings and will be able to take remote sessions of devices if they have the Remote Help license assigned to them.

Now that we have successfully enabled Remote Help in the tenant, the next step involves getting Remote Help ready for different operating systems in our environment, which we will cover in the next section.

Remote Help for different operating systems

The capability and the usage of Remote Help in different operating systems vary; hence, we will be discussing all of them one by one.

Remote Help for Windows

In order to use Remote Help on Windows devices, the Remote Help app needs to be there on the user's device. While the end user can always install the same manually, we, as admins, would like to exercise our control and push the Remote Help application *as required* so that we are not dependent on the end user. Once that is done, the end users can utilize it to establish the remote connection. In this section, we will be covering the steps for deploying the Remote Help app to Windows devices and the connection experience.

Deploying the Remote Help app

The Remote Help app is available in the **Enterprise App Management (EAM)** catalog, and its latest version can be deployed using the same without needing to download and package it. This topic is covered in *Chapter 3* of this book in detail. If we do not have the EAM licenses, we can manually download, package the app, and deploy it through the Intune portal. The Remote Help app can be downloaded for free from https://aka.ms/downloadremotehelp. The link provides us with an executable (.exe), and since it cannot be deployed directly from Intune, we need to convert it into an .intunewin file and deploy it as a Win32 app.

The Remote Help executable can be converted into a Win32 app by using the Intune Win32 app utility tool, which can be downloaded from the GitHub repository (https://github.com/Microsoft/Microsoft-Win32-Content-Prep-Tool). We need to place the Win32 utility tool and the Remote Help source file in separate folders, as seen here:

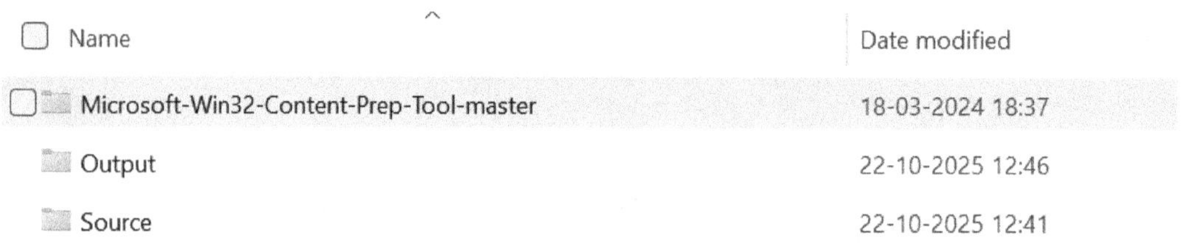

Name		Date modified
☐ Microsoft-Win32-Content-Prep-Tool-master		18-03-2024 18:37
Output		22-10-2025 12:46
Source		22-10-2025 12:41

Figure 6.7: Folder structure for using the Intune Win32 utility tool

Now, we need to run the following command to convert the .exe file to the .intunewin format:

```
.\IntuneWinAppUtil.exe -c "C:\temp\Extra\Source\" -s "C:\temp\Extra\
Source\remotehelpinstaller_bd142b4c833c024a512ed124a1f9058461e18cab.exe"
-o "C:\temp\Extra\Output\" -q
```

Figure 6.8: Command for generating the .intunewin file

We will get the output in the `.intunewin` format in the mentioned folder. Once we have the `.intunewin` file ready, we can deploy it from the Intune portal, as follows:

1. Go to the Intune portal -> **Apps** -> **Windows** -> **+ Create** -> **App type** -> **Windows app (Win32)**:

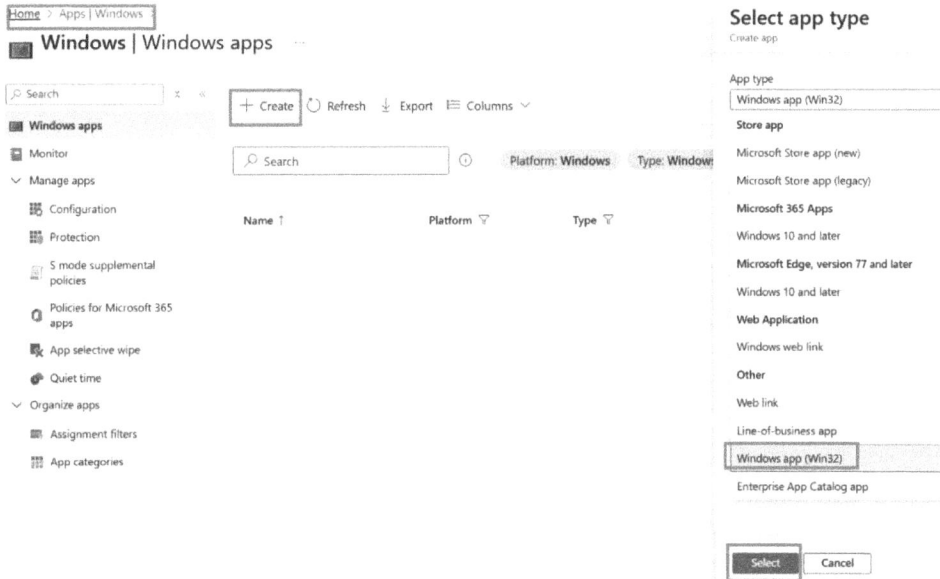

Figure 6.9: Deploying the Win32 app from the Intune portal

2. Click on **Select**, and then in the next screen, as shown here, upload the Remote Help package:

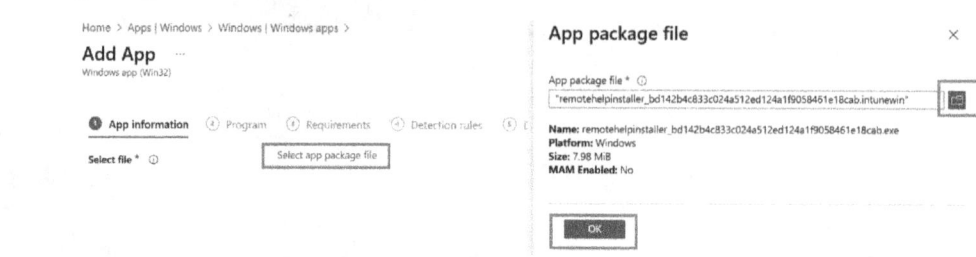

Figure 6.10: Uploading the .intunewin file into the Intune portal

Once uploaded, we have the option of providing the name of the app deployment along with other optional information, such as publisher, logo, and so on. Then, we will move to the next screen.

3. In the next screen, under the **Program** tab, fill in the following information, which is the app installation metadata:

    - **Install command:** `remotehelpinstaller.exe /install /quiet acceptTerms=Yes`
    - **Uninstall command:** `remotehelpinstaller.exe /uninstall /quiet acceptTerms=Yes`
    - **Installation time required (mins): 60** (default value)
    - **Allow available uninstall:** No (this prevents users from uninstalling the app from the company portal)
    - **Install behavior:** System
    - **Device restart behavior: App install may force a device restart**
    - **Return codes:** Default values

Here is a screen capture of these configurations in the Intune portal:

Add App ···
Windows app (Win32)

✅ App information	② **Program**	③ Requirements	④ Detection rules	⑤ Dependencies	⑥ Sup

Specify the commands to install and uninstall this app:

Install command * ⓘ	remotehelpinstaller.exe /install /quiet acceptTerms=Yes ✓
Uninstall command * ⓘ	remotehelpinstaller.exe /uninstall /quiet acceptTerms=Yes ✓
Installation time required (mins) ⓘ	60
Allow available uninstall ⓘ	**Yes** No
Install behavior ⓘ	**System** User
Device restart behavior ⓘ	App install may force a device restart ⌄

Specify return codes to indicate post-installation behavior:

Return code	Code type	
0	Success	⌄ 🗑
1707	Success	⌄ 🗑
3010	Soft reboot	⌄ 🗑
1641	Hard reboot	⌄ 🗑
1618	Retry	⌄ 🗑

+ Add

Previous	**Next**

Figure 6.11: Configuring installation commands and behavior while deploying the Win32 app

4. Click on **Next**, and in the **Requirements** tab, go with the default values.

5. Click on **Next**, and under the **Detection rules** tab, go with the following values:

   - **Rule type: File**
   - **Path:** `C:\Program Files\Remote Help`
   - **File or folder:** `RemoteHelp.exe`
   - **Detection method: String (version)**
   - **Operator: Greater than or equal to**
   - **Value:** `10.0.100110.16384`

Here is a screen capture of these configurations in the Intune portal:

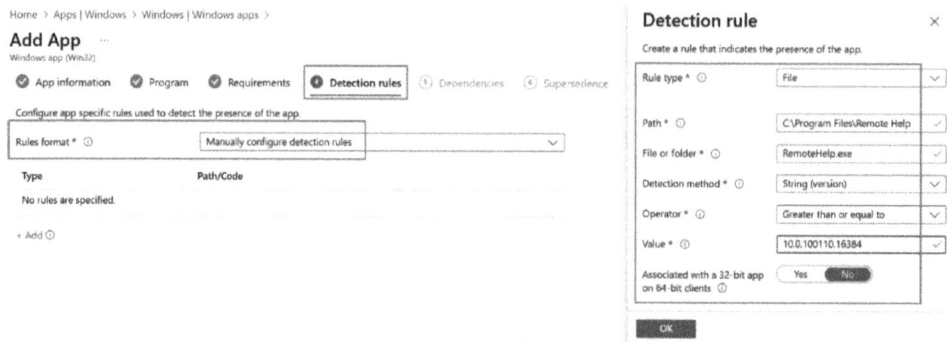

Figure 6.12: Configuring detection logic in the Intune portal

6. Click **OK**, then for the next three tabs (**Dependencies**, **Supersedence**, and **Scope tags**), we can keep the default settings as no changes are required.

7. Click on **Next**, and now this app can be assigned to a user group as required.

Once the Win32 app is pushed as required, the **Intune Management Extension** (**IME**) installed in the device will fetch it, and it will be installed automatically on the device. Once installed, we will be able to view its deployment status in the Intune portal.

The user gets notified during the download and installation of the Remote Help app on the device, as seen here:

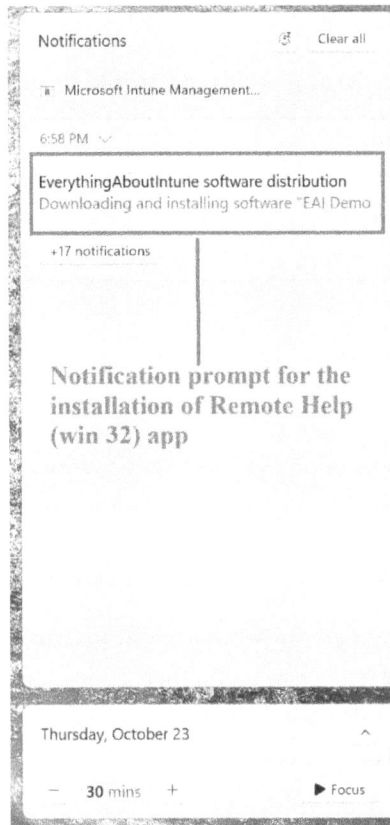

Figure 6.13: Win32 app installation notification on the end device

> If the user's device is not enrolled in Intune, then the admin cannot push the Remote Help application to the same. In that case, the end user has to manually go to https://aka.ms/downloadremotehelp and download the app.

Now that the Remote Help app is installed on the device, in the next section, let's understand how the app can be used by the admin to establish a session.

Establishing a session

Here are the steps the admin needs to follow in order to initiate a successful Remote Help session:

1. The first step involves identifying the Windows device that is impacted and needs troubleshooting from the Intune portal. Navigate to the device under the Intune portal -> **All devices**. Once we have identified the device, we have the option of initiating a new remote assistance session, as seen here:

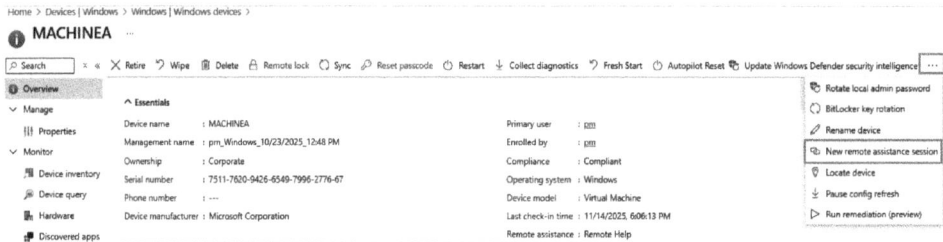

Figure 6.14: Starting a Remote Help session from the Intune portal

2. In the next step, the Intune service sends a notification to the device informing them that an admin wishes to take remote control of their device, and they need to open the Remote Help app and sign in to it. The admin in the Intune portal is informed that the notification is being sent to the end device, as seen here:

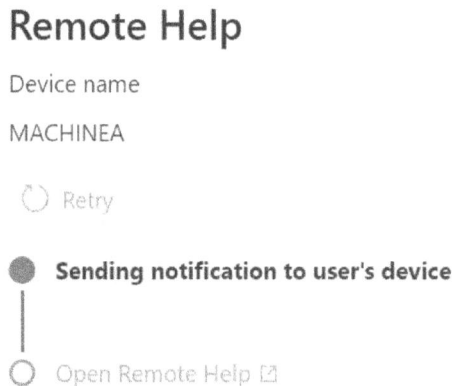

Figure 6.15: Notifying the end user of starting a Remote Help session

The end user gets a notification via WNS, as seen here:

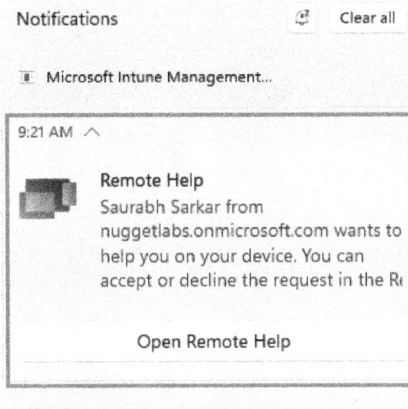

Figure 6.16: Notification to the end user for starting a Remote Help session

Even if the end user has never signed into the Remote Help app post its installation, they receive the preceding notification informing them which admin wishes to take remote control of the device. The end user has the option of launching the Remote Help app directly from the notification.

3. Now, the end user needs to launch the Remote Help app and log in to it. If the app is being launched for the first time, the user has to accept the EULA, as seen here:

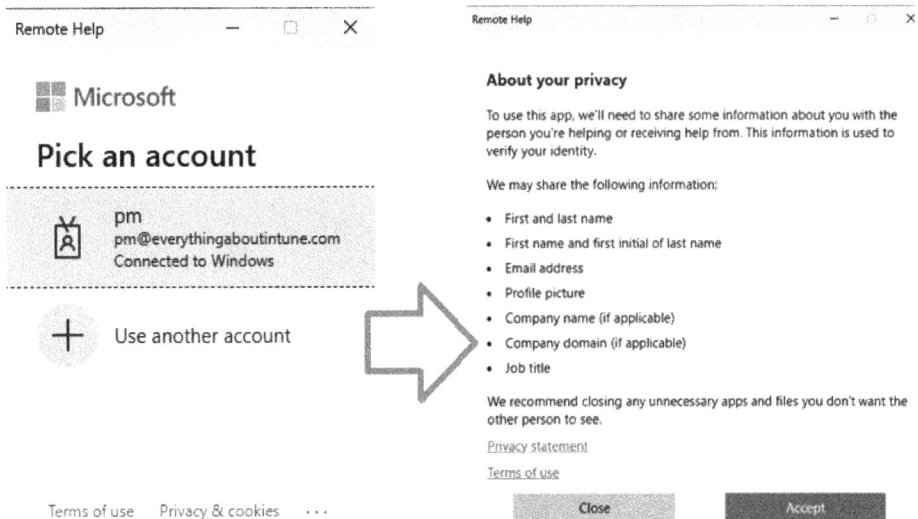

Figure 6.17: EULA prompt for Remote Help

4. A security code is now generated by the helper, which needs to be shared with the end user in order to establish the connection:

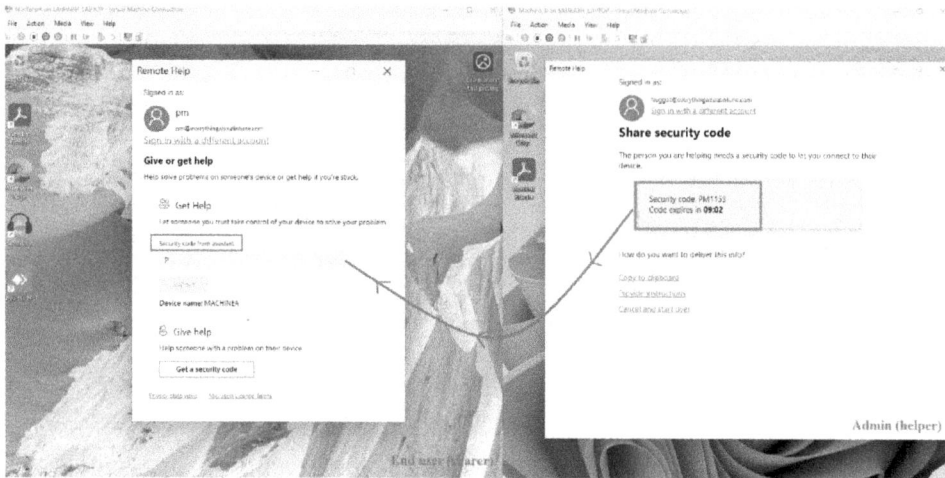

Figure 6.18: Sharing the session code between the sharer and the helper

5. Now, the session gets established. The helper gets an option to choose which kind of control they would like to take of the end user's device: **Take full control** or **View screen**, as seen in the following figure. The options here also depend on the RBAC permissions of the admin:

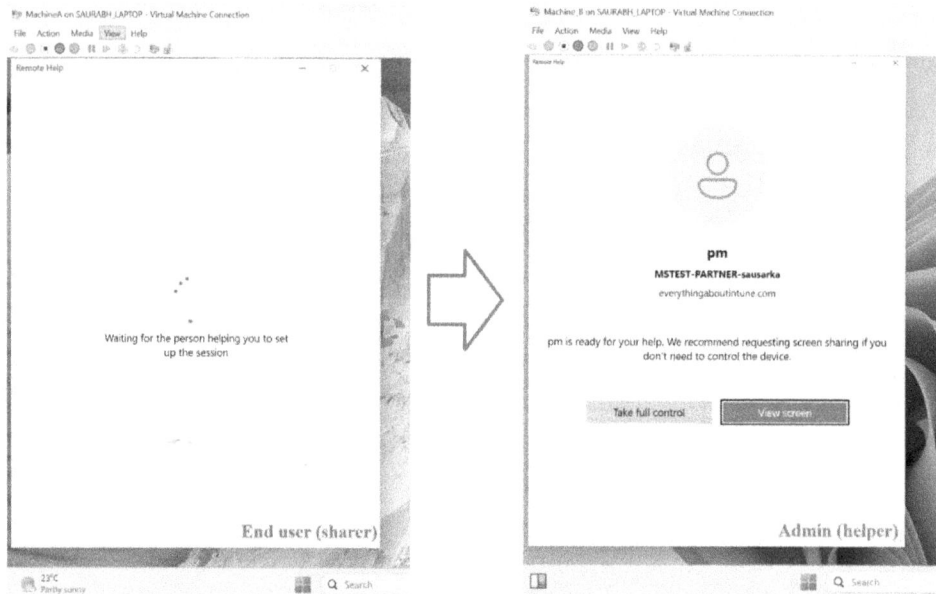

Figure 6.19: Screenshots from the sharer's and helper's devices

If the admin wishes to take full control, the same is informed to the end user, as seen here, and they have to consent to the same by clicking on **Allow**:

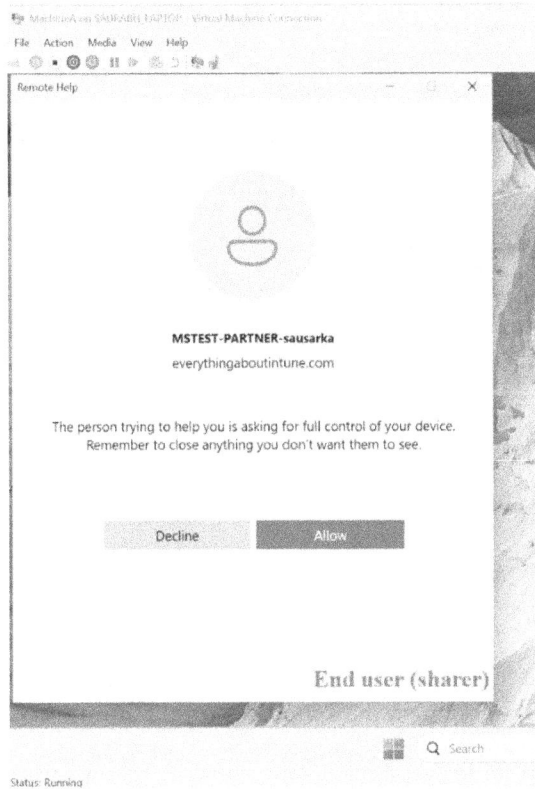

Figure 6.20: Helper's information made visible to the sharer for compliance before the start of the Remote Help session

As seen in the preceding figure, for visibility, the information (such as name, company, and domain) about the requester is shown to the helper, and similarly, the information of the helper is also displayed to the requester as per their profile in Entra ID. This safeguard ensures that only authorized helpers within your organization can provide assistance. Also, both the requester and helper need to sign in to the Remote Help tool with their work or school account and accept the privacy policy.

Once allowed, the end user's (sharer's) device is visible to the admin (helper), as seen here:

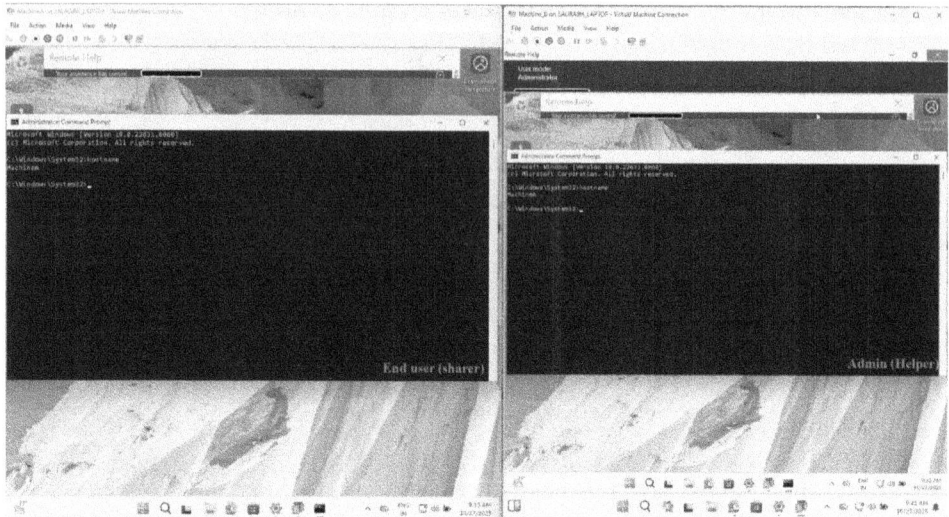

Figure 6.21: Successful Remote Help session established

The helper in this case has full control of the end user's device and can provide the needed help.

Even if the session has started with view-only access, the admin at any point can request full control by clicking on the **Request control** button. This sends a prompt to the end user, which they have to accept in order to grant full control to the helper, as seen here:

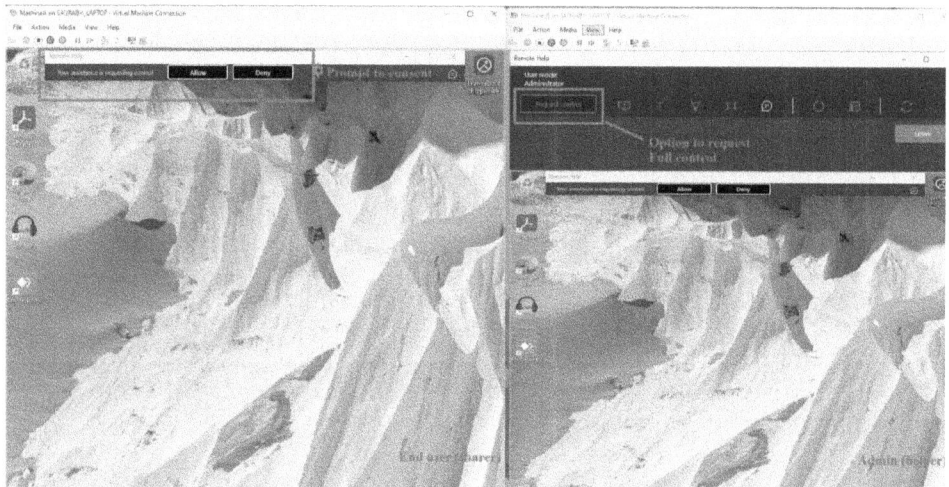

Figure 6.22: Session controls for the helper

In the preceding example, both the helper's and sharer's devices are virtual machines. However, the experience remains the same for physical devices as well.

In some cases, the helper might need to go through an elevated UAC window to make any admin-level change in the device during a session. In the next section, let's discuss UAC-related scenarios on a Windows device during a Remote Help session.

Experience with UAC

If we start an elevated window during a Remote Help session, the UAC prompt will appear on the end user's screen, and the helper's screen view will go black and display a [II] symbol, as seen in the following figure.

This is needed if the end user is not a local admin on the device and the helper wants to make any change that requires admin privileges, for which they have to undergo UAC. Common scenarios wherein the helper might need to go through UAC prompts include installing or updating applications, changing critical system settings such as network configurations or security options, and managing user accounts, such as creating new profiles or resetting passwords within the Remote Help session. These actions trigger UAC to ensure that only authorized changes are made. With UAC enabled, the helper can enter admin credentials if the end user has a standard account.

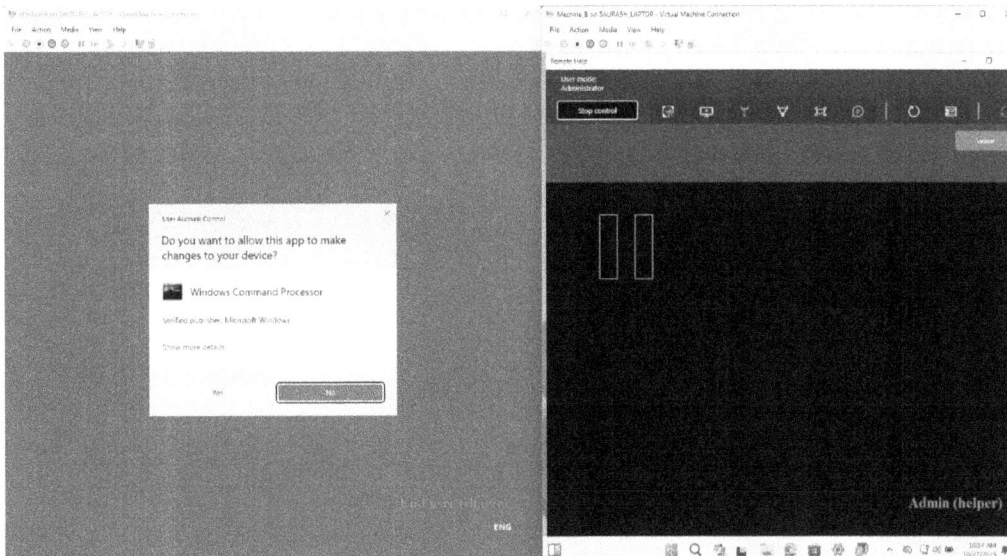

Figure 6.23: UAC prompts during the Remote Help session

The helper (admin) at any time can request access to the UAC prompt for the device by clicking on the following icon:

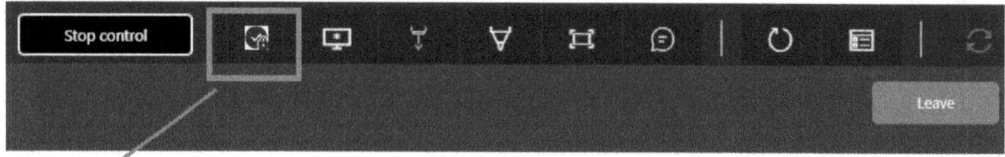

UAC Control

Figure 6.24: Control for requesting UAC during the Remote Help session

Once done, a dialog box pops up that informs the admin to close all windows with admin privileges before ending the session, as seen here:

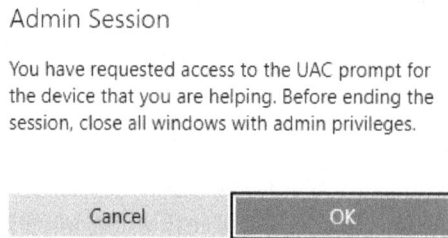

Figure 6.25: UAC prompts for the helper

Once it's enabled, if a UAC prompt appears, the helper can view and interact with it as well, as seen in the following figure, and there won't be a black screen for the admin. Now, if needed, the helper can enter admin credentials at this screen if the user is a standard user and not an admin.

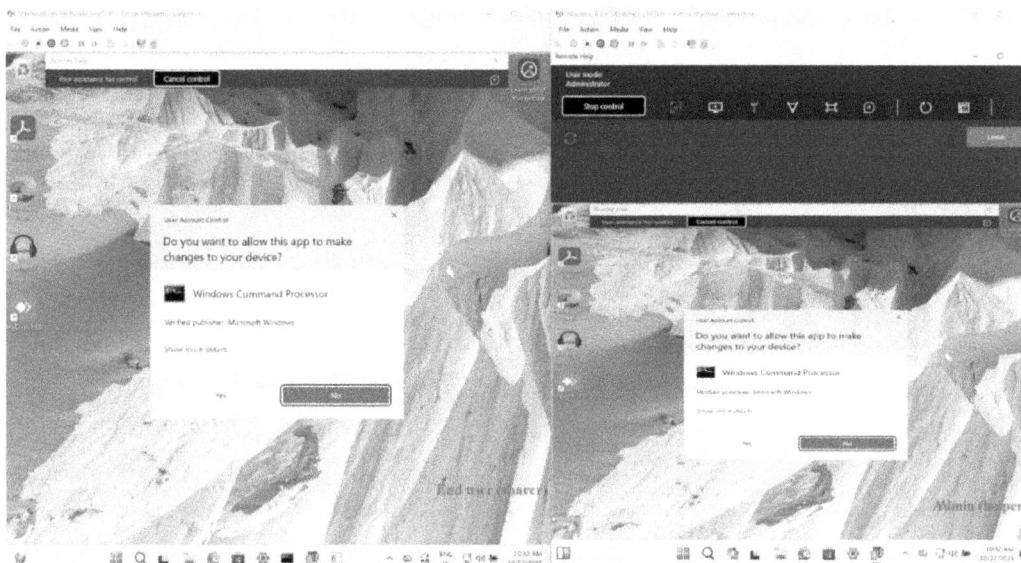

Figure 6.26: Behavior during Remote Help session when UAC is accepted

Now, let's take a close look at the different controls that are available for the helper during a Remote Help session on a Windows device:

1. Taking UAC
2. Changing monitor
3. Laser pointer
4. Pen
5. Screen resize
6. Chatting with the sharer
7. Restarting the PC
8. Opening Task Manager
9. Ending the Remote Help session

Let's take a look at where these controls are located in the user interface, as seen here:

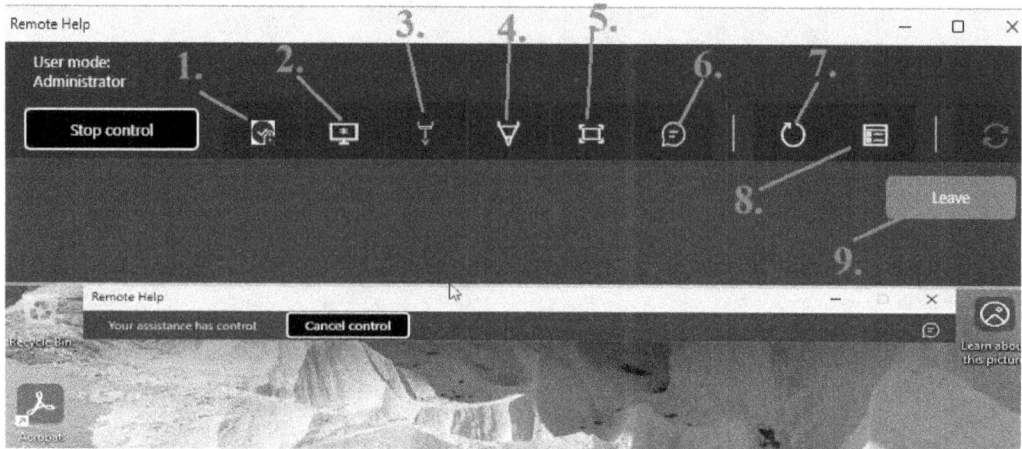

Figure 6.27: Controls for the admin during a Remote Help session

Until now, we have discussed the usage of Remote Help in Windows, where the Remote Help application was installed on the device. In the next section, let's cater to Remote Help scenarios wherein the Remote Help app is not installed on the sharer's device.

Remote Help web app

In some cases, the Remote Help app cannot be installed on the sharer's or helper's device, for example, on a restricted Windows device. To address this, a web-based version of Remote Help is available. Both the helper and the sharer can access the tool via a website. After the helper generates a security code and the sharer enters it, the remote session is established.

Both the helper and the sharer have different URLs for setting up the session, as seen here:

- **Helper**: https://aka.ms/rhh
- **Sharer**: https://aka.ms/rh

The following figure shows what the session looks like when established using the URLs:

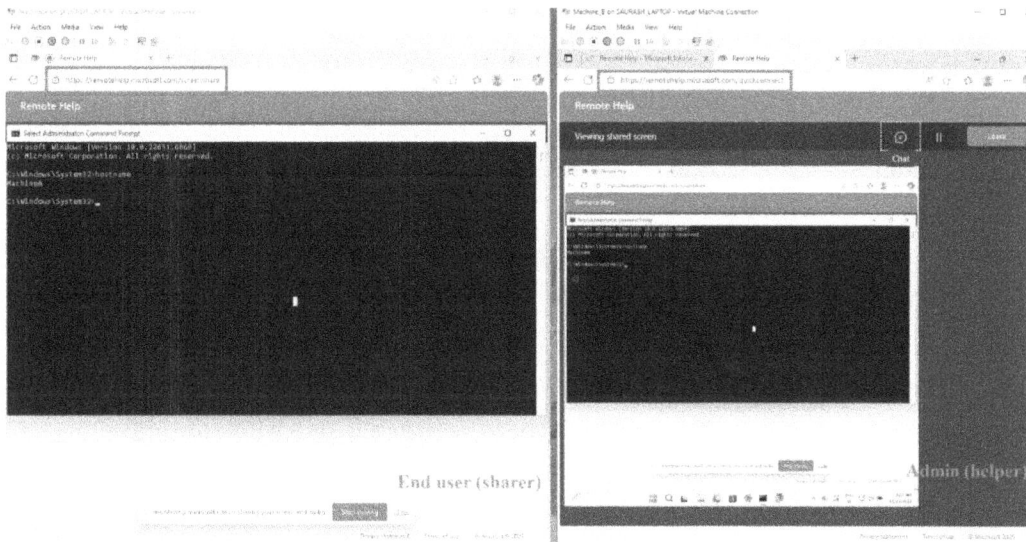

Figure 6.28: Experience while using the Remote Help web app in Windows

Using the Remote Help web app is a quick way of establishing a session, as no app needs to be downloaded and installed. However, the helper can only take a *view-only* session using this methodology.

Unattended Remote Help feature

One of the biggest asks related to Remote Help for Windows is unattended controls. Let's think about a scenario wherein we have Windows devices that don't have any users attributed to them, such as kiosk devices in stores. There are many instances wherein the IT admin needs to check these devices remotely over a screen-sharing session. Since there is no user actively using these devices, it's not possible for anyone to accept the prompts all the time at the sharer's end to establish the remote session. Taking remote access of these machines using RDP is possible however, for Entra-joined devices, RDP can only be achieved by turning off key security features, which is not recommended. Hence, it would be great to have a feature in Remote Help for Windows devices that lets us take the remote session without accepting any prompts at the sharer's end. This functionality already exists in the Remote Help tool for Android devices, and hence, feature parity in Windows is highly anticipated!

Microsoft is working on this ask, and hopefully, we will have this capability by 2026!

Features exclusive to Windows

There are some features in the Remote Help tool that are only available for Windows devices. Let's take a quick look at these in this section:

- **UAC:** This control permits helpers to input UAC credentials on the sharer's device when prompted. With elevation enabled, helpers can also view and control the sharer's device once access is granted.

- **Remote launch:** As already seen in the previous section, the Intune admin can launch the Remote Help app on their device directly from the Intune portal. Also, the admin can send a push notification to the sharer's device and prompt them to launch the Remote Help app.

- **Integration with Conditional Access:** We can use Conditional Access policies, which let us define how helpers and sharers interact with Remote Help. For instance, we can enforce **multifactor authentication (MFA)** for helpers or limit access to approved locations and compliant devices.

- **Chat functionality:** This feature enables the helper and sharer to have a chat conversation within the Remote Help session.

> If the sharer ends the session while an admin session is still active, the user is immediately signed out. This ensures that all elevated windows are closed, thereby protecting admin credentials.

If the sharer's device is not compliant with Intune, the helper gets the following notification message as an alert:

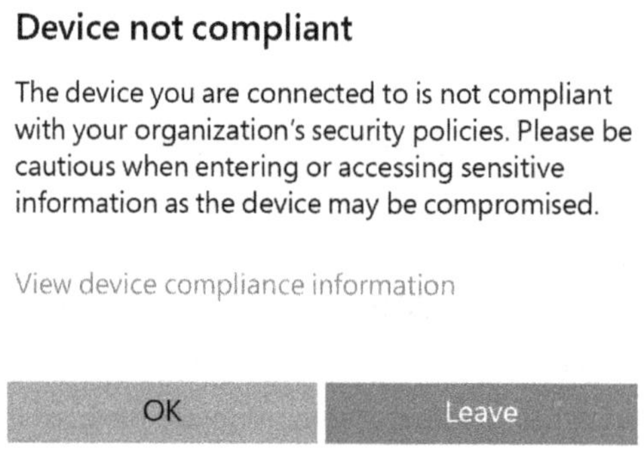

Device not compliant

The device you are connected to is not compliant with your organization's security policies. Please be cautious when entering or accessing sensitive information as the device may be compromised.

View device compliance information

OK   Leave

Figure 6.29: Prompt for helper when the Remote Help session is for a non-compliant device

I recommend exploring an interactive demo walkthrough at `https://regale.cloud/microsoft/ play/1746/remote-help#/0/0`. This resource provides a step-by-step guided experience and simulates the look and feel of the Remote Help tool, without requiring any setup.

Remote Help for Windows in Intune: why pay for it?

One of the most common queries that comes up while using Remote Help on Windows devices, especially from someone who is coming from the SCCM mindset, is that the Remote Help capability in SCCM was bundled with SCCM itself; however, for Intune-managed devices, this feature doesn't come with the base Intune capability, and customers have to purchase additional licenses for the same. Why?

In our opinion, SCCM's remote assistance feature was included within the SCCM tool because it ran in an on-premises environment, leveraging the organization's existing server infrastructure. Intune Remote Help, on the other hand, is a cloud-native solution built on Microsoft Entra ID and tightly integrated with Intune's compliance checks and Conditional Access policies. Delivering these capabilities requires ongoing investment in cloud services, which is why there's an extra associated licensing cost.

Unlike SCCM's Windows-only approach, Intune Remote Help supports Windows, macOS, Android, and even web-based sessions for devices that aren't enrolled. The paid model reflects its role as a premium offering designed for organizations that need enterprise-grade remote support rather than basic assistance. Cloud services bring continuous costs for data storage, encryption, compliance certifications, and global availability—costs that simply don't exist in SCCM's static, on-premises model. Microsoft's pricing ensures sustainability and enables ongoing feature development, including highly requested capabilities such as unattended access for Windows and session recording, both of which are already on the roadmap. Also, we must remember that if a user has multiple devices enrolled with various supported operating systems, only one Remote Help license (assigned to the user) is needed to establish the session.

This completes all the available options and features for using Remote Help on a Windows device using the Remote Help app as well as the web. Now, in the next section, let's see the Remote Help options available for Android devices.

Remote Help for Android

The Remote Help feature in Intune for Android devices is another important capability, especially since these Android devices are mobile and they might not be physically accessible to IT admins all the time. Remote Help for Android includes unattended support as well, which we will discuss later in this chapter.

Before we begin the deployment, there are some prerequisites that Android devices must meet in order to support the Remote Help feature:

- **Managed Google Play setup**: The tenant to which the Android devices are enrolled should have a managed Google Play setup and be linked.
- The Intune app 5.0.5541.0 or later must be installed on the devices.
- Screen captures should not be blocked on the devices via any device configuration policy.
- **The devices should be enrolled as dedicated**: The mode of enrollment of the Android devices to Intune should be **Dedicated** (i.e., COBO). These are userless devices. As of December 2025, fully managed devices are not supported for Remote Help.
- **Zebra or Samsung KNOX devices**: The device must support Samsung Knox. Devices without Knox can only share the screen; they don't allow full control or unattended access. Zebra devices must run MX version 8.3 or later. Unattended control is only supported on Zebra MX version 9.3+ and Samsung OS8+.

Let's start with understanding how we can deploy the Remote Help application from Intune to these Android devices. Once that is covered, we will understand the configuration steps an Intune admin needs to ensure the app works as intended.

Deploying the Remote Help app and configuration from the Intune portal

There are two deployments that we need to do from the Intune portal. First is the Remote Help app, which will be used for the screen-sharing session, and second is an app configuration policy, which will provide the needed microphone and camera access to the app automatically. Let's take a look at both of these in detail next.

Deploying the Remote Help app for Android dedicated devices

The first step is deploying the Remote Help app for Android devices, just like we deployed it for Windows devices in the previous section. The Remote Help app is available in the Google Play store and can be deployed as required from the Intune portal. Let's go through the steps in the Intune portal for deploying the same:

1. First, go to the Intune portal -> **Apps** -> **Android apps** and then **+ Create** -> **Managed Google Play app** and click **Select**, as seen here:

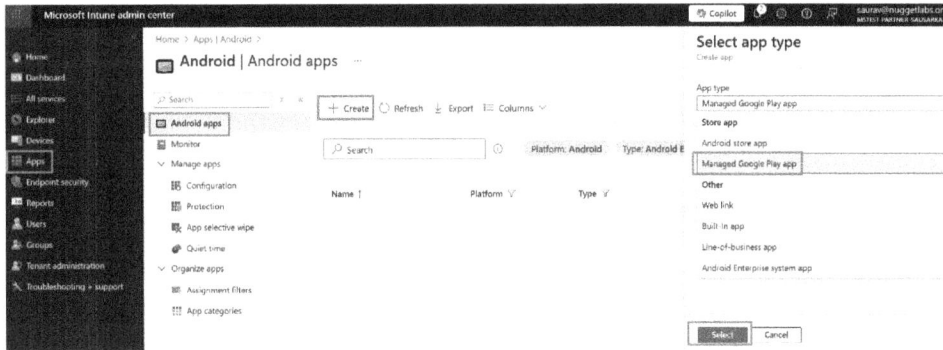

Figure 6.30: Deploying the Remote Help app for Android from the Intune portal

2. Now, on the **Managed Google Play** page, search for the **Remote Help** app, select the app, and click **Sync**:

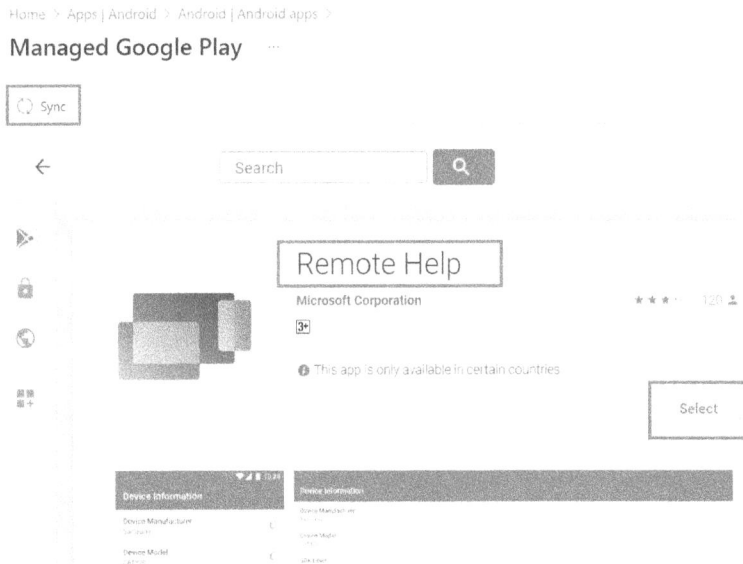

Figure 6.31: Approving the Remote Help app for Android Enterprise devices from the Intune portal

Once done, this app will show as approved, as seen here:

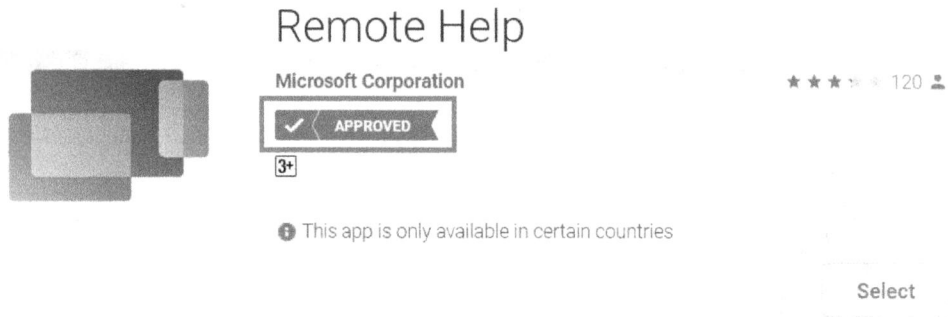

Figure 6.32: Snippet of the approved Remote Help app for Managed Google Play in the Intune portal

Now, this app will be available under the **Android apps** blade, as seen next. We can click on it and edit any of its properties if needed, which are optional.

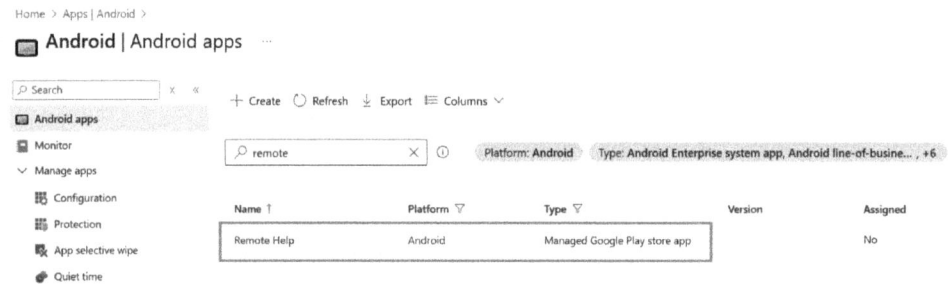

Figure 6.33: Managed Google Play app visible in the Intune portal

3. We need to click on the app and, under **Assignments**, we need to assign the Remote Help app as required to a device group, as seen here:

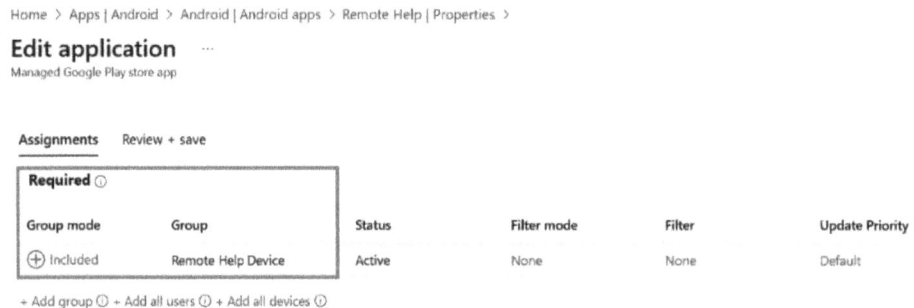

Figure 6.34: Deploying the Remote Help app as required to Android devices from the Intune portal

Once the app is installed, it can be tracked by going to the **Overview** tab of the app in the portal, as seen here:

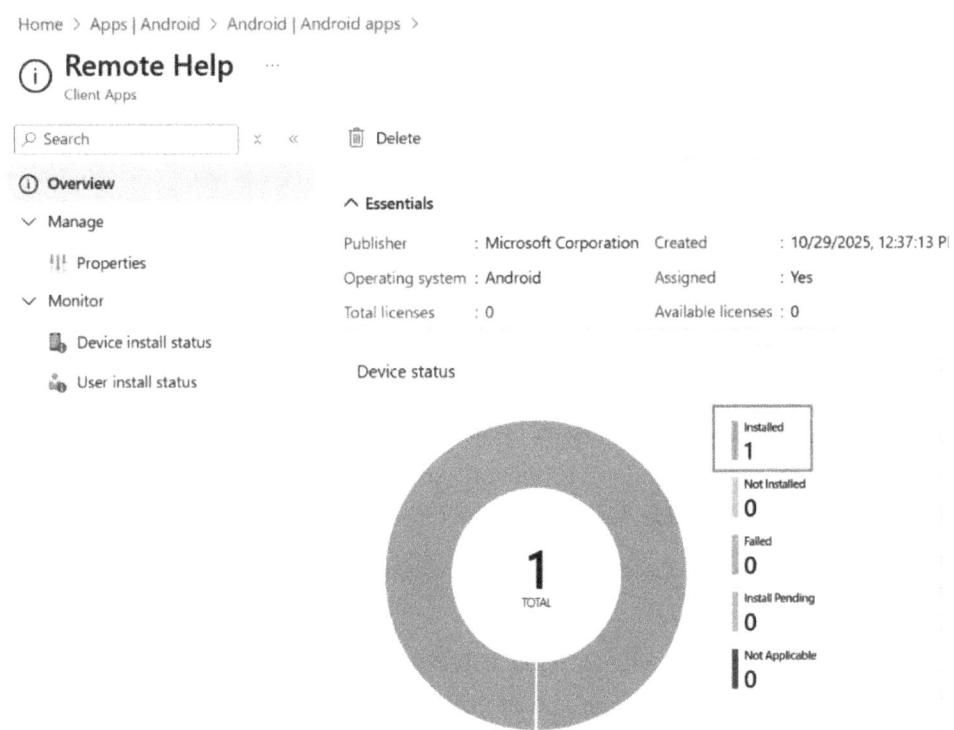

Home > Apps | Android > Android | Android apps >

(i) **Remote Help** ···
Client Apps

| Search | x | « | | 🗑 Delete |

(i) **Overview**

∨ Manage

　⫴ Properties

∨ Monitor

　📱 Device install status

　👥 User install status

∧ **Essentials**

Publisher	: Microsoft Corporation	Created	: 10/29/2025, 12:37:13 PI
Operating system	: Android	Assigned	: Yes
Total licenses	: 0	Available licenses	: 0

Device status

Installed	1
Not Installed	0
Failed	0
Install Pending	0
Not Applicable	0

1
TOTAL

Figure 6.35: Tracking the deployment status of the Remote Help app from the Intune portal

Now that the Remote Help app is successfully deployed to the device, in the next section, let's go through some configuration profiles that also need to be deployed and understand their significance.

Deploying an app configuration policy for Remote Help

Once the Remote Help application is successfully installed on the device, it now needs to have appropriate permissions over audio (microphone) and camera. These permissions can be granted by the end user manually, or they can be set automatically by the admin using an app configuration policy, which reduces the manual actions that the end user has to take. Let's take a look at the steps to create the app configuration policy for Android, which would automatically grant those permissions:

1. Go to the Intune portal and navigate to **Apps** and **Configuration**. Then, click on **+ Create** and select **Managed devices**, as seen here:

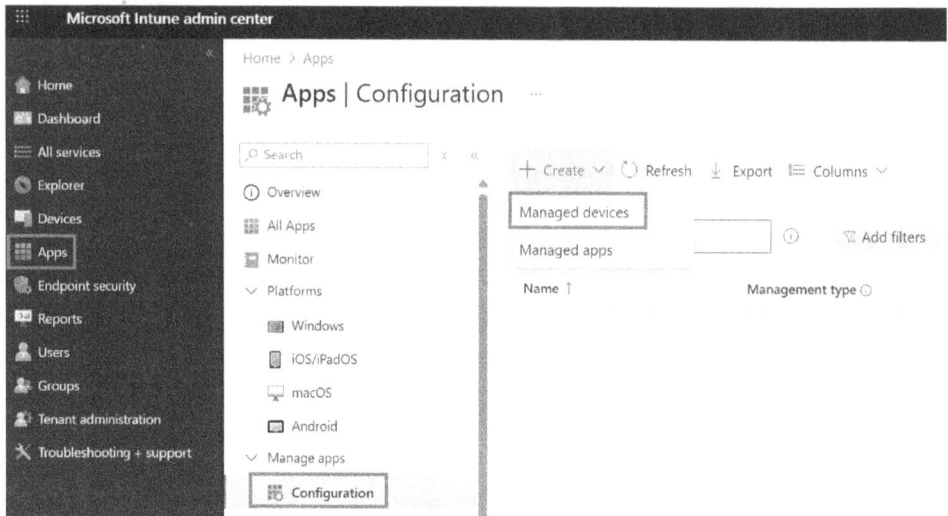

Figure 6.36: Creating an app configuration policy for Remote Help from the Intune portal

2. On the **Basics** page, provide a name for the policy. For **Platform**, choose **Android Enterprise,** and for **Profile Type**, choose **Fully Managed, Dedicated, and Corporate-Owned Work Profile Only**. For **Targeted app**, select **Remote Help**, as seen here, and proceed to the next screen:

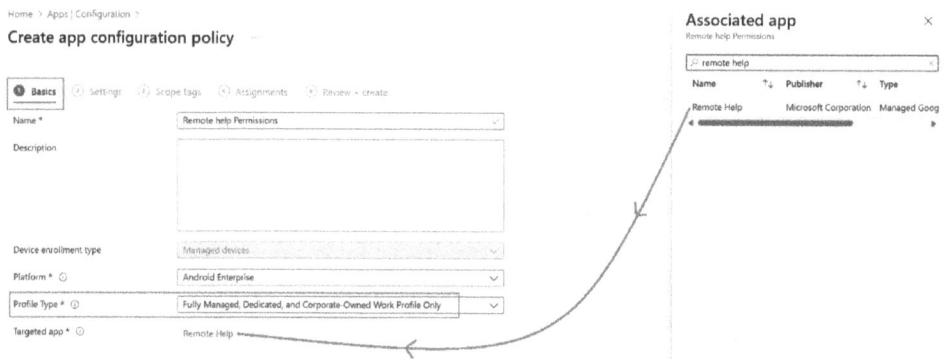

Figure 6.37: Values for the app configuration policy

3. On the next page, on the **Settings** tab, click on + **Add** and select **Record audio** and **Camera** from the list of available options under **Add Permissions**. For both these settings we will select **Auto grant** from the dropdown for **Permission state** as highlighted below:

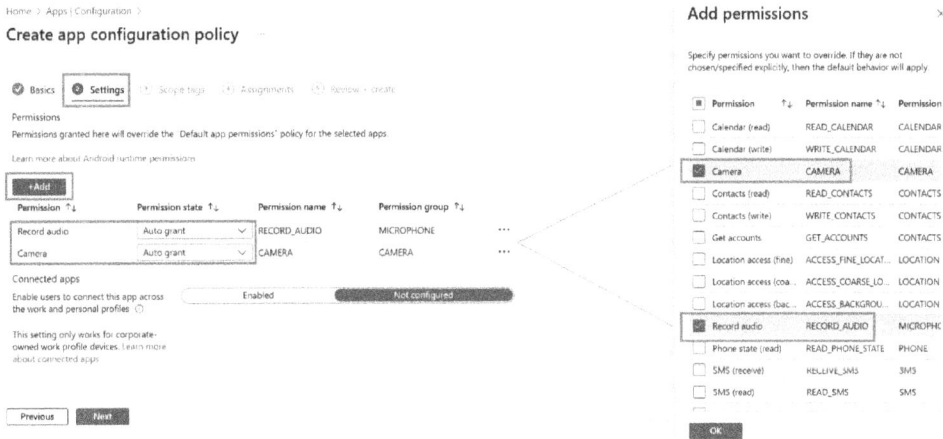

Figure 6.38: Configuring the app configuration policy with the needed values

4. Now, click on **Next**, and this policy will be assigned to a device group containing the Android dedicated devices, as shown here:

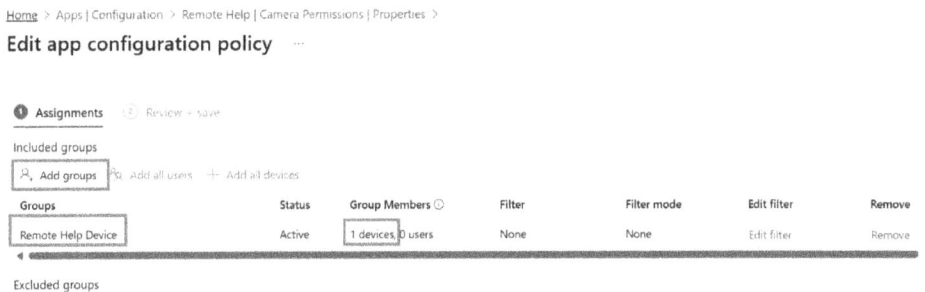

Figure 6.39: Deploying the app configuration policy to the device group

5. If the device is powered on and connected to the internet, it will receive this app configuration policy, and the same can be tracked in the Intune portal under the **Overview** blade of this app configuration deployment, as seen here:

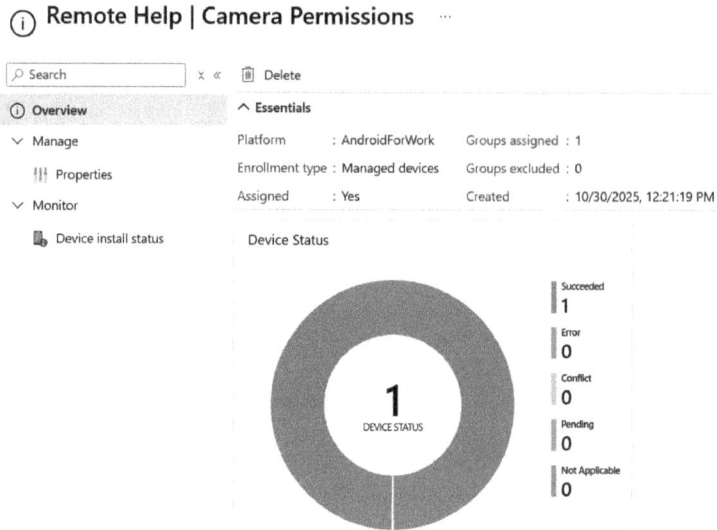

Figure 6.40: Monitoring the status of the app configuration policy deployment from the Intune portal

In this case, since the devices are userless (COBO), we have created a dynamic device group in Entra ID. The group is automatically going to add Android devices to it, based on the enrollment profile name that was used to enroll them. Here is the query for dynamic group membership:

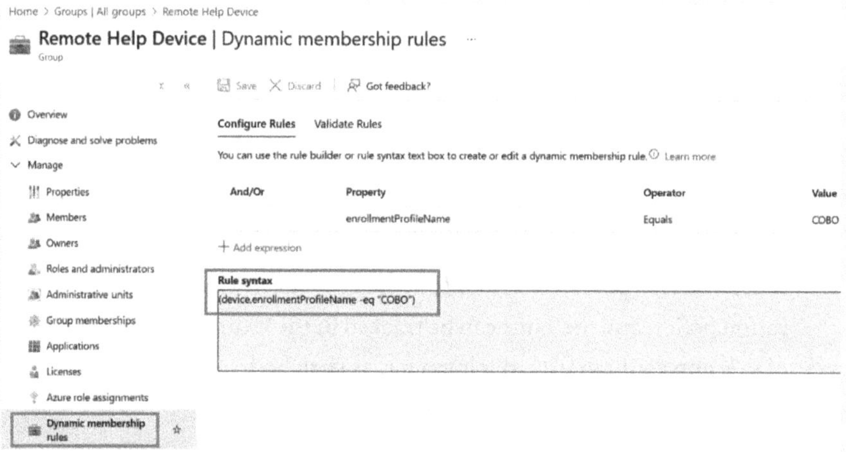

Figure 6.41: Dynamic membership query for a dynamic group containing Android devices enrolled

Once the Remote Help app is installed and the app configuration policy is set, everything is in place for the usage of Remote Help on the device.

This completes the admin side setup steps that were needed to be followed for Remote Help. In the next section, we will take a look at the end user's experience for initiating a Remote Help session.

End user usage and experience

After the app is installed, the user has to launch the Remote Help app and click on **Get Started**. They will be prompted for a couple of permissions that need to be granted manually, which are explained in this section:

1. First, the Remote Help app will ask for overlay permission. This permission is needed so that the Remote Help app can render its features on top of any screen. Click on **Grant**, as seen here:

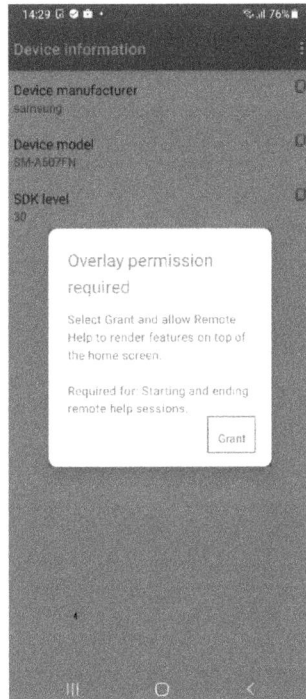

Figure 6.42: Prompt for overlay permission on the end user's device

2. Now, the user will automatically be navigated to the next screen, which is the **Appear on top** settings in the **Settings** app. Here, the user has to simply switch the slider for the **Remote Help** app to the right, which gives the needed overlay permission to the Remote Help app on the device:

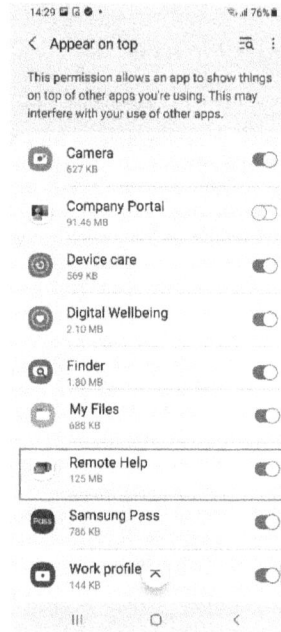

Figure 6.43: Providing permissions for Appear on top on an Android device

3. Now, the Remote Help app shows the second pop-up screen, which states **System Settings permission required** for the Remote Help app. Click on **Grant** and then move the slider to the right for **Remote Help** to allow permission, as shown here:

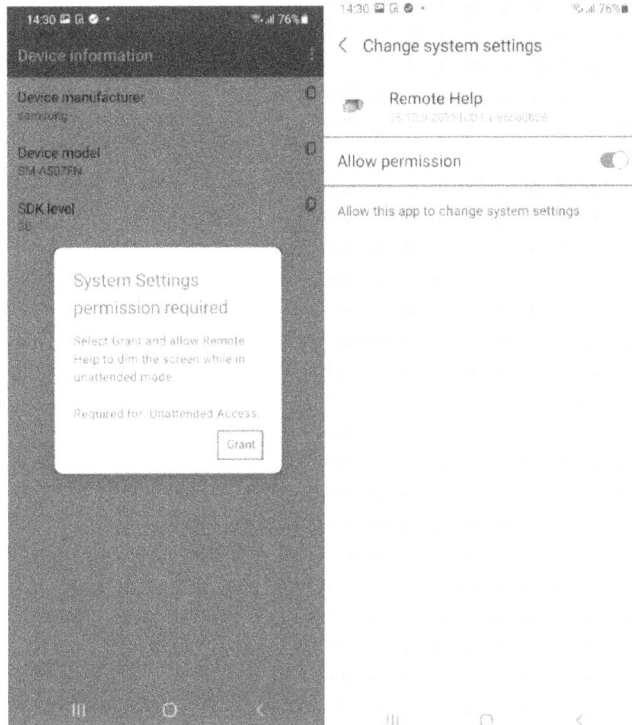

Figure 6.44: Popup for allowing the system settings permission for Remote Help

Accepting these prompts is a one-time action. Once permissions are granted, they remain in place even after the device restarts.

Now, everything is ready, and the Intune admin can start a remote session as per the following steps:

1. In the Intune portal, go to the Android dedicated device you want to take remote control of, and then in the **Overview** pane, click on **New remote assistance session**, as shown here:

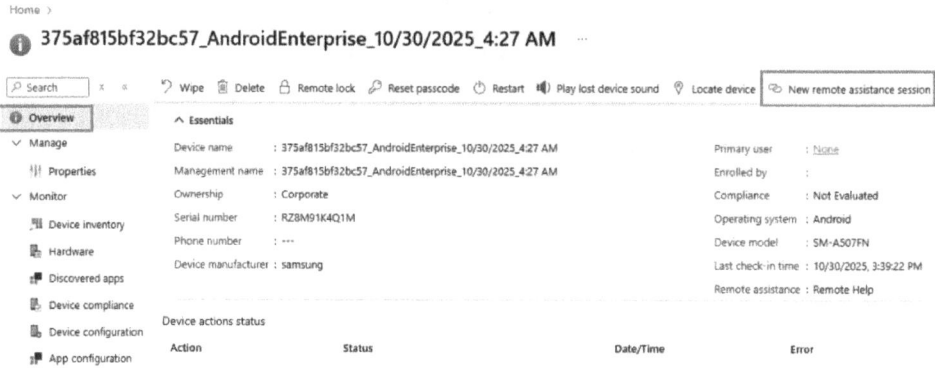

Figure 6.45: Option to start a new Remote Help session for an Android device

2. A new popup appears and the admin can choose which kind of session they want to establish. Select **Request full control** and see the experience:

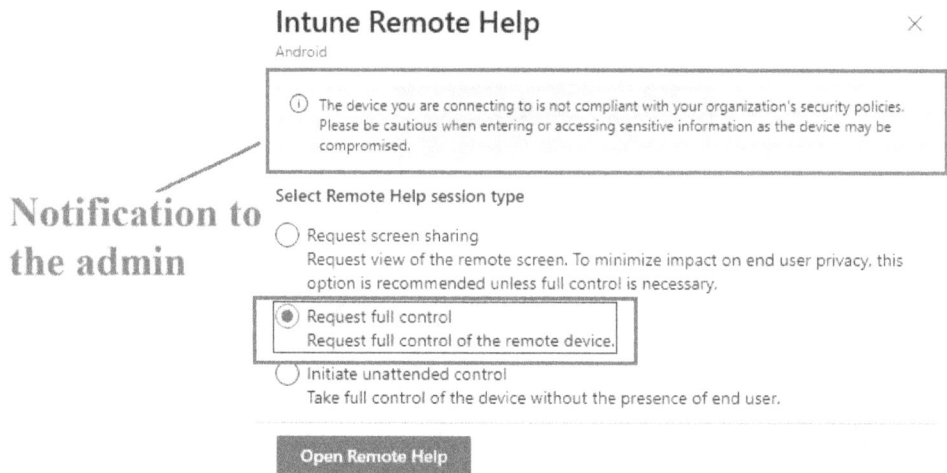

Figure 6.46: Selecting the level of control for the Remote Help session

3. The end user will get a pop-up notification about the Remote Access request, as seen next. This notification contains the name of the admin who is requesting to take the session. The end user needs to click on **ACCEPT**:

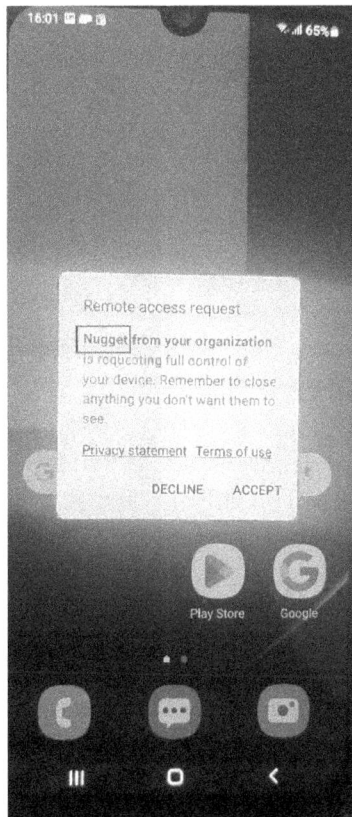

Figure 6.47: Remote Access request prompt to the sharer's device before the start of the Remote Help session

Once accepted, the Remote Help session is established. The user gets a notification mentioning that the remote session is underway, as seen here:

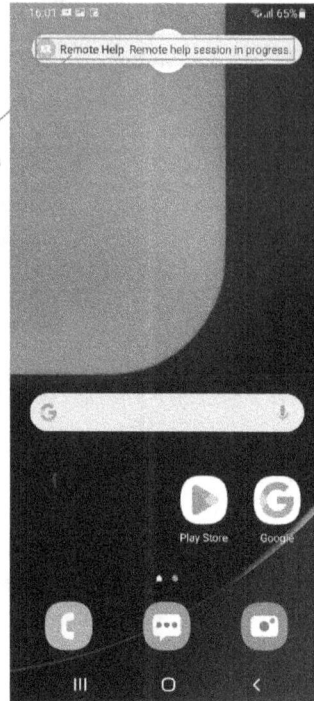

Figure 6.48: Notification to the end user when the Remote Help session starts

For the admin, the remote session is also now visible in the Intune portal. As seen next, the admin has the three default soft key controls (for *Back*, *Home*, and *Overview/Minimize*) along with volume controls and the **Restart** option for the device:

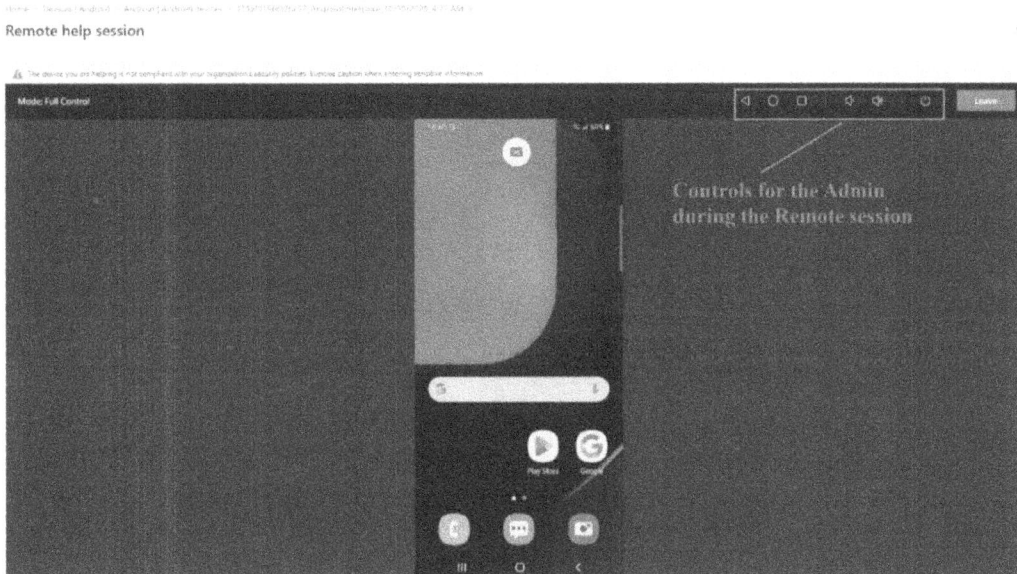

Figure 6.49: Helper's controls during the Remote Help session for Android

The admin can now do the needed troubleshooting on the device and capture any necessary data or screenshots!

The end user always has the option of ending the remote session from their end by clicking on the highlighted icon shown in the following figure. Once done, they get a prompt that they have to accept by clicking on **EXIT**, as seen here:

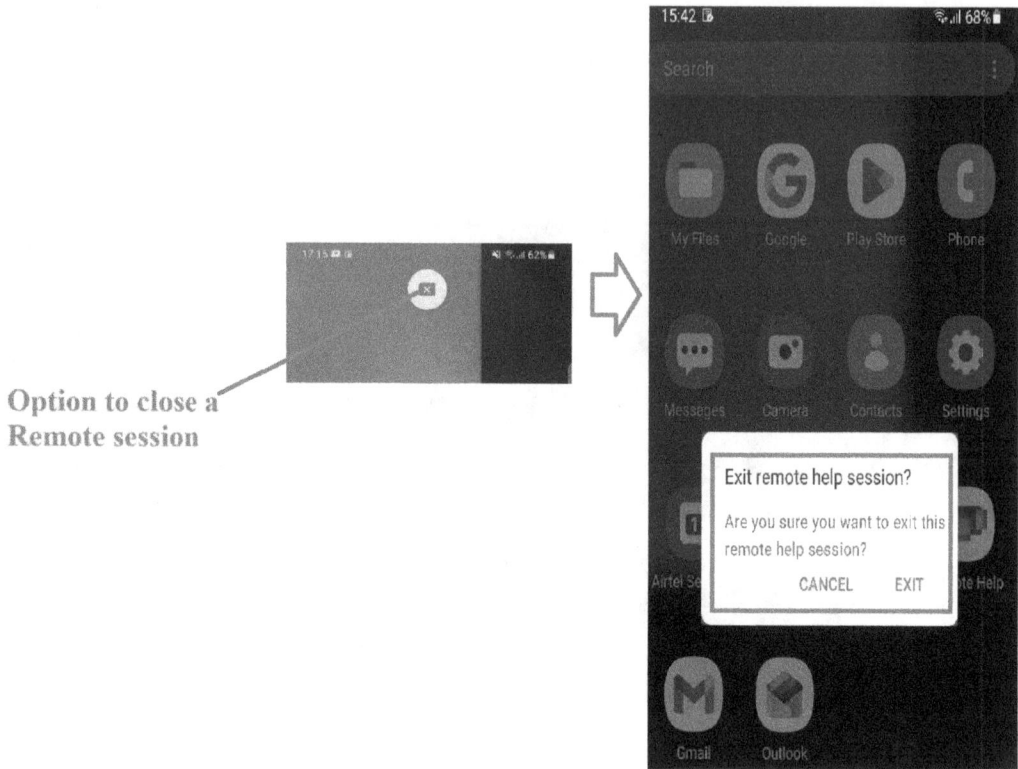

Option to close a Remote session

Figure 6.50: Options for the sharer to end a Remote Help session in Android

Similarly, the admin also has the option of ending the remote session by clicking on **Leave** from the portal:

Figure 6.51: Option for the helper to end a Remote Help session

If a Remote Help session stays idle for over 5 minutes, the user will receive a prompt that it will end automatically. A countdown timer of 3 minutes will appear, and the session will close when it expires. Either the admin or the user can extend the session by clicking **EXTEND**, as seen here:

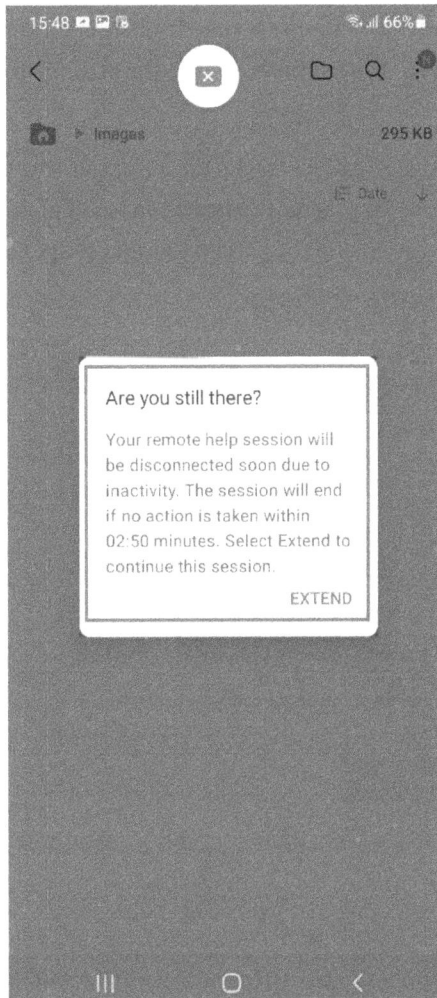

Figure 6.52: Prompt when the Remote Help session is inactive

Remote Help in Android provides us with a very valuable feature called unattended support. Let's understand that in detail and see how it works in the next section.

Unattended Remote Help session

For Android devices (and soon Windows), admins can initiate unattended control. This is especially useful for dedicated (userless) Android devices often used in kiosk scenarios, where no user is present. With unattended control, there's no need for the end user to approve prompts on the device for establishing the session. Let's take a look at the process of establishing an unattended Remote Help session:

1. Just like before, the first step involves the Intune admin locating the device from the portal, and after clicking on **New remote assistance session**, this time, click on the **Initiate unattended control** option and then **Open Remote Help**, as seen here:

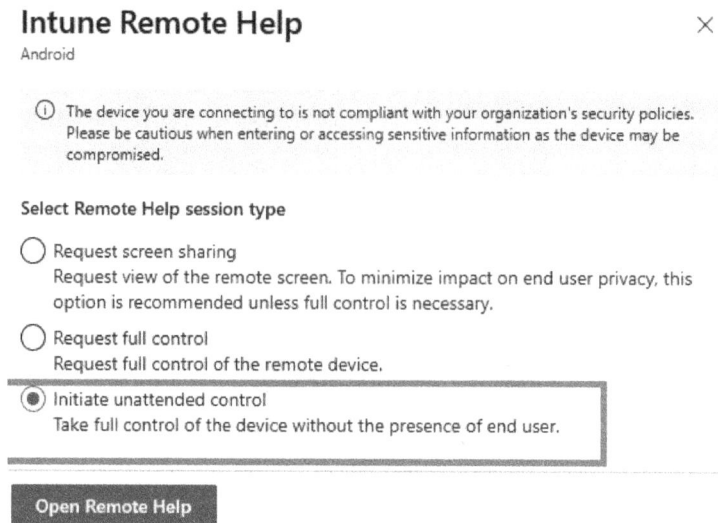

Intune Remote Help   ✕
Android

ⓘ The device you are connecting to is not compliant with your organization's security policies. Please be cautious when entering or accessing sensitive information as the device may be compromised.

Select Remote Help session type

◯ Request screen sharing
Request view of the remote screen. To minimize impact on end user privacy, this option is recommended unless full control is necessary.

◯ Request full control
Request full control of the remote device.

◉ Initiate unattended control
Take full control of the device without the presence of end user.

Open Remote Help

Figure 6.53: Option for the helper to initiate an unattended Remote Help session for Android

2. In this case, the end device still receives a notification, but it includes a 30-second timer. If the user doesn't manually accept or decline within that time, the prompt is automatically accepted, as seen here:

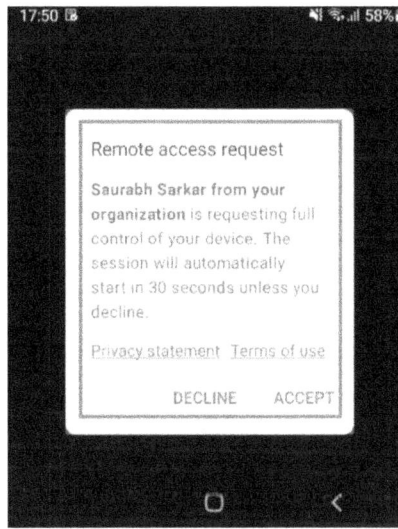

Figure 6.54: Prompt (which gets auto-accepted) in the case of an unattended Remote Help session

3. After the timer runs out, the device gets automatically connected to the Remote Help session, as seen next, without any input from the end user:

Figure 6.55: Successful unattended Remote Help session as viewed from the Intune portal

After connecting, the device is still in a locked state, as seen in the preceding figure. The admin has the option of swiping up and unlocking the device from the portal end, then proceeding with troubleshooting as needed.

When an unattended session is active, it's assumed that no user is present to accept prompts or take action at the device end. During this time, only the admin's controls from the Intune portal are allowed. If a user tries to interact with the device, they will see a prompt stating the device is under maintenance and shouldn't be used. This prompt blocks any activity for 20 seconds, after which the unattended session resumes for the admin, as seen here:

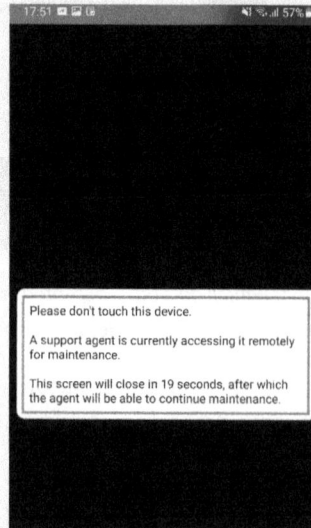

Figure 6.56: Device blocked from usage by the end user during unattended control

This completes all the use cases with Remote Help for Android devices, including kiosk (user-less) devices, that require unattended support. In the next section, let's understand the usage of Remote Help with macOS.

Remote Help for macOS

Remote Help on macOS is a new feature release, and it brings several useful features that improve the support experience. However, just like Windows Remote Help currently doesn't have unattended control functionality, the same is the case for macOS. In this section, we will go through all the steps needed for setting up Remote Help sessions on macOS devices and the available options.

> Apart from RBAC, networking, and licensing requirements, which have already been discussed earlier in this chapter in the *Prerequisites* section, the supported macOS versions for Remote Help are 11 Big Sur, 12 Monterey, 13 Ventura, and future releases.

Similar to Windows, there are two ways to use Remote Help on macOS devices. The end user can either join the session through the Remote Help client or use the web app in a browser. The web app is easier since it doesn't require installation, but it only allows the admin to view the screen. The Remote Help client, on the other hand, is ideal for corporate devices where the app is already deployed or installed by the user. While it depends on having the client present on the device, it gives the helper full control during the session.

Let's now dive into both these options in detail. First, we will cover the Remote Help experience with the web app, which is easier to set up and is ideal for providing support to personal macOS devices.

Using the Remote Help web app

The process of initiating a Remote Help session for macOS devices from Intune is similar to what we have seen before in the case of Windows. Follow these steps in order to establish the same:

1. Go to the Intune admin portal and then locate the macOS device. Then, click on the three dots and select **New remote assistance session**, as seen here:

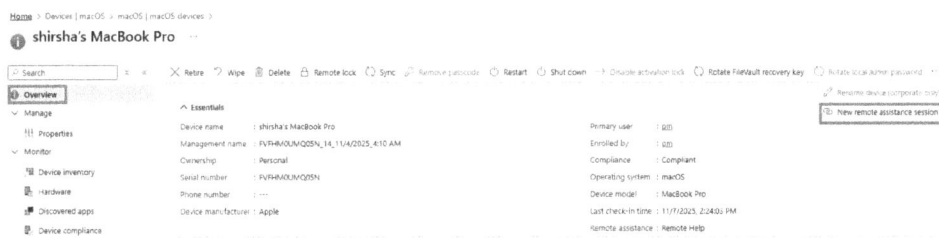

Figure 6.57: Establishing a Remote Help session from the Intune portal for macOS

2. This will generate a passcode and a session link, as seen next, which needs to be shared with the end user:

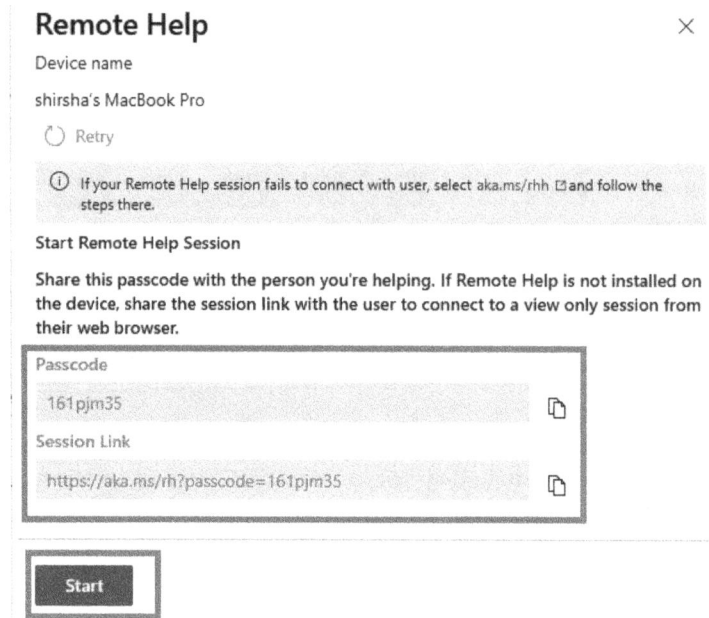

Figure 6.58: Generating the session code and link for a macOS Remote Help session

3. When the user opens the Remote Help app or aka.ms/rh, they must log in, enter the passcode, and allow screen sharing by accepting the prompt from remotehelp.microsoft.com by clicking on **Allow to Share Screen**, as seen here:

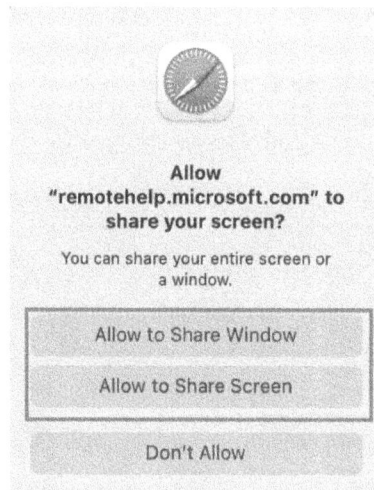

Figure 6.59: Prompt to share the screen or window on the sharer's macOS device

4. There is another prompt for allowing the use of the microphone by remotehelp.microsoft.com, which needs to be accepted, as seen next. Select **Allow** to continue:

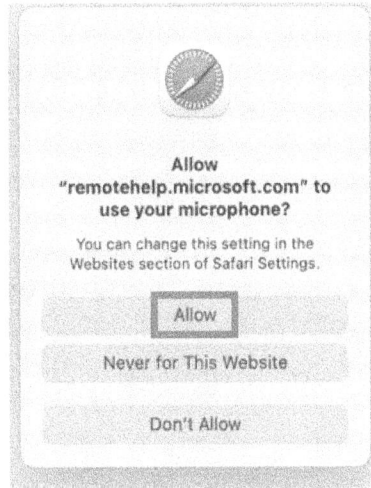

Figure 6.60: Prompt from Remote Help to allow the use of the microphone during a Remote Help session

5. At the helper's end, there will be a prompt for selecting the kind of control they wish to take, which is **Screen sharing** for the web app (and **Screen sharing/Full control** for the native app, which is covered in detail in the next section):

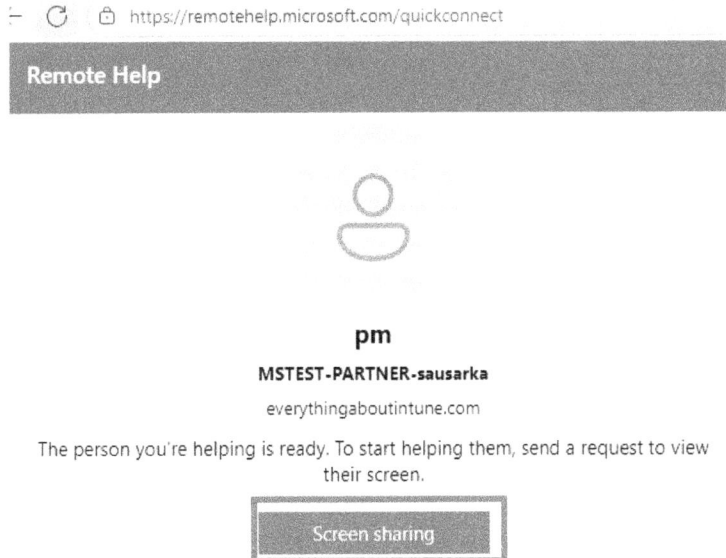

Figure 6.61: Prompt at the sharer's end to share screen and start the Remote Help session

6. The sharer will be able to see the details (photo, name, job title, and domain verification through Entra ID) of the helper to ensure that the correct person is asking for control:

MSTEST-PARTNER-sausarka

everythingaboutintune.com

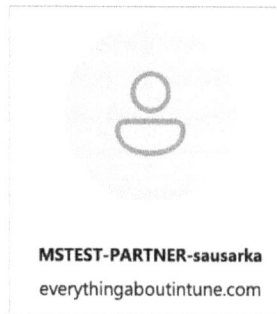

The person trying to help you is asking to see your screen. Remember to close anything you don't want them to see.

Decline   Allow

Figure 6.62: Prompt for the sharer to view the details of the admin before the start
of the Remote Help session

7. The service will check whether the sharer's device is compliant with Intune. When devices are not compliant, the helper will receive a warning, but can still proceed with the session, as seen here:

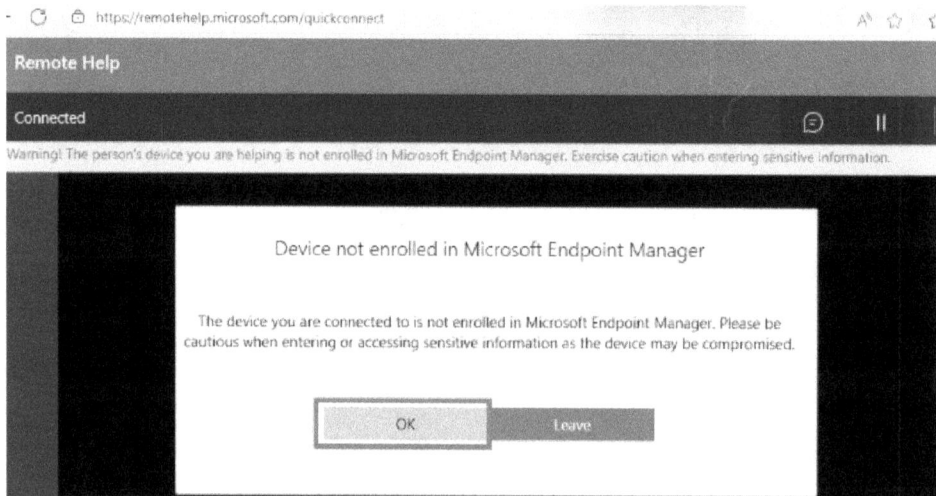

Figure 6.63: Prompt for the helper if the end device is not compliant with Intune

8. Now, the sharer can choose to share a specific window or the entire screen during the session, as seen here:

Figure 6.64: Option for the end user to select the screen/window in macOS

Now, the screen-sharing session is established, and the helper can view the macOS device from their end, as seen next, and guide the end user for troubleshooting:

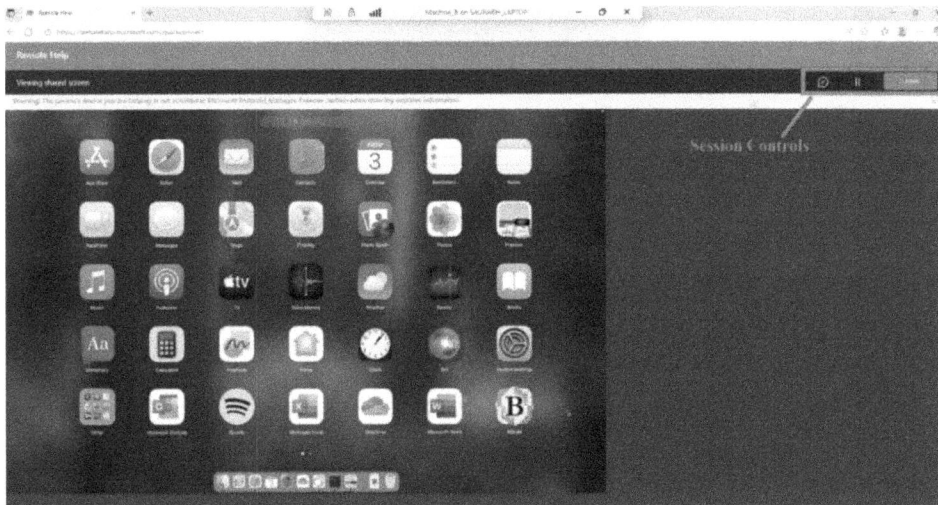

Figure 6.65: Successful Remote Help session for macOS and session controls available for the helper

Until now we have covered the basic Remote Help capabilities for macOS devices. In the next section, let's take a look at an advanced new feature of Remote Help for macOS: full control.

New: full control on the macOS Remote Help native app

Microsoft has taken a significant step forward by introducing full control support for macOS devices in Intune Remote Help, which was rolled out in 2024. This enhancement reflects Intune's broader vision of enabling true cross-platform management, giving IT teams the flexibility to support any device within their environment. With this capability, help desks can go beyond simple screen viewing as they can now take complete control of macOS devices, making troubleshooting faster and more efficient, and enabling them to resolve software issues or assist employees in real time.

If the macOS device is enrolled in Intune, we have the option of deploying the Remote Help package as `.pkg` from the Intune portal, as seen here:

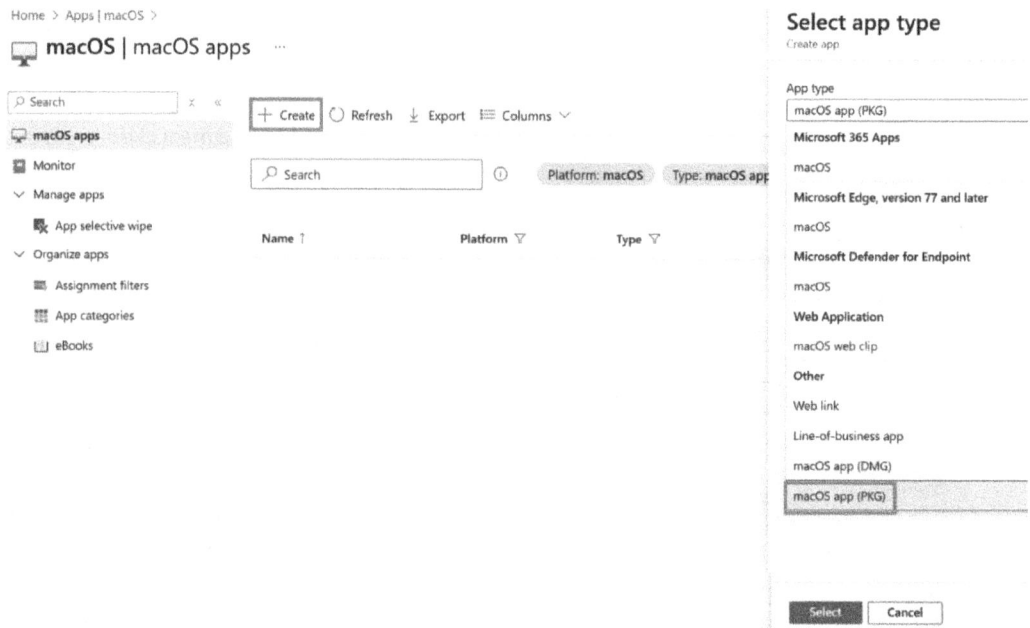

Figure 6.66: Deploying the Remote Help package from the Intune portal to macOS

The end users always have the option of manually downloading the Remote Help package from `aka.ms/downloadremotehelpmacos`.

Once installed, when the sharer launches the app for the very first time, they have to provide permissions for **Screen Recording** and **Accessibility** by clicking on **Set up**. Once they click on **Set up**, the **Accessibility** window opens, and we have to move the slider for the Remote Help app in order to allow the needed permissions.

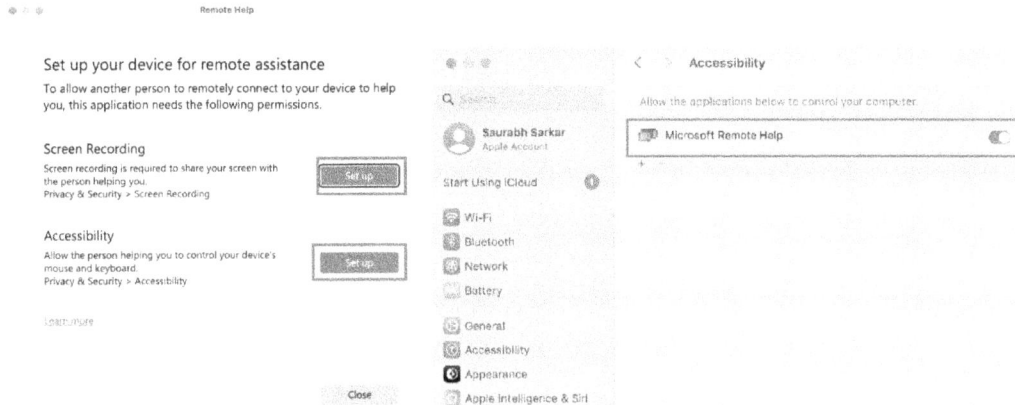

Figure 6.67: Allowing permissions for the Remote Help app for screen recording and accessibility

Now, when the helper launches the Remote Help session, they can see an option for taking full control of the device, as seen here:

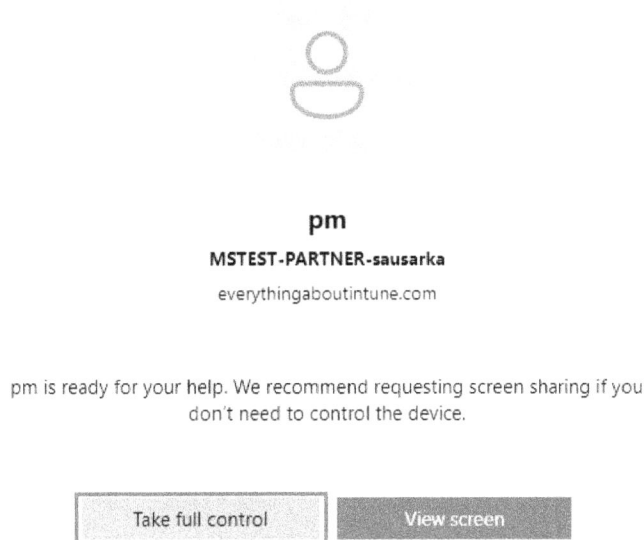

pm

MSTEST-PARTNER-sausarka

everythingaboutintune.com

pm is ready for your help. We recommend requesting screen sharing if you don't need to control the device.

Take full control   View screen

Figure 6.68: Option for the helper to take full control of the macOS device

macOS-specific capabilities

Just like Windows, for macOS, we have the following three capabilities, which are very useful features for the admin:

- **Support for Conditional Access**: We can use a Conditional Access policy for security purposes and configure it to require MFA for helpers or restrict access to specific locations or compliant devices.

- **Chat functionality**: For macOS, there is a chat functionality for the helper to communicate with the sharer.

- **Support for unenrolled devices**: Just like Windows, for macOS, the helper has the option of establishing a remote session with a sharer's device even if the sharer's device is not enrolled in Intune. This is useful for scenarios wherein the end users are using their personal macOS devices for work purposes, and the same is permitted in the organization.

I recommend exploring an interactive demo walkthrough at `https://regale.cloud/microsoft/play/1746/remote-help#/7/0` for an intuitive experience of using the Remote Help native app in macOS. We also have an interactive demo at `https://regale.cloud/microsoft/play/1746/remote-help#/6/0`, which provides a step-by-step guided experience on using the Remote Help web app in macOS and simulates the look and feel of the Remote Help tool, without requiring any setup.

Remote help for iOS

Remote Help does not currently support iOS/iPadOS devices. This gap has been repeatedly flagged as a major blocker for several enterprise customers who are using the Intune suite/Remote Help. Customers compare Intune Remote Help with third-party tools such as TeamViewer and Bomgar, which already support iOS. This gap impacts the Intune suite's competitive positioning. Apple's restrictive APIs for remote control make full control challenging. Microsoft might release view-only Remote Help sessions via web or the app, similar to macOS, in the future; however, as of December 2025, there is no ETA for the same.

This completes the Remote Help setup and its capabilities for macOS devices. In the next section, let's take a quick look at Remote Help's capabilities with the Linux operating system.

Remote Help for Linux

Linux is not officially supported for Remote Help sessions, and there is no native Remote Help app for Linux. This is because Remote Help relies on RDP and OS-level APIs for full control and elevation, which are not available or standardized on Linux. Microsoft's roadmap does not list Linux support for Remote Help as an upcoming feature.

However, the Remote Help web app can technically work in some scenarios on Linux because it runs in a browser. However, the sessions would be limited to *view-only*, as full control is not permitted when using Remote Help in a browser. Also, the behavior is not consistent, as when testing, I saw intermittent issues.

Let's see the steps for establishing a Remote Help session from a Linux device using the Remote Help browser capability:

1. From the Linux device, open a browser and go to aka.ms/rh. You'll see a privacy prompt; click on **OK**:

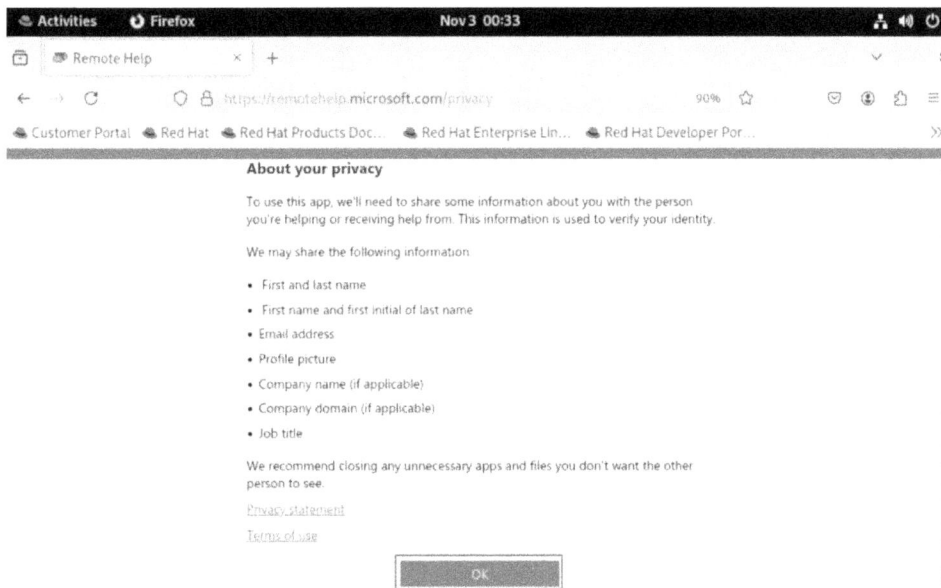

Figure 6.69: Privacy prompt in Linux while starting a Remote Help session

2.   The helper has to visit the Remote Help site to generate a code and share it with the end user. The sharer then sees the helper's details and chooses whether to allow screen sharing, as seen here:

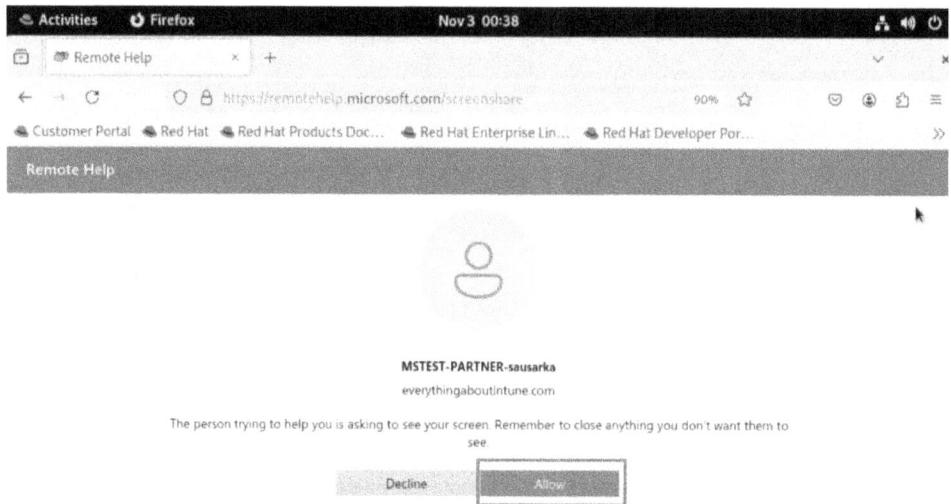

Figure 6.70: Prompt for the sharer to allow a Remote Help session in Linux

3.   If approved, the sharer is asked to grant microphone access for the session:

Figure 6.71: Prompt to allow the use of the microphone in Linux during a Remote Help session

Since the device isn't enrolled in Intune, the helper receives a notification about the un-enrolled status:

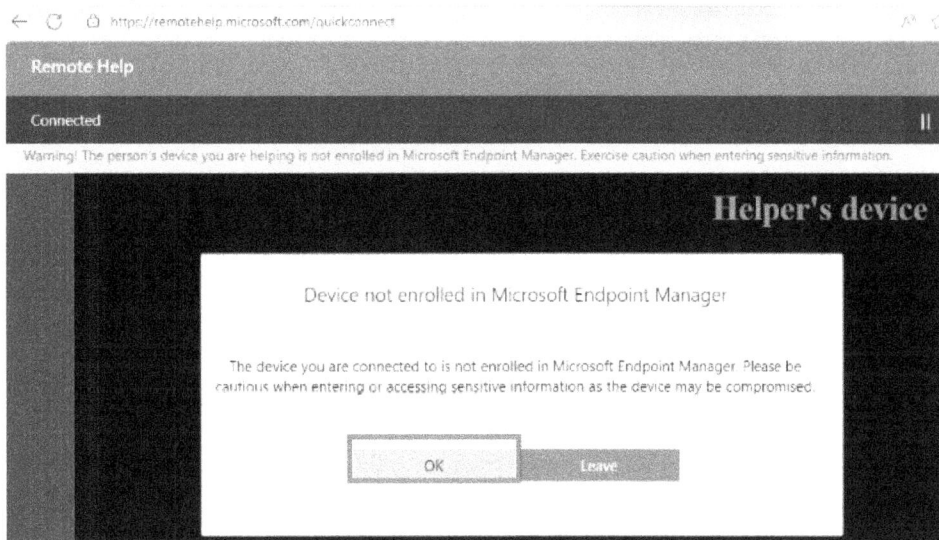

Figure 6.72: Prompt for the helper in case the device is not enrolled in Intune

4. Finally, the sharer gets a prompt to share their screen and confirm, after which the screen-sharing session is fully established, as seen here:

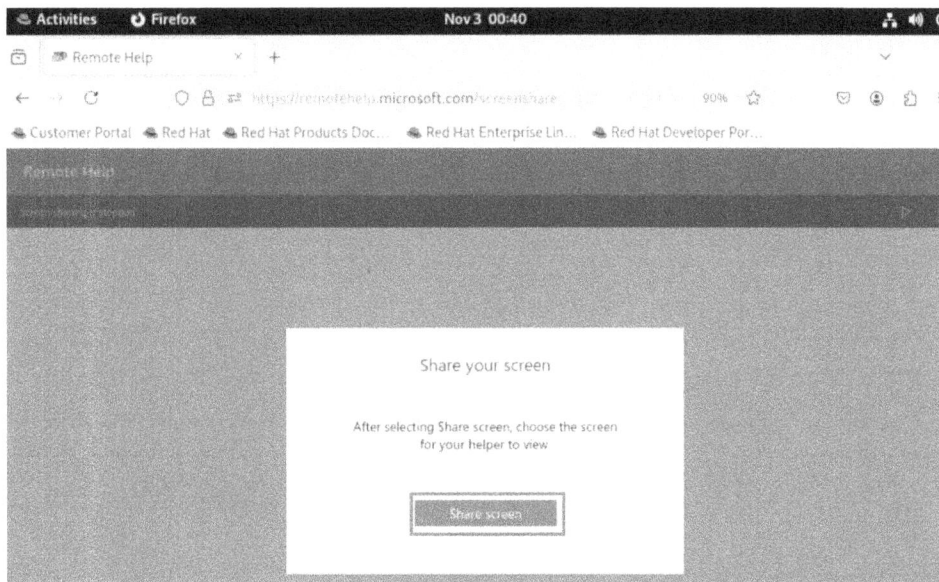

Figure 6.73: Prompt for the end user in Linux to start the screen-sharing session

Given that Linux terminals are not widely used by end users, it's not officially supported by Microsoft yet for Remote Help. However, as we have just established, technically, it's possible to set up a Remote Help session in Linux by using the Remote Help web tool.

In the next section, let's understand how we can integrate Intune with ticketing tools.

Remote Help with ServiceNow

We can integrate ServiceNow with Intune, which allows help desk agents to view open cases in a central Intune console and then use the Remote Help tool to troubleshoot endpoint issues.

This integration is done through the Intune ServiceNow Connector. The detailed steps for setting up this integration are outside the scope of this book, so we won't be covering them here. I recommend referring to Microsoft's official docs (`https://learn.microsoft.com/en-au/intune/intune-service/fundamentals/service-now-integration`) for details on this.

Now, let's explore how to monitor ongoing Remote Help sessions in our tenant, which is a critical step for compliance. We will also dive into the Remote Help telemetry and session logs available in the Intune portal to give us a clear view of Remote Help activity.

Monitoring remote sessions

The Intune portal gives us insights into how Remote Help is being used within the environment. We get a visual of the average session time and total sessions that have concluded and are active currently.

To view the same, we need to go to the Intune portal -> **Tenant administration** -> **Remote Help** -> **Monitor**, as seen here:

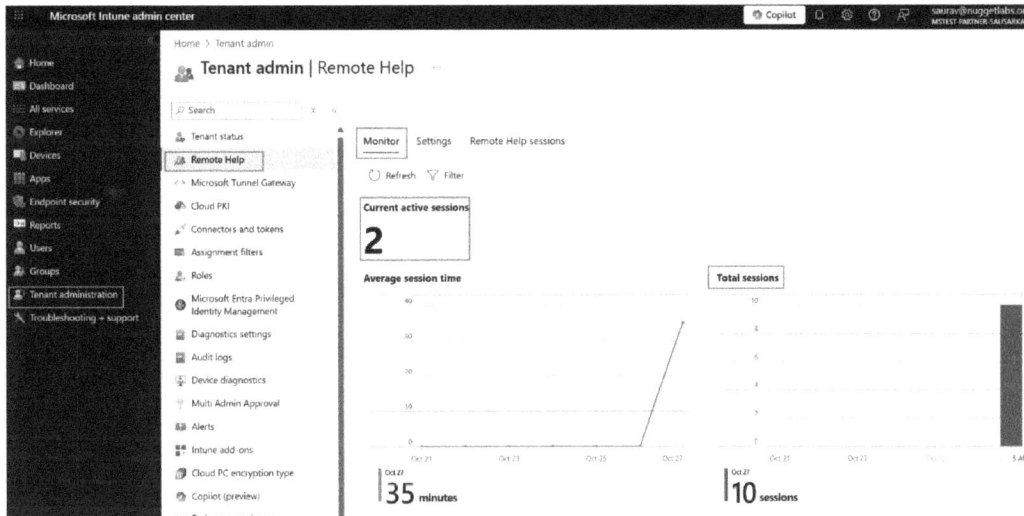

Figure 6.74: Graphical and pictorial view of Remote Help sessions in the tenant via the Intune portal

If we want to view granular details of individual sessions that were established, we can go to the **Remote Help sessions** tab, as seen here:

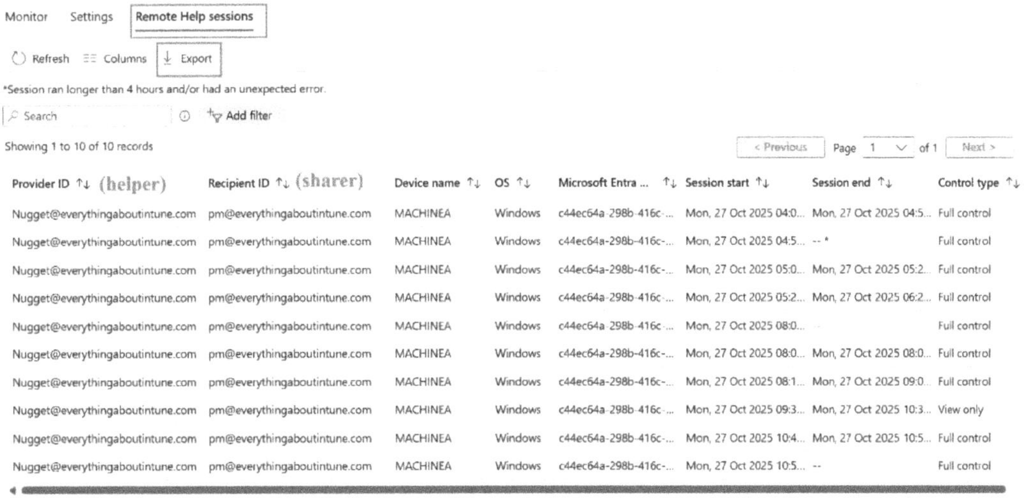

Figure 6.75: Remote Help session logs for the tenant in the Intune portal

This view contains many important details, such as the admin's handling sessions, device info, and session duration information. All this information can be downloaded to an Excel sheet for audit purposes by clicking on the highlighted **Export** option.

Additionally, in the Intune portal, we also have Remote Help-related logs under **Tenant administration -> Audit logs**. This report includes details about the admins who have initiated the remote sessions, along with timestamps and other details, which can be exported, as seen here:

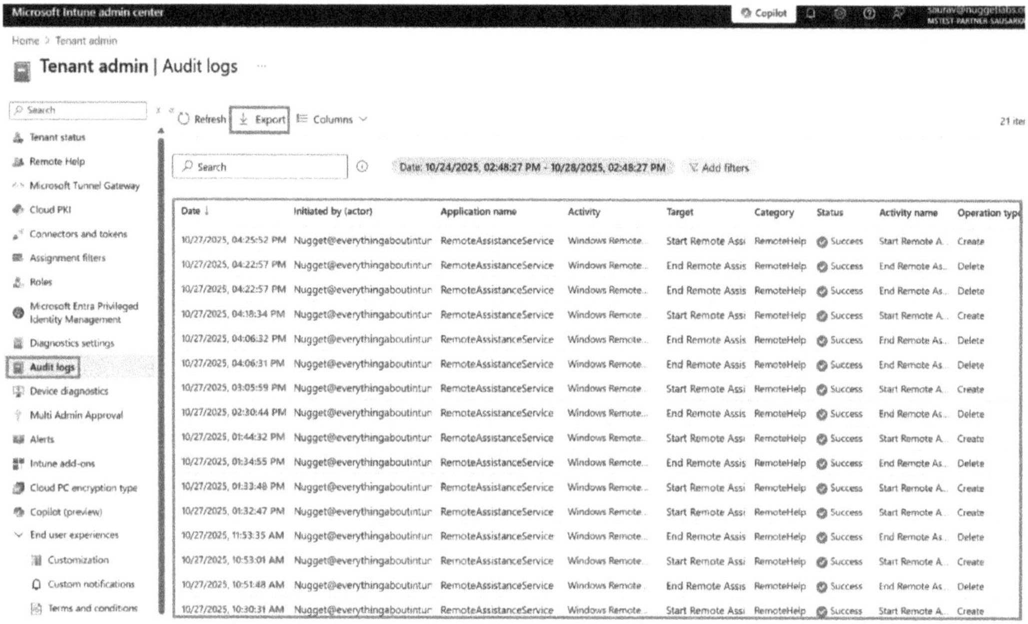

Figure 6.76: Additional audit logs in the Intune portal for Remote Help sessions

> Remote Help can also be used during the OOBE phase of an Autopilot provisioning. This is especially helpful if we need to guide the end user in collecting any logs while they are at the initial setup screen. However, the process for that is currently not very smooth. The sharer will have to open the command prompt in the OOBE screen and download and install the Remote Help app.

Now, in the next section, let's take a look at a few important points we must keep in mind with respect to Remote Help app deployment.

Key considerations before rolling out Remote Help

There are a few things we must keep in mind while setting up Remote Help in our organization. Let's understand those aspects and the following few key considerations:

- **Using least privilege and Zero Trust**: As per Microsoft's Zero Trust model, it's important to set RBAC permissions for helpers so only those who truly need full or unattended control have it. For instance, Level 1 support might be limited to view-only access, while Tier 2 can have full control. This approach helps safeguard user privacy and maintain device integrity.

- **Enforcing Conditional Access**: It's best to use Entra ID Conditional Access policies for Remote Help on Windows and macOS. This adds an extra layer of security by requiring MFA or a compliant helper device, so a compromised account can't be misused to access devices.

- **Enabling unenrolled device support only if needed**: Allowing support for unenrolled devices can be useful, but it needs careful consideration. We should enable it only if our workforce includes users on personal (unenrolled) devices. If we do, we should apply it thoughtfully and consider restricting which support staff can assist these devices by assigning separate RBAC roles.

Remote Help in Intune is a very powerful and essential tool for all IT administrators, offering significant benefits. However, there are still a few feature gaps that Microsoft is reviewing and may address in future updates. Let's discuss the same in the next section.

Current gaps of Remote Help

Remote Help in Intune is ideal for organizations deeply invested in Microsoft 365 and looking for tight integration with Intune policies and compliance. However, Remote Help is missing a few features today that, if added in the future, would make it even stronger, especially when compared to other solutions. Let's take a look at those features next:

- **Cross-tenant support**: Many organizations outsource help desk and routine maintenance to external partners. Currently, Remote Help only works with the account used to enroll the device. This means if a partner's device is enrolled under their own company's tenant, they cannot assist customers in a different tenant. For example, if a helper's device is enrolled in *Tenant A* but they also have an account in *Tenant B*, they cannot sign in to Remote Help with the *Tenant B* account because the device is MDM-enrolled to *Tenant A*. Having this capability will be a good value addition and would ensure that we cater to many such scenarios

- **Recording a session**: It would be great to have the ability to record a Remote Help session to meet regulatory requirements. Ideally, helpers should be able to record these sessions and save them to a SharePoint or OneDrive location, similar to how Teams recordings are handled.

- **File transfer within a Remote Help session**: Adding secure file transfer during a Remote Help session would greatly improve the experience. Many competitors already offer this feature. A typical use case is when the help desk needs to share a file (such as a PDF with instructions, a screenshot, or an Excel sheet) directly within the session. Currently, this gap forces teams to rely on separate tools such as email, Teams, or OneDrive/SharePoint, which disrupts the workflow and adds unnecessary time.

- **Support for iOS**: It will be great to have the ability to provide remote assistance to users who are using iOS/iPadOS devices. Currently, the Remote Help tool doesn't support this feature, as discussed earlier in this chapter.

- **Default Remote Help assistance during OOBE (Autopilot) for Windows**: Very often, remote assistance is needed for users who are provisioning new Windows devices and run into issues. A common scenario is Autopilot provisioning failing, leaving the user stuck and needing help to collect diagnostic logs. Since the user is remote, one option today is to guide them through opening Command Prompt, downloading, installing, and launching the Remote Help tool via the command line. However, this process is cumbersome and not intuitive, as it involves multiple commands. A better approach would be to allow installation and launch of the Remote Help app directly from the OOBE screen, making it simpler and more user-friendly, especially for non-technical users.

All the preceding features that ask for Remote Help are something that Microsoft is already aware of. Though we don't have any ETA, hopefully these features will make it to the product soon!

Our two cents

A remote assistance tool is essential for IT admins and a must-have for any organization. Relying on Microsoft Teams for screen sharing isn't correct because proper logging, reporting, and RBAC controls are critical for security and compliance.

What makes Remote Help stand out is its flexibility, as we can assign just one license to a user and can remotely access their Windows, Android, and macOS devices. Once iOS support is added, this feature set will feel more complete.

From a pricing perspective, keep in mind that both the sharer and the helper need licenses, which can be costlier compared to some competitors that only require the helper to be licensed. That said, the value of having a remote assistance tool fully integrated with Intune, offering a single-pane-of-glass experience, outweighs the price difference (if any). Moreover, if we are going with the entire Intune suite license instead of standalone Remote Help licensing, then the costing is even more efficient.

Summary

Remote Help isn't just another feature in the Intune suite; it's a lifeline for IT admins who are navigating the challenges of today's hybrid environment. In this chapter, we've walked through why Remote Help matters, how it's set up, and what makes it stand out compared to tools such as Quick Assist and TeamViewer. The practical steps for deploying Remote Help across Windows, Android, and macOS are designed to make life easier for admins and end users.

We've also discussed the current gaps in the Remote Help tool, such as the lack of iOS support, session recording, file transfer during a Remote Help session, and why these matter for organizations aiming for seamless support.

Remote Help empowers IT teams to solve problems quickly, keeps users productive, and helps organizations stay secure and compliant. Whether we are rolling it out for the first time or looking to improve our support workflows, the insights in this chapter should give confidence to make Remote Help deployment successful.

This wraps up our in-depth exploration of all the Intune Suite components covered in their respective chapters. In the next chapter, we'll dive into some essential Intune resources that will complement our learning and ensure we are well-prepared for any scenario.

Join us on Discord

For discussions around the book and to connect with your peers, join us on Discord at `https://discord.gg/dygzddgYCR`

7

Go-To Resources for Intune Mastery

When working with Intune, we often run into different kinds of scenarios. An admin might need to troubleshoot a specific issue and figure out why something isn't working. An architect could be planning a migration strategy from third-party products to Intune, while a consultant might be assessing the feasibility of Intune or the Intune Suite. So, depending on the use case and requirement, we need to refer to different types of Intune resources.

In this chapter, you'll find blogs from industry experts and MVPs that dive deep into advanced Windows management topics, offering Level 200+ insights, and blogs that discuss the step-by-step setup guides, complete with visuals and screenshots. There's also tutorial-style video content that explains concepts from the ground up, including migration strategies, and, of course, the official Microsoft documentation remains the ultimate source of truth.

To really understand Microsoft Intune and the Intune Suite, it's important to look at it from multiple angles through different resources. Relying on just one source can limit your perspective.

The goal of this chapter is to bring together a curated list of Intune resources in one place for easy reference.

Highly recommended L200+ resources

The following resources offer deep technical insights into the inner workings of various Intune components. They go beyond surface-level explanations, diving into the logs, registry entries, and background processes that drive Intune functionality. These resources are crafted to help you understand not just what happens, but why it happens, thereby making them invaluable for building a strong foundational understanding.

Whether we're troubleshooting a tricky issue or just curious about how Intune works behind the scenes, these resources offer the kind of in-depth, practical insights that we don't often find in standard guides or documentation. For anyone new to Intune, these are must-have resources that will accelerate your learning and help you develop a more holistic perspective:

Owner	Name	Link	Category	Comments

Saurabh Sarkar	Everything AboutIntune	`aka.ms/intunevideos`
		
		`https://everythingaboutintune.com/`
			Blog site and YouTube channel	Best for structured learning. This resource provides in-depth tutorials on setting up and a deep dive into the workings under the hood. It also focuses on troubleshooting various aspects.

Rudy Ooms	Call4Cloud	`https://call4cloud.nl/`	Blog site	Best for a deep dive into Intune management via Windows-related content and troubleshooting. These blogs are often infused with humor and are very detailed. Highly recommended for learning Intune components at an advanced level
Michael Niehaus	OOFHours	`https://oofhours.com/`	Blog site	Best for a deep dive into Autopilot-related content. This is a bookmark-worthy site for detailed insights into Windows management and patching. Highly recommended for understanding the intricacies of Windows and Intune.
Joy Malya Basu	MDM tech Space- Learn with Joy	`https://joymalya.com/`	Blog site	Best for structured learning and a deep dive into various topics related to Intune. The blogs are very detailed and must-reads for learners seeking clarity and depth. Highly recommended for anyone who wants to learn about any Intune-related topic.

Owner	Name	Link	Category	Comments
Steve Hosking Adam Gross	Intune Training	`https://www.youtube.com/c/IntuneTraining`	YouTube channel	Best for understanding the setup of various Intune components. This is one of the oldest and most subscribed to YouTube channels on Intune, with great technical content and podcasts!
Andrew Taylor	andrewstaylor.com	`https://andrewstaylor.com/category/newsletter/`	Blog site	Best for finding all the content related to Intune every week in one place. Andrew releases a weekly newsletter, which contains links and descriptions of all the Intune content that was posted by different trusted publications in that week. It is a great technical resource since it pulls together everything from the community in one place.

Table 7.1: List of highly recommended L200+ Intune resources

Other important Intune resources

There are also several other resources thoughtfully put together by industry experts and MVPs, which are frequently updated. These cover a wide range of Intune topics, focusing on specific issues and how to resolve them at beginner and intermediate levels. They dive into best practices and troubleshooting tips.

We need to keep in mind that these are individual websites, and each one has 50+ blogs (some even 100+) covering different aspects of Intune. A lot of the content overlaps across these sites. Many of them are beginner-friendly and often cover the same topics in similar ways—just written by different authors in different styles.

Our intention here is simply to highlight trusted blog sites for you to refer to.

This table serves as a reference for those resources:

Owner	Name	Link	Category	Comments
User Community Group HTMD	HowTo Manage Devices	`https://howtomanagedevices.com/`	Blog site	A great resource for structured learning. This blog site, managed by Anoop C Nair along with other contributors, offers both setup/how-to guides and troubleshooting tips. It's updated regularly, so you'll always find fresh content! Plus, it includes job mentorship programs and job listings for the Intune community.
Mattias Melkersen Kalvåg	Mindcore	`https://blog.mindcore.dk/`	Blog site	Very good and detailed resource covering various aspects of Intune management in detail. Recommended for troubleshooting.
Ben Whitmore	ByteBen	`https://byteben.com/`	Blog site	
Adam Gross, Eswar Koneti, and team	System CenterDudes	`https://www.systemcenterdudes.com/`	Blog site	
Nickolaj Andersen	MsEndpoint Mgr	`https://msendpointmgr.com/`	Blog site	
Peter van der Woude	All about Microsoft Intune	`https://petervanderwoude.nl/`	Blog site	
Jannik Reinhard	Transforming Device Management with Intune	`https://jannikreinhard.com/`	Blog site and book	
Joery Van den Bosch	IntuneStuff	`https://intunestuff.com/`	Blog site	

Owner	Name	Link	Category	Comments
Oktay Sari	AllThings Cloud	`https://allthingscloud.blog/`	Blog site	
Torbjörn Granheden	Mr T-Bone	`https://www.tbone.se/`	Blog site	
Michael Meier	MikeMDM	`https://mikemdm.de/`	Blog site	
Prajwal Desai	Prajwal Desai	`https://www.prajwaldesai.com/blog/`	Blog site	

Table 7.2: List of important Intune blog sites for troubleshooting

We would also very strongly advise everyone to join the LinkedIn group *Modern Endpoint Management (SCCM | Intune | W365 | AVD | Security | macOS | iOS)* at `https://www.linkedin.com/groups/8761296/`. It's a great place to be updated with everything that's going on in the Intune space, such as events, announcements, and so on. There are more than 50k members in the group, and it's a great place to have technical discussions.

While blogs are a great source of information, one of the best ways to learn is through YouTube tutorials and videos. Sometimes, reading blogs and documentation can feel a bit monotonous, and that's where structured videos offer a refreshing change. They provide a classroom-like learning experience and make it easier to grasp concepts. Videos give an intuitive view of the setup process, the workflow, and even troubleshooting steps. The next table contains the most popular YouTube channels that discuss various aspects of Intune and the Intune Suite:

Owner	Name	Link	Category	Comments
Dean Ellerby MVP	Dean Ellerby	`https://www.youtube.com/@DeanEllerbyMVP/videos`	YouTube channel	A great resource containing comprehensive walkthroughs, especially focusing on Windows device management via Intune. His 2025 Intune Guide is especially helpful and highly recommended.

Owner	Name	Link	Category	Comments
Anoop C Nair and team	HTMD Community	`https://www.youtube.com/@htmdcommunity`	YouTube channel	Very good resource for understanding the basics of SCCM and Intune. It contains many playlists covering various aspects of device management via Intune.
Steve Weiner	Get Rubix	`https://www.youtube.com/@getrubix`	YouTube channel	A great podcast-style YouTube channel that features demos. It offers short videos on various Intune topics, which makes it perfect for quick, bite-sized learning.
Andy Malone	Andy Malone MVP	`https://www.youtube.com/@AndyMaloneMVP/videos`	YouTube channel	Known for clear, structured tutorials such as The Ultimate Beginners Guide to Intune (2025). It covers device onboarding, security, and Autopilot with practical demos. A great resource covering various topics in one place.

Table 7.3: List of popular Intune-related YouTube channels

Key books on Microsoft Intune

If you're looking to deepen your understanding of Microsoft Intune, exploring books on the subject can be an excellent approach. While blogs, videos, and forums are great for quick tips and real-time updates, they often lack the depth and continuity that books provide. The books listed next were written by experienced professionals who know the subject inside out. They've gone through thorough editing and review, so we can count on them for both accuracy and depth. They are especially valuable if you prefer a more methodical learning experience or want to explore a topic from start to finish without jumping between fragmented sources.

Whether you're preparing for certifications, planning enterprise deployments, or simply wanting to build a solid understanding of Intune, the following books can serve as a reliable and enduring resource.

Here is a curated list of books that cover various aspects of Intune in a structured and comprehensive manner:

Owner	Name	Amazon link
Christiaan Brinkhoff and Per Larsen	Mastering Microsoft Intune	`https://www.amazon.in/Mastering-Microsoft-Intune-Windows-management/dp/1835468519`
Andrew Taylor	Microsoft Intune Cookbook	`https://www.amazon.in/Microsoft-Intune-Cookbook-Andrew-Taylor/dp/1805126547`
Scott Duffey	Learning Microsoft Intune: Unified Endpoint Management	`https://www.amazon.in/Learning-Microsoft-Intune-Endpoint-Management/dp/0645127965`
Paul Winstanley and David Brook	Ultimate: Microsoft Intune for Administrators	`https://www.amazon.in/Ultimate-Microsoft-Intune-Administrators-Enterprise/dp/9348107038`
Manish Bangia	Microsoft Intune Administration: Learning Intune concepts and migrating endpoint devices from SCCM	`https://www.amazon.in/Microsoft-Intune-Administration-Learning-migrating/dp/9355519699`

Table 7.4: List of popular Intune-related books

Our two cents

Intune and the Intune Suite are still relatively new and evolving technologies. Microsoft releases new Intune service updates almost every month, adding fresh features. Similarly, the Intune Suite sees frequent feature rollouts. With so many changes happening so often, it's important to stay on top of everything.

While Microsoft's official documentation under **What's New** covers all the latest updates, there are times when we want something that dives deeper into the details. Often, we'll find the same topic covered by multiple authors, which can feel repetitive, but we need to remember that each author brings a unique perspective and writing style. No single resource is completely comprehensive; they complement each other. The best way to learn is by referencing as many sources as possible. That's why, whether you're preparing for an interview or planning a new deployment, it's important to tap into a mix of reliable resources to get the full picture!

Finally, we want to emphasize the resources listed in the *Highly recommended L200 resources* section of this chapter. These should be your go-to resources for understanding Intune concepts in depth and for understanding the background architecture.

Summary

There are some really valuable resources that complement everything covered in this book. For example, Rudy Ooms shares in-depth content on EPM and EAM at `call4cloud.nl`. If you're looking for detailed tutorials on all Intune Suite topics, along with demo and troubleshooting tips, the YouTube channel *EverythingAboutIntune* is a great place to start. To strengthen your understanding of certificates and Cloud PKI, Joy's blogs on his website are excellent references.

All these resources should be used alongside this book as they help complete the picture and ensure that you cover every aspect thoroughly. This chapter provided you with curated lists of expert blogs, YouTube channels, documentation, and books on Microsoft Intune, offering resources ranging from foundational tutorials to advanced technical insights to support learning and troubleshooting across various Intune topics and scenarios.

If you've made it this far, congratulations! This book wasn't meant to be skimmed, and if you've worked through it chapter by chapter, you're now in a great position to manage and improve any Intune deployment. You're well equipped to deploy any Intune Suite component from scratch. With the architectural diagrams referenced throughout the chapters, you should now have a clear understanding of what happens behind the scenes when these components function. You also have a solid foundation on the logs and registry checks needed for troubleshooting.

Finally, you should have a strong grasp of the use cases for Intune Suite components along with their applications, benefits, and requirements, so you can make informed decisions about when and where Intune Suite should be deployed. This is especially critical if you're working as a consultant or architect.

As next steps, it is recommended to keep an eye on all the resources mentioned in this chapter for future updates. As discussed before, the Intune Suite trial is available for free, and the best way to learn anything is by getting hands-on experience. So, go ahead and grab the trial to explore it and get a real feel for the product.

Get This Book's PDF Version and Exclusive Extras

UNLOCK NOW

Scan the QR code (or go to `packtpub.com/unlock`). Search for this book by name, confirm the edition, and then follow the steps on the page.

Note: Keep your invoice handy. Purchases made directly from Packt don't require an invoice.

8

Unlock Your Exclusive Benefits

Your copy of this book includes the following exclusive benefits:

- ☁ Next-gen Packt Reader
- 📄 DRM-free PDF/ePub downloads

Follow the guide below to unlock them. The process takes only a few minutes and needs to be completed once.

Unlock this Book's Free Benefits in 3 Easy Steps

Step 1

Keep your purchase invoice ready for *Step 3*. If you have a physical copy, scan it using your phone and save it as a PDF, JPG, or PNG.

For more help on finding your invoice, visit `https://www.packtpub.com/unlock-benefits/help`.

> **Note**: If you bought this book directly from Packt, no invoice is required. After *Step 2*, you can access your exclusive content right away.

Step 2

Scan the QR code or go to `packtpub.com/unlock`.

On the page that opens (similar to *Figure 8.1* on desktop), search for this book by name and select the correct edition.

Figure 8.1: Packt unlock landing page on desktop

Step 3

After selecting your book, sign in to your Packt account or create one for free. Then upload your invoice (PDF, PNG, or JPG, up to 10 MB). Follow the on-screen instructions to finish the process.

Need help?

If you get stuck and need help, visit `https://www.packtpub.com/unlock-benefits/help` for a detailed FAQ on how to find your invoices and more. This QR code will take you to the help page.

Note: If you are still facing issues, reach out to `customercare@packt.com`.

Stay Sharp in Cloud and DevOps — Join 44,000+ Subscribers of CloudPro

CloudPro is a weekly newsletter for cloud professionals who want to stay current on the fast-evolving world of cloud computing, DevOps, and infrastructure engineering.

Every issue delivers focused, high-signal content on topics like:

- AWS, GCP & multi-cloud architecture
- Containers, Kubernetes & orchestration
- Infrastructure as Code (IaC) with Terraform, Pulumi, etc.
- Platform engineering & automation workflows
- Observability, performance tuning, and reliability best practices

Whether you're a cloud engineer, SRE, DevOps practitioner, or platform lead, CloudPro helps you stay on top of what matters, without the noise.

Scan the QR code to join for free and get weekly insights straight to your inbox:

https://packt.link/cloudpro

‹packt›

Other Books You May Enjoy

If you enjoyed this book, you may be interested in these other books by Packt:

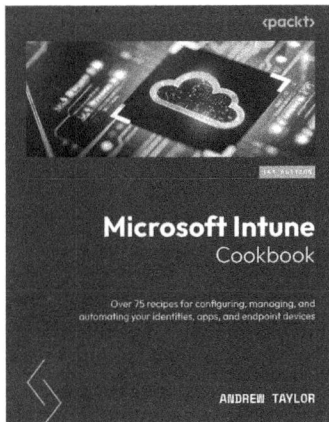

Microsoft Intune Cookbook

Andrew Taylor

ISBN: 978-1-80512-654-6

- Set up your Intune tenant and associated platform connections
- Deploy and manage security and compliance policies of your organization's devices
- Package, deploy, and update your applications using Intune
- Monitor, report, and troubleshoot your environment with advanced tools
- Leverage PowerShell to automate your daily tasks
- Understand the underlying workings of the Microsoft Graph platform and how it interacts with Intune

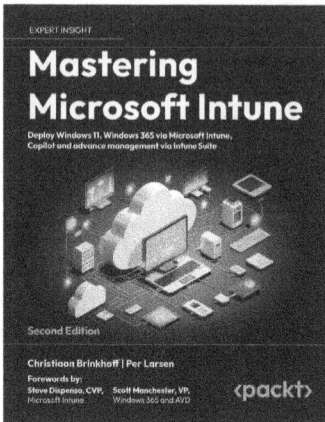

Mastering Microsoft Intune

Christiaan Brinkhoff, Per Larsen

ISBN: 978-1-83546-851-7

- Simplify the deployment of Windows in the cloud with Windows 365 Cloud PCs
- Deliver next-generation security features with Intune Suite
- Simplify Windows Updates with Windows Autopatch
- Configure advanced policy management within Intune
- Discover modern profile management and migration options for physical and Cloud PCs
- Harden security with baseline settings and other security best practices
- Find troubleshooting tips and tricks for Intune, Windows 365 Cloud PCs, and more
- Discover deployment best practices for physical and cloud-managed endpoints

Packt is searching for authors like you

If you're interested in becoming an author for Packt, please visit authors.packt.com and apply today. We have worked with thousands of developers and tech professionals, just like you, to help them share their insight with the global tech community. You can make a general application, apply for a specific hot topic that we are recruiting an author for, or submit your own idea.

Share your thoughts

Now you've finished *Mastering Endpoint Management using Microsoft Intune Suite*, we'd love to hear your thoughts! Scan the QR code below to go straight to the Amazon review page for this book and share your feedback or leave a review on the site that you purchased it from.

https://packt.link/r/1806021951

Your review is important to us and the tech community and will help us make sure we're delivering excellent quality content.

Index

www.ingramcontent.com/pod-product-compliance
Lightning Source LLC
Chambersburg PA
CBHW081043220326
41598CB00038B/6968